3107

Filler, Louis, 1911–   *ed.*
   The President speaks: from William McKinley to Lyndon B. Johnson.   New York, Putnam [1964]

   416 p.   22 cm.

   Bibliographical footnotes.

1. U. S.—Hist.—Sources.   2. Presidents—U. S.   I. Title.

E173.F5   973.082   64–13025

RBP

The President Speaks:

FROM WILLIAM McKINLEY TO LYNDON B. JOHNSON

EDITED WITH AN INTRODUCTION BY

Louis Filler

G. P. Putnam's Sons
New York

ACKNOWLEDGMENTS

Thanks are due to Mr. Steven Frimmer, of G. P. Putnam's Sons, who gave me my head and appreciated the results; to Stephen Pickett, Librarian of Sonoma State College in California, who first helped me lift the tedious Xeroxing job off the ground; and to my student aides who respected significant work and obeyed instructions: a small thing, no doubt, but basic in a sad world which spawned Lee Harvey Oswald, whatever his precise role. Antioch College's excellent research policies worked benignly in my favor, and it is always a pleasure to acknowledge the cooperation of the College's fine Library staff.

L. F.

PART VI

WORLD CRISIS

PART VII

THE COLD WAR

THE SEARCH FOR PEACE

The President as Symbol and as Substance
LOUIS FILLER

I

"Mr. President"

Americans have often been accused of viewing the "presidential sweepstakes" as a sporting event rather than as a decision of high national consequence. It is easy to be disillusioned by some of the cruder manifestations of popular cynicism and irresponsibility when election time comes around again. But even those who believe in our system of popular elections have sometimes had to puzzle how to explain phenomena which seem to do no credit to the democratic process. How, for instance, explain the election of 1840—"Tippecanoe and Tyler, too!"—in a fashion at all creditable to the popular electorate? The ever-increasing voting population was, in that year, sold on the idea that William Henry Harrison, a hero of the War of 1812, was a humble soldier whose major satisfaction was to sit before his log cabin and drink hard cider. Harrison, the son of a signer of the Declaration of Independence, was college-trained and a student of medicine. He had been governor of Indiana, a member of the House of Representatives and the Senate of the United States, and a Minister to Colombia. Moreover, he inhabited a well-appointed fifteen-room mansion. By what stretch of the imagination could he be pictured as a rough old veteran with plebeian tastes?

The Harrison "image" was heightened by the cider vats the Whig campaigners trundled about on wagons carrying replicas of log cabins; these vats contained real cider, and this was freely dispensed to potential voters during political rallies. Harrison was, in fact, a professional soldier with blunt, if shrewd, perceptions. The voters who chose to see him as a simple, democratic fellow, and to denounce his opponent, President Martin Van Buren, as an aristocrat—though he was the son of an upstate-New York farmer and a tavern keeper—were not entirely lost to reason, or to hard cider either.

Americans have the impossible task of electing a President who theoretically represents everybody. They must perceive him as a

9

person and also as the carrier of an idea. How is one to distinguish between candidates seeking pretty much everybody's vote: between a Federalist and a Democrat, a Democrat and a Whig, a Whig and a Republican, a Republican and a Democrat? The voter is constrained to seize upon or create a quality that his candidate can somehow offer, and to highlight it over other qualities he may possess which his opponent also possesses, and which serve to confuse what the voter thinks may be the issues. The Whigs of 1840 were not so much offering Harrison as they were a more democratic version of Whiggism; and a sufficient majority of the electorate in that year preferred it to the (large D) Democratic policies being pursued by incumbent President Van Buren.

Later, a substantial percentage of voters would persist in regarding Abraham Lincoln as a rail splitter, though he had become a successful and well-connected lawyer. They would refer familiarly to Theodore Roosevelt as "Teddy," though this aristocrat's friends called him "Theo." They would, interestingly, refuse to get familiar with Woodrow Wilson or, for that matter, Warren G. Harding, although all types of characters were familiar with him. Yet they chose, in the 1920's, to salute the iceberg from Vermont and Massachusetts as "Cal," and in the 1930's they treated Hoover as a cold-hearted aristocrat, forgetting his humble birth, his very modest background in Iowa and California, his industry and the fact that he had made his reputation as "the great humanitarian." They agreed, too, to regard Franklin D. Roosevelt as a "man of the people."

Americans, then, may be much more subtle than their critics sometimes realize. They do not jeer because a politician avers that he is not running for office when everybody knows he is. They are aware that the politician needs to abide by various rules governing his candidacy, and that these may require him to make ritualistic statements of various sorts. They are not offended when a President tours the country for political purposes while declaring that he has no political purposes. They know that political machines may be engaging in various forms of chicanery in the interests of a man against whom nothing venal can be laid, and they are unimpressed by the dark hints respecting his integrity which the opposition seeks to sow. The public realizes that no man can be elected President without the cooperation of political machines. And once he is elected, he becomes, in some sense, not an ambitious Democrat or Republican, but the nation's President, and, at least during his first days in office, above parties.

10

The President, then, has symbolic weight. He is a unifying center for current circumstances. Whether his is, in fact, "the most important job in the world," as some would have it, is a matter of interpretation. It is an American compulsion to think in terms of VIP's and "nobodies," of losers and winners. One is either up or he is down. Men who have lost an election make a "comeback" by merely having written best-selling books and having enjoyed high corporation salaries and perquisites. Once again they are in the big leagues, runners in the presidential finals. Yet it is probable that actual Presidents have wielded only relative powers—some of them close to no power at all. If we could learn to think of people, let alone of high-ranking officials, as making *contributions* to our civic lives rather than as either dominating them or descending to impotence, we would have a much better perspective on presidential powers. For the moment, it is enough for us to realize that Presidents do indeed wield power—or, at least, have it to wield—but that in our balance-of-power system they function within sets of circumstances that offer boundaries to their power. It helps to think of them *as* boundaries, rather than as limitations: as factors *defining* their role, within which their memorable or mean capacities may be nourished.

II

Who They Are

Our emphasis is on the twentieth century, but it always helps to be conscious of the long shadow of presidential precedents and controversies. It can be an interesting and instructive game to review the sequence of Presidents, their periods of office, and their alleged achievements. It can be even more interesting to examine the incumbents in terms of their changing reputations. Our unhappy educational system encourages our children to concoct mnemonics involving "facts" about the Presidents, meaningless memory aids which suffice for the College Entrance Examinations and disappear from the mind immediately after. The sad fact is that a residue remains in the child's mind to persuade him that he has "known" about the Presidents—and that there was not much to know or remember. But ours is the nation that has done remarkable things in terms of the Executive Office. It elected a Lincoln to the presidency twice—with interesting margins of victory, to be sure—and later

11

elected a Warren G. Harding to the same high office. What had we in mind, in either case? And what, in fact, did these people's choices offer to the voting public? Few candidates are elected President who do not have some remarkable characteristics or who do not wish to be President. *All* of them, without exception, have had to formulate compromise platforms in order to attain their ends. Grover Cleveland's pithy phrase is always memorable: "What is the use of being elected or re-elected, unless you stand for something?"* But such signal expressions of principle aside, Presidents have been complicated equations, products of political professionalism, social circumstances and special-interest and popularity drives which have been welded together by events. The role of accident as it bears on the presidency, is a never-ending study. Some candidates rise and fall with the merest quirks of fate, like James G. Blaine, Cleveland's opponent in 1884. It is always worth recalling that a difference of 575 votes in New York State lost Blaine the election to Cleveland in that year. Henry Clay's forty years of political fame and influence do not permit us to guess what he might or might not have done as Chief Executive had various accidents not obstructed his path to the presidential office. In the twentieth century, numerous public figures impressed politicians and voters as having vital qualities that could affect our history significantly. But Elihu Root, Oscar W. Underwood, Champ Clark, John Hay, Hiram Johnson, among many others, never attained the candidacy of their party, where accident could have opened political doors on their personalities and on ours as voters. Samuel J. Tilden was actually elected President of the United States in 1876, but was not permitted to take office. Would it have made any difference if he had served his term instead of Rutherford B. Hayes? It is difficult to surmise to any purpose. Tilden was far from forceful, during the disputed-election controversy, and he resisted the efforts of leaders of his party to make him the Democratic candidate again in 1880 and 1884. It helps a statesman's cause actively to wish to be President.

Wendell Willkie died suddenly in 1944 leaving an unfulfilled legend of astonishing growth from corporation lawyer to advocate of One

* For Cleveland among the Presidents, see my introduction to Harry Thurston Peck, *Democrats and Republicans: Ten Years of the Republic* (Capricorn Books, 1964). Charles A. Beard suggested, in his *The Presidents in American History* (1935), that Cleveland's most famous act of courage—his attack on the high tariff shortly before he came up, unsuccessfully, for re-election in 1888—was the product of an "unguarded moment." If it was, Cleveland stood by his convictions, as all Presidents have not always done.

World. The needs or preferences of the post-World War I situation did not bring out the civic uses of General John J. Pershing—"Black Jack" Pershing—as they later did of General "Ike" Eisenhower. Thomas E. Dewey was all but ushered into the President's chair; and if he had only . . . but we will never know. The study of personality, of readiness, of desire for office and ability to handle the extraordinary opportunities and risks that result from being in the public eyes—such study goes on. Yet we can never hope for a solution of its enigmas for any ultimate creation of a formula for presidential greatness, or even for election victories.

There have been attempts to fathom the meaning of the presidency and to assay the individual achievements of the Presidents. By and large, they are not very successful. Selected historians have been polled on the comparative merits of Presidents,* but the results are dubious. For example, it has been noted in general studies of popular preferences that voters may be psychologically tempted to voice opinions they imagine are *expected* of them. And historians are, after all, also citizens, subject to the same prejudices, group thinking, assumptions, desire to influence others, that nonhistorians feel. The "greats" they have chosen are (in that order): Lincoln, Washington, Franklin D. Roosevelt, Wilson, Jefferson and Jackson. "Near greats" include (in that order): Theodore Roosevelt, Cleveland, John Adams and James K. Polk. Is there any meaning to these judgments? What were Washington's achievements as *President?* Or did the selected historians rank him so high because they thought it might embarrass their profession to keep the Father of Our Country out of the family of greats? And what did Jefferson *accomplish* that Theodore Roosevelt didn't? Jefferson mediated the Louisiana Purchase, true—an empire, not a state. But he was *offered* it; he did not create conditions for that accession. I suppose we are relieved that he did not bungle that once-in-a-century real-estate bonanza, considering his states-rights fears of an unduly expanded Federal authority. But does that make him a great President? If so, why not add Polk to the list of "greats" at the expense of Jackson? For Polk labored to deliver California and New Mexico to us, to be sure, by means of war and imperialism. Jackson's "great" fight against the Second Bank of the United States has been formidably challenged, and even when

* *Life Magazine*, November 1, 1948, pp. 65 ff., is typical of such efforts. For one interesting "Retrospect and Prospect" which can be measured against later developments, see George Fort Milton, *The Use of Presidential Power, 1789–1943* (1944), pp. 311 ff.

acknowledged only partially compensates for his assault on peaceful Indians, on antislavery champions and on other patently legitimate American-interest elements.

One could go on to ponder the qualities of other Presidents—"near great" and allegedly "average" and "below average" Presidents. But perhaps enough has been said to indicate that the subject is not easily disposed of. The polled historians opined that some Presidents were not "great" because they did not live in times of crisis. But this is a shallow and convenient conjecture. There are desperate times, no doubt, but there are also times of, in Henry D. Thoreau's unforgettable phrase, "quiet desperation." And these can furnish opportunities for truly great men. Can it be *proved* that the period preceding World War I was less significant than the war era? World War I is almost our lost war; we long ago lost our emotional identification with it. President Woodrow Wilson rose on its tide, and his eloquence during its course merits long reconsideration.* But whether his role in it somehow places him above Theodore Roosevelt, for substance or for symbolic significance, remains an open question.

But enough of the historians, with their "below-average" preference for Coolidge over Millard Fillmore (*why?*), and for John Tyler over both Coolidge and Franklin Pierce. We need a poll of ordinary people to determine whether and when they think of the Presidents at all. For example, what would a nondirected poll net us which solicited random ratings of Zachary Taylor, Chester A. Arthur and Benjamin Harrison? Moreover, *sectional* polls would produce surprising results. Warren G. Harding is rather well-regarded, at least among Republicans in Ohio. Andrew Johnson, who fought for the Constitution as Lincoln's successor, is very well-esteemed in his own Tennessee, and at least respected in most of the Nation. William Howard Taft is a distinguished name in Cincinnati; his national reputation could be probed with profit. He is often referred to as a central wheel in a notable family of public servants and elected officials.

III

Power and Purpose

Thus, presidential fame is a function of time and place. All Presidents—and, indeed, all presidential candidates—receive cam-

* See pp. 105 ff.

paign biographies, always interesting, always presenting them in their best light, often with gross exaggeration and sentimental sympathy. At the same time, candidates must all endure the endless vilification of the election campaign. S. I. Hayakawa, a scholar in semantics, has attempted to point out that blind hatred makes us shortsighted. But does shortsightedness necessarily impede presidential aspirations or limit its stature? How does one distinguish shortsightedness from singleminded dedication? Or from concentration on reading the public's will in order to win its confidence? Practically all major candidates are persuaded that they must first be elected before they can hope to carry out any program at all. And to be elected they must satisfy, or appear to satisfy, the preferences, including the "short-sighted" preferences, of enough strategically placed voters to give them a majority of votes in the Electoral College. The real difficulty with semantics as an eye-opener to shortsightedness is that it does not answer the question of shortsightedness *to whom*. Many Mid-westerners see foreign affairs, for example, in ways which vary markedly from the ways they are viewed in New York City or San Francisco. Nor does this mean that the inhabitants of those metro-politan areas necessarily have a larger vision. They may merely be impelled by different social and economic interests. It is the President's or the would-be President's business to understand those interests and minister to them—hopefully in a national and international per-spective.

Presidents have been seen in terms of their individual qualities and also as functions of our political system. The English student of its workings, Viscount Bryce in his *The American Commonwealth* (1888), included a chapter entitled, "Why Great Men Are Not Chosen Presidents." He thought this was "firstly, because great men are rare in politics; secondly, because the method of choice does not bring them to the top; thirdly, because they are not, in quiet times, absolutely needed." We have already rejected this last reason as explaining greatness; it no more than raises the question of whether Presidents associated with crisis periods have really been great. Perhaps they have merely been highlighted by tense and traumatic events. Some students of the Executive Office argue that it has accreted more and more actual responsibilities, and that it is one of our major needs to provide the President with help. Nowadays, says Professor Richard E. Neustadt in his *Presidential Power: the Politics of Leadership* (1960), "he cannot be as small as he might like." His bigness might, however, be illusory. The exercise of presidential power may, in fact, today be a matter of art in administering the constant factors of cold war, the arms race, competition overseas and the problems of inflation and recession, as Professor Neustadt believes. But neither art nor artfulness can overcome the challenge of a Congress drawn from every part of the union, responsive to its throbbings and in ultimate control of the national budget. Presidents have, as we will see, interposed themselves in strategic events, and identified themselves with policies and settlements. They have worked with friends and associates who have influenced large events. But their final achievements are the result of such understanding as they have reached or failed to reach with Congress. Always worth analysis is the fact that William Howard Taft's single term in office resulted in vastly more significant legislation than Theodore Roosevelt's almost two clamorous administrations. Taft's actual relationship to the achievements of Congress during his incumbency can, of course, be debated. But that very fact provides a fresh perspective from which to view presidential accomplishments.

What is the President's actual power? The late John F. Kennedy denied, for instance, that his power of patronage was significant, but he perhaps oversimplified the issue. The question was not so much how many actual jobs he personally filled as, in our society as it now functions, how his stand on particular legislation could affect business and job opportunities which, in turn, would affect the patronage his party associates and supporters could direct. In other words, the President and would-be President are as much servants of the popular will as its potential masters. They can argue, plead, praise, mediate and exercise these functions with resources unavailable to any other group; but they must also abide by a long string of regulations, understandings, prejudices and popular assumptions. Americans seem to be increasingly concerned for the values and program which the President may prefer. The direct reasons involve the augmented welfare aspects of their government and, in varying degree, their intermittent fears of international catastrophe. But it is the *domestic* issues which recent candidates tend to handle with greatest tenderness and relative precision. They are canny and concerned about poverty, or racial dilemmas and the alarm felt by workers everywhere over the effects of automation and population growth. It is unlikely that either Nixon or Kennedy, in 1960, was any clearer on an international program certain to ensure election to the presidency *and* international peace than were the voters to whom they appealed. Their views on Cuba, on Formosa, on Berlin and on the Near East were all formed with an eye on the absentminded voter, alarmed about Sputnik, the space race, U–2 and other matters, yes, but prompt to forget them, and keenly and consistently concerned only for bread-and-butter and regional issues. One definition of an American is that he is a temporarily embarrassed millionaire. As such, he wants a job, but hates to pay taxes. If he needs a job, he demands that the government provide it one way or another. If he needs business, he thinks it is a legitimate lien on government programming that it somehow turn business his way. It is this world of expectations that a President must feed, and since most of it involves funds that only Congress can grant, he must find ways and means to identify himself with fund allocations which will strengthen his entourage and supporters and disarm his detractors.

IV

The Voice of Party, the Voice of the People

Thus, in the last analysis, it is true that the President's most important power is not his patronage. It is not his title of Commander-in-Chief, surrounded as he is with officials and technicians whose memos supply him with the substance of his directives. It is not his nominal role as leader of his party—a doubtful honor, as Nixon discovered, following his defeat in 1960. It is his national forum, his ability to reach his audience through writings and speech. He must find words which will maintain the Northern, Southern, Eastern and Western support of his position which first brought him into the White House.

He starts with positive advantages. "Mr. President" is a unique designation. Moreover, we all have a stake in the dignity of the presidency, and even partisans will attack the man rather than the office. In addition, the gifts that won him the suffrage in the first place can, in some measure, be expected to sustain him in crises and perplexing circumstances.

At the same time, he is fair game for the opposition, who will take advantage of the difficulties he inherited, perhaps from them, and blame him for them, denounce him for doing too little, for lack of understanding, competence or good taste, and for hypocrisy, cowardliness or whatever other qualities they can read into his words. Presidents protect themselves as best they can from inevitable sharp-

17

shooters and deliberate misconstructionists. But their most subtle and practiced phrasings cannot shield them from the subtle and practiced criticisms of their foes. In the last analysis, it will be the people themselves who will decide to remember or forget their particular expressions and in forms which they often cannot have anticipated. George Washington *did not* warn us against "entangling alliances." The phrase can be found nowhere in his Farewell Address, though it does appear in Jefferson's First Inaugural Address. "Speak softly and carry a big stick" is widely imagined to refer to Theodore Roosevelt's policy on trusts, though his five uses of the phrase all related to foreign policy. There are reasons, psychological and practical, why posterity finds it convenient to remember such concepts in the fashion it does. The never-ending study of the Presidents cannot be separated from a never-ending study of the people who have helped make them what they were and are.

Presidents, in their pronouncements, have a number of qualities in common. They aspire to speak for the nation. They assume a cheerful, hard-working, honest and honorable electorate. They take themselves to be spokesmen for their fellow-countrymen, and, as such, offer correct statements on national holidays and heroes, on the virtues of home, patriotism, conservation of natural resources, holiday safety and other concepts and events. They presume to speak for all parties and people; though while mending political fences, and especially during election campaigns, they "take off their gloves," express a sense of outrage and impatience with patent falsehood, and put what they call the truth bluntly and boldly. Such forensic devices are expected and ritualistic; and remarkable indeed is the apparent earnestness with which they are delivered. To simple people it is always astonishing to read the lurid accusations that politicians direct one at another, and then to study photographs showing them shaking hands and smiling fondly into one another's faces.

Beyond this come the individual qualities of the particular President. There has never been a President who did not wish to be well-remembered. There has never been a President who lacked supporters and admirers of even his least well-considered speeches. Cynics sometimes imagine that Presidents employ teams to manufacture the many utterances they are required to produce, either by law, as in their State of the Union addresses, or in their several roles as first citizen and party leader. But cynics, as usual, miss the point. A presidential aide, whatever his talents, must seek to reflect his chief's will. The speech writer who sought to impose his view of affairs upon the

President in place of the President's own would rapidly find himself among the Washington tourists. The aide, the assistant, the idea man, whatever he may be called, studies the President's will, finds phrases for him, acts as a suggestion box and source of information. The speech, in the end, *is* the President's own, for better or for worse.

The President must express himself so often and at such length on so many subjects that he is bound to reveal the cast of his intellectual features. On the other hand, he can hardly avoid uttering a substantial amount of rather predictable phraseology. This is because of the nature of some of his formulations, which must meet legal, Congressional and other expectations, and also seem likely not to offend a significant cross-section of Americans everywhere. These several forces are interrelated. Thus, if the President's messages strike the electorate as wrong, dangerous, offensive, or ineffectual, public discontent will be felt in the deterioration of the President's influence in Congress. The President cannot afford individual eccentricity, and he is likely to indulge in patent flattery of his countrymen. "The American people," averred President Roosevelt, in 1941, "are not easily fooled; they are hard-headed realists and they fear no one." Such a statement, set down in a schoolboy essay, would evoke his teacher's criticisms, on grounds of unproved generalizations, undefined terms and other compositional faults. Yet the President, *as* President of tens of millions of Americans, must generalize, and must think in terms of our ideals as well as of our actual circumstances. Also, he must exhibit qualities that give him a potential for leadership. Just what those qualities may be is debatable. Adlai E. Stevenson was said to have harmed his status with the electorate by being too witty. ("Eggheads of the world, unite. You have nothing to lose but your yolks.") If so, perhaps a drive toward the presidency was the wrong time for his brand of wit. President Kennedy later indulged himself in humor of the "egghead" variety with no apparent loss of prestige, possibly because he waited until after he had won the presidency to relax with correspondents and citizen convocations.

A President must seem strong on important issues if he is to retain his following. It is not generally realized that *all* twentieth-century American Presidents sought to display the colors of strength in speaking on what they thought of as crucial issues. Among the most notable of them, Woodrow Wilson chose an exalted note upon which to exhibit his strength. "There may at any moment come a time when I cannot preserve both the honor and the peace of the United States," he said during his preparedness campaign. His messages were alive with memorable phrases: "Strict accountability," "the fundamental rights of humanity," "peace without victory," "watchful waiting"— these and scores of other expressions roused and directed the thoughts of whole armies of his countrymen. F.D.R. was able to emphasize grim determination, dedicated citizenship or confident good humor for different occasions. Sometimes he mixed all three for major crises, as in his Washington's Birthday address of February 22, 1942:

> From Berlin, Rome and Tokyo we have been described as a nation of weaklings—"playboys"—who would hire British soldiers, or Russian soldiers, or Chinese soldiers to do our fighting for us.
> Let them repeat that now!
> Let them tell that to General MacArthur and his men.
> Let them tell that to the sailors who today are hitting hard in the waters of the Pacific.
> Let them tell that to the boys in the Flying Fortresses.
> Let them tell that to the Marines!

Whether any American President expressed himself with such consistent effectiveness as did Winston Churchill during his many years of Parliamentary address and debate is a moot question. But even Churchill was quite capable of common rhetoric and dubious assertion, though his supreme efforts need little commentary. They are alive with the dedicated efforts of his countrymen; they echo the finer aspirations of his class. The student of our own presidential utterances can properly match them against the Churchillian measure —and find some of them far from unworthy of the comparison.

The very least of the presidential speeches and writings merit an American's attention, and the following selections are not from the least of them. Hardly a year has passed in the twentieth century that has not required extraordinary statements from our highest political office. It should be noted that the selections in this volume do not always necessarily focus on celebrated pronouncements. Time passes. A "famous" issue dwindles into obscurity. It is the business of a live reader to seek out the life in past situations and past commentary and ponder its meaning for modern times. I have sought characteristic utterances, evocative statements, statements shedding light on their own times, their own leaders and also on ours. Major crises and famous quotations are given due regard. But other illuminating statements, highlighting the personalities of the Presidents and the character of their administrations, and tracing the changing interests and attitudes of the American public have also received appropriate attention. The President is never alone. His words acquire character from their surroundings and associations. The President is indeed a person, and merits individual appreciation proportionate to his role at the center of a major American odyssey. But it blurs reality to conceive of him apart from the environment which molded him, and on which he becomes a commentary.

And now: "The President of the United States." But two thoughts, first. A President must stand for something or lose outline or body in the public mind. This has happened to such worthies as Tyler, Fillmore, Buchanan, Hayes, Arthur, Benjamin Harrison and Taft. We have too much of a stake in the presidency to live comfortably with slurs about Presidents, and we tend to forget doubtful figures rather than pillory them. Events sometimes make apparently uneventful presidencies somewhat memorable, as with "Cool Cal" Coolidge, who symbolizes the thoughtless twenties. Even Buchanan may be recalled as a judgment on weakness and indecisiveness in the face of our greatest threat to survival as a nation.

And, finally, *all presidential terms of office are different,* for each term must be won at the polls. Thus, all incumbent Presidents must refresh their image for the electorate. They will jettison doubtful appendages of their administration, take on new associates and new slogans thought to be good for votes. And though they protest that everything done in the last administration was the best that could have been done, they are prepared to be born anew on Election Day.

Antioch College

21

PART I

The President Faces
The Twentieth Century

WILLIAM McKINLEY

(1843–1901)

Homespun

When we assembled here on the 4th of March, 1897, there was great anxiety with regard to our currency and credit. None exists now. . . . Then there was deep solicitude because of the long depression in our manufacturing, mining, agricultural, and mercantile industries and the consequent distress of our laboring population. Now every avenue of production is crowded with activity, labor is well employed, and American products find good markets at home and abroad.

Second Inaugural Address, *March 4, 1901*

"NEVER was there a crime more without purpose, more without possible good effect. William McKinley was no oppressor of the people, no irresponsible and cruel autocrat. No act of his had ever, from evil intent, taken bread from one man's hand, the hope from one man's heart. He was the representative of the people's will, not their master." Thus wrote a contemporary journalist, riding the flood of commentary in the days following the President's assassination in 1901. It was a judgment which many Americans shared. He was the son of simple, pious Ohioans, his father's iron foundry made well-to-do by a high protective tariff—the first President whose father was an industrialist. He taught school briefly, then joined the Federal forces, and served with distinction throughout the Civil War. He emerged, aged twenty-two, a brevet major. He became a lawyer and rose in Republican ranks, entering Congress in 1876. His main cause was protection. His loyalty to party understandings distinguished him from eager political opportunists. By 1888 he was known well enough among Republicans to be a favorite son at the nominating convention, but he was committed to the support of his long-time Ohio political leader, John Sherman, and would not desert his cause. As he said: "Is it then such an honorable thing not to do a dishonorable thing?"

His tariff views were unequivocal. In 1888, speaking in Boston, he said:

I would secure the American market to the American producer, and I would not hesitate to raise the duties whenever necessary to secure this patriotic end. I would not have an idle man or an idle mill or an idle spindle in this country if, by holding exclusively the American market, we could keep them employed and running. Every yard of cloth imported here makes a demand for one yard less of American fabrication. Let England take care of herself. Let France look after her own interests. Let Germany take care of her own people; but in God's name let Americans look after America.

In 1890, he sponsored the famous McKinley tariff bill: the highest schedule of duties till that time. Defeated for Congress in that year, he won the Ohio governorship the next; and during the hard times that followed he sought mediation between labor and capital, and exhibited a good will toward the poor that was not shared by all defenders of free enterprise. McKinley defeated Bryan in the bitter election of 1896, and took office as a plain American whose love for his ill wife, made frail by the loss of her children, stirred the tender feelings of the public. McKinley wavered on a policy toward Cuba, but, once launched on war, pursued it without doubts about American virtue and righteousness. His justification for the two-year war to crush Filipino insurrectionists who had expected to assume power in their islands became notorious among anti-imperialists, but did not prevent McKinley's triumphant re-election in 1900. He took pride, too, in his expeditious crushing of the Boxer Rebellion—an uprising of Chinese against foreign interests operating in their country.

In March of 1901, he made a nationwide tour that was a triumphal procession from Alabama to California. Never had he seemed more secure in the hearts of his countrymen. His visit to the Pan-American Exposition on the Niagara frontier seemed like a capstone to his achievement. Suddenly, luridly, he was dead, struck down as he extended his hand in good will to the assassin, Leon Czolgosz. Correspondents everywhere covered the young man with scorn and hatred, and held his deed alien to the American way. His parents, however, had come to America forty-two years before the assassination; he himself had been born and raised in Detroit, and in his twenty-nine years had come to know malcontents in that city, in Cleveland, in Chicago, and elsewhere.

Incipient progressives, unsympathetic to terrorism, but dissatisfied with the late war, with unbridled capitalism, and with the rigors of recurrent depressions, seized on the positive aspects of McKinley's last message, delivered in Buffalo, September 5, 1901, and saw it as a new way for a more international-minded America.

"The Period of Exclusiveness Is Past"

President Milburn, Director General Buchanan, Commissioners, Ladies and Gentlemen:

I am glad to be again in the city of Buffalo and exchange greetings with her people, to whose generous hospitality I am not a stranger and with whose good will I have been repeatedly and signally honored. To-day I have additional satisfaction in meeting and giving welcome to the foreign representatives assembled here, whose presence and participation in this exposition have contributed in so marked a degree to its interest and success. . . . Expositions are the timekeepers of progress. They record the world's advancement. They stimulate the energy, enterprise and intellect of the people and quicken human genius. They go into the home. They broaden and brighten the daily life of the people. They open mighty storehouses of information to the student. Every exposition, great or small, has helped to some onward step. Comparison of ideas is always educational, and as such instruct the brain and hand of man. Friendly rivalry follows, which is the spur to industrial improvement, the inspiration to useful invention and to high endeavor in all departments of human activity. . . .

Business life, whether among ourselves or with other people, is ever a sharp struggle for success. It will be none the less so in the future. Without competition we would be clinging to the clumsy antiquated processes of farming and manufacture and the methods of business of long ago, and the twentieth would be no further advanced than the eighteenth century. But though commercial competitors we are, commercial enemies we must not be.

The Pan-American exposition has done its work thoroughly, presenting in its exhibits evidences of the highest skill and illustrating the progress of the human family in the western hemisphere. This portion of the earth has no cause for humiliation for the part it has performed in the march of civilization. It has not accomplished everything from it. It has simply done its best, and without vanity or boastfulness, and recognizing the manifold achievements of others, it invites the friendly rivalry of all the powers in the peaceful pursuits of trade and commerce, and will co-operate with all in advancing the highest and best interests of humanity. . . .

After all, how near one to the other is every part of the world.

Modern inventions have brought into close relation widely separated peoples and made them better acquainted. Geographic and political divisions will continue to exist, but distances have been effaced. Swift ships and swift trains are becoming cosmopolitan. They invade fields which a few years ago were impenetrable. The world's products are exchanged as never before, and with increasing transportation facilities come increasing knowledge and larger trade. Prices are fixed with mathematical precision by supply and demand. The world's selling prices are regulated by market and crop reports. . . .

We reached General Miles in Puerto Rico by cable, and he was able, through the military telegraph, to stop his army on the firing line with the message that the United States and Spain had signed a protocol suspending hostilities. We knew almost instantly of the first shots fired at Santiago, and the subsequent surrender of the Spanish forces was known at Washington within less than an hour of its consummation. . . .

So accustomed are we to safe and easy communication with distant lands that its temporary interruption, even in ordinary times, results in loss and inconvenience. We shall never forget the days of anxious waiting and awful suspense when no information was permitted to be sent from Pekin, and the diplomatic representatives of the nations in China, cut off from all communication, inside and outside of the walled capital, were surrounded by an angry and misguided mob that threatened their lives; nor the joy that filled the world when a single message from the Government of the United States brought through our minister the first news of the safety of the besieged diplomats. . . .

God and man have linked the nations together. No nation can longer be indifferent to any other. And as we are brought more and more in touch with each other the less occasion there is for misunderstandings and the stronger the disposition, when we have differences, to adjust them in the court of arbitration, which is the noblest forum for the settlement of international disputes.

My fellow citizens, trade statistics indicate that this country is in a state of unexampled prosperity. The figures are almost appalling. They show that we are utilizing our fields and forests and mines and that we are furnishing profitable employment to the millions of workingmen throughout the United States, bringing comfort and happiness to their homes and making it possible to lay by savings for old age and disability. That all the people are participating in this great prosperity is seen in every American community, and shown by the enormous and unprecedented deposits in our savings banks. Our duty is the care and security of these deposits, and their safe investment demands the highest integrity and the best business capacity of those in charge of these depositories of the people's earnings. . . .

By sensible trade arrangements which will not interrupt our home production we shall extend the outlets for our increasing surplus. A system which provides a mutual exchange of commodities, a mutual exchange is manifestly essential to the continued and healthful growth of our export trade. We must not repose in fancied security that we can forever sell everything and buy little or nothing. If such a thing were possible, it would not be best for us or for those with whom we deal. We should take from our customers such of their products as we can use without harm to our industries and labor. Reciprocity is the natural outgrowth of our wonderful industrial development under the domestic policy now firmly established. What we produce beyond our domestic consumption must have a vent abroad. The excess must be relieved through a foreign outlet and we should sell everywhere we can, and buy wherever the buying will enlarge our sales and productions, and thereby make a greater demand for home labor.

The period of exclusiveness is past. The expansion of our trade and commerce is the pressing problem. Commercial wars are unprofitable. A policy of good will and friendly trade relations will prevent reprisals. Reciprocity treaties are in harmony with the spirit of the times, measures of retaliation are not. If perchance some of our tariffs are no longer needed, for revenue or to encourage and protect our industries at home, why should they not be employed to extend and promote our markets abroad?

In the furthering of these objects of national interest and concern you are performing an important part. This exposition would have touched the heart of that American statesman whose mind was ever alert and thought ever constant for a larger commerce and a truer fraternity of the republics of the new world. His broad American spirit is felt and manifested here. He needs no identification to an assemblage of Americans anywhere, for the name of Blaine is inseparably associated with the Pan-American movement, which finds this practical and substantial expression, and which we all hope will be firmly advanced by the Pan-American congress that assembles this autumn in the capital of Mexico. The good work will go on. It cannot be stopped. These buildings will disappear; this creation of art and beauty and industry will perish from sight, but their influence will remain to

29

Make it live beyond its too short living
With praises and thanksgiving. . . .

Our earnest prayer is that God will graciously vouchsafe prosperity, happiness and peace to all our neighbors, and like blessings to all the peoples and powers of earth.

PART II
Progressivism

THEODORE ROOSEVELT

(1858–1919)

Big Stick

*Much has been given us, and much will rightfully be expected
from us. We have duties to others and duties to ourselves. We
have become a great nation, . . . and we must behave as beseems
a people with . . . responsibilities. . . . But justice and generosity
in a nation, as in an individual, count most when shown not by
the weak but by the strong. While ever careful to refrain from
wrongdoing others, we must be no less insistent that we are not
wronged ourselves. We wish peace, but we wish the peace of
justice, the peace of righteousness.*

Inaugural Address, *March 4, 1905*

"AND this was the man at whom the assassin struck! . . . There is no
baser deed in all the annals of crime." So Theodore Roosevelt, in
his first Annual Message to Congress, December 3, 1901. He expressed
for the nation a personal pride in the "good and great President who is
dead," as well as "infinite sorrow" for his passing. Yet Lincoln Steffens
was to remember him as dancing with joy at the thought that he had
himself attained the presidential office: a paradox of feeling and deport-
ment that was inherent in much that the nation's idol accomplished.

It took some time for Theodore Roosevelt to become Teddy Roosevelt.
His patrician background was real, the sense of superiority to the run
of mankind substantial. His youthful fight for personal health was to
survive as an inspiration to the young, at least into an era that wondered
whether it mattered if one was healthy or not. Roosevelt read widely
and wrote incessantly, infusing a vigorous self-righteousness into all his
judgments of people and events. At the same time, he learned rapidly to
work with the reigning powers in Republican circles. As a young New
York Assemblyman, he had opposed a two-dollar wage for municipal
workers; but he was persuaded by labor leader Samuel Gompers that
certain obnoxious conditions in the cigar-making industry merited remedy.
He swallowed the presidential candidacy of James G. Blaine in 1884,
though other sensitive Republicans found that tarnished knight unpalat-
able. Labor riots roused every Darwinian impulse in the young crusader,
who had become a Dakota rancher. His cowboys, he wrote, yearned to

try their rifles on workers who resorted to force: "I wish I had them with me," he informed his sister Anna, "and a fair show at ten times our number of rioters; my men shoot well and fear very little." He also saw the criminal as "simply a wolf who preys on society and who should be killed or [here Roosevelt became a trifle confused] imprisoned like the wolf of the forest."

He rose in the 1890's as a vigorous Civil Service Commissioner, then as president of the board of police commissioners of New York City. As Assistant Secretary of the Navy, he had much to do with sending Commodore George Dewey on his fateful journey to attack Manila; he himself rose in Cuba to national fame as head of his First United States Volunteer Regiment of Cavalry. Astute party leaders made him governor of New York, then sought to bury him in the vice presidency in 1900; Mark Hanna said that he was going to Washington to see Roosevelt "take the veil." Soon a chagrined Hanna—who himself nourished presidential hopes—was forced to acknowledge "that damned cowboy" as his chief.

Roosevelt—not yet "T.R.," not yet "Teddy," not yet affectionately symbolized by teddy bears, glasses and flashing teeth—the youngest President of the United States, began cautiously. He retained McKinley's cabinet. He denied that the rich had grown richer and the poor poorer. His first State of the Union address held anarchy to be no more an expression of social discontent than picking pockets or wife beating. The great anthracite coal strike of 1902 was settled by his personal intervention, but with the aid of J. P. Morgan; and the strikers gained no union recognition. As Roosevelt later observed:

I was anxious to save the great coal operators and all of the class of big propertied men, of which they were members, from the dreadful punishment which their own folly would have brought on them if I had not acted; and one of the exasperating things was that they were so blinded that they could not see that I was trying to save them from themselves. . . .

T.R.'s action against the Northern Securities Company, a merger of giant railroad interests, established his popularity as a trust buster, despite his lack of consistent action in the field. An enthusiastic congressman from Indiana was to remark that T.R. had "endeared himself not only to the people of the United States but to the very politicians themselves."

A President Emerges: T.R. on Trusts

[ADDRESS IN BOSTON, AUGUST 25, 1902.]

Governor Crane, Mayor Collins, Men and Women of Boston:

I want to take up this evening the general question of our economic and social relations, with specific reference to that problem with which I think our people are now greatly concerning themselves—the problem of our complex social condition as intensified by the existence of the great corporations which we rather loosely designate as trusts. I have not come here to say that I have discovered a patent cure-all for any evils. When people's minds are greatly agitated on any subject, and especially when they feel deeply but rather vaguely that conditions are not right, it is far pleasanter in addressing them to be indifferent as to what you promise; but it is much less pleasant afterward when you come to try to carry out what has been promised. Of course the worth of a promise consists purely in the way in which the performance squares with it. That has two sides. In the first place, if a man in an honest man he will try just as hard to keep a promise made on the stump as one made off the stump. In the second place, if the people keep their heads they won't wish promises to be made which are impossible of performance. You see, one side of that question represents my duty, and the other side yours. . . .

The first requisite of good citizenship is that the man shall do the homely, every-day, humdrum duties well. . . . But he must do more. In this country of ours the average citizen must devote a good deal of thought and time to the affairs of the State as a whole or those affairs will go backward; and he must devote that thought and that time steadily and intelligently. If there is any one quality that is not admirable, whether in a nation or in an individual, it is hysterics, either in religion or in anything else. The man or woman who makes up for ten days' indifference to duty by an eleventh-day morbid repentance about that duty is of scant use in the world. Now in the same way it is of no possible use to decline to go through all the ordinary duties of citizenship for a long space of time and then suddenly to get up and feel very angry about something or somebody, not clearly defined, and demand reform, as if it were a concrete substance to be handed out forthwith.

This is preliminary to what I want to say to you about the whole question of great corporations as affecting the public. There are very many and very difficult problems with which we are faced as the results of the forces which have been in play for more than the lifetime of a generation. It is worse than useless for any of us to rail at or regret the great growth of our industrial civilization during the last half century. . . . The practical thing to do is to face the conditions as they are and see if we can not get the best there is in them out of them. Now we shall not get a complete or perfect solution for all of the evils attendant upon the development of the trusts by any single action on our part, . . . but I think that those gentlemen, and especially those gentlemen of large means, who deny that the evils exist are acting with great folly. So far from being against property when I ask that the question of the trusts be taken up, I am acting in the most conservative sense in property's interest. When a great corporation is sued for violating the anti-trust law, it is not a move against property, it is a move in favor of property, because when we make it evident that all men, great and small alike, have to obey the law, we put the safeguard of the law around all men. When we make it evident that no man shall be excused for violating the law, we make it evident that every man will be protected from violations of the law.

Now one of the great troubles—I am inclined to think much the greatest trouble—in any immediate handling of the question of the trusts comes from our system of government. Under this system it is difficult to say where the power is lodged to deal with these evils. Remember that I am not saying that even if we had all the power we could completely solve the trust question. If what we read in the papers is true, international trusts are now being planned. It is going to be very difficult for any set of laws on our part to deal completely with a problem which becomes international in its bearings. But a great deal can be done in various ways even now—a great deal is being done—and a great deal more can be done, if we see that the power is lodged somewhere to do it. On the whole, our system of government has worked marvelously well—the system of divided functions of government, of a scheme under which Maine, Louisiana, Oregon, Idaho, New York, Illinois, South Carolina, can all come together for certain purposes, and yet each be allowed to work out its salvation as it desires along certain other lines. On the whole, this has worked well; but in some respects it has worked ill. While I most firmly believe in fixity of policy, I do not believe that that policy should be fossilized, and when conditions change we must change our governmental methods to meet them. . . . Sails, oars, wheels—these were the [old] instruments of commerce. The pack train, the wagon train, the rowboat, the sailing craft—these were the methods of commerce. Everything has been revolutionized in the business world since then, and the progress of civilization from being a dribble has become a torrent. There was no particular need at that time of bothering as to whether the nation or the State had control of corporations. They were easy to control. Now, however, the exact reverse is the case. And remember when I say corporations I do not mean merely trusts technically so-called, merely combinations of corporations, or corporations under certain peculiar conditions. For instance, some time ago the Attorney-General took action against a certain trust. There was considerable discussion as to whether the trust aimed at would not seek to get out from under the law by becoming a single corporation. Now, I want laws that will enable us to deal with any evil no matter what shape it takes. I want to see the government able to get at it definitely, so that the action of the government can not be evaded by any turning within or without Federal or State statutes. At present we have really no efficient control over a big corporation which does business in more than one State. Frequently the corporation has nothing whatever to do with the State in which it is incorporated except to get incorporated; and all its business may be done in entirely different communities—communities which may object very much to the methods of incorporation in the State named. I do not believe that you can get any action by any State, I do not believe it practicable to get action by all the States that will give us satisfactory control of the trusts, of big corporations; and the result is at present that we have a great, powerful, artificial creation which has no creator to which it is responsible. . . .

. . . At present if we pass laws nobody can tell whether they will amount to anything. That has two bad effects. In the first place, the corporation becomes indifferent to the law-making body; and in the next place, the law-making body gets into that most pernicious custom of passing a law not with reference to what will be done under it, but with reference to its effects upon the opinions of the voters. That is a bad thing. When any body of law-makers passes a law, not simply with reference to whether that law will do good or ill, but with the knowledge that not much will come of it, and yet that perhaps the people as a whole will like to see it on the statute books—it does not speak well for the lawmakers, and it does not speak well for the people, either. What I hope to see is power given to the National

Legislature which shall make the control real. . . . Here in Massachusetts you have what I regard as, on the whole, excellent corporation laws. Most of our difficulties would be in a fair way of solution if we had the power to put upon the national statute books, and did put upon them, laws for the nation much like those you have here on the subject of corporations in Massachusetts. So you can see, gentlemen, I am not advocating anything very revolutionary. I am advocating action to prevent anything revolutionary. Now, if we can get adequate control by the nation of these great corporations, then we can pass legislation which will give us the power of regulation and supervision over them. If the nation had that power, mind you, I should advocate as strenuously as I know how that the power should be exercised with extreme caution and self-restraint. No good will come from plunging in without having looked carefully ahead. The first thing we want is publicity; and I do not mean publicity as a favor by some corporations—I mean it as a right from all corporations affected by the law. I want publicity as to the essential facts in which the public has an interest. I want the knowledge given to the accredited representatives of the people of facts upon which those representatives can, if they see fit, base their actions later. The publicity itself would cure many evils. The light of day is a great deterrer of wrongdoing. The mere fact of being able to put out nakedly, and with the certainty that the statements were true, a given condition of things that was wrong, would go a long distance toward curing that wrong; and, even where it did not cure it, would make the path evident by which to cure it. We would not be leaping in the dark; we would not be striving blindly to see what was good and what bad. We would know what the facts were and be able to shape our course accordingly. . . .

Four days before McKinley was shot, T.R. spoke at the Minnesota state fair and quoted a "homely old adage": "Speak softly and carry a big stick—you will go far." It made no notable impression at the time. It was to become one of his most familiar remarks. By September 7, 1903, when, at the state fair in Syracuse, he asserted the need for treating each man on his own merits, and in terms of a "square deal," this first Republican President from the East stood on his own feet and could face the presidential year ahead with confidence.

Roosevelt's view of himself, as leader of the greatest nation in the Western world, was that of a patient and generous master. He was willing to conduct formal negotiations with foreign powers of lowly status with respect to American military needs, but he was not for a moment ready to consider their furthering a matter for questioning. In his first Annual

Message, he congratulated Congress on the nation's splendid policy in the Philippines: "History may safely be challenged to show a single instance in which a masterful race such as ours, having been forced by the exigencies of war to take possession of an alien land, has behaved to its inhabitants with the disinterested zeal for their progress that our people have shown in the Philippines." In a later address, he remarked that Cuba "must be in a sense part of our economic system. We expect her to accept a political attitude toward us which we think wisest both for her and for us." We had no land hunger. "Any country whose people conduct themselves well can count upon our hearty friendship." He pondered the merits of Nicaragua and of Panama—a province of Colombia—for carrying American ships by way of a canal from the Atlantic Ocean to the Pacific, and settled on the Colombian route. The Colombian statesmen became difficult. As T.R. was later to say, in speeches delivered in 1908 and 1911: "I took the Canal Zone. . . . and let Congress debate." This was a bit of boasting which was still later to cost the United States $25,000,000, a sum settled upon during the Woodrow Wilson administration, to Roosevelt's deep anger. He defended or, rather, asserted his position on the Canal question in his third Annual Message to Congress, December 7, 1903.

"I Took the Canal Zone"

. . . In the year 1846 this Government entered into a treaty with New Granada, the predecessor upon the Isthmus of the Republic of Colombia and of the present Republic of Panama, by which treaty it was provided that the Government and citizens of the United States should always have free and open right of way or transit across the Isthmus of Panama by any modes of communication that might be constructed, while in turn our Government guaranteed the perfect neutrality of the above-mentioned Isthmus with the view that the free transit from the one to the other sea might not be interrupted or embarrassed. The treaty vested in the United States a substantial property right carved out of the rights of sovereignty and property which New Granada then had and possessed over the said territory. The name of New Granada has passed away and its territory has been divided. Its successor, the Government of Colombia, has ceased to own any property in the Isthmus. A new Republic, that of Panama, which was at one time a sovereign state, and at another time a mere department of the successive confederations known as New Granada and Columbia, has now succeeded to the rights which first one and then the other formerly exercised over the Isthmus. But as long as the Isthmus endures, the mere geographical fact of its existence, and the peculiar interest therein which is required by our position, perpetuate the solemn contract which binds the holders of the territory to respect our right to freedom of transit across it, and binds us in return to safeguard for the Isthmus and the world the exercise of that inestimable privilege. The true interpretation of the obligations upon which the United States entered in this treaty of 1846 has been given repeatedly in the utterances of Presidents and Secretaries of State. . . .

Last spring, under the act above referred to, a treaty concluded between the representatives of the Republic of Colombia and of our Government was ratified by the Senate. This treaty was entered into at the urgent solicitation of the people of Colombia and after a body of experts appointed by our Government especially to go into the matter of the routes across the Isthmus had pronounced unanimously in favor of the Panama route. In drawing up this treaty every concession was made to the people and to the Government of Colombia. We were more than just dealing with them. . . . Nevertheless the Government of Colombia not merely repudiated the treaty, but repudiated it in such manner as to make it evident by the time the Colombian Congress adjourned that not the scantiest hope remained of ever getting a satisfactory treaty from them. The Government of Colombia made the treaty, and yet when the Colombian Congress was called to ratify it the vote against ratification was unanimous. It does not appear that the Government made any real effort to secure ratification.

Immediately after the adjournment of the Congress a revolution broke out in Panama. The people of Panama had long been discontented with the Republic of Colombia, and they had been kept quiet only by the prospect of the conclusion of the treaty, which was to them a matter of vital concern. When it became evident that the treaty was hopelessly lost, the people of Panama rose literally as one man. Not a shot was fired by a single man on the Isthmus in the interest of the Colombian Government. Not a life was lost in the accomplishment of the revolution. The Colombian troops stationed on the Isthmus, who had long been unpaid, made common cause with the people of Panama, and with astonishing unanimity the new Republic was started. The duty of the United States in the premises was clear. . . . The United States gave notice that it would permit the landing of no expeditionary force, the arrival of which would mean chaos and destruction along the line of the railroad and of the proposed canal, and an interruption of transit as an inevitable consequence. The de facto Government of Panama was recognized in the following telegram to Mr. Ehrman:

"The people of Panama have, by apparently unanimous movement, dissolved their political connection with the Republic of Colombia and resumed their independence. When you are satisfied that a de facto government, republican in form and without substantial opposition from its own people, has been established in the State of Panama, you will enter into relations with it as the responsible government of the territory and look to it for all due action to protect the persons and property of citizens of the United States and to keep open the isthmian transit, in accordance with the obligations of existing treaties governing the relations of the United States to that Territory."

The Government of Colombia was notified of our action by the following telegram to Mr. Beaupre:

"The people of Panama having, by an apparently unanimous movement, dissolved their political connection with the Republic of Colombia and resumed their independence, and having adopted a Government of their own, republican in form, with which the Government of the United States of America has entered into relations, the President of the United States, in accordance with the ties of friendship which have so long and so happily existed between the respective nations, most earnestly commends to the Governments of Colombia and of Panama the peaceful and equitable settlement of all questions at issue between them. He holds that he is bound not merely by treaty obligations, but by the interests of civilization, to see that the peaceful traffic of the world across the Isthmus of Panama shall not longer be disturbed by a constant succession of unnecessary and wasteful civil wars."

When these events happened, fifty-seven years had elapsed since the United States had entered into its treaty with New Granada. During that time the Governments of New Granada and of its successor, Colombia, have been in a constant state of flux. The following is a partial list of the disturbances on the Isthmus of Panama during the period in question as reported to us by our consuls. It is not possible to give a complete list, and some of the reports that speak of "revolutions" must mean unsuccessful revolutions.

May 22, 1850.—Outbreak; two Americans killed. War vessel demanded to quell outbreak.

41

October, 1850.—Revolutionary plot to bring about independence of the Isthmus.

July 22, 1851.—Revolution in four southern provinces.

November 14, 1851.—Outbreak at Chagres. Man-of-war requested for Chagres.

June 27, 1853.—Insurrection at Bogota, and consequent disturbance on Isthmus. War vessel demanded.

May 23, 1854.—Political disturbances; war vessel requested.

June 28, 1854.—Attempted revolution.

October 24, 1854.—Independence of Isthmus demanded by provincial legislature.

April, 1856.—Riot, and massacre of Americans.

May 4, 1856.—Riot.

May 18, 1856.—Riot.

June 3, 1856.—Riot.

October 2, 1856.—Conflict between two native parties. United States forces landed.

December 18, 1858.—Attempted secession of Panama.

April, 1859.—Riots.

September, 1860.—Outbreak.

October 4, 1860.—Landing of United States forces in consequence.

May 23, 1861.—Intervention of the United States forces required by intendente.

October 2, 1861.—Insurrection and civil war.

April 4, 1862.—Measures to prevent rebels crossing Isthmus.

June 13, 1862.—Mosquera's troops refused admittance to Panama.

March, 1865.—Revolution, and United States troops landed.

August, 1865.—Riots; unsuccessful attempt to invade Panama.

March, 1866.—Unsuccessful revolution.

April, 1867.—Attempt to overthrow Government.

August, 1867.—Attempt at revolution.

July 5, 1868.—Revolution; provisional government inaugurated.

August 29, 1868.—Revolution; provisional government overthrown.

April, 1871.—Revolution; followed apparently by counter revolution.

April, 1873.—Revolution and civil war which lasted to October, 1875.

August, 1876.—Civil war which lasted until April, 1877.

July, 1878.—Rebellion.

December, 1878.—Revolt.

April, 1879.—Revolution.
June, 1879.—Revolution.
March, 1883.—Riot.
May, 1883.—Riot.
June, 1884.—Revolutionary attempt.
December, 1884.—Revolutionary attempt.
January, 1885.—Revolutionary disturbances.
March, 1885.—Revolution.
April, 1887.—Disturbance on Panama Railroad.
November, 1887.—Disturbance on line of canal.
January, 1889.—Riot.
January, 1895.—Revolution which lasted until April.
March, 1895.—Incendiary attempt.
October, 1899.—Revolution.
February, 1900, to July, 1900.—Revolution.
January, 1901.—Revolution.
July, 1901.—Revolutionary disturbances.
September, 1901.—City of Colon taken by rebels.
March, 1902.—Revolutionary disturbances.
July, 1902.—Revolution.

The above is only a partial list of the revolutions, rebellions, insurrections, riots, and other outbreaks that have occurred during the period in question; yet they number 53 for the 57 years. It will be noted that one of them lasted for nearly three years before it was quelled; another for nearly a year. In short, the experience of over half a century has shown Colombia to be utterly incapable of keeping order on the Isthmus. Only the active interference of the United States has enabled her to preserve so much as a semblance of sovereignty. . . .

The above recital of facts establishes beyond question: First, that the United States has for over half a century patiently and in good faith carried out its obligations under the treaty of 1846; second, that when for the first time it became possible for Colombia to do anything in requital of the services thus repeatedly rendered to it for fifty-seven years by the United States, the Colombian Government peremptorily and offensively refused thus to do its part, even though to do so would have been to its advantage and immeasurably to the advantage of the State of Panama, at that time under its jurisdiction; third, that throughout this period revolutions, riots, and factional disturbances of every kind have occurred one after the other in almost uninterrupted succession, some of them lasting for months and even for years, while the central government was unable to put them down or to make peace with the rebels; fourth, that these disturbances instead of showing any sign of abating have tended to grow more numerous and more serious in the immediate past; fifth, that the control of Colombia over the Isthmus of Panama could not be maintained without the armed intervention and assistance of the United States. In other words, the Government of Colombia, though wholly unable to maintain order on the Isthmus, has nevertheless declined to ratify a treaty the conclusion of which opened the only chance to secure its own stability and to guarantee permanent peace on, and the construction of a canal across, the Isthmus. . . .

Every effort has been made by the Government of the United States to persuade Colombia to follow a course which was essentially not only to our interests and to the interests of the world, but to the interests of Colombia itself. These efforts have failed; and Colombia, by her persistence in repulsing the advances that have been made, has forced us, for the sake of our own honor, and of the interest and well-being, not merely of our own people, but of the people of the Isthmus of Panama and the people of the civilized countries of the world, to take decisive steps to bring to an end a condition of affairs which had become intolerable. The new Republic of Panama immediately offered to negotiate a treaty with us. This treaty I herewith submit. By it our interests are better safeguarded than in the treaty with Colombia which was ratified by the Senate at its last session. It is better in its terms than the treaties offered to us by the Republics of Nicaragua and Costa Rica. At last the right to begin this great undertaking is made available. Panama has done her part. All that remains is for the American Congress to do its part, and forthwith this Republic will enter upon the execution of a project colossal in its size and of well-nigh incalculable possibilities for the good of this country and the nations of mankind. . . .

T.R. insinuated himself into numerous aspects of world affairs. His work in obtaining a peace treaty between Russia and Japan in 1905 won him the Nobel peace prize, though he viewed the entire war from the vantage point of another war lord. In 1907, he was to send the American battleship fleet around the world, mainly to impress the Japanese. Central America interested him intensely, and toward it he took the familiar and domineering stance which has already been noted. "[S]ooner or later," he wrote his son, "it seems to me inevitable that the United States should assume an attitude of protection and regulation in regard to all these little states in the neighborhood of the Caribbean." Officially he wrote more respectfully, though no less energetically, in the formulation of what came to be known as the Roosevelt Corollary to the Monroe Doctrine; it warned off foreign powers from intervening in Latin American affairs, and also denied Latin American countries the right to place themselves in embarrassing positions that might tempt intervention. His views of such circumstances—formulated over the period of more than a year—were outlined to Congress in his Annual Message of December 5, 1905; the immediate occasion was United States intervention in the financial affairs of the Dominican Republic, the chaos of which had threatened to open financial doors to European creditors that could lead them toward political authority in the Caribbean, challenging American pre-eminence in the area.

Little Brown Men: The Monroe Doctrine Plus

. . . One of the most effective instruments for peace is the Monroe Doctrine as it has been and is being gradually developed by this Nation and accepted by other nations. No other policy could have been as efficient in promoting peace in the Western Hemisphere and in giving to each nation thereon the chance to develop along its own lines. If we had refused to apply the doctrine to changing conditions it would now be completely outworn, would not meet any of the needs of the present day, and, indeed, would probably by this time have sunk into complete oblivion. It is useful at home, and is meeting with recognition abroad because we have adapted our application of it to meet the growing and changing needs of the hemisphere. When we announce a policy such as the Monroe Doctrine we thereby commit ourselves to the consequences of the policy, and those consequences from time to time alter. . . .

That our rights and interests are deeply concerned in the maintenance of the doctrine is so clear as hardly to need argument. This is especially true in view of the construction of the Panama Canal. As a mere matter of self-defense we must exercise a close watch over the approaches to this canal; and this means that we must be thoroughly alive to our interests in the Caribbean Sea.

There are certain essential points which must never be forgotten as regards the Monroe Doctrine. In the first place we must as a Nation make it evident that we do not intend to treat it in any shape or way as an excuse for aggrandizement on our part at the expense of the republics to the south. We must recognize the fact that in some South

American countries there has been much suspicion lest we should interpret the Monroe Doctrine as in some way inimical to their interests, and we must try to convince all the other nations of this continent once and for all that no just and orderly Government has anything to fear from us. There are certain republics to the south of us which have already reached such a point of stability, order, and prosperity that they themselves, though as yet hardly consciously, are among the guarantors of this doctrine. These republics we now meet not only on a basis of entire equality, but in a spirit of frank and respectful friendship, which we hope is mutual. If all of the republics to the south of us will only grow as those to which I allude have already grown, all need for us to be the especial champions of the doctrine will disappear, for no stable and growing American Republic wishes to see some great non-American military power acquire territory in its neighborhood. All that this country desires is that the other republics on this continent shall be happy and prosperous; and they cannot be happy and prosperous unless they maintain order within their boundaries and behave with a just regard for their obligations toward outsiders. It must be understood that under no circumstances will the United States use the Monroe Doctrine as a cloak for territorial aggression. We desire peace with all the world, but perhaps most of all with the other peoples of the American Continent. There are, of course, limits to the wrongs which any self-respecting nation can endure. It is always possible that wrong actions toward this Nation, or toward citizens of this Nation, in some State unable to keep order among its own people, unable to secure justice from outsiders, and unwilling to do justice to those outsiders who treat it well, may result in our having to take action to protect our rights; but such action will not be taken with a view to territorial aggression, and it will be taken at all only with extreme reluctance and when it has become evident that every other resource has been exhausted.

Moreover, we must make it evident that we do not intend to permit the Monroe Doctrine to be used by any nation on this Continent as a shield to protect it from the consequences of its own misdeeds against foreign nations. If a republic to the south of us commits a tort against a foreign nation, such as an outrage against a citizen of that nation, then the Monroe Doctrine does not force us to interfere to prevent punishment of the tort, save to see that the punishment does not assume the form of territorial occupation in any shape. The case is more difficult when it refers to a contractual obligation. Our own Government has always refused to enforce such contractual obligations on behalf of its citizens by an appeal to arms. It is much to be wished that all foreign governments would take the same view. But they do not; and in consequence we are liable at any time to be brought face to face with disagreeable alternatives. On the one hand, this country would certainly decline to go to war to prevent a foreign government from collecting a just debt; on the other hand, it is very inadvisable to permit any foreign power to take possession, even temporarily, of the custom houses of an American Republic in order to enforce the payment of its obligations; for such temporary occupation might turn into a permanent occupation. The only escape from these alternatives may at any time be that we must ourselves undertake to bring about some arrangement by which so much as possible of a just obligation shall be paid. It is far better that this country should put through such an arrangement, rather than allow any foreign country to undertake it. To do so insures the defaulting republic from having to pay debt of an improper character under duress, while it also insures honest creditors of the republic from being passed by in the interest of dishonest or grasping creditors. Moreover, for the United States to take such a position offers the only possible way of insuring us against a clash with some foreign power. The position is, therefore, in the interest of peace as well as in the interest of justice. It is of benefit to our people; it is of benefit to foreign peoples; and most of all it is really of benefit to the people of the country concerned. . . .

Santo Domingo, in her turn, has now made an appeal to us to help her, and not only every principle of wisdom but every generous instinct within us bids us respond to the appeal. . . . The conditions in Santo Domingo have for a number of years grown from bad to worse until a year ago all society was on the verge of dissolution. Fortunately, just at this time a ruler sprang up in Santo Domingo, who, with his colleagues, saw the dangers threatening their country and appealed to the friendship of the only great and powerful neighbor who possessed the power, and as they hoped also the will to help them. There was imminent danger of foreign intervention. The previous rulers of Santo Domingo had recklessly incurred debts, and owing to her internal disorders she had ceased to be able to provide means of paying the debts. The patience of her foreign creditors had become exhausted, and at least two foreign nations were on the point of intervention, and were only prevented from intervening by the unofficial assurance of this Government that it would itself strive to help Santo Domingo in her hour of need. In the case of one of these nations, only the actual opening of negotiations to this end by our Government prevented the seizure of territory in Santo Domingo by a European power. Of the debts incurred some were just, while some were not of a character which really renders it obligatory on or proper for Santo Domingo to pay them in full. But she could not pay any of them unless some stability was assured her Government and people.

Accordingly, the Executive Department of our Government negotiated a treaty under which we are to try to help the Dominican people to straighten out their finances. This treaty is pending before the Senate. In the meantime a temporary arrangement has been made which will last until the Senate has had time to take action upon the treaty. Under this arrangement the Dominican Government has appointed Americans to all the important positions in the customs service, and they are seeing to the honest collection of the revenues, turning over 45 per cent to the Government for running expenses and putting the other 55 per cent into a safe depository for equitable division in case the treaty shall be ratified, among the various creditors, whether European or American. . . .

Under the course taken, stability and order and all the benefits of peace are at last coming to Santo Domingo, danger of foreign intervention has been suspended, and there is at last a prospect that all creditors will get justice, no more and no less. . . .

By now, T.R. stood in vibrant and individual splendor before the American and world public, a figure of constant storm and excitement, hatred and adoration. The cowboy and Rough Rider had become the many-sided President, who commented not only on domestic and international issues, but on much of everything else. Journalists were kept busy following up his views on fiction that depicted animals as talking, on phonetic spelling, on "race suicide." It was a sign of his genius for equivocation that, although he stirred unprecedented controversy and harbored racist and aristocratic views, he did not offend substantial sections of the populace. Americans evidently preferred his powerful and unequivocal nationalism to the principled internationalism of the anti-imperialists and socialists. T.R.'s notion that Americans were not bearing enough children for the uses of the republic obviously referred to his Oyster Bay neighbors, rather than to the teeming immigrant hordes of the growing cities. But this fact did not turn foreign-language newspaper editors, or their readers, against him. His majority in the election of 1904 was of landslide proportions. He was, to a degree, consistent with his moralistic view of life, an "egg head" whose interest in fiction, history and natural phenomena did not repel his more earth-bound constituents. An unsolicited article of his praising Edwin

48

Arlington Robinson raised that poet out of failure and despondency and started him on the major phase of his career.

T.R. was surrounded by whirlwinds of reform that had raised a host of crusaders: Lincoln Steffens and others of *McClure's* magazine, Charles Edward Russell, David Graham Phillips, Edwin Markham and still others of a militant, western, Populist persuasion. Stirrers-up of the people on *Collier's, Everybody's* and a dozen other popular magazines ministered to a hunger for reform that effected even pages of the *Saturday Evening Post* and the *Ladies' Home Journal*. T.R. was identified with this impulse by intransigent defenders of the *status quo*, but some of the reformers knew that he rode the whirlwind, rather than directed it. He was a follower rather than a leader in the pure food agitation that made Upton Sinclair's *The Jungle* a sensation. He was separated from the lurid insurance scandals touched off by Thomas W. Lawson's exposé in *Frenzied Finance*. He contributed nothing to the furtherance of child labor laws, women's rights, labor unions, and factory legislation. His denunciation of "malefactors of great wealth" was too generally couched to be useful. Yet he may have helped make the idea of reform respectable. In his most famous speech, delivered April 14, 1906, at the dedication of the Congressional office building in Washington, he denounced the magazine reforms, his immediate target being David Graham Phillips, whose series on "The Treason of the Senate" was placing *Cosmopolitan* magazine in the forefront of unprecedentedly successful periodicals. T.R.'s speech was hailed nationally as having given the *coup de grâce* to the sensationalists. Historically, the word "muckraking" accreted honor, though it was used popularly to designate irresponsible newspaper campaigns.

"The Man with the Muckrake"

Over a century ago Washington laid the corner stone of the Capitol in what was then little more than a tract of wooded wilderness here beside the Potomac. We now find it necessary to provide by great additional buildings for the business of the government.

This growth in the need for the housing of the government is but a proof and example of the way in which the nation has grown and the sphere of action of the national government has grown. We now administer the affairs of a nation in which the extraordinary growth of population has been outstripped by the growth of wealth in complex interests. The material problems that face us today are not such as they were in Washington's time, but the underlying facts of human nature are the same now as they were then. Under altered external form we war with the same tendencies toward evil that were evident in Washington's time, and are helped by the same tendencies for good. It is about some of these that I wish to say a word today.

In Bunyan's "Pilgrim's Progress" you may recall the description of the Man with the Muck Rake, the man who could look no way but downward, with the muck rake in his hand; who was offered a celestial crown for his muck rake, but who would neither look up nor regard the crown he was offered, but continued to rake to himself the filth of the floor.

In "Pilgrim's Progress" the Man with the Muck Rake is set forth as the example of him whose vision is fixed on carnal instead of spiritual things. Yet he also typifies the man who in this life consistently refuses to see aught that is lofty, and fixes his eyes with solemn intentness only on that which is vile and debasing.

Now, it is very necessary that we should not flinch from seeing what is vile and debasing. There is filth on the floor, and it must be scraped up with the muck rake; and there are times and places where this service is the most needed of all the services that can be performed. But the man who never does anything else, who never thinks or speaks or writes, save of his feats with the muck rake, speedily becomes, not a help but one of the most potent forces for evil.

There are in the body politic, economic and social, many and grave evils, and there is urgent necessity for the sternest war upon them. There should be relentless exposure of and attack upon every evil man, whether politician or business man, every evil practice, whether in politics, business, or social life. I hail as a benefactor every writer or speaker, every man who, on the platform or in a book, magazine, or newspaper, with merciless severity makes such attack, provided always that he in his turn remembers that the attack is of use only if it is absolutely truthful.

The liar is no whit better than the thief, and if his mendacity takes the form of slander he may be worse than most thieves. It puts a premium upon knavery untruthfully to attack an honest man, or even with hysterical exaggeration to assail a bad man with untruth. . . .

Now, it is easy to twist out of shape what I have just said, easy to affect to misunderstand it, and if it is slurred over in repetition not difficult really to misunderstand it. Some persons are sincerely incapable of understanding that to denounce mud slinging does not mean the endorsement of whitewashing; and both the interested individuals who need whitewashing and those others who practice mud slinging like to encourage such confusion of ideas.

50

One of the chief counts against those who make indiscriminate assault upon men in business or men in public life is that they invite a reaction which is sure to tell powerfully in favor of the unscrupulous scoundrel who really ought to be attacked, who ought to be exposed, who ought, if possible, to be put in the penitentiary. If Aristides is praised overmuch as just, people get tired of hearing it; and over-censure of the unjust finally and from similar reasons results in their favor.

Any excess is almost sure to invite a reaction; and, unfortunately, the reaction, instead of taking the form of punishment of those guilty of the excess, is apt to take the form either of punishment of the unoffending or of giving immunity, and even strength, to offenders. The effort to make financial or political profit out of the destruction of character can only result in public calamity. Gross and reckless assaults on character, whether on the stump or in newspaper, magazine, or book, create a morbid and vicious public sentiment, and at the same time act as a profound deterrent to able men of normal sensitiveness and tend to prevent them from entering the public service at any price.

As an instance in point, I may mention that one serious difficulty encountered in getting the right type of men to dig the Panama canal is the certainty that they will be exposed, both without, and, I am sorry to say, sometimes within, Congress, to utterly reckless assaults on their character and capacity. . . .

It is because I feel that there should be no rest in the endless war against the forces of evil that I ask the war be conducted with sanity as well as with resolution.

The men with the muck rakes are often indispensable to the well being of society; but only if they know when to stop raking the muck, and to look upward to the celestial crown above them, to the crown of worthy endeavor. There are beautiful things above and round about them; and if they gradually grow to feel that the whole world is nothing but muck, their power of usefulness is gone.

If the whole picture is painted black there remains no hue whereby to single out the rascals for distinction from their fellows. Such painting finally induces a kind of moral color blindness; and people affected by it come to the conclusion that no man is really black, and no man really white, but they are all gray.

In other words, they neither believe in the truth of the attack, nor in the honesty of the man who is attacked; they grow as suspicious of the accusation as of the offense; it becomes well nigh hopeless to stir them either to wrath against wrongdoing or to enthusiasm for what is right; and such a mental attitude in the public gives hope to every knave, and is the despair of honest men. . . .

There is any amount of good in the world, and there never was a time when loftier and more disinterested work for the betterment of mankind was being done than now. The forces that tend for evil are great and terrible, but the forces of truth and love and courage and honesty and generosity and sympathy are also stronger than ever before. It is a foolish and timid, no less than a wicked thing, to blink the fact that the forces of evil are strong, but it is even worse to fail to take into account the strength of the forces that tell for good. . . .

In his Ecclesiastical Polity that fine old Elizabethan divine, Bishop Hooker, wrote:

> He that goeth about to persuade a multitude that they are not so well governed as they ought to be shall never want attentive and favorable hearers, because they know the manifold defects whereunto every kind of regimen is subject, but the secret lets and difficulties, which in public proceedings are innumerable and inevitable, they have not ordinarily the judgment to consider.

. . . At this moment we are passing through a period of great unrest—social, political, and industrial unrest. It is of the utmost importance for our future that this should prove to be not the unrest of mere rebelliousness against life, of mere dissatisfaction with the inevitable inequality of conditions, but the unrest of a resolute and eager ambition to secure the betterment of the individual and the nation.

So far as this movement of agitation throughout the country takes the form of a fierce discontent with evil, of a determination to punish the authors of evil, whether in industry or politics, the feeling is to be heartily welcomed as a sign of healthy life.

If, on the other hand, it turns into a mere crusade of appetite against appetite, of a contest between the brutal greed of the "have nots" and the brutal greed of the "haves," then it has no significance for good, but only for evil. If it seeks to establish a line of cleavage, not along the line which divides good men from bad, but along that other line, running at right angles thereto, which divides those who are well off from those who are less well off, then it will be fraught with immeasurable harm to the body politic.

We can no more and no less afford to condone evil in the man of capital than evil in the man of no capital. The wealthy man who exults because there is a failure of justice in the effort to bring some trust magnate to account for his misdeeds is as bad as, and no worse than, the so-called labor leader who clamorously strives to excite a foul class feeling on behalf of some other labor leader who is implicated in murder. One attitude is as bad as the other, and no worse; in each case the accused is entitled to exact justice; and in neither case is there need of action by others which can be construed into an expression of sympathy for crime. . . .

We should discriminate in the sharpest way between fortunes well won and fortunes ill won; between those gained as an incident to performing great services to the community as a whole and those gained in evil fashion by keeping just within the limits of mere law honesty. Of course, no amount of charity in spending such fortunes in any way compensates for misconduct in making them.

As a matter of personal convinction, and without pretending to discuss the details or formulate the system, I feel that we shall ultimately have to consider the adoption of some such scheme as that of a progressive tax on all fortunes, beyond a certain amount, either given in life or devised or bequeathed upon death to any individual—a tax so framed as to put it out of the power of the owner of one of these enormous fortunes to hand on more than a certain amount to any one individual; the tax, of course, to be imposed by the national and not the state government. Such taxation should, of course, be aimed merely at the inheritance or transmission in their entirety of those fortunes swollen beyond all healthy limits.

Again, the national government must in some form exercise supervision over corporations engaged in interstate business—and all large corporations engaged in interstate business—whether by license or otherwise, so as to permit us to deal with the far reaching evils of overcapitalization.

This year we are making a beginning in the direction of serious effort to settle some of these economic problems by the railway rate legislation. Such legislation, if so framed, as I am sure it will be, as to secure definite and tangible results, will amount to something of itself; and it will amount to a great deal more in so far as it is taken as a first step in the direction of a policy of superintendence and control over corporate wealth engaged in interstate commerce; this superintendence and control not to be exercised in a spirit of malevolence toward the men who have created the wealth, but with the firm purpose both to do justice to them and to see that they in their turn do justice to the public at large. . . .

Roosevelt took what he and his set believed to be a statesmanlike attitude toward the problems faced by American Negroes. He recognized their inferior status and doubtless inferior abilities, was realistic and to a degree

53

sympathetic with white, Southern determination to keep the Negro in firm control, but believed Negroes should be encouraged to be self-supporting, self-respecting, and ambitious to advance materially, thanks to sober middle-class virtues and heightened educational standards that emphasized utilitarian talents. He approved the goals of Booker T. Washington, distinguished Negro founder of Tuskegee Institute in Alabama, which sought to instill workaday habits in its students, rather than stress equal rights or professional capacities. T.R.'s dinner engagement with Washington was treated by white Southerners as a studied insult, and their aggravated criticism of the President caused Finley Peter Dunne's Mr. Dooley to observe that Southerners who would under no condition have voted for Roosevelt were now vowing that under no condition would they vote for him.

The Brownsville incident was another matter. The situation was generally as Roosevelt stated in his December 19, 1908, report. Apologists for the Negroes raised various arguments in their behalf, some of which Roosevelt dealt with according to his lights in separate special messages. A striking historical fact was that it did not occur to the President to note or apologize for the existence of segregated Negro units in the army of the United States.

The Brownsville Incident

In response to Senate resolution of December 6 addressed to me, and to the two Senate resolutions addressed to him, the Secretary of War has, by my direction, submitted to me a report which I herewith send to the Senate, together with several documents, including a letter of General Nettleton and memoranda as to precedents for the summary discharge or mustering out of regiments or companies, some or all of the members of which had been guilty of misconduct.

I ordered the discharge of nearly all the members of Companies B, C, and D of the Twenty-fifth Infantry by name, in the exercise of my constitutional power and in pursuance of what, after full consideration, I found to be my constitutional duty as Commander in Chief of the United States Army. I am glad to avail myself of the opportunity afforded by these resolutions to lay before the Senate the following facts as to the murderous conduct of certain members of the companies in question and as to the conspiracy by which many of the other members of these companies saved the criminals from justice, to the disgrace of the United States uniform.

I call your attention to the accompanying reports of Maj. Augustus P. Blocksom, of Lieut. Col. Leonard A. Lovering, and of Brig. Gen. Ernest A. Garlington, the Inspector-General of the United States Army, of their investigation into the conduct of the troops in question. An effort has been made to discredit the fairness of the investigation into the conduct of these colored troops by pointing out that General Garlington is a Southerner. Precisely the same action would have been taken had the troops been white—indeed, the discharge would probably have been made in more summary fashion. General Garlington is a native of South Carolina; Lieutenant-Colonel Lovering is a native of New Hampshire; Major Blocksom is a native of Ohio. As it happens, the disclosure of the guilt of the troops was made in the report of the officer who comes from Ohio, and the efforts of the officer who comes from South Carolina were confined to the endeavor to shield the innocent men of the companies in question, if any such there were, by securing information which would enable us adequately to punish the guilty. But I wish it distinctly understood that the fact of the birthplace of either officer is one which I absolutely refuse to consider. The standard of professional honor and of loyalty to the flag and the service is the same for all officers and all enlisted men of the United States Army, and I resent with the keenest indignation any effort to draw any line among them based upon birthplace, creed, or any other consideration of the kind. I should put the same entire faith in these reports if it had happened that they were all made by men coming from some one State, whether in the South or the North, the East or the West, as I now do, when, as it happens, they were made by officers born in different States.

Major Blocksom's report is most careful, is based upon the testimony of scores of eye-witnesses—testimony which conflicted only in non-essentials and which established the essential facts beyond chance of successful contradiction. Not only has no successful effort been made to traverse his findings in any essential particular, but, as a matter of fact, every trustworthy report from outsiders amply corroborates them, by far the best of these outside reports being that of Gen. A. B. Nettleton, made in a letter to the Secretary of War, which I herewith append; General Nettleton being an ex-Union soldier, a consistent friend of the colored man throughout his life, a lifelong Republican, a citizen of Illinois, and Assistant Secretary of the Treasury under President Harrison.

It appears that in Brownsville, the city immediately beside which Fort Brown is situated, there had been considerable feeling between the citizens and the colored troops of the garrison companies. Difficulties had occurred, there being a conflict of evidence as to whether the citizens or the colored troops were to blame. My impression is that, as a matter of fact, in these difficulties there was blame attached to both sides; but this is a wholly unimportant matter for our present purpose, as nothing that occurred offered in any shape or way an excuse or justification for the atrocious conduct of the troops when, in lawless and murderous spirit, and under cover of the night, they made their attack upon the citizens.

The attack was made near midnight on August 13. The following facts as to this attack are made clear by Major Blocksom's investigation and have not been, and, in my judgment, can not be, successfully controverted. From 9 to 15 or 20 of the colored soldiers took part in the attack. They leaped over the walls from the barracks and hurried through the town. They shot at whomever they saw moving, and they shot into houses where they saw lights. In some of these houses there were women and children, as the would-be murderers must have known. In one house in which there were two women and five children some ten shots went through at a height of about 4½ feet above the floor, one putting out the lamp upon the table. The lieutenant of police of the town heard the firing and rode toward it. He met the raiders, who, as he stated, were about 15 colored soldiers. They instantly started firing upon him. He turned and rode off, and they continued firing upon him until they had killed his horse. They shot him in the right arm (it was afterwards amputated above the elbow). A number of shots were also fired at two other policemen. The raiders fired several times into a hotel, some of the shots being aimed at a guest sitting by a window. They shot into a saloon, killing the bartender and wounding another man. At the same time other raiders fired into another house in which women and children were sleeping, two of the shots going through the mosquito bar over the bed in which the mistress of the house and her two children were lying. Several other houses were struck by bullets. It was at night, and the streets of the town are poorly lighted, so that none of the individual raiders were recognized; but the evidence of many witnesses of all classes was conclusive to the effect that the raiders were negro soldiers. The shattered bullets, shells, and clips of the Government rifles, which were found on the ground, are merely corroborative. So are the bullet holes in the houses; some of which it appears must, from the direction, have been fired from the fort just at the moment when the soldiers left it. Not a bullet hole appears in any of the structures of the fort.

The townspeople were completely surprised by the unprovoked and murderous savagery of the attack. The soldiers were the aggressors from start to finish. They met with no substantial resistance, and one and all who took part in that raid stand as deliberate murderers, who did murder one man, who tried to murder others, and who tried to murder women and children. The act was one of horrible atrocity, and so far as I am aware, unparalleled for infamy in the annals of the United States Army.

The white officers of the companies were completely taken by surprise, and at first evidently believed that the firing meant that the townspeople were attacking the soldiers. It was not until 2 or 3 o'clock in the morning that any of them became aware of the truth. I have directed a careful investigation into the conduct of the officers, to see if any of them were blameworthy, and I have approved the recommendation of the War Department that two be brought before a courtmartial.

As to the noncommissioned officers and enlisted men, there can be no doubt whatever than many were necessarily privy, after if not before the attack, to the conduct of those who took actual part in this murderous riot. I refer to Major Blocksom's report for proof of the fact that certainly some and probably all of the noncommissioned officers in charge of quarters who were responsible for the gun-racks and had keys thereto in their personal possession knew what men were engaged in the attack.

Major Penrose, in command of the post, in his letter . . . gives the reasons why he was reluctantly convinced that some of the men under him—as he thinks, from 7 to 10—got their rifles, slipped out of quarters to do the shooting, and returned to the barracks without being discovered, the shooting all occurring within two and a half short blocks of the barracks. It was possible for the raiders to go from the fort to the farthest point of firing and return in less than ten minutes, for the distance did not exceed 350 yards.

Such are the facts of this case. . . .

The effort to confute this testimony so far has consisted in the assertion or implication that the townspeople shot one another in order to discredit the soldiers—an absurdity too gross to need discussion, and unsupported by a shred of evidence. There is no question as to the murder and the attempted murders; there is no question that some of the soldiers were guilty thereof; there is no question that many of their comrades privy to the deed have combined to shelter the criminals from justice. These comrades of the murderers, by their own action, have rendered it necessary either to leave all the men, including the murderers, in the Army, or to turn them all out; and under such circumstances there was no alternative, for the usefulness of the Army would be at an end were we to permit such an outrage to be committed with impunity.

. . . So much for the original crime. A blacker never stained the annals of our Army. It has been supplemented by another, only less black, in the shape of a successful conspiracy of silence for the purpose of shielding those who took part in the original conspiracy of murder. These soldiers were not school boys on a frolic. They were full-grown men, in the uniform of the United States Army, armed with deadly weapons, sworn to uphold the laws of the United States, and under every obligation of oath and honor not merely to refrain from criminality, but with the sturdiest rigor to hunt down criminality; and the crime they committed or connived at was murder. They perverted the power put into their hands to sustain the law into the most deadly violation of the law. The noncommissioned officers are primarily responsible for the discipline and good conduct of the men; they are appointed to their positions for the very purpose of preserving this discipline and good conduct, and of detecting and securing the punishment of every enlisted man who does what is wrong. They fill, with reference to the discipline, a part that the commissioned officers are of course unable to fill, although the ultimate responsibility for the discipline can never be shifted from the shoulders of the latter. Under any ordinary circumstances the first duty of the noncommissioned officers, as of the commissioned officers, is to train the private in the ranks so that he may be an efficient fighting man against a foreign foe. But there is an even higher duty, so obvious that it is not under ordinary circumstances necessary so much as to allude to it—the duty of training the soldier so that he shall be a protection and not a menace to his peaceful fellow-citizens, and above all to the women and children of the nation. . . .

Yet some of the noncommissioned officers and many of the men of the three companies in question have banded together in a conspiracy to protect the assassins and would-be assassins who have disgraced their uniform by the conduct above related. Many of these non-commissioned officers and men must have known, and all of them may have known, circumstances which would have led to the conviction of those engaged in the murderous assault. They have stolidly and as one man broken their oaths of enlistment and refused to help discover the criminals.

By my direction every effort was made to persuade those innocent of murder among them to separate themselves from the guilty by helping bring the criminals to justice. They were warned that if they did not take advantage of the offer they would all be discharged from the service and forbidden again to enter the employ of the Government. They refused to profit by the warning. I accordingly had them discharged. If any organization of troops in the service, white or black, is guilty of similar conduct in the future I shall follow precisely the some course. Under no circumstances will I consent to keep in the service bodies of men whom the circumstances show to be a menace to the country. Incidentally I may add that the soldiers of longest service and highest position who suffered because of the order, so far from being those who deserve most sympathy, deserve least, for they are the very men upon whom we should be able especially to rely to prevent mutiny and murder.

People have spoken as if this discharge from the service was a punishment. I deny emphatically that such is the case, because as punishment it is utterly inadequate. The punishment meet for mutineers and murderers such as those guilty of the Brownsville assault is death; and a punishment only less severe ought to be meted out to those who have aided and abetted mutiny and murder and treason by refusing to help in their detection. I would that it were possible for me to have punished the guilty men. I regret most keenly that I have not been able to do so. . . .

Any assertion that these men were dealt with harshly because they were colored men is utterly without foundation. Officers or enlisted men, white men or colored men, who were guilty of such conduct, would have been treated in precisely the same way; for there can be nothing more important than for the United States Army, in all its membership, to understand that its arms cannot be turned with impunity against the peace and order of the civil community.

There are plenty of precedents for the action taken. I call your attention to the memoranda herewith submitted from The Military Secretary's office of the War Department, and a memorandum from The Military Secretary enclosing a piece by ex-Corporal Hesse, now chief of division in The Military Secretary's office, together with a letter from District Attorney James Wilkinson, of New Orleans. . . .

During the civil war numerous precedents for the action taken by me occurred in the shape of the summary discharge of regiments or companies because of misconduct on the part of some or all of their members. . . . Three companies of the Fifth Missouri Cavalry and one company of the Fourth Missouri Cavalry were mustered out of the service of the United States without trial by court-martial by reason of mutinous conduct and disaffection *of the majority of the members of these companies* (an almost exact parallel to my action). Another Missouri regiment was mustered out of service because it was in a state bordering closely on mutiny. Other examples, including New Jersey, Maryland, and other organizations, are given in the enclosed papers.

I call your particular attention to the special field order of Brig. Gen. U. S. Grant, issued from the headquarters of the Thirteenth Army Corps on November 16, 1862, in reference to the Twentieth Illinois. Members of this regiment had broken into a store and taken goods to the value of some $1,240, and the rest of the regiment, including especially two officers, failed, in the words of General Grant, to "exercise their authority to ferret out the men guilty of the offenses." General Grant accordingly mustered out of the service of the United States the two officers in question, and assessed the sum of $1,240 against the said regiment as a whole, officers and men to be assessed pro rata on their pay. In its essence this action is precisely similar to that I have taken; although the offense was of course trivial compared to the offense with which I had to deal. . . .

When General Lee was in command of the Army of Northern Virginia, as will appear from the inclosed clipping from the Charlotte Observer, he issued an order in October, 1864, disbanding a certain battalion for cowardly conduct, stating at the time his regret that there were some officers and men belonging to the organization who, although not deserving it, were obliged to share in the common disgrace because the good of the service demanded it.

In addition to the discharges of organizations, which are of course infrequent, there are continual cases of the discharge of individual enlisted men without honor and without trial by court-martial. The official record shows that during the fiscal year ending June 30, last, such discharges were issued by the War Department without trial by court-martial in the cases of 352 enlisted men of the Regular Army, 35 of them being on account of "having become disqualified for service through own misconduct." . . .

So much for the military side of the case. But I wish to say something additional, from the standpoint of the race question. In my message at the opening of the Congress I discussed the matter of lynching. In it I gave utterance to the abhorrence which all decent citizens should feel for the deeds of the men (in almost all cases white men) who take part in lynchings, and at the same time I condemned, as all decent men of any color should condemn, the action of those colored men who actively or passively shield the colored criminal from the law. In the case of these companies we had to deal with men who in the first place were guilty of what is practically the worst possible form of lynching—for a lynching is in its essence lawless and murderous vengeance taken by an armed mob for real or fancied wrongs—and who in the second place covered up the crime of lynching by standing with a vicious solidarity to protect the criminals.

It is of the utmost importance to all our people that we shall deal with each man on his merits as a man, and not deal with him merely as a member of a given race; that we shall judge each man by his conduct and not his color. This is important for the white man, and it is far more important for the colored man. More evil and sinister counsel never was given to any people than that given to colored men by those advisers, whether black or white, who, by apology and condonation, encourage conduct such as that of the three companies in question. If the colored men elect to stand by criminals of their own race because they are of their own race, they assuredly lay up for themselves the most dreadful day of reckoning. Every farsighted friend of the colored race in its efforts to strive onward and upward, should teach first, as the most important lesson, alike to the white man and the black, the duty of treating the individual man strictly on his worth as he shows it. Any conduct by colored people which tends to substitute for this rule the rule of standing by and shielding an evil doer because he is a member of their race, means the inevitable degradation of the colored race. It may and probably does mean damage to the white race, but it means ruin to the black race.

Throughout my term of service in the Presidency I have acted on the principle thus advocated. In the North as in the South I have appointed colored men of high character to office, utterly disregarding the protests of those who would have kept them out of office because they were colored men. So far as was in my power, I have sought to secure for the colored people all their rights under the law. I have done all I could to secure them equal school training when young, equal opportunity to earn their livelihood, and achieve their happiness when old. I have striven to break up peonage; I have upheld the hands of those who, like Judge Jones and Judge Speer, have warred against this peonage, because I would hold myself unfit to be President if I did not feel the same revolt at wrong done a colored man as I feel at wrong done a white man. I have condemned in unstinted terms the crime of lynching perpetrated by white men, and I should take instant advantage of any opportunity whereby I could bring to justice a mob of lynchers. In precisely the same spirit I have now acted with reference to these colored men who have been guilty of a black and dastardly crime. In one policy, as in the other, I do not claim as a favor, but I challenge as a right, the support of every citizen of this country, whatever his color, provided only he has in him the spirit of genuine and farsighted patriotism.

Conservation brought out the very best in the President; it was his most sincere, his most disinterested crusade. He freely admitted his debt of understanding of its meaning and implications to his Secretary of the Interior James R. Garfield and especially his friend and Chief Forester in the Department of Agriculture Gifford Pinchot. T.R. labored to set aside game preserves, parks, forests, to inform the public on the state of its natural resources, to develop reclamation policies, inland waterways, waterpower. His patrician temper was outraged by the attitude of upstarts who could destroy the nation's heritage for personal profit. The "majestic beauty" of Yosemite and the Grand Canyon was his theme in 1905. By 1908 he was ready to bring together his "Congress of Governors" of all the states, along with experts in natural resources and representatives of national organizations. Congress, the Supreme Court, his cabinet and the Inland Waterway Commission were also invited to a national conference of unprecedented scope which was intended to review and revise policy on the public domain. Roosevelt saw this convocation as the capstone of his administration's achievements. Natural resources were being rapidly expended; nothing could be done about the using up of minerals, oil, and gas. But trees could be replenished, soil could be reclaimed for future generations. Some of T.R.'s predictions would be confounded by future developments—he did not, for example, foresee farm surpluses—but his general program of conservation was essentially sound. His Special Message to Congress, January 22, 1909, reviewing the work of the "Congress of Governors" furnished him with an occasion to review also his own achievements as President.

Public Domain: The People's Heritage

I transmit herewith a report of the National Conservation Commission, together with the accompanying papers. This report, which is the outgrowth of the conference of governors last May, was unanimously approved by the recent joint conference held in this city between the National Conservation Commission and governors of States, state conservation commissions, and conservation committees of great organizations of citizens. It is therefore in a peculiar sense representative of the whole nation and all its parts.

With the statements and conclusions of this report I heartily concur, and I commend it to the thoughtful consideration both of the Congress and of our people generally. It is one of the most fundamentally important documents ever laid before the American people. It contains the first inventory of its natural resources ever made by any nation. In condensed form it presents a statement of our available capital in material resources, which are the means of progress, and calls attention to the essential conditions upon which the perpetuity, safety and welfare of this nation now rest and must always continue to rest. It deserves, and should have, the widest possible distribution among the people.

The facts set forth in this report constitute an imperative call to action. The situation they disclose demands that we, neglecting for a time, if need be, smaller and less vital questions, shall concentrate an effective part of our attention upon the great material foundations of national existence, progress and prosperity.

This first inventory of natural resources prepared by the National Conservation Commission is undoubtedly but the beginning of a series which will be indispensable for dealing intelligently with what we have. It supplies as close an approximation to the actual facts as it was possible to prepare with the knowledge and time available. The progress of our knowledge of this country will continually lead to more accurate information and better use of the sources of national strength. But we can not defer action until complete accuracy in the estimates can be reached, because before that time many of our resources will be practically gone. . . .

The great basic facts are already well known. We know that our population is now adding about one-fifth to its numbers in ten years and that by the middle of the present century perhaps one hundred and fifty million Americans, and by its end very many millions more must be fed and clothed from the products of our soil. With the steady growth in population and the still more rapid increase in consumption our people will hereafter make greater and not less demands per capita upon all the natural resources for their livelihood, comfort and convenience. It is high time to realize that our responsibility to

63

the coming millions is like that of parents to their children, and that in wasting our resources we are wronging our descendants.

We know now that our rivers can and should be made to serve our people effectively in transportation, but that the vast expenditures for our waterways have not resulted in maintaining, much less in promoting, inland navigation. Therefore, let us take immediate steps to ascertain the reasons and to prepare and adopt a comprehensive plan for inland-waterway navigation that will result in giving the people the benefits for which they have paid, but which they have not yet received. We know now that our forests are fast disappearing, that less than one-fifth of them are being conserved, and that no good purpose can be met by failing to provide the relatively small sums needed for the protection, use and improvement of all forests still owned by the Government, and to enact laws to check the wasteful destruction of the forests in private hands. There are differences of opinion as to many public questions; but the American people stand nearly as a unit for waterway development and for forest protection.

We know now that our mineral resources once exhausted are gone forever, and that the needless waste of them costs us hundreds of human lives and nearly $300,000,000 a year. Therefore, let us undertake without delay the investigations necessary before our people will be in position, through state action or otherwise, to put an end to this huge loss and waste, and conserve both our mineral resources and the lives of the men who take them from the earth. . . .

The unchecked existence of monopoly is incompatible with equality of opportunity. The reason for the exercise of government control over great monopolies is to equalize opportunity. We are fighting against privilege. It was made unlawful for corporations to contribute money for election expenses in order to abridge the power of special privilege at the polls. Railroad-rate control is an attempt to secure an equality of opportunity for all men affected by rail transportation; and that means all of us. The great anthracite coal strike was settled, and the pressing danger of a coal famine averted, because we recognized that the control of a public necessity involves a duty to the people, and that public intervention in the affairs of a public-service corporation is neither to be resented as usurpation nor permitted as a privilege by the corporations, but on the contrary to be accepted as a duty and exercised as a right by the Government in the interest of all the people. The efficiency of the army and the navy has been increased so that our people may follow in peace the great work of making this country a better place for Americans to live in, and our navy was sent round the world for the same ultimate purpose. All the acts taken by the Government during the last seven years, and all the policies now being pursued by the Government, fit in as parts of a consistent whole.

Our public-land policy has for its aim the use of the public land so that it will promote local development by the settlement of home makers; the policy we champion is to serve all the people legitimately and openly, instead of permitting the lands to be converted, illegitimately and under cover, to the private benefit of a few. Our forest policy was established so that we might use the public forests for the permanent public good, instead of merely for temporary private gain. The reclamation act, under which the desert parts of the public domain are converted to higher uses for the general benefit, was passed so that more Americans might have homes on the land.

These policies were enacted into law and have justified their enactment. Others have failed, so far, to reach the point of action. Among such is the attempt to secure public control of the open range and thus to convert its benefits to the use of the small man, who is the home maker, instead of allowing it to be controlled by a few great cattle and sheep owners.

The enactment of a pure food law was a recognition of the fact that the public welfare outweighs the right to private gain, and that no man may poison the people for his private profit. The employers' liability bill recognized the controlling fact that while the employer usually has at stake no more than his profit, the stake of the employee is a living for himself and his family.

We are building the Panama Canal; and this means that we are engaged in the giant engineering feat of all time. We are striving to add in all ways to the habitability and beauty of our country. We are striving to hold in the public hands the remaining supply of unappropriated coal, for the protection and benefit of all the people. We have taken the first steps toward the conservation of our natural resources, and the betterment of country life, and the improvement of our waterways. We stand for the right of every child to a childhood free from grinding toil, and to an education; for the civic responsibility and decency of every citizen; for prudent foresight in public matters, and for fair play in every relation of our national and economic life. . . .

The National Conservation Commission wisely confined its report to the statement of facts and principles, leaving the Executive to recommend the specific steps to which these facts and principles inevitably lead. Accordingly, I call your attention to some of the larger features of the situation disclosed by the report, and to the action thereby clearly demanded for the general good.

The report says:

"Within recent months it has been recognized and demanded by the people, through many thousand delegates from all States assembled in convention in different sections of the country, that the waterways should and must be improved promptly and effectively as a means of maintaining national prosperity.

"The first requisite for waterway improvement is the control of the waters in such manner as to reduce floods and regulate the regimen of the navigable rivers. The second requisite is development of terminals and connection in such manner as to regulate commerce."

Accordingly, I urge that the broad plan for the development of our waterways, recommended by the Inland Waterways Commission, be put in effect without delay. It provides for a comprehensive system of waterway improvement extending to all the uses of the waters and benefits to be derived from their control, including navigation, the development of power, the extension of irrigation, the drainage of swamp and overflow lands, the prevention of soil wash, and the purification of streams for water supply. It proposes to carry out the work by co-ordinating agencies in the federal departments through the medium of an administrative commission or board, acting in cooperation with the States and other organizations and individual citizens. . . .

FORESTS.

I urge that provision be made for both protection and more rapid development of the national forests. Otherwise, either the increasing use of these forests by the people must be checked or their protection against fire must be dangerously weakened. If we compare the actual fire damage on similar areas on private and national forest lands during the past year, the government fire patrol saved commerical timber worth as much as the total cost of caring for all national forests at the present rate for about ten years.

I especially commend to the Congress the facts presented by the commission as to the relation between forests and stream flow in its bearing upon the importance of the forest lands in national ownership. Without an understanding of this intimate relation the conservation of both these natural resources must largely fail.

The time has fully arrived for recognizing in the law the

responsibility to the community, the State, and the nation which rests upon the private owners of private lands. The ownership of forest land is a public trust. The man who would so handle his forest as to cause erosion and to injure stream flow must be not only educated, but he must be controlled.

The report of the National Conservation Commission says:

"Forests in private ownership can not be conserved unless they are protected from fire. We need good fire laws, well enforced. Fire control is impossible without an adequate force of men whose sole duty is fire patrol during the dangerous season."

I hold as first among the tasks before the States and the nation in their respective shares in forest conservation the organization of efficient fire patrols and the enactment of good fire laws on the part of the States.

The report says further:

"Present tax laws prevent reforestation of cut-over land and the perpetuation of existing forests by use. An annual tax upon the land itself, exclusive of the timber, and a tax upon the timber when cut is well adapted to actual conditions of forest investment and is practicable and certain. It is far better that forest land should pay a moderate tax permanently than that it should pay an excessive revenue temporarily and then cease to yield at all."

Second only in importance to good fire laws well enforced is the enactment of tax laws which will permit the perpetuation of existing forests by use.

LANDS.

With our increasing population the time is not far distant when the problem of supplying our people with food will become pressing. The possible additions to our arable area are not great, and it will become necessary to obtain much larger crops from the land, as is now done in more densely settled countries. To do this, we need better farm practice and better strains of wheat, corn and other crop plants, with a reduction in losses from soil erosion and from insects, animals and other enemies of agriculture. The United States Department of Agriculture is doing excellent work in these directions and it should be liberally supported.

The remaining public lands should be classified and the arable lands disposed of to home makers. In their interest the timber and stone act and the commutation clause of the homestead act should be repealed, and the desert-land law should be modified in accordance with the recommendations of the Public Lands Commission.

The use of the public grazing lands should be regulated in such ways as to improve and conserve their value.

Rights to the surface of the public land should be separated from rights to forests upon it and to minerals beneath it, and these should be subject to separate disposal.

The coal, oil, gas and phosphate rights still remaining with the Government should be withdrawn from entry and leased under conditions favorable for economic development.

MINERALS.

The accompanying reports show that the consumption of nearly all of our mineral products is increasing more rapidly than our population. Our mineral waste is about one-sixth of our product, or nearly $1,000,000 for each working day in the year. The loss of structural materials through fire is about another million a day. The loss of life in the mines is appalling. The larger part of these losses of life and property can be avoided.

Our mineral resources are limited in quantity and can not be increased or reproduced. With the rapidly increasing rate of consumption the supply will be exhausted while yet the nation is in its infancy, unless better methods are devised or substitutes are found. Further investigation is urgently needed in order to improve methods and to develop and apply substitutes.

It is of the utmost importance that a Bureau of Mines be established in accordance with the pending bill to reduce the loss of life in mines and the waste of mineral resources and to investigate the methods and substitutes for prolonging the duration of our mineral supplies. Both the need and the public demand for such a bureau are rapidly becoming more urgent. It should co-operate with the States in supplying data to serve as a basis for state mine regulations. The establishment of this bureau will mean merely the transfer from other bureaus of work which it is agreed should be transferred and slightly enlarged and reorganized for these purposes.

CONCLUSIONS.

The joint conference already mentioned adopted two resolutions to which I call your special attention. The first was intended to promote co-operation between the States and the nation upon all of the great questions here discussed. It is as follows:

"*Resolved,* That a joint committee be appointed by the chairman, to consist of six members of state conservation commissions and three members of the National Conservation Commission, whose duty it shall be to prepare and present to the state and national commissions, and through them to the governors and the President, a plan for united action by all organizations concerned with the conservation of natural resources. (On motion of Governor Noel, of Mississippi, the chairman and secretary of the conference were added to and constituted a part of this committee.)"

The second resolution of the joint conference to which I refer calls upon the Congress to provide the means for such co-operation. The principle of the community of interest among all our people in the great natural resources runs through the report of the National Conservation Commission and the proceedings of the joint conference. These resources, which form the common basis of our welfare, can be wisely developed, rightly used, and prudently conserved only by the common action of all the people, acting through their representatives in State and nation. Hence the fundamental necessity for co-operation. Without it we shall accomplish but little, and that little badly. The resolution follows:

"We also especially urge on the Congress of the United States the high desirability of maintaining a national commission on the conservation of the resources of the country, empowered to co-operate with state commissions to the end that every sovereign commonwealth and every section of the country may attain the high degree of prosperity and the sureness of perpetuity naturally arising in the abundant resources and the vigor, intelligence and patriotism of our people."

In this recommendation I most heartily concur, and I urge that an appropriation of at least $50,000 be made to cover the expenses of the National Conservation Commission for necessary rent, assistance and traveling expenses. This is a very small sum. I know of no other way in which the appropriation of so small a sum would result in so large a benefit to the whole nation.

WILLIAM HOWARD TAFT

(1857–1930)

The Judicial Outlook

I have had the honor to be one of the advisers of my distin-
guished predecessor, and, as such, to hold up his hands in the
reforms he has initiated. I should be untrue to myself, to my
promises, and to the declarations of the party platform upon
which I was elected to office, if I did not make the maintenance
and enforcement of those reforms a most important feature of
my administration. . . .
    To render the reforms lasting, . . . and to secure at the same
time freedom from alarm on the part of those pursuing proper
and progressive business methods, further legislative and execu-
tive action are needed.

Inaugural Address, *March 4, 1909*

Some Progressives later resented that Roosevelt had, as they interpreted
it, foisted Taft upon them as an inadequately weighed shadow of himself.
They thus forgot that T.R. had long voiced publicly his admiration for his
friend and social peer, and that Taft's reputation for competence, public
service, and uprightness had been widely established. The collapse of Taft's
fame—not into disrepute, but nullity—was remarkable. All twentieth-
century presidents left, for better or worse, a residue: all except Taft. Yet
it became a cliché among professional historians that more had been
legislatively accomplished during his one administration than in T.R.'s
almost two.

Part of Taft's problem was temperamental. Though he put on a merry
air during the presidential campaign of 1908, and had a touch of social
wit and good humor, he viewed life coldly and as a legalist. Law and
order were sacrosanct to him. During the campaign, and before their
separation, Taft referred repeatedly to his "distinguished predecessor."
Thereafter, he emphasized T.R.'s impetuous lack of regard for sober legal
processes and slow and deliberate progress. This unbending insistence on
punctilious right was his undoing; he later stood glaringly embarrassed,
in appearing to have deviated from it himself.

His talents were real enough. He came of highly respected forebears in
Cincinnati, was a brilliant Yale student, Solicitor-General of the United

70

States under President Benjamin Harrison at the age of thirty-three in 1890, and both United States circuit judge and dean of the law department of the University of Cincinnati, thereafter. President McKinley in 1901 appointed him first civil governor of the Philippine Islands, and the then Vice President Roosevelt hailed him in print as almost alone in his virtues of courage, rectitude, and capacity among public servants.

His actual achievements want definition. He believed the war against Spain had been undertaken from a position of "pure altruism." Of the bitter and gory struggle which continued for over two years between American soldiers and Filipino insurrectos he gave it as his "deliberate judgment" that: "there never was a war conducted, whether against inferior races or not, in which there was more compassion and more restraint and more generosity, *assuming that there was a war at all* [italics added], than there have been in the Philippine Islands."*

Nevertheless, despite his contempt for anti-imperialists as such, he strove to establish peace, diminish disease, increase education, and build up a civil service and political interest of Filipinos, looking forward to increased trade relations between the United States and the islands and ultimate—though very ultimate—freedom for its inhabitants. In these goals he was sharply opposed by other Americans stationed or situated in the islands who detested his paternalism, and despised his appeal in behalf of their "little brown brothers." Americans on the mainland also failed to appreciate his combination of good will and good business, and sang the popular song: "He may be a brother of William H. Taft/ But he ain't no friend of mine."

In his zeal to advance his Philippine policy, Taft twice turned down appointments offered him by Roosevelt to the Supreme Court, association with which he sincerely cherished. But, esteeming himself a soldier, he accepted T.R.'s charge that he assume the Secretaryship of War. T.R. employed him in setting up policy for the building of the Panama Canal, and in other responsible capacities which utilized his judicial and conservative assumptions. These, however, threatened to bar him from presidential aspirations. For Taft had been an "injunction judge," intervening in strike and union efforts with cease-and-desist orders which were the bane of organized labor. Taft asserted his sympathy with labor. He agreed that judges must be responsible and even the law might properly curb their injunction-issuing proclivities, though he was not active in spelling out such limitations. Roosevelt backed him in his appeal to the labor electorate: "On the bench Judge Taft showed the two qualities which make a great judge: wisdom and moral courage. They are also the two qualities which make a great President." Enough laborers agreed to bury

* "The war is seldom described in American history books. Before it was over, more than a quarter-million people had died, most of them Filipino refugees killed by disease, starvation and exposure," New York *Times*, February 6, 1964, obituary of General Emilio Aguinaldo.

Bryan at the polls. But the problem of Taft's attitude toward labor and capital continued to stir a conjecture and unrest with which T.R. had not had to cope.

The key to Taft's legislative achievements was the fact that the reform movement was rolling on, that militant journalists and militant Progressive politicians were agitating for progressive laws and laws binding business and enhancing government prerogatives. Taft's natural associations were with the conservative branch of Congress, which he sought conscientiously to serve. His genuine integrity was frayed by his inability to put its stamp upon their actions. The Republican Party platform had declared "unequivocally for a revision of the tariff by a special session of Congress immediately following the inauguration of the next President." There came, instead, the Payne-Aldrich bill, which Taft signed into law, and which juggled with the infinite complexities of tariff schedules pretending to offer relief to the consumer, but failing to do so. In a notoriously heavy-handed address, September 17, 1909, Taft compounded his unfortunate imperception by labeling it (what was technically though insignificantly true) "the best bill that the Republican Party ever passed," and including other inept phrases calculated to annoy his auditors and rouse his opponents.

Tariff Fiasco: The Winona Address

My Fellow Citizens:

As long ago as August, 1906, in the Congressional campaign in Maine, I ventured to announce that I was a tariff revisionist and thought that the time had come for readjustment of the schedules. I pointed out that it had been ten years prior to that time that the Dingley Bill had been passed; that great changes had taken place in the conditions surrounding the productions of the farm, the factory, and the mine, and that under the theory of protection in that time the rates imposed in the Dingley Bill in many instances might have become excessive; that is, might have been greater than the difference between the cost of production abroad and the cost of production at home with a sufficient allowance for a reasonable rate of profit to the American producer. I said that the party was divided on the issue, but that in my judgment the opinion of the party was crystallizing and would probably result in the near future in an effort to make such revision. I pointed out the difficulty that there always

72

was in a revision of the tariff, due to the threatened disturbance of industries to be affected and the suspension of business, in a way which made it unwise to have too many revisions. . . .

It will be observed that the object of the revision under such a statement was not to destroy protected industries in this country, but it was to continue to protect them where lower rates offered a sufficient protection to prevent injury by foreign competition. That was the object of the revision as advocated by me, and it was certainly the object of the revision as promised in the Republican platform.

I want to make as clear as I can this proposition, because, in order to determine whether a bill is a compliance with the terms of that platform, it must be understood what the platform means. A free trader is opposed to any protective rate because he thinks that our manufacturers, our farmers, and our miners ought to withstand the competition of foreign manufacturers and miners and farmers, or else go out of business and find something else more profitable to do. Now, certainly the promises of the platform did not contemplate the downward revision of the tariff rates to such a point that any industry theretofore protected should be injured. Hence, those who contend that the promise of the platform was to reduce prices by letting in foreign competition are contending for a free trade, and not for anything that they had the right to infer from the Republican platform. . . .

Mr. Payne reported a bill—the Payne tariff bill—which went to the Senate and was amended in the Senate by increasing the duty on some things and decreasing it on others. The difference between the House bill and the Senate bill was very much less than the newspapers represented. It turns out upon examination that the reductions in the Senate were about equal to those in the House, though they differed in character. Now, there is nothing quite so difficult as the discussion of a tariff bill, for the reason that it covers so many different items, and the meaning of the terms and the percentages are very hard to understand. The passage of a new bill, especially where a change in the method of assessing the duties has been followed, presents an opportunity for various modes and calculations of the percentages of increases and decreases that are most misleading and really throw no light at all upon the changes made.

One way of stating what was done is to say what the facts show— that under the Dingley law there were 2,024 items. This included dutiable items only. The Payne law leaves 1,150 of these items unchanged. There are decreases in 654 of the items and increases in 220 of the items. Now, of course, that does not give a full picture, but it does show the proportion of decreases to have been three times those of the increases. Again, the schedules are divided into letters from A to N. The first schedule is that of chemicals, oils, etc. There are 232 items in the Dingley law; of these, 81 were decreased, 22 were increased, leaving 129 unchanged. Under Schedule B—earths, earthenware and glassware—there were 170 items in the Dingley law; 46 were decreased, 12 were increased, and 112 left unchanged. C is the schedule of metals and manufactures. . . .

Now, let us take Schedule A—chemicals, oils, and paints. The articles upon which the duty has been decreased are consumed in this country to the extent of $433,000,000. The articles upon which the duty has been increased are consumed in this country to the extent of $11,000,000. Take Schedule B. The articles on which the duty has been decreased enter into the consumption of the country to the amount of $128,000,000, and there has been no increase in duty on such articles. Take Schedule C—metals and their manufactures. . . .

Now, this statement shows as conclusively as possible the fact that there was a substantial downward revision on articles entering into the general consumption of the country which can be termed necessities, for the proportion is $5,000,000,000 representing the consumption of articles to which decreases applied, to less than $300,000,000 of articles of necessity to which the increases applied.

Now, the promise of the Republican platform was not to revise everything downward, and in the speeches which have been taken as interpreting that platform, which I made in the campaign, I did not promise that everything should go downward. What I promised was, that there should be many decreases, and that in some few things increases would be found to be necessary; but that on the whole I conceived that the change of conditions would make the revision necessarily downward—and that, I contend, under the showing which I have made, has been the result of the Payne bill. I did not agree, nor did the Republican party agree, that we would reduce rates to such a point as to reduce prices by the introduction of foreign competition. That is what the free traders desire. That is what the revenue-tariff reformers desire; but that is not what the Republican platform promised, and it is not what the Republican party wished to bring about. . . .

Now, it is said that there was not a reduction in a number of the schedules where there should have been. It is said that there was no reduction in the cotton schedule. There was not. The House and the Senate took evidence and found from cotton manufacturers and from other sources that the rates upon the lower class of cottons were such as to enable them to make a decent profit—but only a decent profit—and they were contented with it; but that the rates on the higher grades of cotton cloth, by reason of court decisions, had been reduced so that they were considerably below those of the cheaper grades of cotton cloth, and that by undervaluations and otherwise the whole cotton schedule had been made unjust and the various items were disproportionate in respect to the varying cloths. Hence, in the Senate a new system was introduced attempting to make the duties more specific rather than *ad valorem,* in order to prevent by judicial decision or otherwise a disproportionate and unequal operation of the schedule. Under this schedule it was contended that there had been a general rise of all the duties on cotton. This was vigorously denied by the experts of the Treasury Department. . . . I agree that the method of taking evidence and the determination was made in a general way, and that there ought to be other methods of obtaining evidence and reaching a conclusion more satisfactory.

Criticism has also been made of the crockery schedule and the failure to reduce that. The question whether it ought to have been reduced or not was a question of evidence which both committees of Congress took up, and both concluded that the present rates on crockery were such as were needed to maintain the business in this country. . . .

On the whole, however, I am bound to say that I think the Payne tariff bill is the best tariff bill that the Republican party ever passed; that in it the party has conceded the necessity for following the changed conditions and reducing tariff rates accordingly. This is a substantial achievement in the direction of lower tariffs and downward revision, and it ought to be accepted as such. . . .

And now the question arises, what was the duty of a Member of Congress who believed in a downward revision greater than that which has been accomplished, who thought that the wool schedules ought to be reduced, and that perhaps there were other respects in which the bill could be improved? Was it his duty because, in his judgment, it did not fully and completely comply with the promises of the party platform as he interpreted it, and indeed as I had interpreted it, to vote against the bill? I am here to justify those who answer this question in the negative. Mr. Tawney was a downward revisionist like myself. He is a low-tariff man, and has been known to be such in Congress all the time he has been there. He is a prominent Republican, the head of the Appropriations Committee, and when a man votes as I think he ought to vote, and an opportunity such as this presents itself, I am glad to speak in behalf of what he did, not in defense of it, but in support of it. . . .

When I could say without hesitation that this is the best tariff bill that the Republican party has ever passed, and therefore the best tariff bill that has been passed at all, I do not feel that I could have reconciled any other course to my conscience than that of signing the bill. . . . Of course if I had vetoed the bill I would have received the applause of many Republicans who may be called low-tariff Republicans, and who think deeply on that subject, and of all the Democracy. Our friends the Democrats would have applauded, and then laughed in their sleeve at the condition in which the party would have been left; but, more than this, and waiving considerations of party, where would the country have been had the bill been vetoed, or been lost by a vote? It would have left the question of the revision of the tariff open for further discussion during the next session. It would have suspended the settlement of all our business down to a known basis upon which prosperity could proceed and investments be made, and it would have held up the coming of prosperity to this country certainly for a year and probably longer. . . . These are the reasons why I signed it.

I have tried to state as strongly as I can, but not more strongly than I think the facts justify, the importance of not disturbing the business interests of this country by an attempt in this Congress or the next to make a new revision; but in the meantime I intend, so far as in me lies, to secure official data upon the operation of the tariff, from which, when a new revision is attempted, exact facts can be secured.

I have appointed a tariff board that has no brief for either side in respect to what the rates shall be. I hope they will make their observations and note their data in their record with exactly the same impartiality and freedom from anxiety as to result with which the Weather Bureau records the action of the elements or any scientific bureau of the Government records the results of its impartial investigations. Certainly the experience in this tariff justifies the statement that no revision should hereafter be attempted in which more satisfactory evidence of an impartial character is not secured.

I am sorry that I am not able to go further into detail with respect to the tariff bill, but I have neither the information nor the time in which to do it. I have simply stated the case as it seemed to Mr. Tawney in his vote and as it seemed to me in my signing the bill.

Taft's imperceptive views of public affairs fouled his relations with varied elements of the public, and brought techniques that had operated to his advantage as a vice-regent into disrepute when employed by him as President. As governor of the Philippine Islands he had made arbitrary decisions on expeditious grounds. As an overseer of technical questions relating to the Canal Zone, the Vatican, and elsewhere he had mixed protocol with high-level rapport successfully. But now suspicion was engendered that his Secretary of the Interior, Richard A. Ballinger, might be plotting to open Alaskan resources to monopolistic exploitation, at the expense of public weal. The "Ballinger Affair" became a saga in the course of which Taft agreed to the casting off of an over-eager, perhaps, but conscientious young land office employee, and to the dismissal of T.R.'s friend and mentor, Gifford Pinchot. Accusations that he had "whitewashed" Ballinger prompted a Senatorial investigation which brought out the fact that he himself had predated a strategic document. In his blunderings, Taft had opened himself to the interpretation that he had deliberately falsified the record, but not in the interests of those concerned for conservation.*

Catastrophe: The Ballinger Affair

On June 27th last, your honorable body [U. S. Senate] adopted the following resolution:

Resolved, That the President of the United States be, and he is hereby, requested to transmit to the Senate of the United States copies of all letters, maps, executive or departmental orders or instructions, surveys, also applications to enter land, or for rights of way for railroads or otherwise, and all other official reports, recommendations, documents, or records in the Departments of War, Interior, and Agriculture, or by any of the officials or bureaus of these departments, not included in the report of the Secretary of the Interior of April 26, 1911, printed as Senate Document No. 12, Sixty-second

* The Ballinger affair is complex. It involved good intentions and good faith. The public aspects of the matter are reflected in Louis Filler, *Crusaders for American Liberalism* (1961 ed.); Taft is explained and exculpated in Henry F. Pringle, *The Life and Times of William Howard Taft* (1939). Alpheus T. Mason, *Bureaucracy Convicts Itself* (1941), definitively explores the socio-political meaning of the case.

Congress, first session, relating in any way to the elimination from the Chugach National Forest, in Alaska, of land fronting upon Controller Bay, approximating 12,800 acres; especially referring to such papers, documents, etc., as relate to the applications of the Controller Railroad & Navigation Co. for rights of way or confirmation of its maps of rights of way or harbor rights or privileges in or near to the said Controller Bay, or upon the Chugach National Forest, or upon lands eliminated therefrom, or upon the tide lands or shore lands of the said Controller Bay, with such information, if any, as is in the possession of the War Department, relating to the character of Controller Bay as a harbor, its soundings, and a designation of those portions of the harbor which are available for the use of deep-water vessels.

Also, to include in the report hereby requested the names of the soldiers whose claims are to be used as bases for the applications for the land referred to, the mesne and subsequent assignments, and other data relating thereto, with a statement of the present status of all said applications to enter said lands or for rights of way thereon.

I herewith submit copies of all the documents above requested. The records in the Department of Commerce and Labor are not asked for in the resolution, but the Secretary of the Interior has secured from the Secretary of Commerce and Labor certain documents relating to the subject matter on file or of record in the Bureau of Coast and Geodetic Survey, and those are transmitted as part of the documents furnished me by the Secretary of the Interior. I also submit such documents as are on the Executive Office files relating to the Executive order of October 28, last.

I deem it wise and proper to accompany the submission of these documents with a statement in narrative form of the action of the administration with the reasons therefor. . . .

In December, 1909, Mr. Richard S. Ryan, representing the Controller Railway & Navigation Company, applied to Mr. Pinchot, the then Forester, for an elimination from the Chugach Forest Reservation of a tract of land to enable his company to secure railroad terminals, bunkers, railroad shops, etc., on the northeast shore of Controller Bay. This application was referred by the Associate Forester to the District Forester at Portland, Ore., and by him to the Forester in Alaska. The result of these references and the application was that early in 1910 Mr. Graves, who had in the meantime become Forester, reported that there was no objection from the standpoint of forestry interests to the elimination of the tract indicated, or, indeed, of 18,000 acres on the northeast shore of Controller Bay. . . .

It follows from what has been said that the question of how the channel of Controller Bay shall be used is wholly in the control of Congress and nothing that has been done by the executive order or otherwise imperils that control. With the opportunity that any projected railway has to secure access to the harbor by locating its right of way to the line of the shore under supervision of the Secretary of the Treasury, or by application to Congress, the mere private ownership of land abutting on the shore is relatively unimportant. If a railway company thus secures access by trestle and wharf to the deepwater channel, it may conveniently establish its terminal yards, stations, warehouses, and elevators wherever in the eliminated tract it can secure title, and extended frontage on the tidal flats is of no particular advantage. As 12,000 acres in the tract eliminated still remain open to entry, the prospect of a monopoly in one railroad company is most remote. I submit to all fair-minded men who may have been disturbed over the charges made in respect to the executive order of October 28, 1910, that it has been demonstrated by the foregoing that no public interest has suffered from its issue; that great good may come from it; and that no dishonest or improper motive is needed to explain it. . . .

Before closing, I desire to allude to a circumstance which the terms of this resolution make apt and relevant. It is a widely published statement attributed to a newspaper correspondent that in an examination of the files of the Interior Department a few weeks ago a postscript was found attached to a letter of July 13, 1910, addressed by Mr. Richard S. Ryan to Secretary Ballinger—and in the present record—urging the elimination of land enough for terminals for the Controller Railway & Navigation Company. The postscript was said to read as follows:

> DEAR DICK:
> I went to see the President the other day. He asked me who it was I represented. I told him, according to our agreement, that I represented myself. But this didn't seem to satisfy him. So I sent for Charlie Taft and asked him to tell his brother, the President, who it was I really represented. The President made no further objection to my claim.
> Yours,   DICK.

The postscript is not now on the files of the department. If it were, it would be my duty to transmit it under this resolution. Who is really responsible for its wicked fabrication if it ever existed, or for the viciously false statement made as to its authenticity, is immaterial for the purposes of this communication. The purport of the alleged postscript is, and the intention of the fabricator was, to make Mr. Richard S. Ryan testify through its words to the public that although I was at first opposed in the public interest to granting the elimination which he requested, nevertheless through the undue influence of my brother, Mr. Charles P. Taft, and the disclosure of the real persons in interest, I was induced improperly and for the promotion of their private gain, to make the order.

The statement in so far as my brother is concerned—and that is the chief feature of the postscript—is utterly unfounded. He never wrote to me or spoke to me in reference to Richard S. Ryan or on the subject of Controller Bay or the granting of any privileges or the making of any orders in respect to Alaska. He has no interest in Alaska, never had, and knows nothing of the circumstances connected with this transaction. He does not remember that he ever met Richard S. Ryan. He never heard of the Controller Railway & Navigation Company until my cablegram of inquiry reached him, which, with his answer, is in the record.

Mr. Ballinger says in a telegram in answer to my inquiry, both of which are in the record, that he never received such a postscript and that he was in Seattle on the date of July 13th, when it was said to have been written.

Mr. Richard S. Ryan, in a letter which he has sent me without solicitation, and which is in the record, says that he never met my brother, Mr. Charles P. Taft, and that so far as he knows, Mr. Charles P. Taft never had the slightest interest in Controller Bay, in the Controller Railway & Navigation Company, or in any Alaskan company, that he utterly denies writing or signing the alleged postscript. The utter improbability of his writing such a postscript to Mr. Ballinger at Washington, when the latter was away for his vacation for two months, must impress everyone. . . .

The person upon whose statement the existence of what has been properly characterized as an amazing postscript is based, is a writer for newspapers and magazines, who was given permission by Secretary Fisher, after consultation with me, to examine all the files in respect to the Controller Bay matter—and this under the supervision of Mr. Brown, then private secretary to the Secretary of the Interior. After the examination, at which it is alleged this postscript was received from the hand of Mr. Brown, the correspondent prepared an elaborate article on the subject of this order and Controller Bay, which was submitted to Mr. Fisher, and which was discussed with Mr.

Fisher at length, but never in the conversation between them or in the article submitted did the correspondent mention the existence of the postscript. Mr. Brown states that there was no such postscript in the papers when he showed them to the correspondent and that he never saw such a postscript. Similar evidence is given by Mr. Carr and other custodians of the records in the Interior Department.

Stronger evidence of the falsity and maliciously slanderous character of the alleged postscript could not be had. Its only significance is the light it throws on the bitterness and venom of some of those who take active part in every discussion of Alaskan issues. The intensity of their desire to besmirch all who invest in that district, and all who are officially connected with its administration, operates upon the minds of weak human instruments and prompts the fabrication of such false testimony as this postscript. I dislike to dwell upon this feature of the case, but it is so full of a lesson that ought to be taken to heart of every patriotic citizen that I cannot pass it over in silence.

When I made this order, I was aware that the condition of public opinion in reference to investments in Alaska, fanned by charges of fraud—some well founded and others of an hysterical and unjust or false character—would lead to an attack upon it and to the questioning of my motives in signing it. I remarked this when I made the order, and I was not mistaken. But a public officer, when he conceives it his duty to take affirmative action in the public interest, has no more right to allow fear of unjust criticism and attack to hinder him from taking that action than he would to allow personal and dishonest motives to affect him. It is easy in cases like this to take the course which timidity prompts, and to do nothing, but such a course does not inure to the public weal.

I am in full sympathy with the concern of reasonable and patriotic men that the valuable resources of Alaska should not be turned over to be exploited for the profit of greedy, absorbing, and monopolistic corporations or syndicates. Whatever the attempts which have been made, no one, as a matter of fact, has secured in Alaska any undue privilege or franchise not completely under the control of Congress. I am in full agreement with the view that every care, both in administration and in legislation, must be observed to prevent the corrupt or unfair acquisition of undue privilege, franchise, or right from the Government in that district. But everyone must know that the resources of Alaska can never become available either to the people of Alaska or to the public of the United States unless reasonable opportunity is granted to those who would invest their money to secure a return proportionate to the risk run in the investment and reasonable under all the circumstances. . . .

Political misfortune and lack of rapport characterized Taft's presidency. Although he would later claim for his administration credit for the new parcel post, postal savings, the Mann Act, the Bureau of Mines and other new agencies, as well as other new techniques of government, the public failed to be impressed by his relationship to them. Thus, with respect to an income tax amendment being bruited, he declared himself against it on the grounds that it would encourage perjury, and expressed himself further on the general topic of taxation in somewhat less than inspiring prose:

> It seems, therefore, that the present Congress has taken the wisest course in adopting as much of the feature of an income tax as conforms to the Constitution, and by recommending an amendment to the Constitution which shall enable us to round out and perfect this corporation tax so as to make it more equitable, and so as to make it an instrument of supervision of corporate wealth by Federal authority. I doubt not that the information thus obtained may be made a basis for further legislation of a regulative character, applicable only to those corporations whose business is so largely of an interstate character as to justify greater restrictions and more direct supervision.

His sincere effort, too, to further better international relationships by means of a reciprocity agreement with Canada also worked against him. His careless wording of the prospect in a letter to T.R. was cruelly, though perhaps accurately, used against him. He saw Canadian products as being exchanged for American goods in a fashion which "would make Canada *only an adjunct of the United States*"—a phrase which Canadians italicized on innumerable occasions. He offended western Progressives who derogated reciprocity on goods which their constituents produced, and also conservative nationalists who stood for protectionism all along the line. He pleased almost no active political element. His Special Message on the subject, January 26, 1911, gave Canadian nationalists still another phrase to denounce, and helped kill reciprocity.

Canadian Reciprocity: "They Are Coming to the Parting of the Ways"

In my annual message of December 6, 1910, I stated that the policy of broader and closer trade relations with the Dominion of Canada, which was initiated in the adjustment of the maximum and minimum provisions of the tariff act of August 5, 1909, had proved mutually beneficial and that it justified further efforts for the readjustment of the commercial relations of the two countries. I also informed you that, by my direction, the Secretary of State had dispatched two representatives of the Department of State as special commissioners to Ottawa to confer with representatives of the Dominion Government, that they were authorized to take steps to formulate a reciprocal trade agreement, and that the Ottawa conferences thus begun, had been adjourned to be resumed in Washington.

On the 7th of the present month two cabinet ministers came to Washington as representatives of the Dominion Government, and the conferences were continued between them and the Secretary of State. The result of the negotiations was that on the 21st instant a reciprocal trade agreement was reached, the text of which is herewith transmitted with accompanying correspondence and other data.

One by one the controversies resulting from the uncertainties which attended the partition of British territory on the American Continent at the close of the Revolution, and which were inevitable under the then conditions, have been eliminated—some by arbitration and some by direct negotiation. The merits of these disputes, many of them extending through a century, need not now be reviewed. They related to the settlement of boundaries, the definition of rights of navigation, the interpretation of treaties, and many other subjects. . . .

The path having been thus opened for the improvement of commercial relations, a reciprocal trade agreement is the logical sequence of all that has been accomplished in disposing of matters of a diplomatic and controversial character. The identity of interest of two peoples linked together by race, language, political institutions, and geographical proximity offers the foundation. The contribution to the industrial advancement of our own country by the migration across the boundary of the thrifty and industrious Canadians of English, Scotch, and French origin is now repaid by the movement of large numbers of our own sturdy farmers to the northwest of Canada, thus giving their labor, their means, and their experience to the development of that section, with its agricultural possibilities.

The guiding motive in seeking adjustment of trade relations between two countries so situated geographically should be to give play to productive forces as far as practicable, regardless of political boundaries. While equivalency should be sought in an arrangement of this character, an exact balance of financial gain is neither imperative nor attainable. No yardstick can measure the benefits to the two peoples of this freer commercial intercourse and no trade agreement should be judged wholly by custom house statistics. . . .

The Dominion has greatly prospered. It has an active, aggressive, and intelligent people. They are coming to the parting of the ways. They must soon decide whether they are to regard themselves as isolated permanently from our markets by a perpetual wall or whether we are to be commercial friends. If we give them reason to take the former view, can we complain if they adopt methods denying access to certain of their natural resources except upon conditions quite unfavorable to us? . . .

Since becoming a nation, Canada has been our good neighbor, immediately contiguous across a wide continent without artificial or natural barrier except navigable waters used in common.

She has cost us nothing in the way of preparations for defense against her possible assault, and she never will. She has sought to agree with us quickly when differences have disturbed our relations. She shares with us common traditions and aspirations. I feel I have correctly interpreted the wish of the American people by expressing, in the arrangement now submitted to Congress for its approval, their desire for a more intimate and cordial realtionship with Canada. I therefore earnestly hope that the measure will be promptly enacted into law.

Taft intended no more nor less with respect to labor and capital than did his former friend Roosevelt, but here as elsewhere he expressed himself badly. His attitude toward labor was not malign; it was merely myopic. During the campaign of 1908, at Cooper Union in New York, he had emphasized his belief that labor deserved all equity before the law. But what of its rights beyond the law? Asked what solution he offered unemployed workmen with starving families, he had answered: "God knows. They have my deepest sympathy. . . . [O]f course there is the charity. . . ." His attitude toward corporations comported better with the times and the trends. Americans really had no heart for destroying the trust; they too much wanted the benefits of the efficiency and mass production it offered. Taft, in effect, proposed regulation of monopolies, rather than destruction; though with his usual insensitivity, he suggested that "judges have been most reluctant to impose . . . sentences on men of respectable standing in society whose offense has been regarded as merely statutory." Labor, too, sought better statutes.

Still, with the great dissolution proceedings against the Standard Oil and tobacco trusts resounding in public consciousness in 1911, Taft surveyed the situation and submitted one of his more judicious proposals, in his Special Message of December 5, 1911.

Antitrust: "Mere Size Is No Sin"

In May last the Supreme Court handed down decisions in the suits in equity brought by the United States to enjoin the further maintenance of the Standard Oil Trust and of the American Tobacco Trust, and to secure their dissolution. The decisions are epoch-making and serve to advise the business world authoratively of the scope and operation of the anti-trust act of 1890. The decisions do not depart in any substantial way from the previous decisions of the court in construing and applying this important statute, but they clarify those decisions by further defining the already admitted exceptions to the literal construction of the act. By the decrees, they furnish a useful precedent as to the proper method of dealing with the capital and property of illegal trusts. These decisions suggest the need and wisdom of additional or supplemental legislation to make it easier for the entire business community to square with the rule of action and legality thus finally established and to preserve the benefit, freedom, and spur of reasonable competition without loss of real efficiency or progress. . . .

We have been twenty-one years making this statute effective for the purposes for which it was enacted. The Knight case was discouraging and seemed to remit to the States the whole available power to attack and suppress the evils of the trusts. Slowly, however, the error of that judgment was corrected, and only in the last three or four years has the heavy hand of the law been laid upon the great illegal combinations that have exercised such an absolute dominion over many of our industries. Criminal prosecutions have been brought and a number are pending, but juries have felt averse to convicting for jail sentences, and judges have been most reluctant to impose such sentences on men of respectable standing in society whose offense has been regarded as merely statutory. Still, as the offense becomes better understood and the committing of it partakes more of studied and deliberate defiance of the law, we can be confident that juries will convict individuals and that jail sentences will be imposed.

In the Standard Oil case the Supreme and Circuit Courts found the combination to be a monopoly of the interstate business of refining, transporting, and marketing petroleum and its products, effected and maintained through thirty-seven different corporations, the stock of which was held by a New Jersey company. It in effect commanded the dissolution of this combination, directed the transfer and *pro rata* distribution by the New Jersey company of the stock held by it in the thirty-seven corporations to and among its stockholders; and the corporations and individual defendants were enjoined from conspiring or combining to restore such monopoly; and all agreements between the subsidiary corporations tending to produce or bring about further violations of the act were enjoined.

In the Tobacco case, the court found that the individual defendants, twenty-nine in number, had been engaged in a successful effort to acquire complete dominion over the manufacture, sale, and distribution of tobacco in this country and abroad, and that this had been done by combinations made with a purpose and effect to stifle competition, control prices, and establish a monopoly, not only in the manufacture of tobacco, but also of tin-foil and licorice used in its manufacture and of its products of cigars, cigarettes, and snuffs. The tobacco suit presented a far more complicated and difficult case than the Standard Oil suit for a decree which would effectuate the will of the court and end the violation of the statute. There was here no single holding company as in the case of the Standard Oil Trust. The main company was the American Tobacco Company, a manufacturing, selling, and holding company. The plan adopted to destroy the combination and restore competition involved the redivision of the capital and plants of the whole trust between some of the companies constituting the trust and new companies organized for the purposes of the decree and made parties to it, and numbering, new and old, fourteen. . . .

Objection was made by certain independent tobacco companies that this settlement was unjust because it left companies with very large capital in active business, and that the settlement that would be effective to put all on an equality would be a division of the capital and plant of the trust into small fractions in amount more nearly equal to that of each of the independent companies. This contention results from a misunderstanding of the anti-trust law and its purpose. It is not intended thereby to prevent the accumulation of large capital in business enterprises in which such a combination can secure reduced cost of production, sale, and distribution. It is directed against such an aggregation of capital only when its purpose is that of stifling competition, enhancing or controlling prices, and establishing a monopoly. If we shall have by the decree defeated these purposes and restored competition between the large units into which the capital and plant have been divided, we shall have accomplished the useful purpose of the statute.

86

It is not the purpose of the statute to confiscate the property and capital of the offending trusts. Methods of punishment by fine or imprisonment of the individual offenders, by fine of the corporation or by forfeiture of its goods in transportation, are provided, but the proceeding in equity is a specific remedy to stop the operation of the trust by injunction and prevent the future use of the plant and capital in violation of the statute.

I venture to say that not in the history of American law has a decree more effective for such a purpose been entered by a court than that against the Tobacco Trust. As Circuit Judge Noyes said in his judgment approving the decree:

"The extent to which it has been necessary to tear apart this combination and force it into new forms with the attendant burdens ought to demonstrate that the Federal anti-trust statute is a drastic statute which accomplishes effective results; which so long as it stands on the statute books must be obeyed, and which can not be disobeyed without incurring far-reaching penalties. And, on the other hand, the successful reconstruction of this organization should teach that the effect of enforcing this statute is not to destroy, but to reconstruct; not to demolish, but to re-create in accordance with the conditions which the Congress has declared shall exist among the people of the United States." . . .

The effect of these two decisions has led to decrees dissolving the combination of manufacturers of electric lamps, a southern wholesale grocers' association, an interlocutory decree against the Power Trust with directions by the circuit court compelling dissolution, and other combinations of a similar history are now negotiating with the Department of Justice looking to a disintegration by decree and reorganization in accordance with law. It seems possible to bring about these reorganizations without general business disturbance.

But now that the anti-trust act is seen to be effective for the accomplishment of the purpose of its enactment, we are met by a cry from many different quarters for its repeal. It is said to be obstructive of business progress, to be an attempt to restore old-fashioned methods of destructive competition between small units, and to make impossible those useful combinations of capital and the reduction of the cost of production that are essential to continued prosperity and normal growth.

In the recent decisions the Supreme Court makes clear that there is nothing in the statute which condemns combinations of capital or mere bigness of plant organized to secure economy in production and a reduction of its cost. It is only when the purpose or necessary effect of the organization and maintenance of the combination or the aggregation of immense size are the stifling of competition, actual and potential, and the enhancing of prices and establishing a monopoly, that the statute is violated. Mere size is no sin against the law. The merging of two or more business plants necessarily eliminates competition between the units thus combined, but this elimination is in contravention of the statute only when the combination is made for purpose of ending this particular competition in order to secure control of, and enhance, prices and create a monopoly. . . .

In a special message to Congress on January 7, 1910, I ventured to point out the disturbance to business that would probably attend the dissolution of these offending trusts. I said:

"But such an investigation and possible prosecution of corporations whose prosperity or destruction affects the comfort not only of stockholders but of millions of wage earners, employees, and associated tradesmen must necessarily tend to disturb the confidence of the business community, to dry up the now flowing sources of capital from its places of hoarding, and produce a halt in our present prosperity that will cause suffering and strained circumstances among the innocent many for the faults of the guilty few. The question which I wish in this message to bring clearly to the consideration and discussion of Congress is whether, in order to avoid such a possible business danger, something can not be done by which these business combinations may be offered a means, without great financial disturbance, of changing the character, organization, and extent of their business into one within the lines of the law under Federal control and supervision, securing compliance with the anti-trust statute. . . ."

I renew the recommendation of the enactment of a general law providing for the voluntary formation of corporations to engage in trade and commerce among the States and with foreign nations. Every argument which was then advanced for such a law, and every explanation which was at that time offered to possible objections, have been confirmed by our experience since the enforcement of the anti-trust statute has resulted in the actual dissolution of active commerical organizations. . . ."

I do not set forth in detail the terms and sections of a statute which might supply the constructive legislation permitting and aiding the formation of combinations of capital into Federal corporations. They should be subject to rigid rules as to their organization and procedure, including effective publicity, and to the closest supervision as to the issue of stock and bonds by an executive bureau or commission in the Department of Commerce and Labor, to which in times of doubt they might well submit their proposed plans for future business. It must be distinctly understood that incorporation under Federal law could not exempt the company thus formed and its incorporators and managers from prosecution under the anti-trust law for subsequent illegal conduct, but the publicity of its procedure and the opportunity for frequent consultation with the bureau or commission in charge of the incorporation as to the legitimate purpose of its transactions would offer it as great security against successful prosecutions for violations of the law as would be practical or wise. . . .

Taft's most famous phrase, voiced in his Annual Message, December 3, 1912, fittingly climaxed a policy which had found him comfortable as a civil governor and as a Secretary of War. His policy would increasingly be rendered obsolete by time and hang about the neck of the United States Department of State. In effect, Taft wanted law and order under the rule of a dominant class—his own. His views of American interests everywhere were always positive. Nations with which we were at peace always enjoyed prosperity; heads of state who cooperated with us always headed excellent regimes. His biographer, Pringle, properly termed his paternalistic approach an "unhappy marriage between idealism and commercialism." Taft, in brief, would have Americans invest in foreign lands, and bring them into the American sphere of influence. In China, he would have had American capital used in building Chinese railroads, among other enterprises. Taft failed in this objective. He was more successful in encouraging Central and South American penetration by way of the American dollar, especially when, as in the cases of Ecuador, Cuba and Nicaragua, American troops stood behind the penetrators, ready to follow them in when necessary.

Dollar Diplomacy

The foreign relations of the United States actually and potentially affect the state of the Union to a degree not widely realized and hardly surpassed by any other factor in the welfare of the whole Nation. The position of the United States in the moral, intellectual, and material relations of the family of nations should be a matter of vital interest to every patriotic citizen. The national prosperity and power impose upon us duties which we can not shirk if we are to be true to our ideals. The tremendous growth of the export trade of the United States has already made that trade a very real factor in the industrial and commercial prosperity of the country. With the development of our industries the foreign commerce of the United States must rapidly become a still more essential factor in its economic welfare. . . .

The fundamental foreign policies of the United States should be raised high above the conflict of partisanship and wholly dissociated from differences as to domestic policy. In its foreign affairs the United States should present to the world a united front. The intellectual, financial, and industrial interests of the country and the publicist, the wage earner, the farmer, and citizen of whatever occupation must cooperate in a spirit of high patriotism to promote that national solidarity which is indispensable to national efficiency and to the attainment of national ideals. . . .

The diplomacy of the present administration has sought to respond to modern ideas of commercial intercourse. This policy has been characterized as substituting dollars for bullets. It is one that appeals alike to idealistic humanitarian sentiments, to the dictates of sound policy and strategy, and to legitimate commercial aims. It is an effort frankly directed to the increase of American trade upon the axiomatic principle that the Government of the United States shall extend all proper support to every legitimate and beneficial American enterprise abroad. How great have been the results of this diplomacy, coupled with the maximum and minimum provision of the tariff law, will be seen by some consideration of the wonderful increase in the export trade of the United States. Because modern diplomacy is commercial, there has been a disposition in some quarters to attribute to it none but materialistic aims. How strikingly erroneous is such an impression may be seen from a study of the results by which the diplomacy of the United States can be judged.

In the field of work toward the ideals of peace this Government negotiated, but to my regret was unable to consummate, two arbitration treaties which set the highest mark of the aspiration of nations toward the substitution of arbitration and reason for war in the settlement of international disputes. Through the efforts of American diplomacy several wars have been prevented or ended. I refer to the successful tripartite mediation of the Argentine Republic, Brazil, and the United States between Peru and Ecuador; the bringing of the boundary dispute between Panama and Costa Rica to peaceful arbitration; the staying of warlike preparations when Haiti and the Dominican Republic were on the verge of hostilities; the stopping of a war in Nicaragua; the halting of internecine strife in Honduras. The Government of the United States was thanked for its influence toward the restoration of amicable relations between the Argentine Republic and Bolivia. The diplomacy of the United States is active in seeking to assuage the remaining ill-feeling between this country and the Republic of Colombia. . . .

In China the policy of encouraging financial investment to enable that country to help itself has had the result of giving new life and practical application to the open-door policy. The consistent purpose of the present administration has been to encourage the use of American capital in the development of China by the promotion of those essential reforms to which China is pledged by treaties with the United States and other powers. . . .

In Central America the aim has been to help such countries as Nicaragua and Honduras to help themselves. They are the immediate beneficiaries. The national benefit to the United States is twofold. First, it is obvious that the Monroe doctrine is more vital in the neighborhood of the Panama Canal and the zone of the Caribbean than anywhere else. There too, the maintenance of that doctrine falls most heavily upon the United States. It is therefore essential that the countries within that sphere shall be removed from the jeopardy involved by heavy foreign debt and chaotic national finances and from the ever-present danger of international complications due to disorder at home. Hence the United States has been glad to encourage and support American bankers who were willing to lend a helping hand to the financial rehabilitation of such countries because this financial rehabilitation and the protection of their customhouses from being the prey of would-be dictators would remove at one stroke the menace of foreign creditors and the menace of revolutionary disorder. . . .

I wish to call your especial attention to the recent occurrences in Nicaragua, for I believe the terrible events recorded there during the revolution of the past summer—the useless loss of life, the devastation of property, the bombardment of defenseless cities, the killing and wounding of women and children, the torturing of noncombatants to exact contributions, and the suffering of thousands of human beings—might have been averted had the Department of State, through approval of the loan convention by the Senate, been permitted to carry out its now well-developed policy of encouraging the extending of financial aid to weak Central American States with the primary objects of avoiding just such revolutions by assisting those Republics to rehabilitate their finances, to establish their currency on a stable basis, to remove the customhouses from the danger of revolutions by arranging for their secure administration, and to establish reliable banks.

During this last revolution in Nicaragua, the Government of that Republic having admitted its inability to protect American life and property against acts of sheer lawlessness on the part of the malcontents, and having requested this Government to assume that office, it became necessary to land over 2,000 marines and bluejackets in Nicaragua. Owing to their presence the constituted Government of Nicaragua was free to devote its attention wholly to its internal troubles, and was thus enabled to stamp out the rebellion in a short space of time. When the Red Cross supplies sent to Granada had been exhausted, 8,000 persons having been given food in one day upon the arrival of the American forces, our men supplied other unfortunate, needy Nicaraguans from their own haversacks. I wish to congratulate the officers and men of the United States [N]avy and Marine Corps who took part in reestablishing order in Nicaragua upon their splendid conduct, and to record with sorrow the death of seven American marines and bluejackets. Since the reestablishment of peace and order, elections have been held amid conditions of quiet and tranquility. Nearly all the American marines have now been withdrawn. The country should soon be on the road to recovery. The only apparent danger now threatening Nicaragua asises from the shortage of funds. Although American bankers have already rendered assistance, they may naturally be loath to advance a loan adequate to set the country upon its feet without the support of some such convention as that of June, 1911, upon which the Senate has not yet acted. . . .

WOODROW WILSON

(1856–1924)

Covenanter in the High Seat

This is not a day of triumph; it is a day of dedication. Here muster, not the forces of party, but the forces of humanity. Men's hearts wait upon us; men's lives hang in the balance; men's hopes call upon us to say what we will do. Who shall live up to the great trust? Who dares fail to try? I summon all honest men, all patriotic, all forward-looking men, to my side. God helping me, I will not fail them, if they will but counsel and sustain me!

First Inaugural Address, *March 4, 1913*

A S A presidential voice, Wilson was far and away the star among twentieth-century performers. T.R. mixed a combination of vigor and morality with rousing and sometimes memorable effort. F.D.R. managed a clear, forthright prose that met issues and promised action and left a residue of significance and of achievement. John F. Kennedy uttered hopes and promises, and seemed to wistful admirers a rare gift too soon lost. But Wilson coped with issues and was striking in his statement of them. He appealed to people and to humanity. He found phrases that were exalted in rhythm and connotation while seeming not to lose their earthbound substance. No one else but Winston Churchill of his generation infused the democratic ideal with equal drama. Critics might note Wilson's tendency toward words of simple, or simplistic, cast: "home," "hearth," "our boys." But after all criticism had been spoken, his outstanding messages lay somewhere between the history of his times and its culture. It was only after memory drifted out of the century toward Abraham Lincoln that the virtues of moderateness, realism and conciliation began to take on lustre at Wilson's expense.

The birth of a popular tribune who was also an intellectual was not readily apparent in his early career. He lived a happy, healthy Virginia youth in the bosom of his Presbyterian family, playing the violin and enjoying group singing. He never felt called upon to apologize for the South's effort at secession. It was his amazing achievement not to disturb his national following with the fact that he was a Southerner and a racist. As late at 1964, nationally known journalists would state without

93

eliciting criticism or ridicule that between Johnson and Johnson there had been no Southern President.

Wilson's early career was mediocre. He was too thin-skinned to fight the ordinary battle to establish himself as a lawyer, too inept to compete with politicians in politics. He became a history teacher, happy, at least, in the possession of an adoring wife and daughters. He wrote essays, esteeming himself one concerned for literature and the humanities. His works in history and biography lacked sweat and depth. He studied comparative government, setting himself down as an admirer of the British parliamentary system. Wilson believed in policy, though he was later to persuade himself, and his constituents, that he believed in people. He believed in free trade—a hallowed Southern cause—rather than in the earthy problems industry and the city had compounded. A follower of Edmund Burke and other standard theorists of conservatism, he sought constitutional controls as brakes against social disorder.

A gentleman, a graceful lecturer, Wilson also offered criticism of "the scientific spirit of the age" soothing to religious breasts, and he would voice unhappiness over monopoly not unusual in Southerners more concerned over "Wall Street" than over Bourbonism in their own backyards. Princeton University, as it now was, had been his alma mater. It had traditionally attracted Southerners—among many distinguished others, James Madison a century and a quarter earlier. In 1902, aged forty-six, Wilson became its president; a pillar of conservatism in an age of reform. His battles against student and faculty snobbery gave him some standing as a liberal, the state of the colleges being what it then was. But it was because he was perceived as a naive educator that the Democratic Party wheelhorses in New Jersey fatefully chose him to be their candidate for governor. They hoped thus to fend off more sophisticated and resourceful reformers. They had no insight into Wilson's tenacity of character, or his self-esteem. (In *Who's Who*, he listed himself as having been a professor at Bryn Mawr College, though he had in fact ranked only as associate professor. After he attained the presidency, he corrected the point.) They were not aware that, as a Princeton undergraduate, he had experimented with cards written: "Thomas Woodrow Wilson, Senator from Virginia." They did not pause to ponder his books in political science, dealing with the cabinet, Congress, the state and the Constitution, or note his belief in the strong executive acting as a species of prime minister. Wilson proved an able campaigner whose gentility did not offend the more matter-of-fact voters. They found his horsey, homely face pleasing, the laugh wrinkles about his eyes genuine, his interest in football and popular entertainment real. They respected his dissatisfaction with common politics and his moments of high seriousness and idealism. He thrilled liberals by breaking with the Democratic Party leaders of his adopted state, and appealing to the electorate to sustain him in his fight for good government.

Meanwhile, there had been a final break between Taft and Roosevelt, a splitup between old guard Republicans and Progressives. All this practically ensured Wilson's presidential victory, but the contest between T.R.'s "New Nationalism" and Wilson's "New Freedom" produced a fiery election. Unbeknownst to both of them, they were speaking for a new America, not an America of populism and popular agitation—the muckrakers had by now been driven out of public life; the age of consolidated journalism and high-geared magazines was underway. Soon, the *New Republic* would be founded, not to sell to the masses but to the leaders, the cognoscenti, the opinion makers. Young Walter Lippmann would denounce drift and call for mastery—in effect, mastery of the mob.

The journalist William Allen White noted that the difference between Wilson and T.R. was the difference between Tweedledum and Tweedledee. Wilson, now a veteran, was even willing to be called "Woody"; the public tactfully bypassed the suggestion. Wilson called for "the emancipation of the generous energies of a people." T.R. wanted to curb the Supreme Court and to regulate trusts. Wilson said he wished to unleash American inventiveness, and that he opposed monopoly. He gave new and inspiring meanings to free trade, which, he said, could not exist "so long as the established fiscal policy of the federal government is maintained." He denied that Democrats contemplated free trade. "But what we intend to do . . . is to weed this garden that we have been cultivating. Because, if we have been laying at the roots of our industrial enterprises this fertilizer of protection, . . . we have found that the stimulation was not equal in respect of all the growths in the garden, and that there are some growths, which every man can distinguish with the naked eye, which have so overtopped the rest, . . . that it is impossible for the industries of the United States as a whole to prosper under their blighting shade. . . ." He went on to make a new tariff the first major act of his new administration; and to electrify the country by beginning, April 8, 1913, a new tradition of addressing Congress in person, something which had not been done since the administration of John Adams.

The First Address to Congress

Mr. Speaker, Mr. President, Gentlemen of the Congress:

I am very glad indeed to have this opportunity to address the two Houses directly and to verify for myself the impression that the President of the United States is a person, not a mere department of the Government hailing Congress from some isolated island of jealous power, sending messages, not speaking naturally and with his own voice—that he is a human being trying to coöperate with other human beings in a common service. After this pleasant experience I shall feel quite normal in all our dealings with one another.

I have called the Congress together in extraordinary session because a duty was laid upon the party now in power at the recent elections which it ought to perform promptly, in order that the burden carried by the people under existing law may be lightened as soon as possible and in order, also, that the business interests of the country may not be kept too long in suspense as to what the fiscal changes are to be to which they will be required to adjust themselves. It is clear to the whole country that the tariff duties must be altered. They must be changed to meet the radical alteration in the conditions of our economic life which the country has witnessed within the last generation. While the whole face and method of our industrial and commercial life were being changed beyond recognition the tariff schedules have remained what they were before the change began, or have moved in the direction they were given when no large circumstance of our industrial development was what it is today. Our task is to square them with the actual facts. The sooner that is done the sooner we shall escape from suffering from the facts and the sooner our men of business will be free to thrive by the law of nature (the nature of free business) instead of by the law of legislation and artificial arrangement.

We have seen tariff legislation wander very far afield in our day—very far indeed from the field in which our prosperity might have had a normal growth and stimulation. No one who looks the facts squarely in the face or knows anything that lies beneath the surface of action can fail to perceive the principles upon which recent tariff legislation has been based. We long ago passed beyond the modest notion of "protecting" the industries of the country and moved boldly forward to the idea that they were entitled to the direct patronage of the Government. For a long time—a time so long that the men now active in public policy hardly remember the conditions that preceded it—we have sought in our tariff schedules to give each group of manufacturers or producers what they themselves thought that they needed in order to maintain a practically exclusive market as against the rest of the world. Consciously or unconsciously, we have built up a set of privileges and exemptions from competition behind which it was easy by any, even the crudest, forms of combination to organize monopoly; until at last nothing is normal, nothing is obliged to stand the tests of efficiency and economy, in our world of big business, but everything thrives by concerted arrangement. Only new principles of action will save us from a final hard crystallization of monopoly and a complete loss of the influences that quicken enterprise and keep independent energy alive.

It is plain what those principles must be. We must abolish everything that bears even the semblance of privilege or of any kind of artificial advantage, and put our business men and producers under the stimulation of a constant necessity to be efficient, economical, and enterprising, masters of competitive supremacy, better workers and merchants than any in the world. Aside from the duties laid upon articles which we do not, and probably cannot, produce, therefore, and the duties laid upon luxuries and merely for the sake of the revenues they yield, the object of the tariff duties henceforth laid must be effective competition, the whetting of American wits by contest with the wits of the rest of the world.

It would be unwise to move toward this end headlong, with reckless haste, or with strokes that cut at the very roots of what has grown up amongst us by long process and at our own invitation. It does not alter a thing to upset it and break it and deprive it of a chance to change. It destroys it. We must make changes in our fiscal laws, in our fiscal system, whose object is development, a more free and wholesome development, not revolution or upset or confusion. We must build up trade, especially foreign trade. We need the outlet and the enlarged field of energy more than we ever did before. We must build up industry as well, and must adopt freedom in the place of artificial stimulation only so far as it will build, not pull down. In dealing with the tariff the method by which this may be done will be a matter of judgment, exercised item by item. To some not accustomed to the excitements and responsibilities of greater freedom our methods may in some respects and at some points seem heroic, but remedies may be heroic and yet be remedies. It is our business to make sure that they are genuine remedies. Our object is clear. If our motive is above just challenge and only an occasional error of judgment is chargeable against us, we shall be fortunate. . . .

I thank you for your courtesy.

The new administration was under way, an administration that would be hailed by its admirers, and by later academicians, as the greatest reform administration in history, at least until the advent of the New Deal. The administration did, in fact, give evidence of action and achievement, but its real meaning lay beneath the surface. True, Wilson made himself personally responsible for the passage of touted legislation. True, he began the practice of giving statements to the press, through which to appeal for the support of the people. Thus, on May 26, 1913, he warned against "the extraordinary exertions being made by the lobby in Washington to gain recognition for certain alterations of the tariff bill." The Underwood Tariff which passed under his leadership made generous downward revisions on necessary commodities. The Federal Reserve Act promised to curb speculators and money monopolists. The Clayton Act sharpened the old Sherman Anti-Trust Act, and exempted unions from prosecution, holding that "the labor of human beings is not a commodity or article of commerce." Federal aid to education, loans to farmers, the Seamen's Act, promising relief to those hitherto oppressed workers, Wilson's eloquent veto of an immigration act—all these deeds and more seemed to add up to unequivocal, unprecedented achievement.

It was too little noted that their *content* depended on factors that would ultimately reduce them to travesty. Free trade would become a mere figment, as British warships and German submarines paraded the sea lanes. The Clayton Act would be rendered null by aggressive antilabor forces in California, in Colorado—where troops paraded in struck mines —and everywhere, once America declared for war, and vigilantes organized to treat dissident labor as subversive. And so with other seemly legislation. One textbook published in 1928 noted smugly that thanks to the Federal Reserve System, the country had been spared financial panics; had it waited another year, it would have been called upon to reconsider its premises.

Wilsonian reform was reform from above. As an efficiency movement, it modernized and streamlined government's relationship to major social interests, ignoring problems of the Negro, poverty, sectionalism, and international relations. It would take monumental events to reveal how spindly were the legislative acts that were intended to support the weight of democratic action.

The Mexican revolution should have been an event of millenarian grandeur: the creation of a giant engine of liberation for Central and South America. Over a relatively long period of time it was revealed as a movement for adjusting some of Mexico's internal relations, and little more. For the United States it offered a dress rehearsal for the stupendous events in Europe. The Wilson administration did not do too badly—it could not have done worse than it did in the Caribbean, which it freely conceived of as an "American lake"—but it was not overly imaginative in its approach. Wilson, in his address to Congress on August 27, 1913, spoke handsomely of American desire for peace and order in Mexico, and used often such words as "genuine," "disinterested," "neighborly," and "concern." But there were American interests as well as interest; American mine owners sought protection for their properties. They were unhappy about turbulent peasants and their rough-handed chieftains.

Wilson over and over protested that America had no wish to interfere in the internal dissensions of her "sister Republic." There was some justice in his protests (April 20, 1914) over the Tampico incident and later (in a statement released to the press March 26, 1916) the transgression of American soil by the peasant leader Villa, who was still later sentimentalized in American motion pictures. Wilson did, however, permit the sale of arms to the friendly Carranza, and take Vera Cruz to forestall the delivery of German arms to the unfriendly Huerta. His policy did not foresee the day when nations south of the border would require study, rather than disciplining.

Dress Rehearsal:
Troubles with Revolutionary Mexico

PART I: THE TAMPICO INCIDENT

Gentlemen of the Congress:

It is my duty to call your attention to a situation which has arisen in our dealings with General Victoriano Huerta at Mexico City which calls for action, and to ask your advice and coöperation in acting upon it. On the 9th of April a paymaster of the U. S. S. *Dolphin* landed at the Iturbide Bridge landing at Tampico with a whaleboat and boat's crew to take off certain supplies needed by his ship, and while engaged in loading the boat was arrested by an officer and squad of men of the army of General Huerta. Neither the paymaster nor anyone of the boat's crew was armed. Two of the men were in the boat when the arrest took place and were obliged to leave it and submit to be taken into custody, notwithstanding the fact that the boat carried, both at her bow and at her stern, the flag of the United States. The officer who made the arrest was proceeding up one of the streets of the town with his prisoners when met by an officer of higher authority, who ordered him to return to the landing and await orders; and within an hour and a half from the time of the arrest orders were received from the commander of the Huertista forces at Tampico for the release of the paymaster and his men. The release was followed by apologies from the commander and later by an expression of regret by General Huerta himself. General Huerta urged that martial law obtained at the time at Tampico; that orders had been issued that no one should be allowed to land at the Iturbide Bridge; and that our sailors had no right to land there. Our naval commanders at the port had not been notified of any such prohibition; and, even if they had been, the only justifiable course open to the local authorities would have been to request the paymaster and his crew to withdraw and to lodge a protest with the commanding officer of the fleet. Admiral Mayo regarded the arrest as so serious an affront that he was not satisfied with the apologies offered, but demanded that the flag of the United States be saluted with special ceremony by the military commander of the port.

The incident cannot be regarded as a trivial one, especially as two of the men arrested were taken from the boat itself—that is to say, from the territory of the United States—but had it stood by itself it might have been attributed to the ignorance or arrogance of a single officer. Unfortunately, it was not an isolated case. . . .

The manifest danger of such a situation was that such offenses might grow from bad to worse until something happened of so gross and intolerable a sort as to lead directly and inevitably to armed conflict. It was necessary that the apologies of General Huerta and his representatives should go much further, that they should be such as to attract the attention of the whole population to their significance, and such as to impress upon General Huerta himself the necessity of seeing to it that no further occasion for explanations and professed regrets should arise. I, therefore, felt it my duty to sustain Admiral Mayo in the whole of his demand and to insist that the flag of the United States should be saluted in such a way as to indicate a new spirit and attitude on the part of the Huertistas.

Such a salute General Huerta has refused, and I have come to ask your approval and support in the course I now purpose to pursue.

This Government can, I earnestly hope, in no circumstances be forced into war with the people of Mexico. Mexico is torn by civil strife. If we are to accept the tests of its own constitution, it has no government. General Huerta has set his power up in the City of Mexico, such as it is, without right and by methods for which there can be no justification. Only part of the country is under his control. If armed conflict should unhappily come as a result of his attitude of personal resentment toward this Government, we should be fighting only General Huerta and those who adhere to him and give him their support, and our object would be only to restore to the people of the distracted Republic the opportunity to set up again their own laws and their own government. . . .

No doubt I could do what is necessary in the circumstances to enforce respect for our Government without recourse to the Congress, and yet not exceed my constitutional powers as President; but I do not wish to act in a matter possibly of so grave consequence except in close conference and coöperation with both the Senate and House. I, therefore, come to ask your approval that I should use the armed forces of the United States in such ways and to such an extent as may be necessary to obtain from General Huerta and his adherents the fullest recognition of the rights and dignity of the United States, even amidst the distressing conditions now unhappily obtaining in Mexico.

There can in what we do be no thought of aggression or of selfish aggrandizement. We seek to maintain the dignity and authority of the United States only because we wish always to keep our great influence unimpaired for the uses of liberty, both in the United States and wherever else it may be employed for the benefit of mankind.

PART II: THE PURSUIT OF VILLA

As has already been announced, the expedition into Mexico was ordered under an agreement with the *de facto* government of Mexico for the single purpose of taking the bandit Villa, whose forces had actually invaded the territory of the United States, and is in no sense intended as an invasion of that Republic or as an infringement of its sovereignty. I have therefore asked the several news services to be good enough to assist the Administration in keeping this view of the expedition constantly before both the people of this country and the distressed and sensitive people of Mexico, who are very susceptible indeed to impressions received from the American press not only, but also very ready to believe that those impressions proceed from the views and objects of our Government itself. Such conclusions, it must be said, are not unnatural, because the main, if not the only source of information for the people on both sides of the border is the public press of the United States. In order to avoid the creation of erroneous and dangerous impressions in this way, I have called upon the several news agencies to use the utmost care not to give news stories regarding this expedition the color of war,

101

to withhold stories of troop movements and military preparations which might be given that interpretation, and to refrain from publishing unverified rumors of unrest in Mexico. I feel that it is most desirable to impress upon both our own people and the people of Mexico the fact that the expedition is simply a necessary punitive measure, aimed solely at the elimination of the marauders who raided Columbus [New Mexico] and who infest an unprotected district near the border which they use as a base in making attacks upon the lives and property of our citizens within our own territory. It is the purpose of our commanders to co-operate in every possible way with the forces of General Carranza in removing this cause of irritation to both governments and to retire from Mexican territory so soon as that object is accomplished. It is my duty to warn the people of the United States that there are persons all along the border who are actively engaged in originating and giving as wide currency as they can to rumors of the most sensational and disturbing sort which are wholly unjustified by the facts. The object of this traffic in falsehood is obvious. It is to create intolerable friction between the Government of the United States and the *de facto* Government of Mexico, for the purpose of bringing about intervention in the interest of certain American owners of Mexican properties. This object can not be attained so long as sane and honorable men are in control of this Government, but very serious conditions may be created, unnecessary bloodshed may result, and the relations between the two republics may be very much embarrassed. The people of the United States should know the sinister and unscrupulous influences that are afoot and should be on their guard against crediting any story coming from the border; and those who disseminate the news should make it a matter of patriotism and of conscience to test the source and authenticity of every report they receive from that quarter.

PART III
The Great War

"The outbreak of war in 1914 caught this nation by surprise," the Committee on Public Information was to explain in its release of June 25, 1917, its "red, white and blue book" on *How the War Came to America*. "The peoples of Europe had had at least some warnings of the coming storm, but to us such a blind, savage onslaught on the ideals of civilization had appeared impossible."

The two great aggregations of Americans massed separately to assimilate the news. On one hand were the friends of the Allies, mainly pro-British and pro-French, with their memories of Shakespeare and Magna Carta, of Lafayette, of the Holy City of Rome. On the other side were the Irish, the German-Americans, and those who despised the czar's government. So vast a division of sympathies seemed of itself to make intervention on the part of Americans impossible. Wilson's presidential proclamation of August 18, 1914, voiced this initial American response to hostilities, but with a solemnity all Americans did not share.

The Shadow of War:
Neutrality "In Fact as Well as in Name"

I suppose that every thoughtful man in America has asked himself, during these last troubled weeks, what influence the European war may exert upon the United States, and I take the liberty of addressing a few words to you in order to point out that it is entirely within our own choice what its effects upon us will be and to urge very earnestly upon you the sort of speech and conduct which will best safeguard the Nation against distress and disaster.

The effect of the war upon the United States will depend upon what American citizens say and do. Every man who really loves America will act and speak in the true spirit of neutrality, which is the spirit of impartiality and fairness and friendliness to all concerned. The spirit of the Nation in this critical matter will be determined largely by what individuals and society and those gathered in public meetings do and say, upon what newspapers and magazines contain, upon what ministers utter in their pulpits, and men proclaim as their opinions on the street.

The people of the United States are drawn from many nations, and chiefly from the nations now at war. It is natural and inevitable that there should be the utmost variety of sympathy and desire among them with regard to the issues and circumstances of the conflict. Some will wish one nation, others another, to succeed in the momentous struggle. It will be easy to excite passion and difficult to allay it. Those responsible for exciting it will assume a heavy responsibility, responsibility for no less a thing than that the people of the United States, whose love of their country and whose loyalty to its Government should unite them as Americans all, bound in honor and affection to think first of her and her interests, may be divided in camps of hostile opinion, hot against each other, involved in the war itself in impulse and opinion if not in action.

Such divisions among us would be fatal to our peace of mind and might seriously stand in the way of the proper performance of our duty as the one great nation at peace, the one people holding itself ready to play a part of impartial mediation and speak the counsels of peace and accommodation, not as a partisan, but as a friend.

I venture, therefore, my fellow countrymen, to speak a solemn word of warning to you against that deepest, most subtle, most essential breach of neutrality which may spring out of partisanship, out of passionately taking sides. The United States must be neutral in fact as well as in name during these days that are to try men's souls. We must be impartial in thought as well as in action, must put a curb upon our sentiments as well as upon every transaction that might be construed as a preference of one party to the struggle before another.

My thought is of America. I am speaking, I feel sure, the earnest wish and purpose of every thoughtful American that this great country of ours, which is, of course, the first in our thoughts and in our hearts, should show herself in this time of peculiar trial a Nation fit beyond others to exhibit the fine poise of undisturbed judgment, the dignity of self-control, the efficiency of dispassionate action; a Nation that neither sits in judgment upon others nor is disturbed in her own counsels and which keeps herself fit and free to do what is honest and disinterested and truly serviceable for the peace of the world.

Shall we not resolve to put upon ourselves the restraints which will bring to our people the happiness and the great and lasting influence for peace we covet for them?

"We are the mediating nation of the world," Wilson declared on April 20, 1915. "We are compounded of the nations of the world; we mediate their blood, we mediate their traditions, we mediate their sentiments, their tastes, their passions, we are ourselves compounded of these things. . . ."

On May 7, 1915, capping a series of incidents at sea which cost American lives, the *Lusitania* was sunk by a German torpedo, drowning over a thousand passengers, more than a hundred of them Americans. The ship had carried ammunition intended for Allied use. Such militants as Theodore Roosevelt despised Wilson for his persistence in the policy of neutrality, as in his speech, May 10, 1915, to several thousand foreign-born citizens who had just been naturalized.

"Too Proud to Fight"

It warms my heart that you should give me such a reception; but it is not of myself that I wish to think to-night, but of those who have just become citizens of the United States. . . .

You have just taken an oath of allegiance to the United States. Of allegiance to whom? Of allegiance to no one, unless it be God—

certainly not of allegiance to those who temporarily represent this great Government. You have taken an oath of allegiance to a great ideal, to a great body of principles, to a great hope of the human race. You have said, "We are going to America not only to earn a living, not only to seek the things which it was more difficult to obtain where we were born, but to help forward the great enterprises of the human spirit—to let men know that everywhere in the world there are men who will cross strange oceans and go where a speech is spoken which is alien to them if they can but satisfy their quest for what their spirits crave; knowing that whatever the speech there is but one longing and utterance of the human heart, and that is for liberty and justice." And while you bring all countries with you, you come with a purpose of leaving all other countries behind you— bringing what is best of their spirit, but not looking over your shoulders and seeking to perpetuate what you intended to leave behind in them. . . . You cannot become thorough Americans if you think of yourselves in groups. America does not consist of groups. A man who thinks of himself as belonging to a particular national group in America has not yet become an American, and the man who goes among you to trade upon your nationality is no worthy son to live under the Stars and Stripes.

My urgent advice to you would be, not only always to think first of America, but always, also, to think first of humanity. You do not love humanity if you seek to divide humanity into jealous camps. Humanity can be welded together only by love, by sympathy, by justice, not by jealousy and hatred. I am sorry for the man who seeks to make personal capital out of the passions of his fellowmen. He has lost the touch and ideal of America, for America was created to unite mankind by those passions which lift and not by the passions which separate and debase. We came to America, either ourselves or in the persons of our ancestors, to better the ideals of men, to make them see finer things than they had seen before, to get rid of the things that divide and to make sure of the things that unite. . . .

See, my friends, what that means. It means that Americans must have a consciousness different from the consciousness of every other nation in the world. I am not saying this with even the slightest thought of criticism of other nations. You know how it is with a family. A family gets centered on itself if it is not careful and is less interested in the neighbors than it is in its own members. So a nation that is not constantly renewed out of new sources is apt to have the narrowness and prejudice of a family; whereas, America must have this consciousness, that on all sides it touches elbows and touches

107

hearts with all the nations of mankind. The example of America must be a special example. The example of America must be the example not merely of peace because it will not fight, but of peace because peace is the healing and elevating influence of the world and strife is not. There is such a thing as a man being too proud to fight. There is such a thing as a nation being so right that it does not need to convince others by force that it is right. . . .

Pacifists and militarists vied with one another in organizing groups intended to resist or increase American interest in intervention. Those who called for entrance into the war could offer no good reason to the mass of citizens for the sacrifices that intervention would entail. The issue of preparedness breached the wall of isolationism.

On June 17, 1915, the League to Enforce Peace was launched at Independence Hall in Philadelphia. Its president was William Howard Taft, who said: "We are not peace-at-any-price men, because we do not think we have reached the time when a plan based on the complete abolition of war is practicable. As long as nations partake of the frailties of men who compose them war is a possibility. . . . We believe it is still necessary to use a threat of overwhelming force of a great league with a willingness to make the threat good in order to frighten nations into a use of rational and peaceful means."

Roosevelt was the prophet of preparedness. He had urged it in 1897, in 1901, and many times more before the coming of the European war. It was insurance against war, he believed; and it guaranteed that America would be ready if war came. "Fear God and take your own part," he wrote. His antagonism to Wilson mounted with every difference that German-American relations created. Wilson himself changed ground, and in January, 1916, went on a speaking tour to urge national defense. He spoke of character, of the need for justice and liberty. He spoke of the national honor. He was not yet ready, as in his speech to the Railway Business Association, January 27, 1916, to spell out what it was America might be preparing for.

The Shadow Lengthens:
Preparedness

Mr. Toastmaster, Ladies and Gentlemen:

The question, it seems to me, which most demands clarification just now is the question to which your toastmaster has referred, the question of preparation for national defense. I say that it stands in need of clarification because it has been deeply clouded by passion and prejudice. . . . For, gentlemen, while America is a very great nation, while America contains every element of fine force and accomplishment, America does not constitute the major part of the world. We live in a world which we did not make, which we can not alter, which we can not think into a different condition from that which actually exists. It would be a hopeless piece of provincialism to suppose that because we think differently from the rest of the world we are at liberty to assume that the rest of the world will permit us to enjoy that thought without disturbance. . . .

Let no man dare to say, if he would speak the truth, that the question of preparation for national defense is a question of war or of peace. If there is one passion more deepseated in the hearts of our fellow countrymen than another, it is the passion for peace. No nation in the world ever more instinctively turned away from the thought of war than this Nation to which we belong. Partly because in the plentitude of its power, in the unrestricted area of its opportunities, it has found nothing to covet in the possession and power of other nations. There is no spirit of aggrandizement in America. There is no desire on the part of any thoughtful and conscientious American man to take one foot of territory from any other nation in the world. I myself share to the bottom of my heart that profound love for peace. I have sought to maintain peace against very great and sometimes very unfair odds. I have had many a time to use every power that was in me to prevent such a catastrophe as war coming upon this country. It is not permissible for any man to say that anxiety for the defense of the Nation has in it the least tinge of desire for a power that can be used to bring on war.

But, gentlemen, there is something that the American people love better than they love peace. They love the principles upon which their political life is founded. They are ready at any time to fight for the vindication of their character and of their honor. They will not at any time seek the contest, but they will at no time cravenly avoid it; because if there is one thing that the individual ought to fight for, and that the Nation ought to fight for, it is the integrity of its own convictions. We can not surrender our convictions. I would rather surrender territory than surrender those ideals which are the staff of life of the soul itself. . . .

Perhaps when you learned, as I dare say you did learn beforehand, that I was expecting to address you on the subject of preparedness, you recalled the address which I made to Congress something more than a year ago, in which I said that this question of military preparedness was not a pressing question. But more than a year has gone by since then and I would be ashamed if I had not learned something in fourteen months. The minute I stop changing my mind with the change of all the circumstances of the world, I will be a back number. . . .

. . . It goes without saying, though apparently it is necessary to say it to some excited persons, that one thing that this country never will endure is a system that can be called militarism. But militarism consists in this, gentlemen: It consists in preparing a great machine whose only use is for war and giving it no use upon which to expend itself. Men who are in charge of edged tools and bidden to prepare them for exact and scientific use grow very impatient if they are not permitted to use them, and I do not believe that the creation of such an instrument is an insurance of peace. I believe that it involves the danger of all the impulses that skillful persons have to use the things that they know how to use.

But we do not have to do that. America is always going to use her Army in two ways. She is going to use it for the purposes of peace, and she is going to use it as a nucleus for expansion into those things which she does believe in, namely, the preparation of her citizens to take care of themselves. There are two sides to the question of preparation; there is not merely the military side, there is the industrial side; and the ideal which I have in mind is this: We ought to have in this country a great system of industrial and vocational education under Federal guidance and with Federal aid, in which a very large percentage of the youth of this country will be given training in the skillful use and application of the principles of science in manufacture and business; and it will be perfectly feasible and highly desirable to add to that and combine with it such a training in the mechanism and care and use of arms, in the sanitation of camps, in the simpler forms of maneuver and organization, as will make these same men at one and the same time industrially efficient and immediately serviceable for national defense. . . .

But, gentlemen, you can not create such a system overnight; you cannot create such a system rapidly. It has got to be built up, and I hope it will be built up, by slow and effective stages; and there is much to be done in the meantime. We must see to it that a sufficient body of citizens is given the kind of training which will make them efficient now if called into the field in case of necessity. It is discreditable to this country, gentlemen, for this is a country full of intelligent men, that we should have exhibited to the world the example we have sometimes exhibited to it, of stupid and brutal waste of force. Think of asking men who can be easily trained to come into the field, crude, ignorant, inexperienced, and merely furnishing the stuff for camp fever and the bullets of the enemy. The sanitary experience of our Army in the Spanish-American War was merely an indictment of America's indifference to the manifest lessons of experience in the matter of ordinary, careful preparation. We have got the men to waste, but God forbid that we should waste them. Men who go as efficient instruments of national honor into the field afford a very handsome spectacle indeed. Men who go in crude and ignorant boys only indict those in authority for stupidity and neglect. So it seems to me that it is our manifest duty to have a proper citizen reserve.

I am not forgetting our National Guard. I have had the privilege of being governor of one of our great States, and there I was brought into association with what I am glad to believe is one of the most efficient portions of the National Guard of the Nation. I learned to admire the men, to respect the officers, and to believe in the National Guard; and I believe that it is the duty of Congress to do very much more for the National Guard than it has ever done heretofore. I believe that that great arm of our national defense should be built up and encouraged to the utmost; but, you know, gentlemen, that under the Constitution of the United States the National Guard is under the direction of more than twoscore States; that it is not permitted to the National Government directly to have a voice in its development and organization; and that only upon occasion of actual invasion has the President of the United States the right to ask those men to leave their respective States. I, for my part, am afraid, though some gentlemen differ with me, that there is no way in which that force can be made a direct resource as a national reserve under national authority.

What we need is a body of men trained in association with units of the Army, and a body of men organized under the immediate direction of the national authority, a body of men subject to the immediate call to arms of the national authority, and yet men not put into the ranks of the Regular Army; men left to their tasks of civil life, men supplied with equipment and training, but not drawn away from the peaceful pursuits which have made America great and must keep her great. I am not a partisan of any one plan. I have had too much experience to think that it is right to so say that the

111

plan that I propose is the only plan that will work, because I have a shrewd suspicion that there may be other plans that will work. What I am after, and what every American ought to insist upon, is a body of at least half a million trained citizens who will serve under conditions of danger as an immediately available national reserve. . . .

Wilson found a cause. Addressing the League to Enforce Peace, May 27, 1916, he indicated that America must cease to isolate herself from the world, must take up the responsibilities of a world power. The United States, he said, must "become a partner in any feasible association of nations formed in order to [create conditions ensuring peace] and make them secure against violation." But he had, in addition, found a more immediate cause: the freedom of the seas. Theoretically, the United States could traffic with Germany or the Allies. Practically, the British battle fleet sealed off the Continent. In retaliation, German submarines prowled the Atlantic Ocean, seeking to discourage commerce with an enemy that provided England with the sinews of strength, if not of war. Had Germany the right to threaten the lives of citizens of neutral nations? Wilson addressed Congress on this subject, April 19, 1916.

The Freedom of the Seas: The "Sussex" Affair

A situation has arisen in the foreign relations of the country of which it is my plain duty to inform you very frankly.

It will be recalled that in February, 1915, the Imperial German Government announced its intention to treat the waters surrounding Great Britain and Ireland as embraced within the seat of war and to destroy all merchant ships owned by its enemies that might be found within any part of that portion of the high seas, and that it warned all vessels, of neutral as well as of belligerent ownership, to keep out of the waters it had thus proscribed or else enter them at their peril. The Government of the United States earnestly protested. It took the position that such a policy could not be pursued without the practical certainty of gross and palpable violations of the law of nations, particularly if submarine craft were to be employed as its instruments, inasmuch as the rules prescribed by that law, rules founded upon principles of humanity and established for the protection of the lives of non-combatants at sea, could not in the nature of the case be observed by such vessels. It based its protest on the ground that persons of neutral nationality and vessels of neutral ownership would be exposed to extreme and intolerable risks, and that no right to close any part of the high seas against their use or to expose them to such risks could lawfully be asserted by any belligerent government. The law of nations in these matters, upon which the Government of the United States based its protest, is not of recent origin or founded upon merely arbitrary principles set up by convention. It is based, on the contrary, upon manifest and imperative principles of humanity and has long been established with the approval and by the express assent of all civilized nations.

Notwithstanding the earnest protest of our Government, the Imperial German Government at once proceeded to carry out the policy it had announced. . . .

. . . In pursuance of the policy of submarine warfare against the commerce of its adversaries, . . . the commanders of German undersea vessels have attacked merchant ships with greater and greater activity, not only upon the high sea surrounding Great Britain and Ireland but wherever they could encounter them, in a way that has grown more and more ruthless, more and more indiscriminate as the months have gone by, less and less observant of restraints of any kind; and have delivered their attacks without compunction against vessels of every nationality and bound upon every sort of errand. Vessels of neutral ownership, even vessels of neutral ownership bound from neutral port to neutral port, have been destroyed along with vessels of belligerent ownership in constantly increasing numbers. Sometimes the merchantman attacked has been warned and summoned to surrender before being fired on or torpedoed; sometimes passengers or crews have been vouchsafed the poor security of being allowed to take to the ship's boats before she was sent to the bottom. But again and again no warning has been given, no escape even to the ship's boats allowed to those on board. . . .

In February of the present year the Imperial German Government informed this Government and the other neutral governments of the world that it had reason to believe that the Government of Great Britain had armed all merchant vessels of British ownership and had given them secret orders to attack any submarine of the enemy they might encounter upon the seas, and that the Imperial German Government felt justified in the circumstances in treating all armed merchantmen of belligerent ownership as auxiliary vessels of war, which it would have the right to destroy without warning. The law of nations has long recognized the right of merchantmen to carry arms for protection and to use them to repel attack, although to use them, in such circumstances, at their own risk; but the Imperial German Government claimed the right to set these understandings aside in circumstances which it deemed extraordinary. Even the terms in which it announced its purpose thus still further to relax the restraints it had previously professed its willingness and desire to put upon the operation of its submarines carried the plain implication that at least vessels which were not armed would still be exempt from destruction without warning and that personal safety would be accorded their passengers and crews; but even that limitation, if it was ever practicable to observe it, has in fact constituted no check at all upon the destruction of ships of every sort. . . .

One of the latest and most shocking instances of this method of warfare was that of the destruction of the French cross channel steamer *Sussex*. It must stand forth, as the sinking of the steamer *Lusitania* did, as so singularly tragical and unjustifiable as to constitute a truly terrible example of the inhumanity of submarine warfare as the commanders of German vessels have for the past twelvemonth been conducting it. If this instance stood alone, some explanation, some disavowal by the German Government, some evidence of criminal mistake or wilful disobedience on the part of the commander of the vessel that fired the torpedo might be sought or entertained; but unhappily it does not stand alone. Recent events make the conclusion inevitable that it is only one instance, even though it be one of the most extreme and distressing instances, of the spirit and method of warfare which the Imperial German Government has mistakenly adopted, and which from the first exposed that Government to the reproach of thrusting all neutral rights aside in pursuit of its immediate objects.

The Government of the United States has been very patient. . . . It has been willing to wait until the significance of the facts became absolutely unmistakable and susceptible of but one interpretation.

That point has now unhappily been reached. The facts are susceptible of but one interpretation. The Imperial German Government has been unable to put any limits or restraints upon its warfare against either freight or passenger ships. It has therefore become painfully evident that the position which this Government took at the very outset is inevitable, namely, that the use of submarines for the destruction of an enemy's commerce is of necessity, because of the very character of the vessels employed and the very methods of attack which their employment of course involves, incompatible with the principles of humanity, the long established and incontrovertible rights of neutrals, and the sacred immunities of noncombatants.

I have deemed it my duty, therefore, to say to the Imperial German Government that if it is still its purpose to prosecute relentless and indiscriminate warfare against vessels of commerce by the use of submarines, notwithstanding the now demonstrated impossibility of conducting that warfare in accordance with what the Government of the United States must consider the sacred and indisputable rules of international law and the universally recognized dictates of humanity, the Government of the United States is at last forced to the conclusion that there is but one course it can pursue; and that unless the Imperial German Government should now immediately declare and effect an abandonment of its present methods of warfare against passenger and freight carrying vessels this Government can have no choice but to sever diplomatic relations with the Government of the German Empire altogether. . . .

Nineteen hundred and sixteen was an election year. Wilson interested himself in the eight-hour day for railroad workers. He amiably addressed the veteran fighters for woman suffrage, assuring them that "when the forces of nature are steadily working and the tide is rising to meet the moon, you need not be afraid that it will not come to its flood." Accepting his party's renomination, he spoke at length on his administration's achievements. He found much that needed still to be accomplished. He said more about Mexico and the coming peace than about the current war, and his party was to reiterate its immortal contention that he had kept America out of the war, with the full though later denied implication that he would continue to do so. It was a bitter election. Roosevelt had destroyed the Progressive Party, and led his followers back into the Republican column. Charles Evans Hughes, its candidate, went to bed under the impression that he had been elected President of the United States. He woke to discover that a few votes in California had turned the state and the election back to Wilson. And now the President rose to his full sense of power and destiny, and forgot that he led a divided country. America, he thought, must mediate. But an administration which had in fact, if not in words, tipped the balance of sympathy in favor of the allies, could hardly mediate, except in their behalf. "Peace without Victory," which he proposed to the Senate, January 22, 1917, rang with equity. In reality, it no more than opened the door to intervention.

Peace Without Victory

GENTLEMEN OF THE SENATE: On the eighteenth of December last I addressed an identic note to the governments of the nations now at war requesting them to state, more definitely than they had yet been stated by either group of belligerents, the terms upon which they would deem it possible to make peace. I spoke on behalf of humanity and of the rights of all neutral nations like our own, many of whose most vital interests the war puts in constant jeopardy. The Central Powers united in a reply which stated merely that they were ready to meet their antagonists in conference to discuss terms of peace. The Entente Powers have replied much more definitely and have stated, in general terms, indeed, but with sufficient definiteness to imply details, the arrangements, guarantees, and acts of reparation which they deem to be the indispensable conditions of a satisfactory settlement. We are that much nearer a definite discussion of the peace which shall end the present war. We are that much nearer the discussion of the international concert which must thereafter hold the world at peace. . . .

It is inconceivable that the people of the United States should play no part in that great enterprise. To take part in such a service will be the opportunity for which they have sought to prepare themselves by the very principles and purposes of their polity and the approved practices of their Government ever since the days when they set up a new nation in the high and honourable hope that it might in all that it was and did show mankind the way to liberty. They cannot in honour withhold the service to which they are now about to be challenged. They do not wish to withhold it. But they owe it to themselves and to the other nations of the world to state the conditions under which they will feel free to render it.

That service is nothing less than this, to add their authority and their power to the authority and force of other nations to guarantee peace and justice throughout the world. Such a settlement cannot now be long postponed. It is right that before it comes this Government should frankly formulate the conditions upon which it would feel justified in asking our people to approve its formal and solemn adherence to a League for Peace. I am here to attempt to state those conditions.

116

The present war must first be ended; but we owe it to candour and to a just regard for the opinion of mankind to say that, so far as our participation in guarantees of future peace is concerned, it makes a great deal of difference in what way and upon what terms it is ended. The treaties and agreements which bring it to an end must embody terms which will create a peace that is worth guaranteeing and preserving, a peace that will win the approval of mankind, not merely a peace that will serve the several interests and immediate aims of the nations engaged. We shall have no voice in determining what those terms shall be, but we shall, I feel sure, have a voice in determining whether they shall be made lasting or not by the guarantees of a universal covenant; and our judgment upon what is fundamental and essential as a condition precedent to permanency should be spoken now, not afterwards when it may be too late. . . .

I do not mean to say that any American government would throw any obstacle in the way of any terms of peace the governments now at war might agree upon, or seek to upset them when made, whatever they might be. I only take it for granted that mere terms of peace between the belligerents will not satisfy even the belligerents themselves. Mere agreements may not make peace secure. It will be absolutely necessary that a force be created as a guarantor of the permanency of the settlement so much greater than the force of any nation now engaged or any alliance hitherto formed or projected that no nation, no probable combination of nations could face or withstand it. If the peace presently to be made is to endure, it must be a peace made secure by the organized major force of mankind.

The terms of the immediate peace agreed upon will determine whether it is a peace for which such a guarantee can be secured. The question upon which the whole future peace and policy of the world depends is this: Is the present war a struggle for a just and secure peace, or only for a new balance of power? If it be only a struggle for a new balance of power, who will guarantee, who can guarantee, the stable equilibrium of the new arrangement? Only a tranquil Europe can be a stable Europe. There must be, not a balance of power, but a community of power; not organized rivalries, but an organized common peace.

Fortunately we have received very explicit assurances on this point. The statesmen of both of the groups of nations now arrayed against one another have said, in terms that could not be misinterpreted, that it was no part of the purpose they had in mind to crush their antagonists. But the implications of these assurances may

117

not be equally clear to all,—may not be the same on both sides of the water. I think them to be.

They imply, first of all, that it must be a peace without victory. It is not pleasant to say this. I beg that I may be permitted to put my own interpretation upon it and that it may be understood that no other interpretation was in my thought. I am seeking only to face realities and to face them without soft concealments. Victory would mean peace forced upon the loser, a victor's terms imposed upon the vanquished. It would be accepted in humiliation, under duress, at an intolerable sacrifice, and would leave a sting, a resentment, a bitter memory upon which terms of peace would rest, not permanently, but only as upon quicksand. Only a peace between equals can last. Only a peace the very principle of which is equality and a common participation in a common benefit. The right state of mind, the right feeling between nations, is as necessary for a lasting peace as is the just settlement of vexed questions of territory or of racial and national allegiance. . . .

And there is a deeper thing involved than even equality of right among organized nations. No peace can last, or ought to last, which does not recognize and accept the principle that governments derive all their just powers from the consent of the governed, and that no right anywhere exists to hand peoples about from sovereignty to sovereignty as if they were property. . . .

And the paths of the sea must alike in law and in fact be free. The freedom of the seas is the *sine qua non* of peace, equality, and co-operation. No doubt a somewhat radical reconsideration of many of the rules of international practice hitherto thought to be established may be necessary in order to make the seas indeed free and common in practically all circumstances for the use of mankind, but the motive for such changes is convincing and compelling. There can be no trust or intimacy between the peoples of the world without them. The free, constant unthreatened intercourse of nations is an essential part of the process of peace and of development. It need not be difficult either to define or to secure the freedom of the seas if the governments of the world sincerely desire to come to an agreement concerning it.

It is a problem closely connected with the limitation of naval armaments and the co-operation of the navies of the world in keeping the seas at once free and safe. And the question of limiting naval armaments opens the wider and perhaps more difficult question of the limitation of armies and of all programmes of military preparation. Difficult and delicate as these questions are, they must be faced with the utmost candour and decided in a spirit of real accommodation if peace is to come with healing it its wings, and come to stay. Peace cannot be had without concession and sacrifice. There can be no sense of safety and equality among the nations if great preponderating armaments are henceforth to continue here and there to be built up and maintained. The statesmen of the world must plan for peace and nations must adjust and accommodate their policy to it as they have planned for war and made ready for pitiless contest and rivalry. The question of armaments, whether on land or sea, is the most immediately and intensely practical question connected with the future fortunes of nations and of mankind. . . .

I am proposing that all nations henceforth avoid entangling alliances which would draw them into competitions of power, catch them in a net of intrigue and selfish rivalry, and disturb their own affairs with influences intruded from without. There is no entangling alliance in a concert of power. When all unite to act in the same sense and with the same purpose all act in the common interest and are free to live their own lives under a common protection.

I am proposing government by the consent of the governed; that freedom of the seas which in international conference after conference representatives of the United States have urged with the eloquence of those who are the convinced disciples of liberty; and that moderation of armaments which makes of armies and navies a power for order merely, not an instrument of aggression or of selfish violence.

These are American principles, American policies. We could stand for no others. And they are also the principles and policies of forward looking men and women everywhere, of every modern nation, of every enlightened community. They are the principles of mankind and must prevail.

Isolationists were unimpressed by Wilson's fervor. They were not outraged by Germany's proclamation (January 31, 1917), in substance closing the sea to American ships. Wilson broke off diplomatic relations with Germany. He sought Congressional approval for arming American merchantmen. Bitterly, he reported to the country, March 4, 1917, that his bill providing this protection had been filibustered into extinction by a "little group of willful men." (This was the famous phrase that would later be confused with the Senate fight of 1919 over acceptance of the League of Nations.) Yet this group spoke for the Germans of Missouri, the Irish of New York, the German-Swedish elements of the Northwest, and included the honorable and distinguished figure of Robert M. La Follette.

"A Little Group of Willful Men"

The termination of the last session of the Sixty-fourth Congress by constitutional limitation disclosed a situation unparalleled in the history of the country, perhaps unparalleled in the history of any modern Government. In the immediate presence of a crisis fraught with more subtle and far-reaching possibilities of national danger than any other the Government has known within the whole history of its international relations, the Congress has been unable to act either to safeguard the country or to vindicate the elementary rights of its citizens. More than 500 of the 531 members of the two houses were ready and anxious to act; the House of Representatives had acted, by an overwhelming majority; but the Senate was unable to act because a little group of eleven Senators had determined that it should not.

The Senate has no rules by which debate can be limited or brought to an end, no rules by which dilatory tactics of any kind can be prevented. A single member can stand in the way of action, if he have but the physical endurance. The result in this case is a complete paralysis alike of the legislative and of the executive branches of the Government.

This inability of the Senate to act has rendered some of the most necessary legislation of the session impossible at a time when the need of it was most pressing and most evident. The bill which would have permitted such combinations of capital and of organization in the export and import trade of the country as the circumstances of international competition have made imperative—a bill which the business judgment of the whole country approved and demanded —has failed. The opposition of one or two Senators has made it impossible to increase the membership of the Interstate Commerce Commission to give it the altered organization necessary for its efficiency. The Conservation bill, which should have released for immediate use the mineral resources which are still locked up in the public lands, now that their release is more imperatively necessary than ever, and the bill which would have made the unused water power of the country immediately available for industry have both failed, though they have been under consideration throughout the sessions of two Congresses and have been twice passed by the House of Representatives. The appropriations for the army have failed, along with the appropriations for the civil establishment of the Government, the appropriations for the military Academy at West Point and the General Deficiency bill. It has proved impossible to extend the powers of the Shipping Board to meet the special needs of the new situations into which our commerce has been forced or to increase the gold reserve of our national banking system to meet the unusual circumstances of the existing financial situation.

It would not cure the difficulty to call the Sixty-fifth Congress in extraordinary session. The paralysis of the Senate would remain. The purpose and the spirit of action are not lacking now. The Congress is more definitely united in thought and purpose at this moment, I venture to say, than it has been within the memory of any men now in its membership. There is not only the most united patriotic purpose, but the objects members have in view are perfectly clear and definite. But the Senate cannot act unless its leaders can obtain unanimous consent. Its majority is powerless, helpless. In the midst of a crisis of extraordinary peril, when only definite and decided action can make the nation safe or shield it from war itself by the aggression of others, action is impossible.

Although, as a matter of fact, the Nation and the representatives of the Nation stand back of the Executive with unprecedented unanimity and spirit, the impression made abroad will, of course, be that it is not so and that other Governments may act as they please without fear that this Government can do anything at all. We cannot explain. The explanation is incredible. The Senate of the United States is the only legislative body in the world which cannot act when its majority is ready for action. A little group of willful men, representing no opinion but their own, have rendered the great Government of the United States helpless and contemptible.

The remedy? There is but one remedy. The only remedy is that the rules of the Senate shall be so altered that it can act. The country can be relied upon to draw the moral. I believe that the Senate can be relied on to supply the means of action and save the country from disaster.

The Germans assayed the situation and concluded there was nothing to be gained by attempting to keep America technically neutral. Public opinion had been turned against them and their American sympathizers. Uncovering of their intrigues with Mexico and Japan, whom they hoped to encourage to war with the United States, capped propaganda against them. They reasoned that the Americans had a meagre military establishment. Before it could be matured, their submarines would have cleared the seas of ships bearing food and munitions for embattled Britain, their armies would have struck death blows at the allied armies in France. The Germans announced that hereafter their submarines would practice unrestricted warfare. Soon after, a number of American ships were torpedoed and sunk. On April 2, 1917, before a joint session of the two houses of Congress, Wilson delivered his most famous address.

The War Message

I have called the Congress into extraordinary session because there are serious, very serious, choices of policy to be made, and made immediately, which it was neither right nor constitutionally permissible that I should assume the responsibility of making.

On the third of February last I officially laid before you the extraordinary announcement of the Imperial German Government that on and after the first day of February it was its purpose to put aside all restraints of law or of humanity and use its submarines to sink every vessel that sought to approach either the ports of Great Britain and Ireland or the western coasts of Europe or any of the ports controlled by the enemies of Germany within the Mediterranean. That had seemed to be the object of the German submarine warfare earlier in the war, but since April of last year the Imperial Government had somewhat restrained the commanders of its undersea craft in conformity with its promise then given to us that passenger boats should not be sunk and that due warning would be given to all other vessels which its submarines might seek to destroy, when no resistance was offered or escape attempted, and care taken that their crews were given at least a fair chance to save their lives in their open boats. The precautions taken were meager and haphazard enough, as was proved in distressing instance after instance in the progress of the cruel and unmanly business, but a certain degree of restraint was observed. The new policy has swept every restriction aside. Vessels of every kind, whatever their flag, their character, their cargo, their destination, their errand, have been ruthlessly sent to the bottom without warning and without thought of help or mercy for those on board, the vessels of friendly neutrals along with those of belligerents. Even hospital ships and ships carrying relief to the sorely bereaved and stricken people of Belgium, though the latter were provided with safe conduct through the proscribed areas by the

German Government itself and were distinguished by unmistakable marks of identity, have been sunk with the same reckless lack of compassion or of principle.

I was for a little while unable to believe that such things would in fact be done by any government that had hitherto subscribed to the humane practices of civilized nations. International law had its origin in the attempt to set up some law which would be respected and observed upon the seas, where no nation had right of dominion and where lay the free highways of the world. By painful stage after stage has that law been built up, with meager enough results, indeed, after all was accomplished that could be accomplished, but always with a clear view, at least, of what the heart and conscience of mankind demanded. This minimum of right the German Government has swept aside under the plea of retaliation and necessity and because it had no weapons which it could use at sea except these which it is impossible to employ as it is employing them without throwing to the winds all scruples of humanity or of respect for the understandings that were supposed to underlie the intercourse of the world. I am not now thinking of the loss of property involved, immense and serious as that is, but only of the wanton and wholesale destruction of the lives of non-combatants, men, women, and children, engaged in pursuits which have always, even in the darkest periods of modern history, been deemed innocent and legitimate. Property can be paid for; the lives of peaceful and innocent people cannot be. The present German submarine warfare against commerce is a warfare against mankind.

It is a war against all nations. American ships have been sunk, American lives taken, in ways which it has stirred us very deeply to learn of, but the ships and people of other neutral and friendly nations have been sunk and overwhelmed in the waters in the same way. There has been no discrimination. The challenge is to all mankind. Each nation must decide for itself how it will meet it. The choice we make for ourselves must be made with a moderation of counsel and a temperateness of judgment befitting our character and our motives as a nation. We must put excited feeling away. Our motive will not be revenge or the victorious assertion of the physical might of the nation, but only the vindication of right, of human right, of which we are only a single champion. . . .

With a profound sense of the solemn and even tragical character of the step I am taking and of the grave responsibilities which it involves, but in unhesitating obedience to what I deem my constitu-

123

tional duty, I advise that the Congress declare the recent course of the Imperial German Government to be in fact nothing less than war against the government and people of the United States; that it formally accept the status of belligerent which has thus been thrust upon it; and that it take immediate steps not only to put the country in a more thorough state of defense but also to exert all its power and employ all its resources to bring the Government of the German Empire to terms and end the war. . . .

In carrying out the measures by which these things are to be accomplished we should keep constantly in mind the wisdom of interfering as little as possible in our own preparation and in the equipment of our own military forces with the duty,—for it will be a very practical duty,—of supplying the nations already at war with Germany with the materials which they can obtain only from us or by our assistance. They are in the field and we should help them in every way to be effective there. . . .

While we do these things, these deeply momentous things, let us be very clear, and make very clear to all the world what our motives and our objects are. My own thought has not been driven from its habitual and normal course by the unhappy events of the last two months, and I do not believe that the thought of the Nation has been altered or clouded by them. I have exactly the same things in mind now that I had in mind when I addressed the Senate on the twenty-second of January last; the same that I had in mind when I addressed the Congress on the third of February and on the twenty-sixth of February. Our object now, as then, is to vindicate the principles of peace and justice in the life of the world as against selfish and autocratic power and to set up amongst the really free and self-governed peoples of the world such a concert of purpose and of action as will henceforth insure the observance of those principles. Neutrality is no longer feasible or desirable where the peace of the world is involved and the freedom of its peoples, and the menace to that peace and freedom lies in the existence of autocratic governments backed by organized force which is controlled wholly by their will, not by the will of their people. We have seen the last of neutrality in such circumstances. We are at the beginning of an age in which it will be insisted that the same standards of conduct and of responsibility for wrong done shall be observed among nations and their governments that are observed among the individual citizens of civilized states.

We have no quarrel with the German people. We have no feeling towards them but one of sympathy and friendship. It was not upon their impulse that their government acted in entering this war. It was not with their previous knowledge or approval. It was a war determined upon as wars used to be determined upon in the old, unhappy days when peoples were nowhere consulted by their rulers and wars were provoked and waged in the interest of dynasties or of little groups of ambitious men who were accustomed to use their fellow men as pawns and tools. Self-governed nations do not fill their neighbor states with spies or set the course of intrigue to bring about some critical posture of affairs which will give them an opportunity to strike and make conquest. Such designs can be successfully worked out only under cover and where no one has the right to ask questions. Cunningly contrived plans of deception or aggression, carried, it may be, from generation to generation, can be worked out and kept from the light only within the privacy of courts or behind the carefully guarded confidences of a narrow and privileged class. They are happily impossible where public opinion commands and insists upon full information concerning all the nation's affairs.

A steadfast concert for peace can never be maintained except by a partnership of democratic nations. No autocratic government could be trusted to keep faith within it or observe its covenants. It must be a league of honor, a partnership of opinion. Intrigue would eat its vitals away; the plottings of inner circles who could plan what they would and render account to no one would be a corruption seated at its very heart. Only free peoples can hold their purpose and their honor steady to a common end and prefer the interests of mankind to any narrow interest of their own. . . .

Just because we fight without rancor and without selfish object, seeking nothing for ourselves but what we shall wish to share with all free peoples, we shall, I feel confident, conduct our operations as belligerents without passion and ourselves observe with proud punctilio the principles of right and of fair play we profess to be fighting for. . . .

It is a distressing and oppressive duty, Gentlemen of the Congress, which I have performed in thus addressing you. There are, it may be, many months of fiery trial and sacrifice ahead of us. It is a fearful thing to lead this great peaceful people into war, into the most terrible and disastrous of all wars, civilization itself seeming to be in the balance. But the right is more precious than peace, and we shall fight for the things which we have always carried nearest our hearts,—for democracy, for the right of those who submit to authority to have a voice in their own Governments, for the rights and liberties of small nations, for a universal dominion of right by such a concert of free peoples as shall bring peace and safety to all nations and make the world itself at last free. To such a task we can dedicate our lives and our fortunes, everything that we are and everything that we have, with the pride of those who know that the day has come when America is privileged to spend her blood and her might for the principles that gave her birth and happiness and the peace which she has treasured. God helping her, she can do no other.

The great adventure was under way. Americans who had whistled "I Didn't Raise My Boy to Be a Soldier" now sang "Over There." A wave of vigilanteism reduced the opposition to silence. Labor, headed by Samuel Gompers, was enlisted for war. The glad news in March of the overthrow of the Russian czar—an unappetizing partner in the Crusade for Democracy—was succeeded by the unwelcome news of the Bolshevik Revolution in October. The communist leaders deserted the allies, and sought peace with Germany. American industry retooled for war and produced miracles of production. Army units under General John J. Pershing were moving overseas and buttressing the tired allied lines, and were soon to receive the massive German offensives. Wilson pondered peace terms. On January 8, 1918, he presented to Congress his Fourteen Points for peace. The cynic statesman of France, Georges Clemenceau, remarked that God himself had been content with ten.

The Fourteen Points

Once more, as repeatedly before, the spokesmen of the Central Empires have indicated their desire to discuss the objects of the war and the possible bases of a general peace. Parleys have been in progress at Brest-Litovsk between representatives of the Central Powers to which the attention of all the belligerents has been invited for the purpose of ascertaining whether it may be possible to extend these parleys into a general conference with regard to terms of peace and settlement. The Russian representatives presented not only a perfectly definite statement of the principles upon which they would be willing to conclude peace but also an equally definite program of the concrete application of those principles. The repre-

126

sentatives of the Central Powers, on their part, presented an outline of settlement which, if much less definite, seemed susceptible of liberal interpretation until their specific program of practical terms was added. . . .

But, whatever the results of the parleys at Brest-Litovsk, whatever the confusions of counsel and of purpose in the utterances of the spokesmen of the Central Empires, they have again attempted to acquaint the world with their objects in the war and have again challenged their adversaries to say what their objects are and what sort of settlement they would deem just and satisfactory. . . .

We entered this war because violations of right had occurred which touched us to the quick and made the life of our own people impossible unless they were corrected and the world secured once for all against their recurrence. What we demand in this war, therefore, is nothing peculiar to ourselves. It is that the world be made fit and safe to live in; and particularly that it be made safe for every peace-loving nation which, like our own, wishes to live its own life, determine its own institutions, be assured of justice and fair dealing by the other peoples of the world as against force and selfish aggression. All the peoples of the world are in effect partners in this interest, and for our own part we see very clearly that unless justice be done to others it will not be done to us. The program of the world's peace, therefore, is our program; and that program, the only possible program, as we see it, is this:

I. Open covenants of peace, openly arrived at, after which there shall be no private international understandings of any kind but diplomacy shall proceed always frankly and in the public view.

II. Absolute freedom of navigation upon the seas, outside territorial waters, alike in peace and in war, except as the seas may be closed in whole or in part by international action for the enforcement of international covenants.

III. The removal, so far as possible, of all economic barriers and the establishment of an equality of trade conditions among all the nations consenting to the peace and associating themselves for its maintenance.

IV. Adequate guarantees given and taken that national armaments will be reduced to the lowest point consistent with domestic safety.

V. A free, open-minded, and absolutely impartial adjustment of all colonial claims, based upon a strict observance of the principle that in determining all such questions of sovereignty the interests of the populations concerned must have equal weight with the equitable claims of the government whose title is to be determined.

VI. The evacuation of all Russian territory and such a settlement of all questions affecting Russia as will secure the best and freest coöperation of the other nations of the world in obtaining for her an unhampered and unembarrassed opportunity for the independent determination of her own political development and national policy and assure her of a sincere welcome into the society of free nations under institutions of her own choosing; and, more than a welcome, assistance also of every kind that she may need and may herself desire. The treatment accorded Russia by her sister nations in the months to come will be the acid test of their good will, of their comprehension of her needs as distinguished from their own interests, and of their intelligent and unselfish sympathy.

VII. Belgium, the whole world will agree, must be evacuated and restored, without any attempt to limit the sovereignty which she enjoys in common with all other free nations. No other single act will serve as this will serve to restore confidence among the nations in the laws which they have themselves set and determined for the government of their relations with one another. Without this healing act the whole structure and validity of international law is forever impaired.

VIII. All French territory should be freed and the invaded portions restored, and the wrong done to France by Prussia in 1871, in the matter of Alsace-Lorraine, which has unsettled the peace of the world for nearly fifty years, should be righted, in order that peace may once more be made secure in the interest of all.

IX. A readjustment of the frontiers of Italy should be effected along clearly recognizable lines of nationality.

X. The peoples of Austria-Hungary, whose place among the nations we wish to see safeguarded and assured, should be accorded the freest opportunity of autonomous development.

XI. Rumania, Serbia, and Montenegro should be evacuated; occupied territories restored; Serbia accorded free and secure access to the sea; and the relations of the several Balkan states to one another determined by friendly counsel along historically established lines of allegiance and nationality; and international guarantees of the political and economic independence and territorial integrity of the several Balkan states should be entered into.

XII. The Turkish portions of the present Ottoman Empire should be assured a secure sovereignty, but the other nationalities which are now under Turkish rule should be assured an undoubted security of life and an absolutely unmolested opportunity of autonomous development, and the Dardanelles should be permanently opened as a free passage to the ships and commerce of all nations under international guarantees.

XIII. An independent Polish state should be erected which should include the territories inhabited by indisputably Polish populations, which should be assured a free and secure access to the sea, and whose political and economic independence and territorial integrity should be guaranteed by international covenant.

XIV. A general association of nations must be formed under specific covenants for the purpose of affording mutual guarantees of political independence and territorial integrity to great and small states alike. . . .

For such arrangements and covenants we are willing to fight and to continue to fight until they are achieved; but only because we wish the right to prevail and desire a just and stable peace such as can be secured only by removing the chief provocations to war, which this program does remove. We have no jealousy of German greatness, and there is nothing in this program that impairs it. We grudge her no achievement or distinction of learning or of pacific enterprise such as have made her record very bright and very enviable. We do not wish to injure her or to block in any way her legitimate influence or power. We do not wish to fight her either with arms or with hostile arrangements of trade if she is willing to associate herself with us and the other peace-loving nations of the world in covenants of justice and law and fair dealing. We wish her only to accept a place of equality among the peoples of the world,— the new world in which we now live,—instead of a place of mastery. . . .

Americans put away doubts. They went cheerfully and energetically into the business of war. Doubters and dissidents were swept aside. Girls went out into the streets with boxes of white feathers which they pinned on youths not in uniform. Army officers and noncoms devised ways to humiliate and distress "yellowbacks" and other conscientious objectors. Wilson and his assistants sought to give sanity to public enthusiasm. "Every Mob Contributes to German Lies," an official bulletin proclaimed. But patriots carried books in the German language out of libraries and burned them in public streets. They harassed "foreigners," from Union Square in New York City to the towns of California, and they treated even more roughly anticapitalist, antiwar labor and radical militants.

"Germany has once more said that force, and force alone, shall decide . . . the destinies of mankind. There is, therefore, but one response possible from us: Force, force to the utmost. . . ." Yet Wilson had, himself, prophesied, in an interview with the journalist Frank I. Cobb, of the New York *World*, and before his own decision for war had been made, that it would put an end to deliberated thought, to freedom of speech, to reasonable settlements. What, then, sustained him in his decisions? Only his faith in the magical power of a League of Nations that would rise superior to any nation's or group's selfishness, shortsightedness, or wickedness. It was this faith that enabled him to face the war and the peace, despite his awareness of the unidealistic attitudes and programs of his Allied associates, despite the revelations (by the Bolsheviks, who opened the czar's coffers) of secret treaties displaying the plans of England, France and others for dividing the spoils of victory. The people of the world, Wilson persuaded himself, longed for peace and would support him in his demand for an international body that would ensure it.

The war ended. Wilson went to Europe, where he received unprecedented homage from the masses and their leaders. At home, he had suffered a staggering political defeat. The voters had answered his unfortunate appeal for a Democratic Congress by turning over both the Senate and the House of Representatives to the Republicans, in November 1918. Yet Wilson's prestige still sustained his demand that his wartime associates agree to the establishment of a League of Nations. His own eloquence, as exhibited at the Peace Conference, January 25, 1919, seemed to him the voice of humanity.

The League of Nations

MR. CHAIRMAN: I consider it a distinguished privilege to be permitted to open the discussion in this Conference on the League of Nations. We have assembled for two purposes—to make the present settlements which have been rendered necessary by this war, and also to secure the peace of the world not only by the present settlements, but by the arrangements we shall make at this Conference for its maintenance.

The League of Nations seems to me to be necessary for both of these purposes. There are many complicated questions connected with the present settlements, which perhaps cannot be successfully worked out to an ultimate issue by the decisions we shall arrive at here. I can easily conceive that many of these settlements will need subsequent consideration; that many of the decisions we make shall need subsequent alteration in some degree, for if I may judge by my own study of some of these questions they are not susceptible of confident judgments at present.

It is, therefore, necessary that we should set up some machinery by which the work of this Conference should be rendered complete.

We have assembled here for the purpose of doing very much more than making the present settlements that are necessary. We are assembled under very peculiar conditions of world opinion. I may say, without straining the point, that we are not the representatives of governments, but representatives of the peoples.

It will not suffice to satisfy governmental circles anywhere. It is necessary that we should satisfy the opinion of mankind.

The burdens of this war have fallen in an unusual ˋdegree upon the whole population of the countries involved. I do not need to draw for you the picture of how the burden has been thrown back from the front upon the older men, upon the women, upon the children, upon the homes of the civilized world, and how the real strain of the war has come where the eyes of the government could not reach, but where the heart of humanity beats. . . .

The enemy, whom we have just overcome, had at his seats of learning some of the principal centers of scientific study and discovery, and he used them in order to make destruction sudden and complete. And only the watchful and continuous co-operation of men can see to it that science, as well as armed men, is kept within the harness of civilization.

In a sense, the United States is less interested in this subject than the other nations here assembled. With her great territory and her extensive sea borders, it is less likely that the United States should suffer from the attack of enemies than that other nations should suffer. And the ardor of the United States—for it is a very deep and genuine ardor—for the society of nations is not an ardor springing out of fear or apprehension, but an ardor springing out of the ideas which have come in the consciousness of this war.

In coming into this war the United States never for a moment thought that she was intervening in the politics of Europe, or the politics of Asia, or the politics of any part of the world. Her thought was that all the world had now become conscious that there was a single cause of justice and of liberty for men of every kind and place.

Therefore the United States should feel that its part in this war should be played in vain if there ensued upon it abortive European settlements. It would feel that it could not take part in guaranteeing those European settlements unless that guarantee involved the continuous superintendence of the peace of the world by the associated nations of the world. . . .

You can imagine, I dare say, the sentiments and the purpose with which the representatives of the United States support this great project for a League of Nations. We regard it as the key-note of the whole, which expressed our purposes and ideals in this war and which the associated nations have accepted as the basis of a settlement.

If we return to the United States without having made every effort in our power to realize this program, we should return to meet the merited scorn of our fellow citizens. For they are a body that constitute a great democracy. They expect their leaders to speak, their representatives to be their servants.

We have no choice but to obey their mandate. But it is with the greatest enthusiasm and pleasure that we accept that mandate. And because this is the key-note of the whole fabric, we have pledged our every purpose to it, as we have to every item of the fabric.

We would not dare abate a single item of the program which constitutes our instructions. We would not dare to compromise upon any matter as the champion of this thing—this peace of the world, this attitude of justice, this principle that we are the masters of no peoples, but are here to see that every people in the world shall choose its own masters and govern its own destinies, not as we wish, but as they wish.

We are here to see, in short, that the very foundations of the war are swept away. Those foundations were the private choice of a small coterie of civil rulers and military staffs. Those foundations were the aggressions of great powers upon the small. Those foundations were the holding together of empires of unwilling subjects by the duress of arms. Those foundations were the power of small bodies of men to wield their will and use mankind as pawns in a game.

And nothing less than the emancipation of the world from these things will accomplish peace.

Wilson did not impress the statesmen and observers of Europe. John Maynard Keynes was disillusioned. He had expected a scholarly, sensitive type of person. Wilson seemed to him not scholarly, and insensitive to his environment: a nonconformist ministerial type who was easily manipulated by the French for their nationalistic purposes. Winston Churchill saw him as having "consumed his own strength and [that of Clemenceau and Lloyd George] in conflict in which he was always worsted." Wilson returned from his rickety peace settlements with a League of Nations that his own Senate repudiated. The nation was reorganizing for peacetime pursuits that Wilson viewed through consecrated eyes. The heart of the people was sound, he believed; they would support him. He embarked on a tour such as three years before he had initiated in behalf of preparedness. Columbus, Ohio; St. Louis, Missouri; Iowa; the Dakotas; a score more of cities; across to the West Coast and back. He exhausted himself in arguments and explanations intended to build an irresistible public opinion favoring acceptance of the League. Following his Pueblo, Colorado address, September 25, 1919, he was stricken—a prophet voice, a wounded body, a lost cause. Some Americans had cared, but not enough, for they had cared about other things more.

Interrupted Campaign: The Pueblo Speech

Mr. Chairman and Fellow Countrymen:

It is with a great deal of genuine pleasure that I find myself in Pueblo, and I feel it a compliment that I should be permitted to be the first speaker in this beautiful hall. One of the advantages of this hall, as I look about, is that you are not too far away from me, because there is nothing so reassuring to men who are trying to express the public sentiment as getting into real personal contact with their fellow citizens. I have gained a renewed impression as I have crossed the continent this time of the homogeneity of this great people to whom we belong. They come from many stocks, but they are all of one kind. They come from many origins, but they are all shot through with the same principles and desire the same righteous and honest things. I have received a more inspiring impression this time of the public opinion of the United States than it was ever my privilege to receive before.

The chief pleasure of my trip has been that it has nothing to do with my personal fortunes, that it has nothing to do with my personal reputation, that it has nothing to do with anything except great principles uttered by Americans of all sorts and of all parties which we are now trying to realize at this crisis of the affairs of the world. But there have been unpleasant impressions as well as pleasant impressions, my fellow citizens, as I have crossed the continent. I have perceived more and more that men have been busy creating an absolutely false impression of what the treaty of peace and the covenant of the League of Nations contain and mean. . . .

Do not think of this treaty of peace as merely a settlement with Germany. It is that. It is a very severe settlement with Germany, but there is not anything in it that she did not earn. . . . But the treaty is so much more than that. It is not merely a settlement with Germany; it is a readjustment of those great injustices which underlie the whole structure of European and Asiatic society. This is only the first of several treaties. They are all constructed upon the same plan. . . . What are those lines? They are based upon the purpose to see that every government dealt with in this great settlement is put in the hands of the people and taken out of the hands of coteries and of sovereigns who had no right to rule over the people. It is a people's treaty, that accomplishes by a great sweep of practical justice the liberation of men who never could have liberated themselves, and the power of the most powerful nations has been devoted not to their aggrandizement but to the liberation of people whom they could have put under their control if they had chosen to do so. Not one foot of territory is demanded by the conquerors, not one single item of submission to their authority is demanded by them. The men who sat around that table in Paris knew that the time had come when the people were no longer going to consent to live under masters, but were going to live the lives that they chose themselves, to live under such governments as they chose themselves to erect. That is the fundamental principle of this great settlement.

And we did not stop with that. We added a great international charter for the rights of labour. Reject this treaty, impair it, and this is the consequence to the laboring men of the world, that there is no international tribunal which can bring the moral judgments of the world to bear upon the great labour questions of the day. What we need to do with regard to the labour questions of the day, my fellow countrymen, is to lift them into the light, is to lift them out of the haze and distraction of passion, of hostility, not [out?] into the calm spaces where men look at things without passion. . . .

At the front of this great treaty is put the covenant of the League of Nations. It will also be at the front of the Austrian treaty and the Hungarian treaty and the Bulgarian treaty and the treaty with Turkey. Every one of them will contain the covenant of the League of Nations, because you can not work any of them without the covenant of the League of Nations. Unless you get the united, concerted purpose and power of the great Governments of the world behind this settlement, it will fall down like a house of cards. There is only one power to put behind the liberation of mankind, and that is the power of mankind. . . . And what do they unite for? They enter into a solemn promise to one another that they will never use their power against one another for aggression; that they never will impair the territorial integrity of a neighbor; that they never will interfere with the political independence of a neighbor; that they will abide by the principle that great populations are entitled to determine their own destiny and that they will not interfere with that destiny; and that no matter what differences arise amongst them they will never resort to war without first having done one or other of two things—either submitted the matter of controversy to arbitration, in which case they agree to abide by the result without question, or submitted it to the consideration of the council of the League of Nations, laying before that council all the documents, all the facts, agreeing that the council can publish the documents and the facts to the whole world, agreeing that there shall be six months allowed for the mature consideration of those facts by the council, and agreeing that at the expiration of the six months, even if they are not then ready to accept the advice of the council with regard to the settlement of the dispute, they will still not go to war for another three months. . . .

But, you say, "We have heard that we might be at a disadvantage in the League of Nations." Well, whoever told you that either was deliberately falsifying or he had not read the covenant of the League of Nations. I leave him the choice. I want to give you a very simple account of the organization of the League of Nations and let you judge for yourself. It is a very simple organization. The power of the League, or rather the activities of the League, lie in two bodies. There is the council, which consists of one representative from each of the principal allied and associated powers—that is to say, the United States, Great Britain, France, Italy, and Japan, along with four other representatives of smaller powers chosen out of the general body of the membership of the League. The council is the source of every active policy of the League, and no active policy of the league can be adopted without a unanimous vote of the council. That is explicitly stated in the covenant itself. Does it not evidently follow that the League of Nations can adopt no policy whatever without the consent of the United States? The affirmative vote of the representative of the United States is necessary in every case. . . .

135

Look at it in another aspect. The assembly is the talking body. The assembly was created in order that anybody that purposed anything wrong should be subjected to the awkward circumstance that everybody could talk about it. . . .

When you come to the heart of the covenant, my fellow citizens, you will find it in Article X, and I am very much interested to know that the other things have been blown away like bubbles. There is nothing in the other contentions with regard to the League of Nations, but there is something in Article X that you ought to realize and ought to accept or reject. Article X is the heart of the whole matter. What is Article X? I never am certain that I can from memory give a literal repetition of its language, but I am sure that I can give an exact interpretation of its meaning. Article X provides that every member of the League covenants to respect and preserve the territorial integrity and existing political independence of every other member of the League as against external aggression. Not against internal disturbance. There was not a man at that table who did not admit the sacredness of the right of self-determination, the sacredness of the right of any body of people to say that they would not continue to live under the Government they were then living under, and under Article XI of the covenant they are given a place to say whether they will live under it or not. For following Article X is Article XI, which makes it the right of any member of the League at any time to call attention to anything, anywhere, that is likely to disturb the peace of the world or the good understanding between nations upon which the peace of the world depends. . . .

Again and again, my fellow citizens, mothers who lost their sons in France have come to me and, taking my hand, have shed tears upon it not only, but they have added, "God bless you, Mr. President!" Why, my fellow citizens, should they pray God to bless me? I advised the Congress of the United States to create the situation that led to the death of their sons. I ordered their sons oversea. I consented to their sons being put in the most difficult parts of the battle line, where death was certain, as in the impenetrable difficulties of the forest of Argonne. Why should they weep upon my hand and call down the blessings of God upon me? Because they believe that their boys died for something that vastly transcends any of the immediate and palpable objects of the war. They believe, and they rightly believe, that their sons saved the liberty of the world. They believe that wrapped up with the liberty of the world is the continuous protection of that liberty by the concerted powers of all

136

civilized people. They believe that this sacrifice was made in order that other sons should not be called upon for a similar gift—the gift of life, the gift of all that died—and if we did not see this thing through, if we fulfilled the dearest present wish of Germany and now dissociated ourselves from those alongside whom we fought in the war, would not something of the halo go away from the gun over the mantlepiece, or the sword? Would not the old uniform lose something of its significance? These men were crusaders. They were not going forth to prove the might of the United States. They were going forth to prove the might of justice and right, and all the world accepted them as crusaders, and their transcendent achievement has made all the world believe in America as it believes in no other nation organized in the modern world. There seems to me to stand between us and the rejection or qualification of this treaty the serried ranks of those boys in khaki, not only these boys who came home, but those dear ghosts that still deploy upon the fields of France. . . .

You will say, "Is the League an absolute guaranty against war?" No; I do not know any absolute guaranty against the errors of human judgment or the violence of human passion, but I tell you this: With a cooling space of nine months for human passion, not much of it will keep hot. I had a couple of friends who were in the habit of losing their tempers, and when they lost their tempers they were in the habit of using very unparliamentary language. Some of their friends induced them to make a promise that they never would swear inside the town limits. When the impulse next came upon them, they took a street car to go out of town to swear, and by the time they got out of town they did not want to swear. They came back convinced that they were just what they were, a couple of unspeakable fools, and the habit of getting angry and of swearing suffered great inroads upon it by that experience. Now, illustrating the great by the small, that is true of the passions of nations. It is true of the passions of men however you combine them. Give them space to cool off. I ask you this: If it is not an absolute insurance against war, do you want no insurance at all? Do you want nothing? Do you want not only no probability that war will not recur, but the probability that it will recur? The arrangements of justice do not stand of themselves, my fellow citizens. The arrangements of this treaty are just, but they need the support of the combined power of the great nations of the world. And they will have that support. Now that the mists of this great question have cleared away, I believe that men will see the truth, eye to eye and face to face. There is one thing that the

American people always rise to and extend their hand to, and that is the truth of justice and of liberty and of peace. We have accepted that truth and we are going to be led by it, and it is going to lead us, and through us the world, out into pastures of quietness and peace such as the world never dreamed of before.

PART IV
Normalcy

WARREN G. HARDING

(1865–1923)

Good Will Is Not Enough

Mankind needs a world-wide benediction of understanding. . . .

Our supreme task is the resumption of our onward, normal way. Reconstruction, readjustment, restoration—all these must follow. I would like to hasten them. . . .

The normal balances have been impaired, the channels of distribution have been clogged, the relations of labor and management have been strained. We must seek the readjustment with care and courage. Our people must give and take. . . .

Perhaps we never shall know the old levels of wages again, because war invariably readjusts compensations, and the necessaries of life will show their inseparable relationship, but we must strive for normalcy to reach stability.

Inaugural Address, *March 4, 1921*

THE twenty-ninth President of the United States was born on a farm in central Ohio among a people whose farthest fling of imagination reached just about to the borders of their state. They thought well of themselves as inhabiting a land of opportunity and plenty, of independence and the pioneer spirit: this land belonged to them. Harding's father was a doctor, as well as a farmer. His tall, handsome son worked on the farm, in a sawmill, at broom-making and as a laborer. He worked his way through a small and undistinguished Ohio college and then served on the Marion *Mirror,* a Democratic sheet that he left in 1884 for lack of sympathy with its politics. Harding favored James G. Blaine, though some Republicans were unwilling to vote for a knight, plumed or otherwise, whose hands were sticky with the graft of the Little Rock and Fort Smith Railroad.

Harding became proprietor and publisher of the Marion *Star,* which supported him modestly. He lived the careless, personal life of a good fellow. In 1891, he married a widow, Florence Kling De Wolfe, daughter of a local banker, and began to expand his local interests as a successful younger citizen. His oratorical voice and somewhat distinguished bearing, his party regularity, his ability to what he called "bloviate," that is,

141

say little in ringing phrases, made him popular in politics. In 1898, he was elected to the state senate and made floor leader. In 1902, he was run successfully for lieutenant-governor of the state, and could have been renominated. He declined and returned to Marion. Throughout the reform era, he absorbed himself in developing his paper, which grew, and with a remarkable record of good employee relations. In 1910, he was defeated for the governorship. Yet his reputation was such that he was selected to offer Taft for renomination at the Republican convention in 1912. Harding had good friends among the Ohio politicians, notably Harry M. Daugherty. In 1914, they organized to defeat Harding's old master of bloviation, "Fireworks" James B. Foraker, a former governor and discredited United States Senator, for the Senate seat. Two years later, Harding was a dark horse for the Republican presidential nomination, but national politics on the highest level were still too serious to tolerate such a candidate. Harding looked every inch a Roman senator, but his understandings were totally derived from party instructions and his own small-town myopia. Thus, as an adoring biographer later explained his views of one issue: "There was no note of selfishness in . . . Harding's dealings with the Philippines. Even as a Senator he was opposed to cutting the islands loose from the helpful hands of the United States." He voted against the confirmation of Louis D. Brandeis to a seat on the Supreme Court. He protested that Wilson's Mexican policy did not protect American business interests. He supported the war but thought that war profits ought not to be seriously taxed. Although he drank and played cards, and probably continued his youthful philandering, he respected the militant fighters for prohibition—the Anti-Saloon League was mighty in his own Ohio—and supported the Eighteenth Amendment. It reflected American indifference to the world outside that so unqualified a Senator should have been placed on the Senate's Foreign Relations Committee. He believed in League reservations, but also advocated a world court for what he called "justiciable disputes," and as "an agency for the revelation of the moral judgment of the world"; in other words, as a talking, rather than an acting world congress.

His friend Daugherty fought boldly and resourcefully in his behalf at the Republican convention of 1920. Daugherty knew and cared little about the complexities of life at home and abroad, and he knew that his fellow Americans cared just as little. Even so, the party chieftains who decided to fight through in Harding's behalf called the prospective candidate in for questioning, and received his false assurances that there was nothing in his past that might embarrass their campaign.

Harding followed McKinley in conducting a "front porch" campaign. In 1860, there had been two major contenders for the presidency from Illinois; now there were two from Ohio. Harding was opposed by another newspaper proprietor of little more distinction than he himself had to offer. Harding proclaimed that "the big business of America is the little business of America." "I think," he said, "we can and ought to have voluntary volitional arbitration" in labor disputes. "We need fewer land-hogs who menace our future, and more fat hogs for ham and bacon." He offered various messages: for mothers (women had been given the vote), for teachers, and even for actors. Social justice, he declared, in one of those phrases which pleased the ear but baffled the mind, is an obligation, not a right. Competition teaches the square deal. He offered a message for youth on the value of play. American voters gave him a ringing 76 percent of the electoral votes.

Harding's major contemporary biographer, a professor at New York University, quoted without irony the Paris *Figaro's* comment on Harding's Inaugural Address: "Most of the new President's Address was a declaration of faith in God and a hymn to the greatness and wisdom of America." Harding had every President's desire to rank respectably in history. His problem was with his insight and knowledge. He may never have heard of Andrew W. Mellon before he called him to head the Treasury. The same President-elect who chose Charles Evans Hughes to be Secretary of State chose Senator Albert B. Fall, a man of no stature, to be Secretary of the Interior, as well as even shoddier types in lesser but responsible offices.

Carrying the odd distinction of being the first businessman in presidential office, and an employer who paid his employees above the union scale, Harding took office. His Special Message (April 12, 1921) called Congress into extraordinary session and necessarily dealt with extraordinary matters. Most extraordinary was the order of importance given to major items of business, ranging as they did from taxation to world peace. Harding's most notable achievement was the Bureau of the Budget, much of it a product of studies prepared during the Wilson administration. Much of the remainder of his program involved hopes, rather than power and direction, which required prosperity to make tolerable. Fortunately for Harding, as it seemed, prosperity came, enabling his administration to take credit for its presence.

"It Is Our Purpose to Prosper America First"

Members of the Congress:

You have been called in extraordinary session to give your consideration to national problems far too pressing to be long neglected. We face our tasks of legislation and administration amid conditions as difficult as our government has ever contemplated. Under our political system the people of the United States have charged the new Congress and the new Administration with the solution—the readjustments, reconstruction, and restoration which must follow in the wake of war. . . .

The staggering load of war debt must be cared for in orderly funding and gradual liquidation. We shall hasten the solution and aid effectively in lifting the tax burdens if we strike resolutely at expenditure. It is far more easily said than done. In the fever of war our expenditures were so little questioned, the emergency was so impelling, appropriation was so unimpeded that we little noted millions and counted the Treasury inexhaustible. It will strengthen our resolution if we ever keep in mind that a continuation of such a course means inevitable disaster. . . .

It is of less concern whether internal taxation or tariff revision shall come first than has been popularly imagined, because we must do both, but the practical course for earliest accomplishment will readily suggest itself to the Congress. We are committed to the repeal of the excess-profits tax and the abolition of inequities and unjustifiable exasperations in the present system. The country does not expect and will not approve a shifting of burdens. It is more interested in wiping out the necessity for imposing them and eliminating confusion and cost in the collection.

The urgency for an instant tariff enactment, emergency in character and understood by our people that it is for the emergency only, can not be too much emphasized. I believe in the protection of American industry, and it is our purpose to prosper America first. The privileges of the American market to the foreign producer are offered too cheaply today, and the effect on much of our own productivity is the destruction of our self-reliance, which is the foundation of the independence and good fortune of our people. Moreover, imports should pay their fair share of our cost of government.

One who values American prosperity and maintained American standards of wage and living can have no sympathy with the proposal that easy entry and the flood of imports will cheapen our cost of living. It is more likely to destroy our capacity to buy. Today American agriculture is menaced, and its products are down to prewar normals, yet we are endangering our fundamental industry through the high cost of transportation from farm to market and through the influx of foreign farm products, because we offer, essentially unprotected, the best market in the world. It would be better to err in protecting our basic food industry than paralyze our farm activities in the world struggle for restored exchanges. . . .

A very important matter is the establishment of the Government's business on a business basis. There was toleration of the easy-going, unsystematic method of handling our fiscal affairs, when indirect taxation held the public unmindful of the Federal burden. But there is knowledge of the high cost of government today, and high cost of living is inseparably linked with high cost of government. There can be no complete correction of the high living cost until government's cost is notably reduced. Let me most heartily commend the enactment of legislation providing for the national budget system. Congress has already recorded its belief in the budget. It will be a very great satisfaction to know of its early enactment, so that it may be employed in establishing the economies and business methods so essential to the minimum of expenditure. . . .

The great interest of both the producer and consumer—indeed, all our industrial and commercial life, from agriculture to finance—in the problems of transportation will find its reflex in your concern to aid reestablishment, to restore efficiency, and bring transportation cost into a helpful relationship rather than continue it as a hindrance to resumed activities. . . .

During the recent political canvass the proposal was made that a department of public welfare should be created. It was indorsed and commended so strongly that I venture to call it to your attention and to suggest favorable legislative consideration. . . .

Somewhat related to the foregoing human problems is the race question. Congress ought to wipe the stain of barbaric lynching from the banners of a free and orderly, representative democracy. We face the fact that many millions of people of African descent are numbered among our population, and that in a number of states they constitute a very large proportion of the total population. It is unnecessary to recount the difficulties incident to this condition, nor to emphasize the fact that it is a condition which can not be removed. There has been suggestion, however, that some of its difficulties might be ameliorated by a humane and enlightened consideration of it, a study of its many aspects, and an effort to formulate, if not a policy, at least a national attitude of mind calculated to bring about the most satisfactory possible adjustment of relations between the races, and of each race to the national life. One proposal is the creation of a commission embracing representatives of both races, to study and report on the entire subject. The proposal has real merit. I am convinced that in mutual

145

tolerance, understanding, charity, recognition of the interdependence of the races, and the maintenance of the rights of citizenship lies the road to righteous adjustment. . . .

Nearly two and a half years ago the World War came to an end, and yet we find ourselves today in the technical state of war, though actually at peace, while Europe is at technical peace, far from tranquillity and little progressed toward the hoped-for restoration. It ill becomes us to express impatience that the European belligerents are not yet in full agreement, when we ourselves have been unable to bring constituted authority into accord in our own relations to the formally proclaimed peace. Little avails in reciting the causes of delay in Europe or our own failure to agree. But there is no longer excuse for uncertainties respecting some phases of our foreign relationship. In the existing League of Nations, world-governing with its super-powers, this republic will have no part. There can be no misinterpretation, and there will be no betrayal of the deliberate expression of the American people in the recent election; and, settled in our decision for ourselves, it is only fair to say to the world in general, and to our associates in war in particular, that the League covenant can have no sanction by us.

The aim to associate nations to prevent war, preserve peace, and promote civilization our people most cordially applauded. We yearned for this new instrument of justice, but we can have no part in a committal to an agency of force in unknown contingencies; we can recognize no super-authority. . . .

It was a new time, and though Harding spoke freely of such epochal instruments of change as the airplane and the automobile, he did not understand what they did to people and perspectives, at home and abroad. He was, indeed, a McKinley lost among cocktails. Genuinely kindhearted, he freed Eugene V. Debs from prison, whom the liberal, but bitter, Wilson had preferred to see in prison for his opposition to the war. However, Harding pressed a bill establishing immigration quotas such as Wilson, speaking for the Democratic Party and the big city machines, had vetoed. He appointed Taft Chief Justice of the Supreme Court. Harding's advisers bewildered him. One group of businessmen urged him to keep American credit at home to develop American industries. International bankers, on the other hand, urged credit for foreign trade, in some of which they had investments. Harding sincerely felt for the farmers, bankrupted by the collapse of wartime demand for wheat; but his free enterprise principles would not allow him to tamper with price controls in their behalf. Prosperity eluded miners and steelworkers, among others who lived in rigidly policed or controlled industries, but Harding could only plead for arbitration that the embattled principals could not afford, or thought they couldn't. Meanwhile, he could only contribute to appeasing savage strike actions in the mining towns and on the railroads with well-intentioned commissions—and also with purposeful levies of Federal troops.

Most famous of all his actions was his call for a Naval Disarmament conference. Unfriendly critics would not allow him credit even for this accomplishment, seeing him as a follower rather than an innovator. There was even legitimate question of its significance; as a lively skeptic of the time, Clinton Wallace Gilbert, anonymously observed, in his *Mirrors of Washington:*

> The war had left the great sea powers with excessive navies and insupportable naval budgets. All wanted naval limitation. It was only necessary to propose an agreement for reduction to have it accepted. . . .
>
> The results of the Washington Conference were substantial. They put off war where none was threatening.

Nevertheless, the Conference gave a shallow time some pomp and circumstance, offered a change from embarrassing problems of unemployment and civil rights at home, and provided distraction from the chaos of civil war and hunger besetting Germany and eastern Europe. Harding's closing address to the Conference (February 6, 1922) expressed his sincere good will, as well as his naïve understanding of momentous matters.

The Washington Naval Conference

Nearly three months ago it was my privilege to utter to you sincerest words of welcome to the capital of our republic, to suggest the spirit in which you were invited, and to intimate the atmosphere in which you were asked to confer. In a very general way, perhaps, I ventured to express a hope for the things towards which our aspirations led us.

To-day it is my greater privilege, and an even greater pleasure, to come to make acknowledgment. It is one of the supreme compensations of life to contemplate a worth-while accomplishment.

It can not be other than seemly for me, as the only chief of government so circumstanced as to be able to address the Conference, to speak congratulations, and to offer the thanks of our nation, our people, perhaps I dare volunteer to utter them for the world. My own gratification is beyond my capacity to express.

This conference has wrought a truly great achievement. It is hazardous sometimes to speak in superlatives, and I will be restrained. But I will say, with every confidence, that the faith plighted here to-day, kept in national honor, will mark the beginning of a new and better epoch in human progress.

Stripped to the simplest fact, what is the spectacle which has inspired a new hope for the world? Gathered about this table nine great nations of the earth—not all, to be sure, but those most directly concerned with the problems at hand—have met and have conferred on questions of great import and common concern, on problems menacing their peaceful relationship, on burdens threatening a common peril. In the revealing light of the public opinion of the world, without surrender of sovereignty, without impaired nationality or affronted national pride, a solution has been found in unanimity, and to-day's adjournment is marked by rejoicing in the things accomplished. If the world has hungered for new assurance it may feast at the banquet which the Conference has spread. . . .

You have written the first deliberate and effective expression of great Powers, in the consciousness of peace, of war's utter futility, and challenged the sanity of competitive preparation for each other's destruction. You have halted folly and lifted burdens, and revealed to the world that the one sure way to recover from the sorrow and ruin and staggering obligations of a world war is to end the strife in preparation for more of it, and turn human energies to the constructiveness of peace.

Not all the world is yet tranquilized. But here is the example, to imbue with new hope all who dwell in apprehension. At this table came understanding, and understanding brands armed conflict as abominable in the eyes of enlightened civilization.

I once believed in armed preparedness. I advocated it. But I have come now to believe there is a better preparedness in a public mind and a world opinion made ready to grant justice precisely as it exacts it. And justice is better served in conferences of peace than in conflicts at arms.

How simple it all has been. When you met here twelve weeks ago there was not a commitment, not an obligation except that which each delegation owes to the Government commissioning it. But human service was calling, world conscience was impelling, and world opinion directing. . . .

It may be that the naval holiday here contracted will expire with the treaties, but I do not believe it. Those of us who live another decade are more likely to witness a growth of public opinion, strengthened by the new experience, which will make nations more concerned with living to the fulfillment of God's high intent than with agencies of warfare and destruction. Since this conference of nations has pointed with unanimity to the way of peace to-day, like conferences in the future, under appropriate conditions and with aims both well conceived and definite, may illumine the highways and byways of human activity. The torches of understanding have been lighted, and they ought to glow and encircle the globe. . . .

"How simple it all has been." Harding yearned sincerely for a state of affairs that would permit casual living, and, somehow, international concord. He took it as one of his tasks and contributions to exude a spirit of friendliness. Yet he knew no way to formulate a clear or even consistent policy. Though he and his friends drank, he pleaded with the public for compliance to Prohibition. He asked for world cordiality, but, visiting in the Caribbean under sponsorship of American industrialists, and in his role of commander-in-chief of the army and navy, he told men of the Atlantic Fleet that the United States wanted only its own (undefined) just dues, but that we did want "that which is righteously our own; and by the Eternal, we mean to have it."

Yet his vague promises of participation in a world court which would carry no responsibility were meaningful to him, and evoked one of his most earnest appeals, at a luncheon of the Associated Press (April 24, 1923).

The World Court

Mr. President, Members of the Associated Press and Guests: It is inevitable that the President, who happens to be a newspaper man, appearing before a newspaper gathering, must talk some kind of shop. I am willing to make the confession that I would rather talk newspaper shop to you than anything else. I believe I could do it helpfully sometimes, because I have had my viewpoint about journalism broadened while twisting around occasionally in the Executive chair. Frankly, I have never squirmed under the criticism, but I have sometimes been appalled at inaccuracy of statement, and if I were going to lecture on journalism my theme would be "a little less eagerness and much more of accuracy."

Not very long ago I returned from a southern vacation and picked up a copy of a very friendly publication, and in a story on the first page was the statement that during my trip South I had broken all but two of my golf sticks and was in the process of having them replaced. Now, that was not very serious to the country, but it put me out of the duffer class and in among the dubs, and I resented it. Nobody breaks eight golf sticks in five weeks. It cannot be done. And yet, as one of the three golf-playing Presidents, I have been crucified as a destroyer of sticks, eight in number in five weeks.

During the closing days of the last session of Congress I sent to the Senate a communication asking its advice and consent to the adherence by the Government of the United States to a protocol establishing an International Court of Justice. Out of this simple, natural, normal proceeding has developed so much of mystery and so much of misunderstanding and so much of protest and approval and so much of threatened muddying of the political waters, that I welcome this opportunity on so appropriate an occasion to reveal to the American people both the purpose and the motives impelling. . . .

In 1904 the national platform of the Republican Party said "we favor the peaceful settlement of international differences by arbitration." Four years later, in the national convention of 1908, the party in its platform alluded to the progress made in keeping faith with the previous declaration and said:

"The conspicuous contributions of American statesmanship to the cause of international peace so strongly advanced in the Hague Conference are occasions for just pride and gratification. . . . We indorse such achievement as the highest duty of a people to perform and proclaim the obligation of further strengthening the bonds of friendship and good will with all the nations of the world."

Then, in 1912, the Republican platform—the national platform —made a very explicit declaration relating to an international court of justice. I quote again from the party convenant of faith:

"Together with peaceful and orderly development at home, the Republican Party earnestly favors all measures for the establishment and protection of the peace of the world, and for the development of closer relations between the various nations of the earth. It believes most earnestly in the peaceful settlement of international disputes and in the reference of all controversies between nations to an international court of justice."

The next formal and solemn pledge was made in 1916. . . .

In 1920 the question of our foreign relationship was very acute.

150

The Senate had rejected the Versailles treaty and the League of Nations pact. The convention at Chicago voiced its approval of the rejection but was unwilling to pledge aloofness from the world. Therefore it said in its platform pronouncement:

"We pledge the coming Republican administration to such agreements with other nations of the world as shall meet the full duty of America to civilization and humanity, in accordance with American ideals, without surrendering the right of the Amercan people to exercise its judgment and its power in favor of justice and peace."

As a participant in the making of some of these platforms and as the banner bearer in one campaign, I have the right to believe they spoke the party conscience so plainly that it is not easy to misconstrue.

But there are other utterances which it is seemly to recall. I allude to the interpretation of the platform by the candidate in 1920. On August 28, 1920, speaking on the League of Nations proposal I said frankly and very definitely I did not favor the United States entering the League of Nations. It was declared then that the issue, as defined between the candidates, involved the disparity between a world court of justice, supplemented by world association for conference, on the one hand, and the Council of the League on the other. . . .

So much for political party history. I have quoted it because I believe in keeping the faith. If political parties do not mean what they say, and if political candidates do not mean what they say, then our form of government, our form of popular government, is based on fraud and can not hope long to endure.

In compliance with its pledges the new Administration which came into power in March, 1921, definitely and decisively put aside all thought of the United States entering the League of Nations. It does not propose to enter now by the side door, or the back door or the cellar door. . . .

Then in the fulfillment of the pledge of free conference, the international conference on the limitation of armaments was called, not in haste, not because someone was prodding, but as early as the barriers to success could be removed. The spirit of that conference and the achievements wrought have been written into history and will grow immeasurably beyond the almost universal popular favor already accorded. There was not alone the triumph of reducing naval armaments, and ending competition which was leading to oppressive naval strength, and adding staggering burdens to the

151

treasuries of competing powers; not alone the removal of every war cloud and every reason for conflict in the Pacific, so that now accord and concord abide, where suspicion and fear had previously dwelt, but we gave an example to the world of the conference way to peace, which time will appraise as the supreme accomplishment.

Hardly had that gratifying work been accomplished before the Administration began its endeavors for further fulfillment. Meanwhile an International Court of Justice had been established. It was an agency of peaceful settlement which had long been sought. Its establishment previously had failed because no agreement had been possible over the method of electing judges. The existence of the League of Nations offered a solution. Almost all the Members of the League had signed the protocol establishing the Court. The members of the Council, in which the large powers have permanent representation, afforded one voting body with a veto on the members of the Assembly consisting of representatives of all nations, and members of the Assembly could have a veto on the larger powers permanently represented in the Council. Here was a device for electing judges which removed the heretofore unsolvable problem of a satisfactory means of selecting them. Not the Council, but the nations members thereof, must vote in majority for the same candidates for which members of the Assembly vote in majority, else the election is void until a conference points the way to an agreement.

The Court was established and is functioning. An American judge sits on the Court, though we had no part in choosing him.*

Under the provisions of its establishment the United States can apply for a court decision on any justiciable question, even as any nation participating in its establishment. Perhaps the Court is not all that some advocates of the court plan would have it, but it is in a large measure the fulfillment of an aspiration we long have boasted for the United States of America; so I thought, and I still think, we ought to be a party to the agreement and assume our part in its maintenance and give to it the benefit of such influence as our size and wealth and ideals may prove to be.

* The Permanent Court of International Justice was the third arm of the League of Nations, which also included an Assembly and a Council, with the authority to handle international disputes submitted to it and to advise both Assembly and Council. The Court did not supersede the Court of Arbitration set up by the first Hague Peace Conference in 1899. The latter engaged in arbitration; the Court advised on international laws which applied to specific disputes. Its judges were elected by majorities of the Council and Assembly. In 1921, Professor John Bassett Moore, who had long served the Department of State, was added to the Court.

For mere eligibility to appeal to the Court, nothing was needed. But it did not seem fair to seek its advantages without accepting all becoming responsibilities, and here developed the stumbling-block. Naturally, we should wish to participate in selecting the judges, and the electors designated were Members of the League. We had no thought of joining the League, we sought none of its offerings and will accept none of its obligations. The President could propose no solution to the signatory powers, because the world had witnessed in disappointment the spectacle of an executive proposing and the Senate disposing. It was not desirable to make some proposal abroad that could not be carried out; indeed, none would be considered, and it was not pleasing to think of asking the Senate's consent to a program to which the nations concerned would not agree. So, very informally and very discreetly, and over a considerable period of time, the situation was felt out, and when satisfied that there was an appropriate course of action without connection with the League, provided the Senate consented, I proposed adherence to the court protocol, and asked the Senate's consent. . . .

Excessive friends of the League have beclouded the situation by their unwarranted assumption that it is a move toward League membership. Let them disabuse their minds, because there is no such thought among us who must make our commitments abroad. And the situation is likewise beclouded by those who shudder excessively when the League is mentioned, and who assume entanglement is unavoidable. Any entanglement would first require an assent of the Senate, and if by any chance the Senate approved of any entanglement, the present Administration would not complete the ratification. If, in spite of these statements, uttered with full deliberation, there are excessive and unfounded hopes on the one hand, or utterly unjustifiable apprehensions on the other, I know of no words fittingly to apply.

Frankly, there is one political bugbear. When we discussed the League of Nations and its rule of force, with its superpowers through a political council and assembly, I myself contended as a Senator for equal voting power on the part of the United States with any nation in the world. With her dominions members of the League Assembly, the British Empire will have six votes in that branch of the court electorate, but it has only one in the electorate of the Council. In view of the fact that no nation can have more than one judge, it is a less formidable objection than when applied to the League as a super-power, dealing with problems likely to abridge a nation's rights. I appraise the objection now as one who voted against this disparity of power in the League Assembly, but in an appraisal now I do not hesitate to say that if other great powers can accept without fear the voting strength of the British dominions, when these great powers are without the ties of race to minimize international rivalries and suspicions, we ought, in view of the natural ties of English-speaking kinship, to feel ourselves reasonably free from danger.

The perfected Court must be a matter of development. I earnestly commend it because I think it is a great step in the right direction toward peaceful settlement of judiciable questions, toward the elimination of frictions which lead to war, and a surer agency of international justice through the application of law than can be hoped for in arbitration which is influenced by the prejudices of men and the expediency of politics. . . .

Rumors of dubious happening circulated among the knowing in the Capitol. As early as May 1921, at the very inception of his administration, Harding had been persuaded by Secretary of the Interior Fall to sign an executive. order—constitutionally illegal—transferring vast navy oil reserves to the Interior. Fall proceeded to dispense them, including the soon-to-be-famous Teapot Dome reserves in Wyoming, to private hands. Thomas W. Miller, Alien Property Custodian, and Charles R. Forbes, of the Veterans' Bureau, both Harding appointees, were rumored to be handling vast government resources with obscure propriety. Harding's own friend and benefactor, Attorney-General Daugherty—he was later to defend his record with vigor in *The Inside Story of the Harding Tragedy* (1932)—was seen as sitting gingerly on his feebly upholstered prerogatives. Rumors and intimations of disaster appear to have come to Harding. He looked plainly anxious and haggard. On June 20, 1923, with an entourage of some sixty-five associates, including cabinet members, he began a good will tour of the nation. At Cheyenne, Wyoming, he talked on the coal problem, and what the government was doing (mostly in terms of fact finding) to mitigate gloomy and even shocking conditions. At Idaho Falls, Idaho, he spoke in praise of cooperatives as an aid to distraught farmers. Before leaving for Alaska, the President announced with patent satisfaction that the iron and steel owners had agreed to abolish the twelve-hour day in deference to public opinion, as soon as it would be "practical" for them to do so. But Harding himself did not improve in spirits. He asked trusted newspapermen what a President should do who had been betrayed by his friends. The trip continued. His address (July 26, 1923) at Vancouver, British Columbia, was again one of his happier efforts—an expression of friendliness such as Taft had not been able to manage. When Harding suddenly sickened and died at San Francisco, August 2, 1923, his unpretentious friendliness shone out as his major quality, which subsequent revelations did not dim. Harding had not been a knave; he had gained nothing material from the presidency. It had simply been too large a responsibility for him.

Canadian-American Relations

Citizens of Canada: I may as well confess to you at the outset a certain perplexity as to how I should address you. The truth of the matter is that this is the first time I have ever spoken as President in any country other than my own. Indeed, so far as I can recall, I am, with the single exception of my immediate predecessor, the first President in office even to set foot on politically foreign soil.

True, there is no definite inhibition upon one doing so, such as prevents any but a natural born from becoming President, but an early prepossession soon developed into a tradition and for more than a hundred years held the effect of unwritten law. I am not prepared to say that the custom was not desirable, perhaps even needful, in the early days, when time was the chief requisite of travel. Assuredly, too, at present, the Chief Magistrate of a great Republic ought not to cultivate the habit or make a hobby of wandering over all the continents of the earth.

But exceptions are required to prove rules. And Canada is an exception, a most notable exception, from every viewpoint of the United States. You are not only our neighbor, but a very good neighbor, and we rejoice in your advancement and admire your independence, no less sincerely than we value your friendship. . . .

What an object lesson of peace is shown today by our two countries to all the world! No grim-faced fortifications mark our frontiers, no huge battleships patrol our dividing waters, no stealthy spies lurk in our tranquil border hamlets. Only a scrap of paper, recording hardly more than a simple understanding, safeguards lives and properties on the Great Lakes, and only humble mile-posts mark the inviolable boundary line for thousands of miles through farm and forest.

Our protection is in our fraternity; our armor is our faith; the tie that binds more firmly year by year is ever-increasing acquaintance and comradeship through interchange of citizens; and the compact is not of perishable parchment, but of fair and honorable dealing, which, God grant, shall continue for all time.

An interesting and significant symptom of our growing mutuality appears in the fact that the voluntary interchange of residents to which I have referred is wholly free from restrictions. Our national and industrial exigencies have made it necessary for us, greatly to our regret, to fix limits to immigration from foreign countries. But there is no quota for Canada. We gladly welcome all of your sturdy, steady stock who care to come, as a strengthening ingredient and influence. We none the less bid Godspeed and happy days to the thousands of our own folk who are swarming constantly over your land and participating in its remarkable development. Wherever in either of our countries any inhabitant of the one or the other can best serve the interests of himself and his family is the place for him to be.

A further evidence of our increasing interdependence appears in the shifting of capital. Since the armistice, I am informed, approximately $2,500,000,000 has found its way from the United States into Canada for investment. That is a huge sum of money, and I have no doubt is employed safely for us and helpfully for you. Most gratifying to you, moreover, should be the circumstance that one-half of that great sum has gone for purchase of your state and municipal bonds, a tribute, indeed, to the scrupulous maintenance of your credit, to a degree equaled only by your mother country across the sea and your sister country across the hardly visible border. . . .

. . . It is public will, not public force, that makes for enduring peace. And is it not a gratifying circumstance that it has fallen to the lot of us North Americans, living amicably for more than a century, under different flags, to present the most striking example yet produced of that basic fact? If only European countries would heed the lesson conveyed by Canada and the United States, they would strike at the root of their own continuing disagreements and, in their own prosperity, forget to inveigh constantly at ours. . . .

I find that, quite unconsciously, I am speaking of our two countries almost in the singular when perhaps I should be more painstaking to keep them where they belong, in the plural. But I feel no need to apologize. You understand as well as I that I speak in no political sense. The ancient bugaboo of the United States scheming to annex Canada disappeared from all our minds years and years ago. Heaven knows we have all we can manage now, and room enough to spare for another hundred millions, before approaching the intensive stage of existence of many European states.

And if I might be so bold as to offer a word of advice to you, it would be this: Do not encourage any enterprise looking to Canada's annexation of the United States. You are one of the most capable governing peoples in the world, but I entreat you, for your own sakes, to think twice before undertaking management of the territory which lies between the Great Lakes and the Rio Grande.

No, let us go our own gaits along parallel roads, you helping us and we helping you. So long as each country maintains its independence, and both recognize their interdependence, those paths can not fail to be highways of progress and prosperity. Nationality continues to be a supreme factor in modern existence. Make no mistake about that. But the day of the Chinese wall, inclosing a hermit nation, has passed forever. Even though space itself were not in process of annihilation by airplane, submarine, wireless, and broadcasting, our very propinquity enjoins that most effective cooperation which comes only from clasping of hands in true faith and good fellowship.

CALVIN COOLIDGE

(1872–1933)

Hard-Headed Illusions

> *No one can contemplate current conditions without finding much that is satisfying and still more that is encouraging. . . .*
>
> *The Nation believes thoroughly in an honorable peace under which the rights of its citizens are to be everywhere protected. . . . We have never practiced the policy of competitive armaments. We have recently committed ourselves by covenants with the other great nations to a limitation of our sea power. As one result of this, our Navy ranks larger, in comparison, than it ever did before. . . .*
>
> *These policies of better international understandings, greater economy, and lower taxes have contributed greatly to peaceful and prosperous industrial relations. Under the helpful influences of restrictive immigration and a protective tariff, . . . [there is] a state of contentment seldom before seen. . . . Agriculture has been very slow in reviving, but the price of cereals at last indicates that the day of its deliverance is at hand.*

Inaugural Address, *March 4, 1925*

A VOLUME published in 1960, in Brattleboro, Vermont, and titled *Meet Calvin Coolidge,* could persuade even a non-Vermonter that some people sincerely liked and admired its subject. Bernard Baruch, Herbert Hoover, Bruce Barton, Will Rogers, Mark Sullivan and others praised his wit, honesty, virtues of hard work, economy and intelligence. Grace Coolidge wrote with the disarming love of a wife and mother.

Walter Lippmann's essay, "Puritanism de Luxe," was most rewarding for an American concerned for America. He noted Coolidge's genius for inactivity: "a grim, determined, alert inactivity which keeps [him] occupied constantly." There was also his capacity for deflating interest; Coolidge, Lippmann noted, "with an exquisite subtlety that amounts to genius, . . . has used dullness and boredom as political devices." Democrats found it impossible to cash in on the Harding scandals. Coolidge neither denounced the grafters nor defended them. A dreadful strike in the coal regions of Pennsylvania in 1925-1926, lasting five months and costing some $150 million in wages, elicited no action from him at all. And though he spoke continuously of the need for obeying the law, during a period of Prohibition in which automobile manufacturers advertised bullet-proof windows, he would not involve himself in controversy over enforcement of the Volstead Act.

Even as a symbol, he wanted objective analysis. An admirer who compiled his "Wit and Wisdom" told of a newspaperman who visited Coolidge at Plymouth, Vermont, following his retirement, and found him on the porch watching the automobiles roll by. It must make Coolidge proud, he opined, to see all the people who passed by simply in order to see him. "Not as many as yesterday," Coolidge was reported as saying: "There were sixty-three then." He was also reported as "boyish" in his delight in "spoofing" the White House servants; he liked, for example, to ring the alarm and hide while they anxiously looked for him.

Coolidge's silence and succinctness were highly touted; the content of his remarks was little probed. Many of his shattering comments required imperceptive "straight men" for full effect. Thus, one asked him how he had stayed in public life so long with "no money." Coolidge's pithy retort was: "I'm solvent."

He was reputedly down to earth and firm in his views; it was too little noted that these qualities totally depended on his lack of understanding or sensitivity to reality. Whether or not he actually said, "They hired the money, didn't they?" in connection with the war debts, there was no doubt that he saw nothing but dollars and cents in the Great Crusade. He could never understand the bitterness the Allies came to feel toward "Uncle Sham" or the careless electorate who were pleased to see him in the White House. His annals were meagre. He had been a Northampton, Massachusetts, politician, and in the state legislature. He had attained the governorship. During the great strike in 1919 of the underpaid Boston police, he had uttered his program for posterity: "There is no right to strike against the public safety by anybody, anywhere, anytime." Ten years before, the remark would have assured him of a quiet life among second- and third-string politicians. In an America that had quelled labor during the war and was ignoring the Bill of Rights in its drive against "Reds," the sentiment suggested his usefulness on the Republican Party ticket of 1920 beside Harding.

Coolidge viewed American history and life with curious fogginess. Thus, some students of post-Civil War America noticed the reckless proliferation of trusts that threatened traditional American freedoms and opportunities, as well as violent economic depressions, with attendant hunger, strikes, unemployment, tragedy. Not Coolidge. The country in Reconstruction times had "entered an era of great industrial expansion." "Along with this, however, went that spread of culture which wealth brings." "It was no wonder that men . . . sought to increase the means for the production of wealth by great combinations which in some instances [sic] partook of monopoly." "This certainly was well intended and believed to be patriotic. . . ." "Logically developed it would have meant stagnation in business through the loss of initiative. . . ." Fortunately, Theodore Roosevelt "brought the business men of the nation to see that their course was economically unsound, and therefore to be abandoned." Such was the history of the antitrust movement and progressivism, according to the then Vice-President of the United States.

As President, Coolidge was required to deal with vital national and international affairs. His cold and abstemious personality served the republic little more than had Harding's warm and self-indulgent qualities. "Self-government means self-support," said Coolidge. But he would have liked to give over to private industry the Muscle Shoals plant which had been built at enormous government expense for war purposes. "Men do not make laws," he observed. "They do but discover them." He discovered that there was no need for government regulation of business, and earnestly pressed for reduction of taxes. The unprecedented prosperity that followed his election in 1924 seemed to bear out his keen understanding of reality. It would take the crash of 1929 to reveal that prosperity had been a function of speculation—which Coolidge had neither forestalled nor controlled—and of the un-Puritanic operations of the installment plan. But even Coolidge could observe that the farmers were not profiting from prosperity. He was willing to encourage agricultural education, to construct good roads, to offer more credit, which would ultimately ruin great numbers of farmers. But though he was willing to protect industry by raising forbidding tariffs against foreign goods, he was unwilling to cooperate with such "special legislation" as the McNary-Haugen Act, which would have activated the government in raising the prices of farm commodities. His message vetoing the agriculture bill (May 23, 1928) developed points that were muted in the 1930's and during World War II prosperity, but which came to life again in the 1950's.

Vetoing the Farmer: Nonplanning as a Way of Life

Senate bill 3555, called the surplus control act, is in some respects an improvement over Senate bill 4808 of the last Congress. It includes several provisions, which, if unencumbered by objectionable features, would form a basis for a measure that should do much to develop stronger business organizations in agriculture. But the present bill contains not only the so-called equalization fee and other features of the old measure prejudicial, in my opinion, to sound public policy and to agriculture, but also new and highly objectionable provisions. In its entirety it is little less undesirable than the earlier measure. The bill still is unconstitutional. . . .

In its essentials the objectionable plan proposed here is the stimulation of the price of agricultural commodities and products thereof by artificially controlling the surpluses so that there will be an apparent scarcity on the market. This is to be done by means of a board having supposedly adequate powers and adequate funds to accomplish such purpose through various agencies, governmental and private. The surpluses of the different selected commodities so accumulated by the board are then to be sold by export and otherwise directly or through such agencies at whatever loss is necessary in making the disposition. The fund to pay the losses and other costs while at first furnished by the Government is ultimately to be replaced and thereafter replenished from time to time by means of a tax or fee charged against the product. The theory is that the enhanced price of the commodity would enable the producer to pay the equalization fee and still reap a profit. . . .

A detailed analysis of all the objections to the measure would involve a document of truly formidable proportions. However, its major weaknesses and perils may be summarized under six headings:

I. Its attempted price-fixing fallacy.

II. The tax characteristics of the equalization fee.

III. The widespread bureaucracy which it would set up.

IV. Its encouragement to profiteering and wasteful distribution by middlemen.

V. Its stimulation of overproduction.

VI. Its aid to our foreign agricultural competitors.

These topics by no means exhaust the list of fallacious and indeed dangerous aspects of the bill, but they afford ample ground for its emphatic rejection.

I. *Price fixing.*—This measure is as cruelly deceptive in its disguise as governmental price-fixing legislation and involves quite as unmistakably the impossible scheme of attempted governmental control of buying and selling of agricultural products through political agencies as any of the other so-called surplus control bills. In fact, in certain respects it is much broader and more flagrant in its scope. The heights to which price lifting might be *promised* are freed from the limitations fixed in previous measures. The bill carefully avoids any direct allusion to such price-fixing functions, but there can be no doubt about its intentions and authorizations to the Federal farm board in this respect. There is apparently no change in the import of the bill in the resolution to impose upon the farmer and upon the consumers of farm produce a régime of futile, delusive experiments with price fixing, with indirect governmental buying and selling, and with a nation-wide system of regulatory policing, intolerable espionage, and tax collection on a vast scale. . . .

The board would be compelled to arrive in some way at the premium on the domestic price which would be demanded from the consumer, and this figure would have to be fixed in the contracts which it would make with the millers, packers, canners, spinners, and other processors. Such prices and other terms fixed in the contracts would be used by the board to calculate the losses upon which it will base the size of the equalization fee. This procedure is the very essence of price fixing no matter how cumbersome and crudely camouflaged it may be. By throwing the very large resources of the Government into this operation the present bill gives the widest latitude for the most vicious temptations adherent in autocratic authority in complete command of vast industries and trades. . . .

II. *The equalization fee,* which is the kernel of this legislation, is a sales tax upon the entire community. It is in no sense a mere contribution to be made by the producers themselves, as has been represented by supporters of the measure. It can be assessed upon the commodities in transit to the consumer and its burdens can often unmistakably be passed on to him.

Furthermore, such a procedure would certainly involve an extraordinary relinquishment of the taxing power on the part of Congress, because the tax would not only be levied without recourse to legislative authority but its proceeds would be expended entirely without the usual safeguards of congressional control of appropriations. This would be a most dangerous nullification of one of the essential checks and balances which lie at the very foundation of our Government. . . .

III. *Widespread bureaucracy.*—A bureaucratic tyranny of unprecedented proportions would be let down upon the backs of the farm industry and its distributors throughout the Nation in connection with the enforcement of this measure. Thousands of contracts involving scores of different grades, quantities, and varieties of products would have to be signed by the board with the 4,400 millers, the 1,200 meat-packing plants, the 3,000 or more cotton and woolen mills, and the 2,700 canners. If this bill had been in operation in

1925 it would have involved collections upon an aggregate of over 16,000,000,000 units of wheat, corn, and cotton.

The bill undertakes to provide insurance against loss, but presumably only against reasonable and unavoidable loss. Just what this might be would involve judgment on the part of Government employees upon tens of thousands of transactions running into billions of dollars. This is bureaucracy gone mad. Cooperative associations, flour mills, packing plants, and grain elevators will cease to be private and become public agencies. If there is any conclusion that we can announce as final with regard to governmental business operations, particularly after the bitter and excessively costly war-time experiences with such enterprises, it is that we can not maintain a bureaucracy of such vast proportions engaged in buying and selling without constant danger of corruption, mismanagement, and prodigious tax burdens. No private agency of so gigantic and complex a character attempting to juggle with profound economic principles in such fashion could survive under such circumstances, and the chances for a governmental trading organization would be even less. . . .

IV. *Encouragement to profiteering and wasteful distribution by middlemen.*—As was pointed out in the veto last year, it seems almost incredible that the farmers of this country are being offered this scheme of legislative relief in which the only persons who are guaranteed to benefit are the exporters, packers, millers, canners, spinners, and other processors. Their profits are definitely assured. They have, in other words, no particular incentive toward careful operation, since each of them holding a contract, no matter how unscrupulous, wasteful, or inefficient his operations may have been, would be fully reimbursed for all of his losses. . . .

The packers could be commanded by the board to buy hogs enough to create a near shortage at home and then raise the prices to a fixed level. The unsalable surplus would then be dumped abroad at a loss, which would thereupon be made good out of the pockets of all taxpayers, including the farmers. The operations would involve an impenetrable maze of contracts between the board and hundreds of packers and provisioners. . . .

V. *Stimulation of overproduction.*—The bill runs counter to an economic law as well settled as the law of gravitation. Increased prices decrease consumption; they also increase production. These two conditions are the very ones that spell disaster to the whole program. The vaguely drawn clause in the measure to meet this

163

obvious danger merely amounts to moral suasion and as a last resort the withdrawal of the equalization fee. Thus if 90 per cent of the growers of a given commodity heed the admonitions of the board and refrain from production, they will, nevertheless, be punished because of the evasions of the remaining 10 per cent who have ignored the board's requests. In other words, no farmer will be safe in directing his planning upon his individual judgment, for should the result be a stimulation of an increased yield the board will be likely to withdraw the support which encouraged the surpluses and allow the prices to collapse under the weight of that artificially created excess. The annals of the industrial and agricultural world are replete with the catastrophes that have come in the wake of such attempted distortions of one of the most fundamental principles of commercial relations.

VI. *Aid to our foreign agricultural competitors.*—This measure continues, as did its predecessor, to give substantial aid to the foreign competitors of American agriculture and industry. It continues the amazing proposal to supply foreign workers with cheaper food than those of the United States, and this at the expense of the American farm industry, thereby encouraging both the foreign peasant, whose produce is not burdened with the costs of any equalization fees, and also affording through reduced food prices the means of cutting the wage rates paid by foreign manufacturers. The latter step would promptly impair the prosperity of our manufacturing population, which is by far the leading and most profitable market for our farm produce. It is nonsense to say that our farmers are not interested in such a development, which can only result in unemployment and in consequent decreases in food consumption in the great industrial districts. It is surely poor business to transfer the farmer's market from an employed American workman to the latter's competitor in the low wage scale countries across the seas, whose potential buying power and standards of living even at best are far below those of this country. . . .

By the inevitable stimulation of production the bill can only mean an increase of exportable surplus to be dumped in the world market. This in turn will bring about a constantly decreasing world price, which will soon reach so low a figure that a wholesale curtailment of production in this country with its attendant demoralization and heavy losses would be certain. Where is the advantage of dragging our farmers into such folly? . . .

In conclusion, if the measure is enacted one would be led to wonder how long it would be before producers in other lines would clamor for similar "equalizing" subsidies from the public coffers. The lobbies of Congress would be filled with emissaries from every momentarily distressed industry demanding similar relief of a burdensome surplus at the expense of the Treasury. Once we plunged into the futile sophistries of such a system of wholesale commercial doles for special groups of middlemen and distributors at the expense of farmers and other producers, it is difficult to see what the end might be.

I have believed at all times that the only sound basis for further Federal Government action in behalf of agriculture would be to encourage its adequate organization to assist in building up marketing agencies and facilities in the control of the farmers themselves. I want to see them undertake, under their own management, the marketing of their products under such conditions as will enable them to bring about greater stability in prices and less waste in marketing, but entirely within unalterable economic laws. Such a program, supported by a strong protective tariff on farm products, is the best method of effecting a permanent cure of existing agricultural ills. Such a program is in accordance with the American tradition and the American ideal of reliance on and maintenance of private initiative and individual responsibility, and the duty of the Government is discharged when it has provided conditions under which the individual can achieve success. . . .

Coolidge's idealism—his view that the armed forces of the United States were "the forces of peace"—did him no harm with his constituency. The still, small voice of anti-imperialism never reached him. Mexican relations had continued strained since the days of Wilson. Coolidge passed by a Senate resolution suggesting arbitration; Mexico's nationalizing program made her plainly guilty of having confiscated mines and other properties which were "legally owned by American citizens." There was nothing to arbitrate. He was reluctant to carry out the terms of the Jones Act (1916) which had promised independence to the Philippines: "[T]he Government of the United States would not feel that it had performed its full duty by the Filipino people, or discharged all its obligations to civilization, if it should yield at this time to . . . aspirations for national independence." Our protracted Nicaraguan intervention was embarrassed by peasant leaders. Despite strong protests from civic and liberal bodies and notable Senators, Coolidge expressed himself firmly and according to his best lights, in his Message to Congress (January 10, 1927).

Neighbors and Strangers:
Ways to Peace

While conditions in Nicaragua and the action of this Government pertaining thereto have in general been made public, I think the time has arrived for me officially to inform the Congress more in detail of the events leading up to the present disturbances and conditions which seriously threaten American lives and property, endanger the stability of all Central America, and put in jeopardy the rights granted by Nicaragua to the United States for the construction of a canal. It is well known that in 1912 the United States intervened in Nicaragua with a large force and put down a revolution, and that from that time to 1925 a legation guard of American marines was, with the consent of the Nicaraguan Government, kept in Managua to protect American lives and property. In 1923 representatives of the five Central American countries, namely, Costa Rica, Guatemala, Honduras, Nicaragua, and Salvador, at the invitation of the United States, met in Washington and entered into a series of treaties. These treaties dealt with limitation of armament, a Central American tribunal for arbitration, and the general subject of peace and amity. The treaty last referred to specifically provides in Article II that the Governments of the contracting parties will not recognize any other government which may come into power in any of the five Republics through a coup d'état or revolution and disqualifies the leaders of such coup d'état or revolution from assuming the presidency or vice presidency. . . .

The United States was not a party to this treaty, but it was made in Washington under the auspices of the Secretary of State, and this Government has felt a moral obligation to apply its principles in order to encourage the Central American States in their efforts to prevent revolution and disorder. The treaty, it may be noted in passing, was signed on behalf of Nicaragua by Emiliano Chamorro himself, who afterwards assumed the presidency in violation thereof and thereby contributed to the creation of the present difficulty.

In October, 1924, an election was held in Nicaragua for President, Vice President, and members of the Congress. This resulted in the election of a coalition ticket embracing Conservatives and Liberals. Carlos Solorzano, a Conservative Republican, was elected President and Juan B. Sacasa, a Liberal, was elected Vice President. This

166

Government was recognized by the other Central American countries and by the United States. It had been the intention of the United States to withdraw the marines immediately after this election, and notice was given of the intention to withdraw them in January, 1925. At the request of the President of Nicaragua this time was extended to September 1, 1925. Pursuant to this determination and notice, the marines were withdrawn in August, 1925, and it appeared at that time as though tranquillity in Nicaragua was assured. Within two months, however, further disturbances broke out between the supporters of General Chamorro and the supporters of the President, culminating in the seizure of the Loma, a fortress dominating the city of Managua. Once in possession of the Loma, General Chamorro dictated an agreement which President Solorzano signed the next day. According to the terms of this agreement the President agreed to substitute supporters of General Chamorro for certain members of his cabinet, to pay General Chamorro $10,000 for the expenses of the uprising, and to grant amnesty to all those who participated in it. Vice President Sacasa thereupon left the country. In the meantime General Chamorro, who, while he had not actually taken over the office of President, was able to dictate his will to the actual Executive, brought about the expulsion from the Congress of 18 members, on the ground that their election had been fraudulent, and caused to be put in their places candidates who had been defeated at the election of 1924. Having thus gained the control of Congress, he caused himself to be appointed by the Congress as designate on January 16, 1926. On January 16, 1926, Solorzano resigned as President and immediately General Chamorro took office. The four Central American countries and the United States refused to recognize him as President. . . .

Notwithstanding the refusal of this Government and of the other Central American Governments to recognize him, General Chamorro continued to exercise the functions of President until October 30, 1926. In the meantime, a revolution broke out in May on the east coast in the neighborhood of Bluefields and was speedily suppressed by the troops of General Chamorro. However, it again broke out with considerable more violence. The second attempt was attended with some success and practically all of the east coast of Nicaragua fell into the hands of the revolutionists. Throughout these events Sacasa was at no time in the country, having remained in Mexico and Guatemala during this period.

Repeated requests were made of the United States for protection, especially on the east coast, and, on August 24, 1926, the Secretary of State addressed to the Secretary of the Navy the following communication:

"I have the honor to suggest that war vessels of the Special Service Squadron proceed as soon as possible to the Nicaraguan ports of Corinto and Bluefields for the protection of American and foreign lives and property in case that threatened emergencies materialize. The American Chargé d'Affaires at Managua has informed the Department that he considers the presence of war vessels at these ports desirable, and the American Consul at Bluefields has reported that a warship is urgently needed to protect life and property at that port. An attack on The Bluff and Bluefields is expected momentarily."

Accordingly, the Navy Department ordered Admiral Latimer, in command of the special service squadron, to proceed to Bluefields. Upon arriving there he found it necessary for the adequate protection of Amreican lives and property to declare Bluefields a neutral zone. This was done with the consent of both factions, afterwards, on October 26, 1926, reduced to a written agreement, which is still in force. . . .

According to our reports, the Sacasa delegates . . . stated freely that to accept any government other than one presided over by Doctor Sacasa himself would be a breach of faith with their Mexican allies. Hostilities were resumed on October 30, 1926. On the same date General Chamorro formally turned over the executive power to Sebastian Uriza, who had been appointed designate by the Congress controlled by General Chamorro. The United States Government refused to recognize Señor Uriza, on the ground that his assumption of the Presidency had no constitutional basis. Uriza thereupon convoked Congress in extraordinary session, and the entire 18 members who had been expelled during the Chamorro régime were notified to resume their seats. The Congress which met in extraordinary session on November 10 had, therefore, substantially the same membership as when first convened following the election of 1924. This Congress, whose acts may be considered as constitutional, designated Señor Adolfo Diaz as first designate. At this session of Congress 53 members were present out of a total membership of 67, of whom 44 voted for Diaz and 2 for Solorzano. The balance abstained from voting. On November 11 Señor Uriza turned over the executive power to Diaz, who was inaugurated on the 14th.

The Nicaraguan constitution provides in article 106 that in the absence of the President and Vice President the Congress shall designate one of its members to complete the unexpired term of President. As President Solorzano had resigned and was then residing in California, and as the Vice President, Doctor Sacasa, was in Guatemala, having been out of the country since November, 1925, the action of Congress in designating Señor Diaz was perfectly legal and in accordance with the constitution. Therefore the United States Government on November 17 extended recognition to Señor Diaz. . . .

Immediately following the inauguration of President Diaz and frequently since that date he has appealed to the United States for support, has informed this Government of the aid which Mexico is giving to the revolutionists, and has stated that he is unable solely because of the aid given by Mexico to the revolutionists to protect the lives and property of American citizens and other foreigners. When negotiations leading up to the Corinto conference began, I immediately placed an embargo on the shipment of arms and ammunition to Nicaragua. The Department of State notified the other Central American States, to wit, Costa Rica, Honduras, Salvador, and Guatemala, and they assured the department that they would cooperate in this measure. So far as known, they have done so. The State Department also notified the Mexican Government of this embargo and informally suggested to that Government like action. The Mexican Government did not adopt the suggestion to put on an embargo, but informed the American ambassador at Mexico City that in the absence of manufacturing plants in Mexico for the making of arms and ammunition the matter had little practical importance.

As a matter of fact, I have the most conclusive evidence that arms and munitions in large quantities have been on several occasions since August, 1926, shipped to the revolutionists in Nicaragua. Boats carrying these munitions have been fitted out in Mexican ports, and some of the munitions bear evidence of having belonged to the Mexican Government. It also appears that the ships were fitted out with the full knowledge of and, in some cases, with the encouragement of Mexican officials and were in one instance, at least, commanded by a Mexican naval reserve officer. At the end of November, after spending some time in Mexico City, Doctor Sacasa went back to Nicaragua, landing at Puerto Cabezas, near Bragmans Bluff. He immediately placed himself at the head of the insurrection and declared himself President of Nicaragua. He has never been recognized by any of the Central American Republics nor by any other Government, with the exception of Mexico, which recognized him immediately. As arms and munitions in large quantities were reaching the revolutionists, I deemed it unfair to prevent the recognized Government from purchasing arms abroad, and, accordingly, the Secretary of State has notified the Diaz Government that licenses would be issued for the export of arms and munitions purchased in this country. It would be thoroughly inconsistent for this country not to support the Government recognized by it while the revolutionists were receiving arms and munitions from abroad.

During the last two months the Government of the United States has received repeated requests from various American citizens, both directly and through our consuls and legation, for the protection of their lives and property. The Government of the United States has also received requests from the British chargé at Managua and from the Italian ambassador at Washington for the protection of their respective nationals. Pursuant to such requests, Admiral Latimer, in charge of the special service squadron, has not only maintained the neutral zone at Bluefields under the agreement of both parties but has landed forces at Puerto Cabezas and Rio Grande, and established neutral zones at these points where considerable numbers of Americans live and are engaged in carrying on various industries. He has also been authorized to establish such other neutral zones as are necessary for the purposes above mentioned.

For many years numerous Americans have been living in Nicaragua developing its industries and carrying on business. At the present time there are large investments in lumbering, mining, coffee growing, banana culture, shipping, and also in general mercantile and other collateral business. All these people and these industries have been encouraged by the Nicaraguan Government. That Government has at all times owed them protection, but the United States has occasionally been obliged to send naval forces for their proper protection. In the present crisis such forces are requested by the Nicaraguan Government, which protests to the United States its inability to protect these interests and states that any measures which the United States deems appropriate for their protection will be satisfactory to the Nicaraguan Government.

In addition to these industries now in existence, the Government of Nicaragua, by a treaty entered into on the 5th day of August, 1914, granted in perpetuity to the United States the exclusive proprietary rights necessary and convenient for the construction, operation, and maintenance of an oceanic canal. . . .

The consideration paid by the United States to Nicaragua was the sum of $3,000,000. At the time of the payment of this money a financial plan was drawn up between the Nicaraguan Government and its creditors which provided for the consolidation of Nicaragua's obligations. At that time the bondholders holding the Nicaraguan external debt consented to a reduction in interest from 6 to 5 per cent, providing the service of this loan was handled through the American collector of customs, and at the same time a series of internal guaranteed customs bonds amounting to $3,744,000 was issued by the Nicaraguan Government to pay off the claims which had arisen against it because of revolutionary disturbances from 1909 to 1912. . . . The internal revenues were, as heretofore, to be collected by the Government. Collection of the internal revenue, however, was to be taken over by the collector general of customs, an American citizen appointed by the Nicaraguan Government and approved by the Secretary of State of the United States, if the product should average less than $60,000 a month for three consecutive months. This has never yet been necessary. . . .

There is no question that if the revolution continues American investments and business interests in Nicaragua will be very seriously affected, if not destroyed. The currency, which is now at par, will be inflated. American as well as foreign bondholders will undoubtedly look to the United States for the protection of their interests.

It is true that the United States did not establish the financial plan by any treaty, but it nevertheless did aid through diplomatic channels and advise in the negotiation and establishment of this plan for the financial rehabilitation of Nicaragua. . . .

Consequently, I have deemed it my duty to use the powers committed to me to insure the adequate protection of all American interests in Nicaragua, whether they be endangered by internal strife or by outside interference in the affairs of that Republic.

Coolidge liked a good, firm statement: "The Government does not want war anywhere. It wants peace everywhere." The Washington Conference of 1922, he thought, "did a great deal to restore harmony and good will among the nations." Yet there were steps making for peace still to be explored. Coolidge continued to voice his generalities, while various enthusiasts worked to initiate legislation outlawing war. Coolidge himself made efforts to interest France, England, Italy and Japan in further naval cutbacks, but was disappointed. He became an advocate of preparedness, and of augmented American seapower. The Message to Congress of February 10, 1927, is a sample of his thinking in the area.

In the spring of 1927, French Premier Briand, proposed a treaty with the United States setting an example of a turn away from war as an instrument of national policy. Intricate negotiations broadened the proposal to include other nations. The Kellogg-Briand Pact of Paris was largely a product of American efforts, notably those of Frank B. Kellogg, the Secretary of State. It ultimately received the signatures of sixty-two nations, and was ratified by the Senate on January 15, 1929. On February 5, the Senate passed a bill providing for the building of fifteen war-ready cruisers and one aircraft carrier.

The Limitation of Armaments

Pursuant to my instructions the American ambassadors at London, Paris, Rome, and Tokyo will to-day present to the Governments of Great Britain, France, Italy, and Japan a memorandum suggesting that they empower their delegates at the forthcoming meeting of the Preparatory Commission for the Disarmament Conference at Geneva to negotiate and conclude at an early date an agreement further limiting naval armament, supplementing the Washington treaty on that subject, and covering the classes of vessels not covered by that treaty. . . .

The support of all measures looking to the preservation of the peace of the world has been long established as a fundamental policy of this Government. The American Government and the people are convinced that competitive armaments constitute one of the most dangerous contributing causes of international suspicion and discord and are calculated eventually to lead to war. A recognition of this fact and a desire as far as possible to remove this danger led the American Government in 1921 to call the Washington conference.

At that time we were engaged in a great building program which, upon its completion, would have given us first place on the sea. We felt then, however, and feel now, that the policy we then advocated—that of deliberate self-denial and limitation of naval armament by the great naval powers—promised the attainment of at least one guarantee of peace, an end worthy of mutual adjustment and concession.

At the Washington conference we found the other nations animated with the same desire as ourselves, to remove naval competition from the list of possible causes of international discord. Unfortunately, however, it was not possible to reach agreements at Washington covering all classes of naval ships. The Washington treaty provided a specific tonnage limitation upon capital ships and aircraft carriers, with certain restrictions as to size and maximum caliber of guns for other vessels. Every nation has been at complete liberty to build any number of cruisers, destroyers, and submarines. Only size and armament of cruisers were limited. The signatories of the Washington treaty have fulfilled their obligations faithfully and there can be no doubt that that treaty constitutes an outstanding success in its operation.

It has been the hope of the American Government, constantly expressed by the Congress since the Washington conference, that a favorable opportunity might present itself to complete the work begun here by the conclusion of further agreements covering cruisers, destroyers, and submarines. The desirability of such an agreement has been apparent, since it was only to be expected that the spirit of competition, stifled as regards capital ships and aircraft carriers by the Washington treaty, would sooner or later show itself with regard to the other vessels not limited under the treaty. Actually, I do not believe that competitive building of these classes of ships has begun. Nevertheless, far-reaching building programs have been laid down by certain powers, and there has appeared in our own country, as well as abroad, a sentiment urging naval construction on the ground that such construction is taking place elsewhere. In such sentiments lies the germ of renewed naval competition. . . .

The moment seems particularly opportune to try to secure further limitation of armament in accordance with the expressed will of the Congress. The earnest desire of the nations of the world to relieve themselves in as great a measure as possible of the burden of armaments and to avoid the dangers of competition has been shown by the establishment of the preparatory commission for the disarmament conference, which met in Geneva last May, and which is continuing its work with a view of preparing the agenda for a final general conference. For more than six months, representatives of a score or more of nations have examined from all points of view the problem of the reduction and limitation of armaments. In these discussions it was brought out very clearly that a number of nations felt that land, sea, and air armaments were interdependent and that it would be difficult, if not impossible, to agree upon the limitation of one type of armament without simultaneously limiting the other types.

The consequence to be feared is that a deadlock will be reached, should even partial progress in the reduction of armaments be conditioned upon the acceptance of some universal plan covering land, sea, and air forces together. If the prospective deadlock can not be broken, it is probable that little progress will be made for the time being. It appears to me to be the duty of this Government, which has always advocated limitation of armaments, to endeavor to suggest some avenue by which concrete results may be achieved, even though such results may be short of an ultimate ideal solution for the threefold problem of land, sea, and air armament. . . .

PART V
The Depression

HERBERT HOOVER

(1874–   )

Freedom and Free Enterprise

In the large view, we have reached a higher degree of comfort and security than ever existed before in the history of the world. Through liberation from wide-spread poverty we have reached a higher degree of individual freedom than ever before. . . . We are steadily building a new race—a new civilization great in its own attainments. . . . For wise guidance in this great period of recovery the Nation is deeply indebted to Calvin Coolidge.

Inaugural Address, *March 4, 1929*

MORE than thirty years after he had been ushered out of public office by an anxious and embittered electorate, Herbert Hoover could look back at his decades of public service from a pinnacle of almost universal approval. His reputation had suffered extremes of heat and cold. In 1918, "Hooverize" meant to be saving and thoughtful in terms of war needs. Hoover had gradually become "the great humanitarian," by reason of his World War I work of feeding the Belgians and his postwar aid to hungry nations, including Russia, which had come out of the throes of civil war and gone into the throes of communist economics. In the 1930's, the resourceful Democrats had identified him with the shabby huts and other housing which demoralized people had been driven to inhabit. "Hooverize" had been forgotten; "Hoovervilles" had, perhaps, attained a certain historical permanency. But, in later years, there were few in America who could whip up a tithe of their old indignation, satire and invective to refer to the ex-President whom they had once held to be the author of their ills. They themselves had since gained from wartime prosperity and postwar economics. Depression days were far off.

Three decades before the anxious years of the 1930's, Hoover had started his career as a young mining engineer; a boy who had been born not exactly in a log cabin, but in a Midwestern equivalent of one, and who had lived poorly and stringently before working his way through Stanford University. In 1897, two years after graduation and in his first association with a mining company, he began his career in the Western Australia goldfields. Succeeding in this difficult, speculative area required all his energy and resourcefulness, but he did well in that raw mining country. And he did well in other consultantships which carried him to China—where he helped defend the foreign settlement at Tientsin, during the Boxer Rebellion—and to London. His foes were later to complain that he was scarcely an American, at this point. He seems, in fact, to have got back home to California as regularly as anywhere else.

His business as a consulting engineer took him all over the world in the interests of numerous mining companies. His operations involved properties in South Africa, Colorado, Mexico, Russia, Korea, the Malay Straits Settlement, and India. He may have become something less than aware of the endless diversity of life. One unfriendly critic noted raucously that he had had occasion to say that he *believed* he had once visited a particular country. Didn't one *know* when one had been abroad? Not, perhaps, when one had, like Hoover, been everywhere, and was concentrating on technical problems of ore deposits, transportation, labor costs, and other factors which entered into mining. In 1914, Hoover and his associates are said to have employed some 175,000 men over the world. Hoover was a very rich man. He was also well read for a man with his professional responsibilities. He had published *Principles of Mining* (1909), composed of a series of lectures given at Stanford and Columbia Universities. And with his wife, he had translated Agricola's *De Re Metallica* (1912). World War I gave him a new career.

He began unofficially as an aid to Americans stranded in Europe. He then organized a committee to help feed Belgians under the German occupation. His work made him famous. When the United States entered the war, he was placed in charge of food administration. Americans responded to Hoover's appeal that they make do with plain coffee and unsweetened grapefruit, that they support meatless days and the patriotic saving of fats—all, significantly, on a *voluntary* basis. Hoover feared bloated government authority. With the war over, he became head of the American Relief Administration, and fed the Germans, the Russians, and the varied peoples of Central Europe. A biography of him published in 1920—and possibly considering him as a candidate for President— treated him as a great man.

There was malice and suspicion of Hoover's motives and activities, after he became a public figure of consequence. He seems to have answered all charges satisfactorily. It was his *principles* that were and would continue to be controversial. Hoover assumed the transcendent virtues of free enterprise. He believed in the rectitude of the Allied cause in World War I. He conceived of the Bolshevik revolution in Russia as a nest of horrors from which only horrors could arise. Socialism was slavery, anywhere and everywhere. No one in his generation fought as wholeheartedly and determinedly to support these premises.

As Secretary of Commerce under Harding, he made his office a central post in government. He was not antilabor, but he did believe that the key to its well-being was efficient business management. Accordingly, he arranged conferences between industrial leaders, in order to help them create order in their affairs; to make standards for production more uniform; to develop economic methods of manufacture and distribution that would result in savings to the consumer; to further scientific research. In the course of his work, Hoover persuaded his capitalist aides to create hundreds of codes for industries, some of which were taken over wholesale by the NRA of the later Roosevelt administration. Hoover saw clearly the difference between government competing with private industry—he was opposed to government ownership of railroads, for instance—and government *stimulation* of private industry. He opposed aid to the unemployed, but believed in public works privately constructed and presumably encouraging the increased employment of those needing work. He made an exception of children; he favored health and education for the underprivileged, and helped organize the American Child Health Association.

Hoover assumed the presidency in a blaze of popular confidence and well-being, on which he congratulated the nation. He warned it against the weakness of our criminal justice and emphasized the need to enforce the Eighteenth Amendment. He spoke of the need for education, public health, world peace. He himself had, as President-elect, taken a good will tour through Central and South America. His apologists were later to say that he foresaw the Great Depression, but he offered no evidence that this had been the case. He had, apparently, really believed that America had discovered the secret of perpetual prosperity. He met the stock market crash and subsequent business collapse with firmness and dispatch, but his program involved holding the line of government credit rather than ministering to the victims of the nationwide layoffs and bankruptcies. He urged leaders of labor and capital to hold the line on personnel and salary reduction on the one hand, strikes on the other. He prophesized often and long the return of prosperity. Above all, he urged public works calculated to swell industrial activity and considered how the credit structure of the country could be adjusted to retard unwarranted speculation.

Hoover, as it turned out, simply had no understanding of the depth of the social disorder, and, in terms of the human suffering involved, held grimly to his old shibboleth: the need for voluntary action by the citizens. For him, the situation was only hungry Belgium all over again. A glaring point he could never fathom was that *talents* were being corroded, as well as personalities. A surgeon without a patient was worse than hungry, and would soon have lost his skill forever. Thus, a social convulsion faced Hoover, as well as physical need. He marched on bravely, denouncing "unwarranted pessimism." Soon, he would have his stock answer to all criticism: America was

179

always about to resume prosperity, but relapsed from new economic shocks generated abroad. A friendly critic noted how puzzling it was that Hoover, who had always insisted on the interrelatedness of world affairs, "should attempt to free his own country from responsibility for a world-wide situation. . . ."

Hoover had what seemed to him to be a broad based program. One major plank related to foreign debts, which he explained in a press statement (July 6, 1931).

Moratorium

I am glad to announce that the American proposal for one year's postponement of all intergovernmental debts and reparations has now been accepted in principle by all of the important creditor governments.

The terms of acceptance by the French Government are, of course, subject to the approval of the other interested powers, for whom the American Government naturally cannot speak. Without going into technical terms, while certain payments are made by Germany for reparations account, the substance of the President's proposal is retained as the sums so paid are immediately reloaned to Germany.

The technical difficulties arising from many complicated international agreements which involve the aggregate payment between governments of over $800,000,000 per annum are now in the course of solution by the good-will and earnest cooperation of governmental leaders everywhere.

The American part of the plan is, of course, subject to the approval by Congress, but I have received the individual assurances of support from a very large majority of the members of both Senate and House, irrespective of political affiliations.

The acceptance of this proposal has meant sacrifices by the American people and by the Allied Governments, who are with all others suffering from world-wide depression and deficits in governmental budgets. The economic load most seriously oppressing the peoples of Germany and Central Europe will be immensely lightened.

While the plan is particularly aimed to economic relief, yet economic relief means the swinging of men's minds from fear to confidence, the swinging of nations from the apprehension of disorder and governmental collapse to hope and confidence of the future. It means tangible aid to unemployment and agriculture.

The almost unanimous support in the United States is again profound evidence of the sincere humanity of the American people. And in this year, devoted to economic upbuilding, the world has need of solemn thought on the causes which have contributed to the depression. I need not repeat that one of these causes is the burdens imposed and the fears aroused by competitive armament.

Contemplation of the past few weeks should bring a realization that we must find relief from these fundamental burdens which today amount to several times the amount of intergovernmental debts.

Hoover was far from being a stipendiary of big business or a tool of politicians. One of his first acts as President had been to stop the leasing of oil resources and put outstanding oil-exploring permits under government review. National resources, he asserted, were limited and had to be administered under strict supervision in the public interest. But Hoover's limitations were fundamental. *Mirrors of Washington* (1921) had taken him off very shrewdly. Whatever his gifts, it pointed out, he lacked political intelligence. He was indecisive; during the campaign of 1920, he had found difficulty in deciding whether he was a Democrat or a Republican, since both parties had wooed him. Furthermore, he lacked personality: "[H]e is disappointing, without charm, given to silence, as if he had nothing for ordinary human relations which had no profitable bearing on the task in hand." And again: "It is characteristic of him that he always speaks of the relief of starving populations not in terms of human suffering, but in terms of chemistry."

In his February 12, 1931, Lincoln Day address Hoover sought to be inspirational, but he saw the Illinois statesman as a Republican, an advocate of the protection tariff, of government aid for waterways and roads, and of constitutional processes. Hoover fought fiercely for the American way, and evidently expected that Americans would admire the battle he had waged in their behalf. Yet his pronouncements took on an air of the bizarre, as the depression crisis wore on.

May 1, 1930, at the annual dinner of the United States Chamber of Commerce: "While the crash only took place six months ago, I am convinced that we have now passed the worse and with continued unity of effort we shall rapidly recover."

October 2, 1930, at the annual convention of the American Bankers' Association: "During the past year you have carried the credit system of the Nation safely through a most difficult crisis. In this success you have demonstrated not alone the soundness of the credit system but also the capacity of our bankers in emergency."

June 16, 1931, at the dedication of the Harding Memorial, Marion,

Ohio: "He succeeded in [his] tasks. When in two years [of his Presidency] he died, new peace treaties had been made . . . tranquillity had been restored at home, employment had been renewed, and a long period of prosperity had begun."

Hoover did not know how to dramatize his causes. His denunciations of hoarding sounded insulting to the millions who had nothing to hoard. His Surgeon-General's Report (January 2, 1932) that so far as health was concerned, "the country has never been as prosperous in its history," was calculated to make readers rub their eyes with disbelief. He called industrialists to head his unemployment committees. His Moratorium had rung no bells for gladness. His battle with the Senate in behalf of World Court affiliation made as little impression. His great effort, institution of the Reconstruction Finance Corporation—destined to accomplish little before it was galvanized by the New Deal—elicited few hosannas from the disturbed victims of the social convulsion.

RFC

I

Press Statement, January 22, 1932.

I have signed the Reconstruction Finance Corporation act.

It brings into being a powerful organization with adequate resources, able to strengthen weaknesses that may develop in our credit, banking and railway structure, in order to permit business and industry to carry on normal activities free from the fear of unexpected shocks and retarding influences.

Its purpose is to stop deflation in agriculture and industry and thus to increase employment by the restoration of men to their normal jobs.

It is not created for the aid of big industries or big banks. Such institutions are amply able to take care of themselves. It is created for the support of the smaller banks and financial institutions and, through rendering their resources liquid, to give renewed support to business, industry, and agriculture. It should give opportunity to mobilize the gigantic strength of our country for recovery.

In attaching my signature to this extremely important legislation, I wish to pay tribute to the patriotism of the men in both houses of Congress who have given proof of their devotion to the welfare of their country irrespective of political affiliation.

II

Press Statement, January 23, 1932.

The President said:

I am glad to sign the third of our reconstruction measures, that providing additional capital to the Federal Land banks. It should (a) reinforce the credit of the Federal Land Bank system and reassure investors in Land Bank bonds; (b) thus enable the banks to obtain capital for farmers at reasonable rates, and (c) above all, bring relief and hope to many borrowers from the banks who had done their honest best, but, because of circumstances beyond their control, have been unable temporarily to make the grade.

III

Report of Activities, March 25, 1932.

The President provided the press with the following statement of allocations of funds:

	Number of Institutions	Loans Authorized	Average per Institution
Banks and Trust Companies	587	$126,895,073	216,162
Building and Loan Associations	18	2,917,000	162,055
Insurance Companies	13	5,765,000	443,461
Railroads	13	46,975,557	3,613,504
Joint Stock Land Banks	2	775,000	287,500
Mortgage Loan Companies	3	1,362,000	454,000
Livestock Credit Associations	1	292,084	292,084
Secretary of Agriculture		50,000,000	
Total,		$234,981,714	

He observed that the banks and trust companies receiving the loans totalling $126,000,000, are located in 45 States. The great majority of these loans are to smaller communities. Less than $3,500,000 has been authorized in cities of over 1,000,000 population; more than $116,000,000 has been authorized in towns of under 600,000 population.

IV

Press Statement, July 6, 1932. The Garner-Wagner Relief Bill.

I regret that the conferences in endeavor to arrive at a basis of a workable relief bill did not succeed. It is all the more regrettable, since the deliberations this morning made it clear that it was possible to harmonize conflicting views and so reach an agreement, were it not for the insistence of the Speaker on one point. The bill, as reported by the conferees, provides:

First, provision for expanding the borrowing authority of the Reconstruction Corporation by $1,500,000,000, to be used for temporary financing of self-liquidating construction projects of public and semi-public character to increase employment.

Second, Speaker Garner insists that the corporation shall also make loans to any individual, any private corporation, any partnership, any State, or any municipality on any conceivable kind of security and for any conceivable purpose.

Third, provision of a fund by the Reconstruction Corporation of $100,000,000 for the President, to be disposed of either as charity or as loans, and one of $200,000,000 to be loaned to State Governments who are unable to finance themselves to care for distress, but such loans to be apportioned amongst the states on a per capita basis of population.

Fourth, $322,000,000 of additional public works beyond the $500,000,000 of construction work now provided for in the budget.

As to the first provision, the Reconstruction Corporation authority to make loans today is practically limited to institutions under State and Federal regulation, that is—banks, savings banks, building and loan associations, agricultural credit corporations and railways. It is serving to protect the credit structure of the nation whose collapse would mean the complete disaster to all and the savings of all the people that directly or indirectly are in the safe-keeping of the great fiduciary institutions, savings banks, insurance companies, building and loan associations. That is, the whole people.

The provision to finance $1,500,000,000 self-liquidating construction projects for relief of unemployment comprised part of the proposals I had already made to the Congress.

The fatal difficulty is the Speaker's insistence upon provision that loans should also be made to individuals, private corporations, partnerships, States and municipalities on any conceivable security and for every purpose. Such an undertaking by the United States Government makes the Reconstruction Corporation the most gigantic banking and pawn-broking business in all history.

There are forty-eight States and 16,000 municipalities who could under its terms dump their responsibilities upon the Federal Government. The purpose to take care of unemployment distress in such centers is provided for in the proposals of employment and loans to the states.

The Speaker's proposal in no sense contributes to relieve such distress. It would compel the Reconstruction Corporation to attempt to deal with millions of people in terms of hundreds of thousands of small and large loans. It would result in dumping a vast amount of doubtful private and corporation debts on the Federal treasury to no national purpose of relieving unemployment.

It would require the extension of branch offices in every town and county in the United States and set up a huge bureaucracy able to dictate the welfare of millions of people and at the will of its agents deal favor and disaster amongst them. No group of seven men can so organize as not to discriminate unfairly between competitive enterprises. There is no body of men who could physically administer such a gigantic project.

The board of the Reconstruction Corporation, except one absent member, informs me unanimously that the making of loans to individuals is totally unworkable. It would undermine Federal credit and bring a vast increase in unemployment.

I wish to emphasize what it means. Such a proposal means that the Reconstruction Finance Corporation is to take over an impossible task and most difficult part of the banking business that is to deal with the doubtful credits in the whole United States. To carry out such a purpose it would be necessary, as I have said, for the board of seven men to set up branch banks in practically every community and to direct their operations from Washington. It would be dependent upon men in these thousand branches.

The task of organization and of finding competent personnel would not be a matter of months, but of years. From an organization and administrative standpoint, it is self-evident that the proposal is impossible of execution, and huge losses and great scandals must inevitably result from any attempt to do so.

Any attempt to carry out such a law under these circumstances must mean the squandering of hundreds of millions of dollars of public funds. The board would be flooded with hundreds of thousands of applications. There would be serious interference, if not a complete breakdown, of the vital activities it is now carrying on under high pressure. And there would be disappointment on the part of hundreds and thousands of individuals and thousands of businesses who will have been led to believe that the credit of the United States Government was made available for their individual purposes. There

185

would be inevitable discriminations. The organization would be subject to predatory corporations and interests everywhere.

Aside from the utter impracticability of the proposal, no funds, or totally inadequate funds, are provided for the making of these loans. The bill as it came from the Senate provided for increasing the authority of the Reconstruction Finance Corporation to borrow by $1,500,000,000 for certain self-liquidating construction projects enumerated in the bill. Presumably the Senate did not provide more than it thought was necessary for these purposes.

Not one penny is to be added for the making of these individual, private, corporation and public loans. In other words, the Reconstruction Corporation is to be charged with a duty which is impossible to carry out in practice, and it is to be furnished with no additional funds with which to make the loans, unless the Senate unemployment projects are to be abandoned.

Some conception of the credit needs of the people of the United States may be had from the following figures:

Total bank loans on Dec. 31 last aggregated over $31,600,000,000. This does not take into consideration loans made by insurance companies running into the billions, loans made by savings banks, mortgage companies, building and loan associations amounting of $9,000,000,000, or the funded debt of corporations running into further billions.

To hold out the hope to the people of the United States that the United States Government is prepared to take care of their credit needs with the ridiculously small sum provided, or the impossible organization urged, must be condemned, in addition to every other reason as a deception. Furthermore, the statement of the Speaker that the board can determine if it should enter upon such loans is a shifting of responsibility from the Congress to the board, which is itself misleading the hopes of the people. . . .

My objection to the second proposal of placing $100,000,000 at the disposal of the President was that the Federal Government should not make direct charitable gifts to individuals and that such responsibility should not be placed on the President; a further objection is that the $200,000,000 of loans to States were allocated on a population basis, or $1.66 per capita. A large part of the States are able to take care of their own and to finance their relief needs, and probably three-fourths of the total amount would be unused by such states or alternatively there would be every pressure upon state officials to demand the money, even though there was no need. . . .

As to the third point, that is, the provisions to spend additional $322,000,000 on public works, my objections were that the cost of these works ultimately comes from the taxpayer and will produce a deficit in the budget by just the amount expended; that it discards to the winds every effort made to balance the budget. . . .

There is unquestioned need for the passage of legislation to take care of unemployment and such cases of destitution as the resources of the States are unable to meet. I have recommended such legislation. While I am determined that there shall be relief legislation at this session of Congress, I cannot accept the proposal up to now insisted upon by Speaker Garner as a condition to securing his support, for I do not propose to further increase unemployment by such disastrous action as is now proposed through jeopardizing the whole credit of the government and laying our people open to every kind of injustice and loss.

It was not RFC for which Hoover would be remembered; many Americans imagined it had been instituted by Roosevelt—it was the Bonus Marchers. Had Hoover appointed a committee to determine how he could make himself least popular with the nation, he could not have arrived at a better solution than he achieved. His opposition to the bonus measure was technically sound. His effort, during his campaign for re-election (October 28, 1932) to explain his position was reasonable: A father has offered his son a bonus of $100, to accumulate at the rate of $5 per annum plus compound interest. He cannot give him the $100 now; he doesn't have it to give. The illustration was interesting. Unfortunately for Hoover, the veterans were not children, but fathers; Hoover's explanations were only calculated to enrage his hard-pressed auditors, his actions calculated to stimulate vengeful thought.

The Bonus Marchers

I

July 3, 1930

The Honorable James E. Watson,
United States Senate

My dear Mr. Senator:

You request my views on the effect of the Senate amendments to the new House veterans' bill.

I must say at once that these amendments again re-establish injustices and discriminations between veterans, impose unwarranted burdens on the taxpayer and perpetuate entirely wrong principles in such legislation. There are many points of criticism in this direction.

For instance, under these amendments the average allowance to veterans whose disabilities were incurred in civil life subsequent to the war will work out very close to the same average payment as that given to veterans who actually suffered from battle and in the trenches. This is an injustice both to the men who suffered in the war and the public.

The amendments reverse the House action limiting allowances to men who are exempt from income tax. From this removal of the indication of the necessity, a wealthy veteran, if he becomes permanently disabled, either partially or wholly, as a result of an automobile accident next week, may draw a life allowance from the United States Treasury.

The Senate amendments seriously affect the men who were enrolled after the armistice and who never heard a shot fired. They seriously modify the clauses in respect to venereal diseases and impose a burden upon the treasury therefor, which must be condemned from the point of view of family life.

General Hines estimates the cost [of] the first year of this bill, as passed by the Senate, will be $70,000,000, rising to about $175,-000,000 in five years and thereafter. This represents an increase on the House bill by about 250 per cent. These are sums wholly uncalled for by the need of the situation and probably imply an increase in taxes.

There are many other objections to the Senate amendments, such as renewal of certain presumptions, but perhaps this will indicate my views. The bill as passed by the House, before [being] amended by the Senate, was in itself a generous national action, based upon sound principles.

Except for some minor technical points, the House bill met the entire approval of the representatives of the American Legion and the Veterans of Foreign Wars. They did not ask for any more. They have shown a sense of responsibility not only to the country but to the veterans by unhesitatingly expressing their opposition to the major Senate amendments.

Yours faithfully,
HERBERT HOOVER

II

Press Statement, February 27, 1931.

Although I have been greatly opposed to the passage of the bonus legislation in its provisions for loans from the treasury to people not in need, now that it is a law we propose to facilitate the working of it in every way possible.

Inasmuch as the physical task of making loans to 3,500,000 veterans, or even half that number, who might apply, will require many months, even with the most intensive organization, I have requested General Hines to give complete priority to applications from veterans who are in need, and have asked him to set up some machinery for the certification of these cases, especially giving regard to the certification of the veterans' serving organizations and the various relief organizations dealing with unemployment.

The recent survey of the larger cities shows, in the opinion of the administrator of veterans' affairs, that about 6 per cent of the total number of veterans in industrial centers are now receiving support from the local unemployment and other relief committees. This bill will relieve some of the burden now being carried by these committees, but, as the amount possible for many veterans to borrow under the bill is so small, it is urgently necessary that the local committees shall continue their service to many veterans.

I wish to compliment the veterans' service organizations for their co-operation in undertaking a campaign among all veterans, urging them not to take advantage of the loan provisions except in cases of absolute necessity. I understand they are placing it on the ground of assistance to the Federal Government in minimizing the amount of money we shall be called upon to borrow and upon the fact that loans upon the bonus certificates exhaust the protection to veterans' families under the endowment insurance features of the certificates.

Taking General Hines's survey of the number of veterans being assisted by local committees as a basis, it would appear that, if all loans were confined to need, the drain on the treasury may be limited to 10 per cent of the potential liability created by the law.

III

Press Statement, March 29, 1932.

Informal polls of the House of Representatives have created apprehension in the country that a further bonus bill of $2,000,000,000 or thereabouts for World War veterans will be passed.

I wish to state again that I am absolutely opposed to any such legislation. I made this position clear at the meeting of the American Legion in Detroit last September 21 and the Legion has consistently supported that position. I do not believe any such legislation can become law.

Such action would undo every effort that is being made to reduce Government expenditures and balance the budget. The first duty of every citizen of the United States is to build up and sustain the credit of the United States Government. Such an action would irretrievably undermine it.

IV

Press Statement, July 28, 1932.

For some days police authorities and Treasury officials have been endeavoring to persuade the so-called bonus marchers to evacuate certain buildings which they were occupying without permission.

These buildings are on sites where Government construction is in progress and their demolition was necessary in order to extend employment in the district and to carry forward the government's construction program.

This morning the occupants of these buildings were notified to evacuate and at the request of the police did evacuate the buildings concerned. Thereafter, however, several thousand men from different camps marched in and attacked the police with brickbats and otherwise injured several policemen, one probably fatally. . . .

In order to put an end to this rioting and defiance of civil authority, I have asked the army to assist the District authorities to restore order.

Congress made provision for the return home of the so-called bonus marchers, who have for many weeks been given every opportunity of free assembly, free speech and free petition to the Congress. Some 5,000 took advantage of this arrangement and have returned to their homes. An examination of a large number of names discloses the fact that a considerable part of those remaining are not veterans; many are communists and persons with criminal records.

The veterans amongst these numbers are no doubt unaware of the character of their companions and are being led into violence which no government can tolerate.

I have asked the Attorney General to investigate the whole incident and to cooperate with the District civil authorities in such measures against leaders and rioters as may be necessary.

190

July 29, 1932.

Hon. Luther H. Reichelderfer,
Commissioner, District of Columbia,
Washington, D. C.

My dear Mr. Commissioner:

In response to your information that the police of the District were overwhelmed by an organized attack by several thousand men, and were unable to maintain law and order, I complied with your request for aid from the army to the police. It is a matter of satisfaction that, after the arrival of this assistance, the mobs which were defying the municipal government were dissolved without the firing of a shot or the loss of a life.

I wish to call attention of the District Commissioners to the fact that martial law has not been declared; that responsibility for order still rests upon your commission and the police. The civil government of Washington must function uninterrupted. The Commissioners, through their own powers, should now deal with this question decisively.

It is the duty of the authorities of the District to at once find the instigators of this attack on the police and bring them to justice. It is obvious that, after the departure of the majority of the veterans, subversive influences obtained control of the men remaining in the District, a large part of whom were not veterans, secured repudiation of their elected leaders and inaugurated and organized this attack.

They were undoubtedly led to believe that the civil authorities could be intimidated with impunity because of attempts to conciliate by lax enforcement of city ordinances and laws in many directions. I shall expect the police to strictly enforce every ordinance of the District in every part of the city. I wish every violator of the law to be instantly arrested and prosecuted under due process of law.

I have requested the law enforcement agencies of the Federal Government to cooperate with the District authorities to this end.

There is no group, no matter what its origins, that can be allowed either to violate the laws of this city or to intimidate the government.

> Yours faithfully,
> HERBERT HOOVER

VI

Press Statement, September 14, 1932.

It is due to the country and to the veterans that there should be no misunderstanding of my position upon payment of the face value of the adjusted service certificates prior to maturity, as recommended in the resolution pending before the convention at Portland. I have consistently opposed it. In public interest I must continue to oppose it.

I have the duty not alone to see that justice and a sympathetic attitude is taken by this nation toward the 4,000,000 veterans and their families but also to exert myself for justice to the other 21,-000,000 families to whom consummation of this proposal at this time would be a calamity. Cash payment of face value of certificates today would require an appropriation from the Treasury of about $2,300,000,000.

No matter how or in what form the payment to the veterans is imposed it will come out of all these families, but of more importance it will indefinitely set back any hope of recovery for employment, agriculture or business and will impose infinite distress upon the whole country. We owe justice and generosity to the men who have served under our flag. Our people have tried to discharge that obligation. Regular expenditures on account of the veterans already constitute nearly a billion a year or almost one-fourth of our whole Federal budget.

Every right-thinking man has the deepest sympathy for the veteran suffering from disability, for those out of work or for veterans on farms struggling with the adversities of the depression. No one who began life in the humble circumstances that I did, and who at the earliest and most impressionable age learned the meaning of poverty from actual experience, can be lacking in feeling and understanding of the problems and sufferings of these men and their families. I have seen war at first hand. I know the courage, the sacrifice of our soldiers.

But there are many million others in the same circumstances. They, too, must be entitled to consideration. Their employment and their farm recovery, as well as that of the veterans, can be secured only by the restoration of the normal economic life of the nation. To that end we have been and are devoting our best efforts. Anything that stands in the way must be opposed. The welfare of the nation as a whole must take precedence over the demands of any particular group.

I do not believe that the veterans generally really understand the adjusted service certificate law (so-called bonus law) which was proposed by themselves. In its simplest terms that law provides that an annual sum of about $112,000,000 is to be paid into a fund which, with compound interest, is calculated to amount to a total of $3,500,000,000, the face value of certificates to be distributed in

192

1945. Approximately $1,300,000,000 has been paid into this fund. Under the law of last year authorizing loans up to 50 per cent of the face amount of the certificates, if we take into consideration loans made through the veterans' life insurance fund which will have to be paid, all this accumulated sum and more has already been distributed. If the government distributed to the veterans the $112,000,000 annually from now on, it would represent the government's obligation. If these sums be kept in the fund the government adds compound interest on each installment and gives a life insurance right. By paying the adjusted service certificates at their face value now, the government would not only be paying all remaining thirteen annual installments in advance but would be paying the compound interest upon them in advance.

This would, I am advised, add about $2,250,000,000 to the amount which the people of the United States, acting through Congress, undertook to pay when they gave the certificates.

No such sum is available. It cannot be raised by adding to the crushing burden of taxes which drain every family budget in our country today and weigh heavily on business struggling in the midst of depression. It cannot be borrowed without impairment of the credit of the National Government and thus destroy that confidence upon which our whole system depends.

It is unthinkable that the government of the United States should resort to the printing press and the issuance of fiat currency as provided in the bill which passed the House at the last session of Congress, under the leadership of the Democratic Vice Presidential candidate. Such an act of moral bankruptcy would depreciate and might ultimately destroy the value of every dollar in the United States. It would cause the collapse of all confidence in our government and would bring widespread ruin to the entire country and to every one of our citizens. . . .

Hoover expended more eloquence during his campaign for re-election than he had ever mustered before. He challenged his opponent's accuracy, his sincerity, his responsibility. He fought off the slurs and slights of the many intellectuals who adhered to the Democratic Party, whose wit and observations had stirred him to nothing but resentment. In a remarkable passage of his speech to the Gridiron Club (April 9, 1932), in which he called for a "saving sense of humor" to help lighten the rigors of depression, he confided: "I could not turn for help to the so-called intellectuals with their unbroken record of total abstinence from constructive joy over our whole national history."

He criticized his opponent for lack of consistency; he missed the note of tentativeness in his opponent's speeches, their promise of flexibility, experiment, change. Hoover himself stood on his record, in his October 31, 1932 address on "The Consequences of the Proposed New Deal." He praised the work of the Republican Party during the 1920's and in his administration as having created a new kind of voluntary cooperation. It had transformed America with new roads, homes, telephones, automobiles, and it had reduced the work day and multiplied municipal facilities. Hoover warned that what the Democratic Party envisioned was nothing less than a change in the American system. Democrats in power would make "group raids on the Public Treasury" which, in effect, would enslave citizens to work in the government's behalf to pay off the public debt. Inflating the currency would still further deprive the citizen of his earnings. Government entry into the power business would put it in competition with private businesses. And so with other issues and enterprises. Hoover prophesied: "This election is not a mere shift from the ins to the outs. It means deciding the direction our Nation will take over a century to come."

At St. Paul, on November 5, he made his final major appeal to that nation.

Hoover Stands on the Record

In these closing hours of the campaign I am conscious that the American people are summing up in their minds the candidates' statements, the issues; weighing the expositions of the party policy, making their appraisals of party measures and of men, and thus preparing themselves individually for their final personal decision to be expressed by their ballots at the polls next Tuesday.

I stated a few days ago that the most important issue before the American people at this moment is to overcome this crisis. What our people need is the restoration of their normal jobs and the recovery of agricultural prices and of business. They need help in the meantime to tide them over their difficulties in order that they may not suffer privation or lose their farms and homes.

There are other measures which concern the more distant future. We must not lose sight of them. But the great balance in which to weigh the two great political parties today is in their attitude toward this immediate problem, because in this attitude lies their philosophy of government, their ability to penetrate into causes, their capacity to meet emergency and to translate measures into action. And in these balances should also be weighed the question of honesty in presentation to the people of the facts so that they may formulate a proper judgment. . . .

We are part of a world, the disturbance of whose remotest population affects our own financial system, our markets, our employment and the prices of our farm products. And we have many problems of our own growing out of the great war, the inflation of values during the war and the stupendous increase of our debt; the failure of foreign countries to respond to their debt obligations to us. Finally, with the desperate crisis abroad the whole world scrambled to convert their property into gold and thus withdrew from us suddenly over $2,400,000,000 of exchange and gold. These fears, spreading to our own citizens, caused them to withdraw $1,600,000,000 in currency from circulation. The effect of this was to withdraw vast sums of gold from our own use as we must protect the gold convertibility of our currency, with further repercussions of credit stringency, unemployment and dropping prices.

Our own economists overlooked one great fundamental factor— that while our own people consume 90 per cent of their production, yet no one calculated the effect of world-wide fear upon our credit system, which thereby suddenly undermined our industry and commerce.

In the face of these gigantic, appalling world-wide forces our opponents set up the Hawley-Smoot tariff bill, changing as it did the tariffs on less than one-sixth of our own imports, one one-hundredth of the world's imports, and introduced long after the collapse started as the cause of all this world catastrophe. What an unspeakable travesty upon reason this explanation is!

Suppose that we had never had the Hawley-Smoot tariff bill. Do you think for one moment that this crushing collapse in the structure of the world, these revolutions, these perils to civilization would not have happened and would not have reached the United States? . . .

I would recall to you the unprecedented measures which we have introduced by which we have brought the full reserve powers of the Federal Government to save community values and protect every family and fireside, so far as it was humanly possible, from deterioration. . . .

1. The first of our measures, which subsequently proved of great emergency service, was the revision of the tariff. By this act we gave protection to our agriculture, from a world demoralization which would have been far worse than anything we have suffered and we prevented unemployment to millions of workmen.

2. We have secured extension of authority to the Tariff Com-

mission by which the adjustments can be made to correct inequities in the tariff, and to make changes to meet economic tides, thereby avoiding the national disturbance of general revision of the tariff, with all its greed and log-rolling. That authority becomes of vital importance today in the face of depreciated currencies abroad.

3. At the outset of the depression we brought about an understanding between employers and employees that wages should be maintained. They were maintained until the cost of living had decreased and the profits had practically vanished. They are now the highest real wages in the world. . . .

4. An agreement to a spread of work where employers were compelled to reduce production was brought about in order that none might be deprived of all their living and all might participate in the existing jobs and thus give real aid to millions of families.

5. We have mobilized throughout the country private charity and Local and State support for the care of distress under which our women and men have given such devoted service that the health of our country has actually improved.

6. By the expansion of State, municipal, and private construction work as an aid to employment, and by the development of an enlarged program of Federal construction, which has been maintained at the rate of $600,000,000 a year throughout the depression, we have given support to hundreds of thousands of families.

7. By the negotiation of the German moratorium and the standstill agreements upon external debts of that country we saved their people from a collapse that would have set a prairie afire and possibly have involved all civilization itself.

8. We created the National Credit Association by cooperation of the bankers of the country, with a capital of $500,000,000, which prevented the failure of a thousand banks with all the tragedies to their depositors and borrowers.

9. By drastic reduction of the ordinary operating expenses of the Federal Government, together with the increasing of the revenues in the year 1932, we contributed to balancing the Federal budget, and thus held impregnable the credit of the United States.

10. We created the Reconstruction Finance Corporation, originally with $2,000,000,000 of resources, in order that, having maintained national credit, we should thrust the full resources of public credit behind private credit of the country and thus re-establish and maintain private enterprise in an unassailable position; that, with this backing of the Federal credit acting through existing institutions,

we might protect depositors in savings banks, insurance policy holders, lenders and borrowers in building and loan associations; through banking institutions expand the funds available for loans to merchants, manufacturers, farmers and marketing associations; that we should protect the railways from receiverships in order that, in turn, railway securities in the great fiduciary institutions such as insurance companies and savings banks might be protected and a score of other services performed. . . .

12. We extended authorities under the Federal Reserve act to protect beyond all question the gold standard of the United States and at the same time expand the credit in counter-action to the strangulation due to the hoarding and foreign withdrawals of gold. . . .

16. We increased the resources to the Reconstruction Corporation by a further $1,500,000,000 for the undertaking of great public works which otherwise would have to await financing due to the stringency of credit. These works are of a character which, by their own earnings, will enable disposal of the repayment of these loans without charge upon the taxpayer. . . .

20. We have developed, together with European nations, a world-wide economic conference with a view to relieving pressure upon us from foreign countries, to increase their stability, to deal with silver, and to prevent recurrence of these calamities for the future.

21. We have given American leadership in the development of drastic reductions of armament in order to reduce our own expenditures by $200,000,000 a year and to increase the financial stability of foreign nations and to relieve the world of fear and political friction.

These are a part of the great and effective weapons with which we have fought the battle that has saved the American people from disaster and chaos. They are still in action and advancing along the whole front to the restoration of recovery. . . .

I recently enumerated at Detroit some of the evidences of recuperation of the country under these measures in so short a period as four months since the destruction of public confidence by the Democratic House of Representatives ceased.

Not to weary you with statistics, but to show the validity of that progress I may mention that in employment over a million men have now returned to work in these four months. This is the estimate of our Government departments. The estimate of our employers place the number at a million and a half. Certainly, we are now gaining a half million a month. . . .

And now in contrast with this construction program of the Republican Party, I wish to develop for you the Democratic program to meet this depression as far as we have been able to find any definition to it.

I would again call your attention to the fact that with the Democratic victory in congressional elections of 1930 their leaders promised to produce a program which would redeem this country from the depression. No such program was produced until we were well into the Winter of 1932.

Their program, as developed under the leadership of Mr. Garner by the Democratic House of Representatives, was:

1. They passed the Collier bill, providing for destruction of the Tariff Commission by reducing it again to a mere statistical body controlled by the Congress. Had they succeeded, the relief which you so sorely require from competition from countries or depreciated currencies would now be impossible.

2. They attempted to instruct me by legislation to call an international conference through which the aid of foreign nations was requested to lower American tariffs, by which the independence of the United States in control of its domestic policies was to be placed in the hands of an international body.

3. They passed an act instructing me to negotiate reciprocal tariffs, the result of which could only be to deprive some locality of its tariff protection for the benefit of another, and by which the only possible agreements would involve the reduction of farm tariffs in order to build up markets for other goods. . . .

8. They defeated a large part of the national economy measure proposed by the administration, by reduction of ordinary expenditures from $250,000,000 to less than $50,000,000, a part of which we subsequently rescued in the Senate.

9. They passed the Garner-Rainey pork barrel bill, increasing expenditures by $1,200,000,000 for unnecessary, non-productive public works, purely for the benefit of favored localities. We stopped this bill, but it is still on their political calendar.

10. They passed the cash prepayment of the bonus calling for immediate expenditure of $2,300,000,000 and for actual increase in liabilities of the Federal Government over the original act over $1,300,000,000. We stopped this bill, but it is still on their political calendar.

11. They passed the provision for the issuance of over $2,-200,000,000 of greenback currency, a reversion to vicious practices

already demonstrated in the last hundred years as the most destructive to labor, agriculture and business. We stopped this bill and even as late as last night the Democratic candidate failed to frankly disown it. . . .

13. They injected an expenditure of $322,000,000 for entirely unnecessary purposes in time of great emergency. They complain daily that we do not spend it fast enough. . . .

15. The Democratic candidate eloquently urges the balancing of the budget, but nowhere disavows these gigantic raids on the Treasury, under which a budget cannot be balanced.

Thus far is the program of the Democratic House under the leadership of Mr. Garner, whose policies the Democratic Party ratified by nominating him Vice President.

16. The Democratic candidate adds to this program the proposal to plant a billion trees and thereby immediately employ a million men, but the Secretary of Agriculture has shown that the trees available to plant will give them a total less than three days work.

17. The candidate promises to relieve agriculture with a six-point program which amounts to envisaging to distressed farmers a great structure of agricultural relief, but he has refused to submit it to debate. He disclosed no details of the plan except six methods by which he can escape from the promise.

18. The candidate has promised the immediate inauguration of a program of self-liquidating public works, such as utilization of our water resources, flood control and land reclamation, to provide "employment for all surplus labor at all times." It would exceed in cost $9,000,000,000 a year. The works are unavailable, the cost would destroy the credit of the government, deprive vast numbers of the men now working of their jobs and thus destroy the remedy itself. . . .

FRANKLIN D. ROOSEVELT

(1882–1945)

Dr. New Deal and Dr. Win-the-War

I am certain that my fellow Americans expect that on my induction into the Presidency I will address them with a candor and a decision which the present situation of our Nation impels. This is pre-eminently the time to speak the truth, the whole truth, frankly and boldly. Nor need we shrink from honestly facing conditions in our country today. This great Nation will endure as it has endured, will revive and will prosper. So, first of all, let me assert my firm belief that the only thing we have to fear is fear itself—nameless, unreasoning, unjustified terror which paralyzes needed efforts to convert retreat into advance. In every dark hour of our national life a leadership of frankness and vigor has met with that understanding and support of the people themselves which is essential to victory. I am convinced that you will again give that support to leadership in these critical days.

First Inaugural Address, *March 4, 1933*

IN 1930, there was still only one Roosevelt, and no one had to be told his first name; in the Fall of 1932, there was only one Roosevelt again, but his given name had changed. F.D.R. ("Frank" never went well with the strong, aristocratic voice, for all the good fellowship it exuded) had become the hope of a nation, or, it might be, its Nemesis. In any event, the other Roosevelt's vigor and individualism echoed aimlessly in forgotten corridors.

As late as the summer of 1931, Roosevelt seemed, at least to Ray Thomas Tucker in his *Mirrors of 1932,* no more than the "fifth cousin of Theodore the First," and that, despite the fact that as governor of New York he had struggled determinedly with the effects of depression in a grimly individualistic state and in the country's greatest city. He had instituted what would later be called a "little New Deal," offering relief to New York's farmers and state aid to the unemployed. He had also sought development of New York's water power resources and old age pensions. Already at his side was Francis Perkins, who had been galvanized in the 1910's to institute laws that would curb the incidence of sweatshop and factory horrors—such as had resulted in the Triangle Waistshirt Company fire of 1911, in which 146 girls died. Harry Hopkins, a quiet, competent social worker, was engaged in studying ways to handle unemployment and welfare problems.

Mirrors of 1932 saw Roosevelt as having been pushed into everything he had done: "He has the heart, he has the head—with some reservations—but he lacks guts." This portrait noted various points about Roosevelt, but it did not cope with the effects upon him of polio. There were, indeed, two Roosevelts. One was the good-natured, pampered, and somewhat vain patrician—who had played politics with Democratic politicians in the 1910's, and had been Assistant Secretary of the Navy during World War I—and the tall, handsome vice-presidential candidate for the Democrats in 1920. And there was the stricken Roosevelt, compelled to reorganize his life and determine what could be done with it. This Roosevelt was grim, purposeful, and indomitable, fighting endlessly, sleeplessly, to recover the use of his legs and to maintain his hold on life. He labored to keep his name in the public eye. He engaged in endless exercises intended to bring life back into his limbs. They never did; but in the course of his exertions, Roosevelt developed the upper torso of an athlete, and the powerful control of his feelings and relations that characterized his associations. Disillusioned admirers later saw him as selfish, fickle, even hypocritical. They missed his will to power, his urge to lead; qualities which would later serve a nation of individuals who needed nothing so much as a leader who would, nevertheless, respect their deeper preferences.

Walter Lippmann in his New York *Herald* column of January 8, 1932, voiced a view that was fated to become notorious: that Roosevelt was "no crusader. He is no tribune of the people. He is no enemy of entrenched privilege. He is a pleasant man who, without any important qualifications for the office, would like very much to be President." The latter part of the judgment was certainly true. Roosevelt was his own chief of staff, his own aider and abettor. He made his own deals, plotted his own strategy. He campaigned earnestly and hopefully for the Democratic nomination. On April 7, 1932, he offered his plea for "the forgotten man at the bottom of the economic pyramid," a phrase that endured.* It seemed to his more needy and experimental fellow countrymen that Governor Roosevelt promised action as President of the United States, and he was an early favorite for the Democratic nomination. His lieutenants fought bravely and without qualms in his behalf at

* That it did endure in this form was a comment on American preferences. For the phrase, as originally expressed by the social Darwinist William Graham Sumner referred to the independent American who desired neither aid nor comfort from government or humanitarians, but asked only to be let alone to tend to his own affairs.

their party's convention. They persuaded Huey P. Long, dictator of Louisiana, that he would be of consequence in the coming Roosevelt administration. Long threw his influence among Southern politicians into the New Yorker's camp, in a move that turned the nomination in F.D.R.'s direction.

During the furious campaign that followed, Roosevelt made much of Hoover's failure to economize. Without burdening himself with specifics, he emphasized the need for new policies respecting transportation, utilities, banking and investment frauds. He, like Hoover, made much of the tariff issue. But he gave a different tone to his views of the depression crisis, in asserting that "the national government has a positive duty to see that no citizen shall starve." Elected President by an overwhelming majority, he prepared to assume power. His often quoted First Inaugural Address thrilled the nation. His view that "our common difficulties . . . concern, thank God, only material things," did not sound like an evasion of essentials, but a call to action. His derogation of credit as a means for overcoming the economic stalemate struck at a major premise of 1920's economics. He pointed to the "overbalance of population in our industrial centers" in a gesture that brought rural and urban problems into focus. And he recognized that the people demanded action. He was prepared to ask Congress to enact measures that would minister to a stricken world. And such measures, "or such other measures as the Congress may build out of its experience and wisdom," he was prepared to put into motion. But, he warned, with a resoluteness which forced attention:

in the event that the Congress shall fail to take one of these two courses, and in the event that the national emergency is still critical, I shall not evade the clear course of duty that will then confront me. I shall ask the Congress for the one remaining instrument to meet the crisis—broad Executive power to wage a war against the emergency, as great as the power that would be given to me if we were in fact invaded by a foreign foe.

Roosevelt and his advisers and Cabinet members, including such brilliant names as Ickes, Wallace, Perkins, Tugwell, Moley, Harry Hopkins, and A. A. Berle, as well as more pedestrian but dependable names, such as Hull, Morganthau, Averell Harriman, and "Corcoran and Cohen," among many others, gained headlines and wielded influence. Roosevelt's first, famous "hundred days" brought action, though much of it was stopgap action. Roosevelt proclaimed a bank holiday, and began a series of monetary experiments, none of which substantially affected the course of the depression crisis. He instituted the memorable CCC—the Civilian Conservation Corps—which intended to take young men off the streets and employ them usefully on constructive projects.

Operated as they were under the army, they gave concern to left-wing elements who feared incipient fascistic organization such as never materialized. The Federal Emergency Relief Administration hastily set up projects for some of the unemployed. The Public Works Administration continued Hoover's policy of seeking to encourage private enterprise through expanded public building.

So far as Europe was concerned, Roosevelt's New Deal was taking a hands-off attitude; his eyes were fixed on domestic problems. Central and South America were a different story. Their increasing strength, their vulnerability in case of war suggested that the United States could no longer afford a truculent or patronizing attitude toward them. Roosevelt was prepared to disavow his earlier imperialism, as Assistant Secretary of the Navy—his cheerful quip that Haiti had an excellent constitution; he knew, since he had written it himself. In his Inaugural Address, he had spoken of a "good neighbor" policy. On April 12, 1933, at a meeting of the governing board of the Pan-American Union, he made a more explicit statement of a policy thereafter destined to vie with the not wholly defunct Monroe Doctrine.

Good Neighbor

I rejoice in this opportunity to participate in the celebration of "Pan-American Day" and to extend on behalf of the people of the United States a fraternal greeting to our sister American Republics. The celebration of "Pan-American Day" in this building, dedicated to international good-will and cooperation, exemplifies a unity of thought and purpose among the peoples of this hemisphere. It is a manifestation of the common ideal of mutual helpfulness, sympathetic understanding and spiritual solidarity.

There is inspiration in the thought that on this day the attention of the citizens of the twenty-one Republics of America is focused on the common ties—historical, cultural, economic, and social— which bind them to one another. Common ideals and a community of interest, together with a spirit of cooperation, have led to the realization that the well-being of one Nation depends in large measure upon the well-being of its neighbors. It is upon these foundations that Pan Americanism has been built.

This celebration commemorates a movement based upon the policy of fraternal cooperation. In my Inaugural Address I stated that I would "dedicate this Nation to the policy of the good neighbor —the neighbor who resolutely respects himself and, because he does so, respects the rights of others—the neighbor who respects his obligations and respects the sanctity of his agreements in and with a world of neighbors." Never before has the significance of the words "good neighbor" been so manifest in international relations. Never have the need and benefit of neighborly cooperation in every form of human activity been so evident as they are today.

Friendship among Nations, as among individuals, calls for constructive efforts to muster the forces of humanity in order that an atmosphere of close understanding and cooperation may be cultivated. It involves mutual obligations and responsibilities, for it is only by sympathetic respect for the rights of others and a scrupulous fulfillment of the corresponding obligations by each member of the community that a true fraternity can be maintained.

The essential qualities of a true Pan Americanism must be the same as those which constitute a good neighbor, namely, mutual understanding, and, through such understanding, a sympathetic appreciation of the other's point of view. It is only in this manner that we can hope to build up a system of which confidence, friendship and good-will are the cornerstones.

In this spirit the people of every Republic on our continent are coming to a deep understanding of the fact that the Monroe Doctrine, of which so much has been written and spoken for more than a century, was and is directed at the maintenance of independence by the peoples of the continent. It was aimed and is aimed against the acquisition in any manner of the control of additional territory in this hemisphere by any non-American power.

Hand in hand with this Pan-American doctrine of continental self-defense, the peoples of the American Republics understand more clearly, with the passing years, that the independence of each Republic must recognize the independence of every other Republic. Each one of us must grow by an advancement of civilization and social well-being and not by the acquisition of territory at the expense of any neighbor.

In this spirit of mutual understanding and of cooperation on this continent you and I cannot fail to be disturbed by any armed strife between neighbors. I do not hesitate to say to you, the distinguished members of the Governing Board of the Pan-American Union, that I regard existing conflicts between four of our sister Republics as a backward step.

Your Americanism and mine must be a structure built of confidence, cemented by a sympathy which recognizes only equality and fraternity. It finds its source and being in the hearts of men and dwells in the temple of the intellect.

We all of us have peculiar problems, and, to speak frankly, the interest of our own citizens must, in each instance, come first. But it is equally true that it is of vital importance to every Nation of this Continent that the American Governments, individually, take, without further delay, such action as may be possible to abolish all unnecessary and artificial barriers and restrictions which now hamper the healthy flow of trade between the peoples of the American Republics.

I am glad to deliver this message to you, Gentlemen of the Governing Board of the Pan-American Union, for I look upon the Union as the outward expression of the spiritual unity of the Americas. It is to this unity which must be courageous and vital in its element that humanity must look for one of the great stabilizing influences in world affairs. . . .

Roosevelt's first massive hopes for a revived economy centered on two measures: the AAA—the Agricultural Adjustment Act—which received his signature on May 12, 1933, and NRA, product of the National Industrial Recovery Act, which he signed into law on June 16. AAA was intended, as he said, "to increase the purchasing power of our farmers and the consumption of articles manufactured in our industrial communities," as well as to provide easier mortgage and loan terms for the harassed farmer. In effect, farm production was to be curbed through subsidies, raising the price of farm commodities, and the government was to find money for such subsidies in a "processing tax" laid on the manufacturer of farm products.

As for the NRA it was, no doubt, as awkwardly constructed as its critics believed. It was prone to "crazy antics," even as the bitter John T. Flynn, humanitarian liberal turned Manchester liberal, later saw, in his mordant, *The Roosevelt Myth* (1948). NRA adopted methods of "moral coercion" of industry, according to Walter Lippmann, and, he added sharply, undermined the law as Congress had intended it. Herbert Hoover saw liberty itself placed in jeopardy. Administration supporters viewed the matter differently. An unparalleled economic breakdown had to be overcome. Industry had to cooperate in order to set standards of fair profits. It had to offer fair wages for a fair day's work. It had to create fair working conditions.

What was "fair"? How could it be determined? There was no time for lengthy studies and preparations. Commissions of experts could not conduct national surveys in order to set up schedules of scientifically determined codes of production and distribution that took into account the peculiar factors separating small business from large, Southern manufacturing plants from Northern, tariff-supported products from those subject to free trade. Codes had to be fixed and administered *now*. And so some codes were borrowed wholesale from those which had been drawn up during Hoover's service as Secretary of Commerce. Other codes were hastily constructed by agents of industries, and rarely conflicted with the interests of their firms. Employers set up regulations governing their employees. Here was industry's opportunity to create its version of a modern economy: one that gave due regard to individualism and free enterprise, but recognized that neither had been able to forestall the hideous stoppage of work or start it circulating again through social conduits. General Hugh S. Johnson, picturesque army man and businessman, organized as for war, forcing regulations on hard-pressed retail merchants and large-scale executives. Alarmists left and right remembered that the Italian dictator, Benito Mussolini, had also organized industry, by means of his "corporate state." Was that Roosevelt's goal? Roosevelt went on the radio, July 24, 1933, to defend his program.

Fireside Chat: AAA and NRA

After the adjournment of the historical special session of the Congress five weeks ago I purposely refrained from addressing you for two very good reasons.

First, I think that we all wanted the opportunity of a little quiet thought to examine and assimilate in a mental picture the crowding events of the hundred days which had been devoted to the starting of the wheels of the New Deal.

Secondly, I wanted a few weeks in which to set up the new administrative organization and to see the first fruits of our careful planning.

I think it will interest you if I set forth the fundamentals of this planning for national recovery; and this I am very certain will make it abundantly clear to you that all of the proposals and all of the legislation since the fourth day of March have not been just a collection of haphazard schemes, but rather the orderly component parts of a connected and logical whole.

Long before Inauguration Day I became convinced that individual effort and local effort and even disjointed Federal effort had failed and of necessity would fail and, therefore, that a rounded leadership by the Federal Government had become a necessity both of theory and of fact. Such leadership, however, had its beginning in preserving and strengthening the credit of the United States Government, because without that no leadership was a possibility. For years the Government had not lived within its income. The immediate task was to bring our regular expenses within our revenues. That has been done.

It may seem inconsistent for a government to cut down its regular expenses and at the same time to borrow and to spend billions for an emergency. But it is not inconsistent because a large portion of the emergency money had been paid out in the form of sound loans which will be repaid to the Treasury over a period of years; and to cover the rest of the emergency money we have imposed taxes to pay the interest and the installments on that part of the debt.

So you will see that we have kept our credit good. We have built a granite foundation in a period of confusion. That foundation of the Federal credit stands there broad and sure. It is the base of the whole recovery plan.

Then came the part of the problem that concerned the credit of the individual citizens themselves. You and I know of the banking crisis and of the great danger to the savings of our people. On March sixth every national bank was closed. One month later ninety per cent of the deposits in the national banks had been made available to the depositors. Today only about five per cent of the deposits in the national banks are still tied up. The condition relating to State banks, while not quite so good on a percentage basis, is showing a steady reduction in the total of frozen deposits —a result much better than we had expected three months ago.

The problem of the credit of the individual was made more difficult because of another fact. The dollar was a different dollar from the one with which the average debt had been incurred. For this reason large numbers of people were actually losing possession of and title to their farms and homes. All of you know the financial steps which have been taken to correct this inequality. In addition the Home Loan Act, the Farm Loan Act and the Bankruptcy Act were passed.

It was a vital necessity to restore purchasing power by reducing the debt and interest charges upon our people, but while we were helping people to save their credit it was at the same time absolutely essential to do something about the physical needs of hundreds of thousands who were in dire straits at that very moment. Municipal and State aid were being stretched to the limit. We appropriated half a billion dollars to supplement their efforts and in addition, as you know, we have put three hundred thousand young men into practical and useful work in our forests and to prevent flood and soil erosion. The wages they earn are going in greater part to the support of the nearly one million people who constitute their families.

In this same classification we can properly place the great public works program running to a total of over three billion dollars—to be used for highways and ships and flood prevention and inland navigation and thousands of self-sustaining State and municipal improvements. Two points should be made clear in the allotting and administration of these projects: first, we are using the utmost care to choose labor-creating, quick-acting, useful projects, avoiding the smell of the pork barrel; and second, we are hoping that at least half of the money will come back to the Government from projects which will pay for themselves over a period of years.

Thus far I have spoken primarily of the foundation stones—the measures that were necessary to reestablish credit and to head people in the opposite direction by preventing distress and providing as much work as possible through governmental agencies. Now I come to the links which will build us a more lasting prosperity. I have said that we cannot attain that in a Nation half boom and half broke. If all of our people have work and fair wages and fair profits, they can buy the products of their neighbors, and business is good. But if you take away the wages and the profits of half of them, business is only half as good. It does not help much if the fortunate half is very prosperous; the best way is for everybody to be reasonably prosperous.

For many years the two great barriers to a normal prosperity have been low farm prices and the creeping paralysis of unemployment. These factors have cut the purchasing power of the country in half. I promised action. Congress did its part when it passed the Farm and the Industrial Recovery Acts. Today we are putting these two Acts to work and they will work if people understand their plain objectives.

First, the Farm Act: It is based on the fact that the purchasing power of nearly half our population depends on adequate prices for farm products. We have been producing more of some crops than we consume or can sell in a depressed world market. The cure is not to produce so much. Without our help the farmers cannot get together and cut production, and the Farm Bill gives them a method of bringing their production down to a reasonable level and of obtaining reasonable prices for their crops. I have clearly stated that this method is in a sense experimental, but so far as we have gone we have reason to believe that it will produce good results.

It is obvious that if we can greatly increase the purchasing power of the tens of millions of our people who make a living from farming and the distribution of farm crops, we shall greatly increase the consumption of those goods which are turned out by industry.

That brings me to the final step—bringing back industry along sound lines.

Last autumn, on several occasions, I expressed my faith that we can make possible by democratic self-discipline in industry general increases in wages and shortening of hours sufficient to enable industry to pay its own workers enough to let those workers buy and use the things that their labor produces. This can be done only if we permit and encourage cooperative action in industry, because it is obvious that without united action a few selfish men in each competitive group will pay starvation wages and insist on long hours of work. Others in that group must either follow suit or close up shop. We have seen the result of action of that kind in the continuing descent into the economic hell of the past four years.

There is a clear way to reverse that process: If all employers in each competitive group agree to pay their workers the same wages —reasonable wages—and require the same hours—reasonable hours —then higher wages and shorter hours will hurt no employer. Moreover, such action is better for the employer than unemployment and low wages, because it makes more buyers for his product. That is the simple idea which is the very heart of the Industrial Recovery Act.

On the basis of this simple principle of everybody doing things together, we are starting out on this nationwide attack on un-employment. It will succeed if our people understand it—in the big industries, in the little shops, in the great cities and in the small villages. There is nothing complicated about it and there is nothing particularly new in the principle. It goes back to the basic idea of society and of the Nation itself that people acting in a group can accomplish things which no individual acting alone could even hope to bring about.

Here is an example. In the Cotton Textile Code and in other agreements already signed, child labor has been abolished. That makes me personally happier than any other one thing with which I have been connected since I came to Washington. In the textile industry—an industry which came to me spontaneously and with a splendid cooperation as soon as the Recovery Act was signed— child labor was an old evil. But no employer acting alone was able to wipe it out. If one employer tried it, or if one State tried it, the costs of operation rose so high that it was impossible to compete with the employers or States which had failed to act. The moment the Recovery Act was passed, this monstrous thing which neither opinion nor law could reach through years of effort went out in a flash. As a British editorial put it, we did more under a Code in one day than they in England had been able to do under the common law in eighty-five years of effort. I use this incident, my friends, not to boast of what has already been done but to point the way to you for even greater cooperative efforts this summer and autumn.

We are not going through another winter like the last. I doubt if ever any people so bravely and cheerfully endured a season half so bitter. We cannot ask America to continue to face such needless hardships. It is time for courageous action, and the Recovery Bill gives us the means to conquer unemployment with exactly the same weapon that we have used to strike down child labor.

The proposition is simply this: . . .

We have sent out to all employers an agreement which is the result of weeks of consultation. This agreement checks against the voluntary codes of nearly all the large industries which have already been submitted. This blanket agreement carries the unanimous approval of the three boards which I have appointed to advise in this, boards representing the great leaders in labor, in industry, and in social service. The agreement has already brought a flood of approval from every State, and from so wide a cross-section of the common calling of industry that I know it is fair for all. It is a plan—deliberate, reasonable and just—intended to put into effect at once the most important of the broad principles which are being established, industry by industry, through codes. Naturally, it takes a good deal of organizing and a great many hearings and many months, to get these codes perfected and signed, and we cannot wait for all of them to go through. The blanket agreements, however, which I am sending to every employer will start the wheels turning now, and not six months from now.

There are, of course, men, a few men, who might thwart this great common purpose by seeking selfish advantage. There are adequate penalties in the law, but I am now asking the cooperation that comes from opinion and from conscience. These are the only instruments we shall use in this great summer offensive against unemployment. But we shall use them to the limit to protect the willing from the laggard and to make the plan succeed. . . .

When Andrew Jackson, "Old Hickory," died, someone asked, "Will he go to Heaven?" and the answer was, "He will if he wants to." If I am asked whether the American people will pull themselves out of this depression, I answer, "They will if they want to." The essence of the plan is a universal limitation of hours of work per week for any individual by common consent, and a universal payment of wages above a minimum, also by common consent. I cannot guarantee the success of this nationwide plan, but the people of this country can guarantee its success. I have no faith in "cure-alls" but I believe that we can greatly influence economic forces. I have no sympathy with the professional economists who insist that things must run their course and that human agencies can have no influence on economic ills. One reason is that I happen to know that professional economists have changed their definition of economic laws every five or ten years for a very long time, but I do have faith, and retain faith, in the strength of the common purpose, and in the strength of unified action taken by the American people. . . .

The New Deal rolled on. The giant construction work of the Tennessee Valley Authority began. The Soviet Union was recognized. RFC operations were kept under surveillance. The Securities Exchange Act of 1934 finally brought the government into the problem of controlling speculative practices. Reciprocity was instituted in international trade agreements. AAA and NRA struggled on, the processors resisting being taxed for subsidies to farmers. As for NRA, it had indeed created codes for industry, and its famous section 7(a) had approved union organization for workers. But, though law implemented the industrial codes, it did not support labor efforts to organize in the face of armed company guards and city and state police. The Roosevelt administration created various boards, among others, the first National Labor Relations Board (June 29, 1934) and the National Resources Board (June 30, 1934).

Roosevelt had gone on the air two days before to ask: "Are You Better Off Than You Were Last Year?" If anyone was, he avoided making a public display of the fact. For darkness and tragedy still lay heavy on Americans, and political desperadoes of every stripe found ready audience. Father Coughlin, the "Radio Priest," a formidable demagogue, Huey P. Long of "Share the Wealth" fame, Upton Sinclair who offered to "End

Poverty in California" (EPIC) were among many Messiahs who quickened the hopes and urge to action of the hungry and the malcontented. Particularly disturbing to F.D.R. and his followers was Dr. Francis E. Townsend, whose simple "plan" dazzled the needy hordes who adhered to his gospel: a $200 monthly pension for persons of sixty years of age and over that would guarantee (it was alleged) a rapid turnover of money and goods and start the economy on its way. Townsend's popularity constituted a positive threat to the Democratic Party machine. It was in part to drain off that threat that F.D.R. gave his support to the principle of social security, in a Message to Congress, January 17, 1935.

Social Security

In addressing you on June eighth, 1934, I summarized the main objectives of our American program. Among these was, and is, the security of the men, women, and children of the Nation against certain hazards and vicissitudes of life. This purpose is an essential part of our task. In my annual message to you I promised to submit a definite program of action. This I do in the form of a report to me by a committee on Economic Security, appointed by me for the purpose of surveying the field and of recommending the basis of legislation. . . .

It is my best judgment that this legislation should be brought forward with a minimum of delay. Federal action is necessary to, and conditioned upon, the action of States. Forty-four legislatures are meeting or will meet soon. In order that the necessary State action may be taken promptly it is important that the Federal Government proceed speedily.

The detailed report of the Committee sets forth a series of proposals that will appeal to the sound sense of the American people. It has not attempted the impossible, nor has it failed to exercise sound caution and consideration of all of the factors concerned: the national credit, the rights and responsibilities of States, the capacity of industry to assume financial responsibilities and the fundamental necessity of proceeding in a manner that will merit the enthusiastic support of citizens of all sorts.

It is overwhelmingly important to avoid any danger of permanently discrediting the sound and necessary policy of Federal legislation for economic security by attempting to apply it on too ambitious a scale before actual experience has provided guidance for the permanently safe direction of such efforts. The place of such a fundamental in our future civilization is too precious to be jeopardized now by extravagant action. It is a sound idea—a sound ideal. Most of the other advanced countries of the world have already adopted it and their experience affords the knowledge that social insurance can be made a sound and workable project.

Three principles should be observed in legislation on this subject. First, the system adopted, except for the money necessary to initiate it, should be self-sustaining in the sense that funds for the payment of insurance benefits should not come from the proceeds of general taxation. Second, excepting in old-age insurance, actual management should be left to the States subject to standards established by the Federal Government. Third, sound financial management of the funds and the reserves, and protection of the credit structure of the Nation should be assured by retaining Federal control over all funds through trustees in the Treasury of the United States.

At this time, I recommend the following types of legislation looking to economic security:

1. Unemployment compensation.

2. Old-age benefits, including compulsory and voluntary annuities.

3. Federal aid to dependent children through grants to States for the support of existing mothers' pension systems and for services for the protection and care of homeless, neglected, dependent, and crippled children.

4. Additional Federal aid to State and local public-health agencies and the strengthening of the Federal Public Health Service. I am not at this time recommending the adoption of so-called "health insurance," although groups representing the medical profession are cooperating with the Federal Government in the further study of the subject and definite progress is being made.

With respect to unemployment compensation, I have concluded that the most practical proposal is the levy of a uniform Federal payroll tax, ninety per cent of which should be allowed as an offset to employers contributing under a compulsory State unemployment compensation act. The purpose of this is to afford a requirement of a reasonably uniform character for all States cooperating with the Federal Government and to promote and encourage the passage of unemployment compensation laws in the States. The ten per cent not thus offset should be used to cover the costs of Federal and

213

State administration of this broad system. Thus, States will largely administer unemployment compensation, assisted and guided by the Federal Government. An unemployment compensation system should be constructed in such a way as to afford every practicable aid and incentive toward the larger purpose of employment stabilization. This can be helped by the intelligent planning of both public and private employment. It also can be helped by correlating the system with public employment so that a person who has exhausted his benefits may be eligible for some form of public work as is recommended in this report. Moreover, in order to encourage the stabilization of private employment, Federal legislation should not foreclose the States from establishing means for inducing industries to afford an even greater stabilization of employment.

In the important field of security for our old people, it seems necessary to adopt three principles: First, noncontributory old-age pensions for those who are now too old to build up their own insurance. It is, of course, clear that for perhaps thirty years to come funds will have to be provided by the States and the Federal Government to meet these pensions. Second, compulsory contributory annuities which in time will establish a self-supporting system for those now young and for future generations. Third, voluntary contributory annuities by which individual initiative can increase the annual amounts received in old age. It is proposed that the Federal Government assume one-half of the cost of the old-age pension plan, which ought ultimately to be supplanted by self-supporting annuity plans. . . .

We pay now for the dreadful consequences of economic insecurity —and dearly. This plan presents a more equitable and infinitely less expensive means of meeting these costs. We cannot afford to neglect the plain duty before us. I strongly recommend action to attain the objectives sought in this report.

F.D.R. took the attitude that businessmen as a class were humanitarian and socially responsible, but that their organizations did not accurately represent their views. He was frankly critical of the United States Chamber of Commerce in its opposition to the New Deal. As he said, at a press conference on May 3, 1935, their annual convention had not offered "a single speech which took the human side, the old-age side, the unemployment side. There were some glittering generalities, yes, 'we hate to see old people starve,' 'we would not willingly throw people out of work,' and so forth and so on—not exactly what you could call a constructive contribution."

He faced the fact that, for all his politically unavoidable self-congratulation on the alleged pickup of business and employment—a matter of technical definition that could satisfy only loyal partisans of the New Deal —that unemployment continued to be a patent and malignant fact in American life only meagerly affected by stopgap measures. He concluded that direct relief could be left to the states, and that the Federal government ought to "establish a larger Works Program for the unemployed who were employable." From his dry Executive Order No. 7034 (May 6, 1935) proliferated a vast network of projects that quietly transformed America. Only perhaps one-fourth of the needy unemployed were affected by WPA, but these laid down roads, built bridges, post offices, school gymnasiums, and tennis courts. They helped to clear away the debris of storm-struck towns. Artists on the most famous element of WPA—the Federal Arts Projects—created, at absurdly low cost, the murals outside the Catalog Room of the New York Public Library and the base-reliefs that added distinction to the public buildings on Pennsylvania Avenue in Washington, D.C. Grant Wood, Dong Kingman, Jack Levine, and, as far away as San Francisco, Beniamino Bufano lent their talents to works that were derogated by the Hearst Press and, later, by the artistic *avant garde*.

The "Right to Work" was given significant meaning in that era, being the title of a book by Nels Anderson, WPA's Director of the Section on Labor Relations. In his book (1938), Anderson asked: "What should the unemployed workers expect of the government and what are the responsibilities of government to the unemployed?" His answer was that people had a right to jobs and training. "If industry cannot or will not recognize that right, they must look to the government." He recognized that there was alarm in certain quarters for the security of capitalism. It seemed to him, on the contrary, that work relief was "the best possible insurance against more drastic changes in the existing economic order."

WPA

By virtue of and pursuant to the authority vested in me under the "Emergency Relief Appropriation Act of 1935," approved April 8, 1935 (Public Resolution No. 11, 74th Congress), and of all other authority vested in me, it is hereby ordered as follows:

I. I hereby establish within the Government certain agencies, and prescribe their respective functions and duties, as follows: . . .

(C) A Works Progress Administration, which shall be responsible to the President for the honest, efficient, speedy, and coordinated execution of the work relief program as a whole, and for the execution of that program in such manner as to move from the relief rolls to work on such projects or in private employment the maximum number of persons in the shortest time possible.

To this end, the Works Progress Administration shall have the following powers and duties:

1. To establish and operate a division of progress investigation, and to coordinate the pertinent work of existing investigative agencies of the Government, so as to insure the honest execution of the work relief program.

2. To formulate, and, with the approval of the President, to require uniform periodic reports of progress on all projects; and, where any avoidable delay appears, forthwith to recommend to the President appropriate measures for eliminating such delay, and, similarly, to recommend the termination of projects where it develops that they are not affording the amount of employment warranting their continuance.

3. With the approval of the President, to prescribe rules and regulations:

  a. To assure that as many of the persons employed on all work projects as is feasible shall be persons receiving relief; and
  b. To govern the selection of such persons for such employment.

4. To formulate and administer a system of uniform periodic reports of the employment on such projects of persons receiving relief.

5. To investigate wages and working conditions and to make and submit to the President such findings as will aid the President in prescribing working conditions and rates of pay on projects.

In addition to the foregoing powers and duties, the Works Progress Administration shall:

1. Provide for the coordination of such data compiling projects as form a part of the work relief program and of such portions of other research activities as may be necessary or useful in carrying out such program.

2. Coordinate all requests for opinions and decisions addressed to the Executive departments or independent establishments of the Government on questions affecting the administration of the Act or of orders issued thereunder.

3. Recommend and carry on small useful projects designed to assure a maximum of employment in all localities.

The Federal Emergency Relief Administrator shall serve also as Administrator of the Works Progress Administration. . . .

Still, what had the New Deal accomplished? Critics of the NRA claimed that it had created an intolerable bureaucracy and legalized monopoly. The AAA, in its eagerness to cut production in order to raise farm prices, had slaughtered pigs and dumped potatoes into the Mississippi River. Or, as Benjamin Stolberg and Warren Jay Vinton charged, in their *The Economic Consequences of the New Deal* (1935): "There is nothing [it] has so far done that could not have been done better by an earthquake. A first-rate earthquake, from coast to coast, could have reestablished scarcity much more effectively, and put all the survivors to work for the greater glory of Big Business—with far more speed and far less noise than the New Deal."

The Supreme Court struck down the NRA. It struck down the AAA. The latter was revived under the technical guise of soil conservation. But NRA stayed down. The New Deal had given up hope that big business could minister to the needs of labor. Instead, it sanctioned the Wagner Labor Relations Act, which dramatically raised the status of labor in government and the courts. In effect, labor could fight for its own advancement and find a friend in law.

The Republicans chose, in 1936, to put their faith in what seemed to them a return to sound principles. They would prove the New Deal a failure and a disgrace. Roosevelt fought them confidently, vigorously, with all his ability to make contact with the masses, which was the despair of his foes.

Campaign for Re-election

During the past month I have seen a great deal of our country and a great many of our people. Both the America and the Americans I have seen look very different from three and a half years ago.

Many important things have happened to them in those three and a half years. I could talk to you for hours about this better, happier America. What I am going to talk to you about for a few minutes, however, is some of the things that have brought about that better, happier America. I want to tell you in terms of actual achievement what we in Washington have done, what we have done to restore prosperity, what we have done to end abuses.

The first thing before us on that famous fourth of March, 1933, was to give aid to those overtaken by disaster. We did that, and we are not ashamed of giving help to those who needed help. We furnished food relief, drought relief, flood relief, work relief. We established the Federal Emergency Relief Administration; the Public Works Administration; the Civilian Conservation Corps; the Works Progress Administration. Some people ridicule them as alphabetical agencies. But you and I know that they are the agencies that have substituted food for starvation; work for idleness; hope instead of dull despair.

And on November 3d, America will say that that was a job well done!

The second thing we did was to help our stalled economic engine to get under way again. We knew enough about the mechanism of our economic order to know that we could not do that one wheel at a time. We had had enough of one-wheel economics. We proposed to get all four wheels started at once. We knew that it was no good to try to start only the wheel of finance. At the same time we had to start the wheels of agriculture, of workers of all classes, of business and industry.

By democratizing the work of the Reconstruction Finance Corporation and redirecting it into more practical and helpful channels we furnished fuel for the machine.

We primed the pump by spending Government money in direct relief, in work relief, in public works.

We established the Agricultural Adjustment Administration; the National Recovery Administration; the Farm Credit Administration; the Soil Conservation Program; the Home Owners Loan Corporation; the Federal Housing Administration; the Tennessee Valley Authority; the Resettlement Administration; the Rural Electrification Administration. We set up a sound monetary policy; a sound banking structure; reciprocal trade agreements; foreign exchange accords.

We created a National Labor Relations Board to improve working conditions and seek industrial peace. We brought the business men of the Nation together to encourage them to increase wages, to shorten working hours, to abolish child labor. With labor's aid and backing we took the first great step for workers' security by the Social Security Act—an act which is now being misrepresented to the workers in a pay-envelope propaganda by a few employers whom you will easily recognize as old time exploiters of labor who have always fought against contributing anything themselves to a sound security for the laboring man and his wife and children.

That Act is a new Magna Charta for those who work. In its preparation and in its enactment, it was supported not only by organized labor but by those other liberal groups—workers, employers, churches, private charities, educators who for many years have believed that modern Government can make provision against the hardship of unemployment and the terrors of old age.

On the passage of this law, in addition to overwhelming support on the part of Democrats in both the House and Senate, the country should note that seventy-seven Republican Representatives voted for it and only eighteen against it, and that in the Senate fifteen Republican Senators voted for it and only five against it.

This fact is perhaps illustrative of the paradox that in the closing days of the campaign, a distraught Republican leadership, driven to desperation and urged on by the same sinister forces which generation after generation have opposed all social legislation, now repudiates its own Representatives and Senators in the halls of the Congress and leaves them looking positively silly. . . .

To return to what the Federal Government has done in the past three and one-half years, some people call these things waste. You and I know that they are the means by which our stalled machine has been started on the road once more.

And on November 3d America will say that that was a job well done!

The third thing we did was to look to the future, to root out abuses, to establish every possible defense against a return of the evils which brought the crash. We established the Securities Exchange Commission; banking reforms; a sound monetary policy; deposit insurance for fifty million bank accounts—all aimed to safeguard the thrift of our citizens.

By our tax policy and by regulating financial markets, we loosened the grip which monopolies had fastened upon independent American business. We began also to free American business and American labor from the unfair competition of a small unscrupulous minority. We established by a statute a curb upon the overweening power and unholy practices of some utility holding companies.

By the Rural Electrification Act, by the Tennessee Valley Authority and similar projects we set up yardsticks to bring electricity at cheaper rates to the average American farm and the average American home. Through loans to private enterprise and in cooperation with cities, we promoted slum-clearance and established low-cost modern housing. We set up a National Youth Administration to help keep our youth in school and to hold open for them the door of opportunity. By a successful war on crime we have made America's homes and places of business safer against the gangster, the kidnapper and the racketeer.

Some people call these things meddling and interference. You and I know them to be new stones in a foundation on which we can, and are determined to, build a structure of economic security for all our people—a safer, happier, more American America.

On November 3d, the American people will say that that is a job well begun! . . .

Unfortunately, those who now raise the cry of class distinctions are the very leaders whose policies in the past have fostered such distinctions. When they were in power, they were content in the belief that the chief function of Government was to help only those at the top in the pious hope that the few at the top would in their benevolence or generosity pass that help on.

That theory of Government has been banished from Washington. It did not work. It was not and cannot be the answer to our problem. We have united all classes in the Nation in a program for the Nation. In doing that, we are bridging the gulf of antagonism which twelve years of neglect had opened up between them.

An equally important task remains to be done: to go forward, to consolidate and to strengthen these gains, to close the gaps by destroying the glaring inequalities of opportunity and of security which, in the recent past, have set group against group and region against region.

By our policies for the future we will carry forward this program of unity. We will not be content until all our people fairly share in the ever-increasing capacity of America to provide a high standard of living for all its citizens.

On November 3d, the American people will say that our policy for the future is their policy for the future.

F.D.R. came back into office with a renewed mandate, and a fresh determination to cope with the depression crisis. His eyes were still fixed upon domestic affairs, even though Germany was now in the hands of the Nazi Party, though Mussolini's legions had invaded Ethiopia, though Spain was in the throes of civil war, and though mighty Japanese air, land and sea forces threatened the entire Far East. American communists might dream of great world convulsions that would augment their significance in American life. Native fascist groups might negotiate with the Ku Klux Klan, seeking a basis for rapport. Roosevelt's followers con-

220

tinued, for the most part, to investigate means for dealing decisively with the tenacious sicknesses that accompanied a stalled economy. Roosevelt's Second Inaugural Address (January 20, 1937) pointed the way for them, and provided them with their rationale.

"One-Third of a Nation"

When four years ago we met to inaugurate a President, the Republic, single-minded in anxiety, stood in spirit here. We dedicated ourselves to the fulfillment of a vision—to speed the time when there would be for all the people that security and peace essential to the pursuit of happiness. We of the Republic pledged ourselves to drive from the temple of our ancient faith those who had profaned it; to end by action, tireless and unafraid, the stagnation and despair of that day. We did those first things first.

Our covenant with ourselves did not stop there. Instinctively we recognized a deeper need—the need to find through government the instrument of our united purpose to solve for the individual the ever-rising problems of a complex civilization. Repeated attempts at their solution without the aid of government had left us baffled and bewildered. For, without that aid, we had been unable to create those moral controls over the services of science which are necessary to make science a useful servant instead of a ruthless master of mankind. To do this we knew that we must find practical controls over blind economic forces and blindly selfish men.

We of the Republic sensed the truth that democratic government has innate capacity to protect its people against disasters once considered inevitable, to solve problems once considered unsolvable. We would not admit that we could not find a way to master economic epidemics just as, after centuries of fatalistic suffering, we had found a way to master epidemics of disease. We refused to leave the problems of our common welfare to be solved by the winds of chance and the hurricanes of disaster.

In this we Americans were discovering no wholly new truth; we were writing a new chapter in our book of self-government.

This year marks the one hundred and fiftieth anniversary of the Constitutional Convention which made us a nation. At that Convention our forefathers found the way out of the chaos which

221

followed the Revolutionary War; they created a strong government with powers of united action sufficient then and now to solve problems utterly beyond individual or local solution. A century and a half ago they established the Federal Government in order to promote the general welfare and secure the blessings of liberty to the American people.

Today we invoke those same powers of government to achieve the same objectives.

Four years of new experience have not belied our historic instinct. They hold out the clear hope that government within communities, government within the separate States, and government of the United States can do the things the times require, without yielding its democracy. Our tasks in the last four years did not force democracy to take a holiday.

Nearly all of us recognize that as intricacies of human relationships increase, so power to govern them also must increase—power to stop evil; power to do good. The essential democracy of our Nation and the safety of our people depend not upon the absence of power, but upon lodging it with those whom the people can change or continue at stated intervals through an honest and free system of elections. The Constitution of 1787 did not make our democracy impotent.

In fact, in these last four years, we have made the exercise of all power more democratic; for we have begun to bring private autocratic powers into their proper subordination to the public's government. The legend that they were invincible—above and beyond the processes of a democracy—has been shattered. They have been challenged and beaten.

Our progress out of the depression is obvious. But that is not all that you and I mean by the new order of things. Our pledge was not merely to do a patchwork job with second-hand materials. By using the new materials of social justice we have undertaken to erect on the old foundations a more enduring structure for the better use of future generations. . . .

Among men of good will, science and democracy together offer an ever-richer life and ever-larger satisfaction to the individual. With this change in our moral climate and our rediscovered ability to improve our economic order, we have set our feet upon the road of enduring progress.

Shall we pause now and turn our back upon the road that lies ahead? Shall we call this the promised land? Or, shall we continue on our way? For "each age is a dream that is dying, or one that is coming to birth."

Many voices are heard as we face a great decision. Comfort says, "Tarry a while." Opportunism says, "This is a good spot." Timidity asks, "How difficult is the road ahead?"

True, we have come far from the days of stagnation and despair. Vitality has been preserved. Courage and confidence have been restored. Mental and moral horizons have been extended.

But our present gains were won under the pressure of more than ordinary circumstance. Advance became imperative under the goad of fear and suffering. The times were on the side of progress.

To hold to progress today, however, is more difficult. Dulled conscience, irresponsibility, and ruthless self-interest already reappear. Such symptoms of prosperity may become portents of disaster! Prosperity already tests the persistence of our progressive purpose.

Let us ask again: Have we reached the goal of our vision of that fourth day of March, 1933? Have we found our happy valley?

I see a great nation, upon a great continent, blessed with a great wealth of natural resources. Its hundred and thirty million people are at peace among themselves; they are making their country a good neighbor among the nations. I see a United States which can demonstrate that, under democratic methods of government, national wealth can be translated into a spreading volume of human comforts hitherto unknown, and the lowest standard of living can be raised far above the level of mere subsistence.

But here is the challenge to our democracy: In this nation I see tens of millions of its citizens—a substantial part of its whole population—who at this very moment are denied the greater part of what the very lowest standards of today call the necessities of life.

I see millions of families trying to live on incomes so meager that the pall of family disaster hangs over them day by day.

I see millions whose daily lives in city and on farm continue under conditions labeled indecent by a so-called polite society half a century ago.

I see millions denied education, recreation, and the opportunity to better their lot and the lot of their children.

I see millions lacking the means to buy the products of farm and factory and by their poverty denying work and productiveness to many other millions.

223

I see one-third of a nation ill-housed, ill-clad, ill-nourished.

It is not in despair that I paint you that picture. I paint it for you in hope—because the Nation, seeing and understanding the injustice in it, proposes to paint it out. We are determined to make every American citizen the subject of his country's interest and concern; and we will never regard any faithful, law-abiding group within our borders as superfluous. The test of our progress is not whether we add more to the abundance of those who have much; it is whether we provide enough for those who have too little. . . .

Roosevelt had endured the ruminations of the Supreme Court respecting New Deal legislation with increased impatience. Dissatisfaction with the Supreme Court was an old tradition. Thomas Jefferson's administration had sought to undermine it. Andrew Jackson had voiced one of his best-known thoughts on the subject: "John Marshall has made his decision; now let him enforce it." Lincoln's administration had had no time to treat tenderly the Supreme Court's views of civil rights in wartime. F.D.R. reviewed a Supreme Court of "nine old men" who had undermined NRA, the first AAA, the Guffey Soft Coal Act—an effort at creating order and peace in the mining industry—the Railway Pension Act, and others, and he concluded that the New Deal had been more than patient with an agency that impeded progress. He determined to influence the makeup of the Court. Early in February 1937 he began an all out offensive against the Court as it was, asking Congress to permit the President to add one Justice for each of those presently on the bench who, having attained seventy years, had not voluntarily retired. Since six of them were beyond that age, F.D.R. could, given the legislation, have appointed six additional Justices. A political storm blew up. Roosevelt was charged with wishing to undermine the Court. In a "Fireside Chat" (March 9, 1937), he defended himself with his usual energy. No one could foresee that, by the time his presidency was completed, he would have appointed, in more routine fashion, more Justices than any of his predecessors.

"Court Packing":
The Attack on the Supreme Court

Last Thursday I described in detail certain economic problems which everyone admits now face the Nation. For the many messages which have come to me after that speech, and which it is physically impossible to answer individually, I take this means of saying "thank you."

Tonight, sitting at my desk in the White House, I make my first radio report to the people in my second term of office.

I am reminded of that evening in March, four years ago, when I made my first radio report to you. We were then in the midst of the great banking crisis.

Soon after, with the authority of the Congress, we asked the Nation to turn over all of its privately held gold, dollar for dollar, to the Government of the United States.

Today's recovery proves how right that policy was.

But when, almost two years later, it came before the Supreme Court its constitutionality was upheld only by a five-to-four vote. The change of one vote would have thrown all the affairs of this great Nation back into hopeless chaos. In effect, four Justices ruled that the right under a private contract to exact a pound of flesh was more sacred than the main objectives of the Constitution to establish an enduring Nation.

In 1933 you and I knew that we must never let our economic system get completely out of joint again—that we could not afford to take the risk of another great depression.

We also became convinced that the only way to avoid a repetition of those dark days was to have a government with power to prevent and to cure the abuses and the inequalities which had thrown that system out of joint.

We then began a program of remedying those abuses and inequalities—to give balance and stability to our economic system— to make it bomb-proof against the causes of 1929.

Today we are only part-way through that program—and recovery is speeding up to a point where the dangers of 1929 are again becoming possible, not this week or month perhaps, but within a year or two.

National laws are needed to complete that program. Individual or local or state effort alone cannot protect us in 1937 any better than ten years ago.

It will take time—and plenty of time—to work out our remedies administratively even after legislation is passed. To complete our program of protection in time, therefore, we cannot delay one moment in making certain that our National Government has power to carry through. . . .

The Courts, however, have cast doubts on the ability of the

elected Congress to protect us against catastrophe by meeting squarely our modern social and economic conditions.

We are at a crisis in our ability to proceed with that protection. It is a quiet crisis. There are no lines of depositors outside closed banks. But to the far-sighted it is far-reaching in its possibilities of injury to America. . . .

Last Thursday I described the American form of Government as a three horse team provided by the Constitution to the American people so that their field might be plowed. The three horses are, of course, the three branches of government—the Congress, the Executive and the Courts. Two of the horses are pulling in unison today; the third is not. Those who have intimated that the President of the United States is trying to drive that team, overlook the simple fact that the President, as Chief Executive, is himself one of the three horses. . . .

It is the American people themselves who expect the third horse to pull in unison with the other two.

I hope that you have re-read the Constitution of the United States in these past few weeks. Like the Bible, it ought to be read again and again.

It is an easy document to understand when you remember that it was called into being because the Articles of Confederation under which the original thirteen States tried to operate after the Revolution showed the need of a National Government with power enough to handle national problems. In its Preamble, the Constitution states that is was intended to form a more perfect Union and promote the general welfare; and the powers given to the Congress to carry out those purposes can be best described by saying that they were all the powers needed to meet each and every problem which then had a national character and which could not be met by merely local action.

But the framers went further. Having in mind that in succeeding generations many other problems then undreamed of would become national problems, they gave to the Congress the ample broad powers "to levy taxes . . . and provide for the common defense and general welfare of the United States."

That, my friends, is what I honestly believe to have been the clear and underlying purpose of the patriots who wrote a Federal Constitution to create a National Government with national power, intended as they said, "to form a more perfect union . . . for ourselves and our posterity."

For nearly twenty years there was no conflict between the Congress and the Court. Then Congress passed a statute which, in 1803, the Court said violated an express provision of the Constitution. The Court claimed the power to declare it unconstitutional and did so declare it. But a little later the Court itself admitted that it was an extraordinary power to exercise and through Mr. Justice Washington laid down this limitation upon it: "It is but a decent respect due to the wisdom, the integrity and the patriotism of the legislative body, by which any law is passed, to presume in favor of its validity until its violation of the Constitution is proved beyond all reasonable doubt."

But since the rise of the modern movement for social and economic progress through legislation, the Court has more and more often and more and more boldly asserted a power to veto laws passed by the Congress and State Legislatures in complete disregard of this original limitation.

In the last four years the sound rule of giving statutes the benefit of all reasonable doubt has been cast aside. The Court has been acting not as a judicial body, but as a policy-making body.

When the Congress has sought to stabilize national agriculture, to improve the conditions of labor, to safeguard business against unfair competition, to protect our national resources, and in many other ways, to serve our clearly national needs, the majority of the Court has been assuming the power to pass on the wisdom of these Acts of the Congress—and to approve or disapprove the public policy written into these laws.

That is not only my accusation. It is the accusation of most distinguished Justices of the present Supreme Court. I have not the time to quote to you all the language used by dissenting Justices in many of these cases. But in the case holding the Railroad Retirement Act unconstitutional, for instance, Chief Justice Hughes said in a dissenting opinion that the majority opinion was "a departure from sound principles," and placed "an unwarranted limitation upon the commerce clause." And three other Justices agreed with him.

In the case holding the AAA unconstitutional, Justice Stone said of the majority opinion that it was a "tortured construction of the Constitution." And two other Justices agreed with him. . . .

In the face of these dissenting opinions, there is no basis for the claim made by some members of the Court that something in the Constitution has compelled them regretfully to thwart the will of the people. . . .

We have, therefore, reached the point as a Nation where we must take action to save the Constitution from the Court and the

Court from itself. We must find a way to take an appeal from the Supreme Court to the Constitution itself. We want a Supreme Court which will do justice under the Constitution—not over it. In our Courts we want a government of laws and not of men. . . .

When I commenced to review the situation with the problem squarely before me, I came by a process of elimination to the conclusion that, short of amendments, the only method which was clearly constitutional, and would at the same time carry out other much needed reforms, was to infuse new blood into all our Courts. We must have men worthy and equipped to carry out impartial justice. But, at the same time, we must have Judges who will bring to the Courts a present-day sense of the Constitution—Judges who will retain in the Courts the judicial functions of a court, and reject the legislative powers which the courts have today assumed.

In forty-five out of the forty-eight States of the Union, Judges are chosen not for life but for a period of years. In many States Judges must retire at the age of seventy. Congress has provided financial security by offering life pensions at full pay for Federal Judges on all Courts who are willing to retire at seventy. In the case of Supreme Court Justices, that pension is twenty thousand dollars a year. But all Federal Judges, once appointed, can, if they choose, hold office for life, no matter how old they may get to be.

What is my proposal? It is simply this: whenever a Judge or Justice of any Federal Court has reached the age of seventy and does not avail himself of the opportunity to retire on a pension, a new member shall be appointed by the President then in office, with the approval, as required by the Constitution, of the Senate of the United States.

That plan has two chief purposes. By bringing into the judicial system a steady and continuing stream of new and younger blood, I hope, first, to make the administration of all Federal justice speedier and, therefore, less costly; secondly, to bring to the decision of social and economic problems younger men who have had personal experience and contact with modern facts and circumstances under which average men have to live and work. This plan will save our national Constitution from hardening of the judicial arteries. . . .

Those opposing this plan have sought to arouse prejudice and fear by crying that I am seeking to "pack" the Supreme Court and that a baneful precedent will be established.

What do they mean by the words "packing the Court"?

Let me answer this question with a bluntness that will end all *honest* misunderstanding of my purposes.

If by that phrase "packing the Court" it is charged that I wish to place on the bench spineless puppets who would disregard the law and would decide specific cases as I wished them to be decided, I make this answer: that no President fit for his office would appoint, and no Senate of honorable men fit for their office would confirm, that kind of appointees to the Supreme Court.

But if by that phrase the charge is made that I would appoint and the Senate would confirm Justices worthy to sit beside present members of the Court who understand those modern conditions, that I will appoint Justices who will not undertake to override the judgment of the Congress on legislative policy, that I will appoint Justices who will act as Justices and not as legislators—if the appointment of such Justices can be called "packing the Courts," then I say that I and with me the vast majority of the American people favor doing just that thing—now.

Is it a dangerous precedent for the Congress to change the number of the Justices? The Congress has always had, and will have, that power. The number of Justices has been changed several times before, in the Administrations of John Adams and Thomas Jefferson—both signers of the Declaration of Independence—Andrew Jackson, Abraham Lincoln and Ulysses S. Grant. . . .

This plan of mine is no attack on the Court; it seeks to restore the Court to its rightful and historic place in our system of Constitutional Government and to have it resume its high task of building anew on the Constitution "a system of living law." The Court itself can best undo what the Court has done. . . .

PART VI
World Crisis

Americans had noted only in general ways that there was trouble abroad. The Far East still seemed far away. Adolf Hitler, seizing power in Germany early in 1933, made displays of that power that were dramatic and impressive—solemn, torchlit night parades under giant swastika banners; Brown Shirt raids on Jews and communists, who were led, humiliated and with their heads shaved, through the streets; the Reichstag fire trial. But some Americans thought Hitler could be destroyed by ridicule, such as Charles Chaplin's "The Great Dictator" offered. "Left-wing" intellectuals talked of "social fascism," "workers and peasants alliances," of how Chiang Kai-shek had "drowned the Chinese revolution in workers' blood." The Nye-Vandenberg Committee, investigating the "merchants of death" of World War I, helped make war seem a racket: the result of the international skulduggery practiced by munitions manufacturers. Patriotism was at low ebb; Americans thought they would never again be taken in by mere emotionalism and appeals to nationalism.

October 3, 1935, Mussolini's Roman legions invaded Ethiopia and his planes bombed Addis Ababa; but Americans were bemused by the World Series. The next summer, the Spanish fascists rebelled against the constitutional republican regime and began their drive on Madrid. This event activated Italians, Germans, and Russians, all eager to try out their military strategies and resources on the Spanish. American left-wingers sent their "Abraham Lincoln Brigade" as a contribution to the proceedings. In October 1936, the fateful Nazi-Fascist Axis of Hitler and Mussolini was forged; later, Japan would enter into the alliance. The League of Nations, which the late Russian premier, Lenin, had once called "the thieves' kitchen," was patently impotent and unable to influence events.

F.D.R. maintained the attitude that the depression crisis had been conquered, though he warned repeatedly that reform had to continue, that there was always the possibility of a relapse into depression. Resistance to his relief program never diminished. As late as 1940, he was constrained to note: "It is an unfortunate human failing that a full pocketbook often groans more loudly than an empty stomach." Unemployment had not actually been conquered; there were still approximately twelve million unemployed, moving sluggishly about on welfare funds, family handouts, aimless schooling, various forms of charity and common degradation, and other makeshift arrangements, including WPA. It was under such circumstances that Roosevelt announced a new turn of policy. On October 5, 1937, in Chicago, he dedicated its new Outer Drive Bridge and drew international lessons from such a "project of civic betterment."

"Quarantine"

. . . On my trip across the continent and back I have been shown many evidences of the result of common sense cooperation between municipalities and the Federal Government and I have been greeted by tens of thousands of Americans who have told me in every look and word that their material and spiritual wellbeing has made great strides forward in the past few years.

And yet, as I have seen with my own eyes, the prosperous farms, the thriving factories and the busy railroads, as I have seen the happiness and security and peace which covers our wide land, almost inevitably I have been compelled to contrast our peace with very different scenes being enacted in other parts of the world.

It is because the people of the United States under modern conditions must, for the sake of their own future, give thought to the rest of the world, that I, as the responsible executive head of the Nation, have chosen this great inland city and this gala occasion to speak to you on a subject of definite national importance.

The political situation in the world, which of late has been growing progressively worse, is such as to cause grave concern and anxiety to all the peoples and nations who wish to live in peace and amity with their neighbors.

Some fifteen years ago the hopes of mankind for a continuing era of international peace were raised to great heights when more than sixty nations solemnly pledged themselves not to resort to arms in furtherance of their national aims and policies. The high aspirations expressed in the Briand-Kellogg Peace Pact and the hopes for peace thus raised have of late given way to a haunting fear of calamity. The present reign of terror and international lawlessness began a few years ago.

It began through unjustified interference in the internal affairs of other nations or the invasion of alien territory in violation of treaties; and has now reached a stage where the very foundations of civilization are seriously threatened. The landmarks and traditions which have marked the progress of civilization toward a condition of law, order and justice are being wiped away.

Without a declaration of war and without warning or justification of any kind, civilians, including vast numbers of women and children, are being ruthlessly murdered with bombs from the air. In times of so-called peace, ships are being attacked and sunk by submarines without cause or notice. Nations are fomenting and taking sides in civil warfare in nations that have never done them any harm. Nations claiming freedom for themselves deny it to others.

Innocent peoples, innocent nations, are being cruelly sacrificed to a greed for power and supremacy which is devoid of all sense of justice and humane considerations.

To paraphrase a recent author* "perhaps we foresee a time when men, exultant in the technique of homicide, will rage so hotly over the world that every precious thing will be in danger, every book and picture and harmony, every treasure garnered through two millenniums, the small, the delicate, the defenseless—all will be lost or wrecked or utterly destroyed."

If those things come to pass in other parts of the world, let no one imagine that America will escape, that America may expect mercy, that this Western Hemisphere will not be attacked and that it will continue tranquilly and peacefully to carry on the ethics and the arts of civilization. . . .

If those days are not to come to pass—if we are to have a world in which we can breathe freely and live in amity without fear— the peace-loving nations must make a concerted effort to uphold laws and principles on which alone peace can rest secure. . . .

There is a solidarity and interdependence about the modern world, both technically and morally, which makes it impossible for any nation completely to isolate itself from economic and political upheavals in the rest of the world, especially when such upheavals appear to be spreading and not declining. There can be no stability or peace either within nations or between nations except under laws and moral standards adhered to by all. International anarchy destroys every foundation for peace. It jeopardizes either the immediate or the future security of every nation, large or small. It is, therefore, a matter of vital interest and concern to the people of the United States that the sanctity of international treaties and the maintenance of international morality be restored.

The overwhelming majority of the peoples and nations of the world today want to live in peace. They seek the removal of barriers against trade. They want to exert themselves in industry, in agriculture and in business, that they may increase their wealth through the production of wealth-producing goods rather than striving to produce military planes and bombs and machine guns and cannon for the destruction of human lives and useful property.

* James Hilton, in *Lost Horizon* (1933). Roosevelt also found occasion to mention the novel's never-never land, Shangri-La.

In those nations of the world which seem to be piling armament on armament for purposes of aggression, and those other nations which fear acts of aggression against them and their security, a very high proportion of their national income is being spent directly for armaments. It runs from thirty to as high as fifty per cent. We are fortunate. The proportion that we in the United States spend is far less—eleven or twelve per cent.

How happy we are that the circumstances of the moment permit us to put our money into bridges and boulevards, dams and reforestation, the conservation of our soil and many other kinds of useful works rather than into huge standing armies and vast supplies of implements of war.

I am compelled and you are compelled, nevertheless, to look ahead. The peace, the freedom and the security of ninety per cent of the population of the world is being jeopardized by the remaining ten per cent who are threatening a breakdown of all international order and law. Surely the ninety per cent who want to live in peace under law and in accordance with moral standards that have received almost universal acceptance through the centuries, can and must find some way to make their will prevail.

The situation is definitely of universal concern. The questions involved relate not merely to violations of specific provisions of particular treaties; they are questions of war and of peace, of international law and especially of principles of humanity. It is true that they involve definite violations of agreements, and especially of the Covenant of the League of Nations, the Briand-Kellogg Pact and the Nine Power Treaty. But they also involve problems of world economy, world security and world humanity. . . .

It seems to be unfortunately true that the epidemic of world lawlessness is spreading.

When an epidemic of physical disease starts to spread, the community approves and joins in a quarantine of the patients in order to protect the health of the community against the spread of the disease.

It is my determination to pursue a policy of peace. It is my determination to adopt every practicable measure to avoid involvement in war. It ought to be inconceivable that in this modern era, and in the face of experience, any nation could be so foolish and ruthless as to run the risk of plunging the whole world into war by invading and violating, in contravention of solemn treaties, the territory of other nations that have done them no real harm and are too weak to protect themselves adequately. Yet the peace of the world and the welfare and security of every nation, including our own, is today being threatened by that very thing.

No nation which refuses to exercise forbearance and to respect the freedom and rights of others can long remain strong and retain the confidence and respect of other nations. No nation ever loses its dignity or its good standing by conciliating its differences, and by exercising great patience with, and consideration for, the rights of other nations.

War is a contagion, whether it be declared or undeclared. It can engulf states and peoples remote from the original scene of hostilities. We are determined to keep out of war, yet we cannot insure ourselves against the disastrous effects of war and the dangers of involvement. We are adopting such measures as will minimize our risk of involvement, but we cannot have complete protection in a world of disorder in which confidence and security have broken down.

If civilization is to survive, the principles of the Prince of Peace must be restored. Trust between nations must be revived.

Most important of all, the will for peace on the part of peace-loving nations must express itself to the end that nations that may be tempted to violate their agreements and the rights of others will desist from such a course. There must be positive endeavors to preserve peace.

America hates war. America hopes for peace. Therefore, America actively engages in the search for peace.

Abroad, there were stirrings of unrest and war; there was concern that a great war might explode, involving not only Spain or the Continental maneuvers of a patently aggressive Germany, but all of Europe and perhaps the world. There was a striking contrast between the clash of arms and the rumors of plots elsewhere, and the peaceful plans being bruited for a St. Lawrence seaway at home. As Roosevelt said, at the dedication of Thousand Island Bridge, on August 18, 1938:

I look forward to the day when a Canadian Prime Minister and an American President can meet to dedicate, not a bridge across this water, but the very water itself, to the lasting and productive use of their respective peoples. Until that day comes, and I hope it may be soon, this bridge stands as an open door. There will be no challenge at the border, and no guard to ask a countersign. Where the boundary is crossed the only word must be, "pass, friend."

Roosevelt had also taken steps to ensure cooperation elsewhere in the Western Hemisphere. As early as 1936, he had traveled to Buenos Aires to address the Inter-American Conference for the Maintenance of Peace and express his belief that the American nations needed to keep peace among themselves. Now America and F.D.R. adopted the legal stance of neutrality, which sadly (its supporters thought) most acutely harmed the Spanish republican government. Czechoslovakia disappeared, as England's premier, Neville Chamberlain, left it to its fate. In the summer of 1939, Hitler and Stalin stunned the world by joining in a peace pact. Many quasi-liberals who had justified Soviet policy, whatever it might be, on the ground that Russian antifascism was a bulwark of freedom began to retreat from their previous commitments, as public tolerance and admiration of communists diminished. On September 1, 1939, Hitler unleashed his armies against Poland, and Great Britain and France declared war. F.D.R. proclaimed neutrality in behalf of the United States, but also asked for a repeal of its official embargo provisions. In his Message of September 21, he explained that "a belligerent nation often needs wheat and lard and cotton . . . just as much as it needs anti-aircraft guns. . . ." Repeal of the embargo would give greater consistency to our laws, and would better help us to stay at peace: "I say this because with the repeal of the embargo this Government clearly and definitely will insist that American citizens and American ships keep away from the immediate perils of the actual zones of conflict."

Revised legislation gave Roosevelt the discretion to permit American shipping to operate in the combat areas. Russia's attack on Finland (she had already absorbed her share of Poland) and Germany's invasion of Norway and Denmark, and then of the Netherlands, Belgium and Luxembourg, strained F.D.R.'s formal adherence to neutrality. National defense was stepped up, and then stepped up again and again, though Roosevelt also continued to ask for relief funds. He ran for re-election on a dual platform of continued social legislation and dreary but necessary peace promises. ("I have said this before, but I shall say it again and again and again. Your boys are not going to be sent into any foreign wars.") French forces crumbled before the Nazis, and their government retreated to what would ultimately become the ignominious Vichy regime. Mussolini assumed a jackal role, by declaring war on France on grounds that Italy required access to the ocean. As Roosevelt said, in an address at the University of Virginia that rang around the world: "On this tenth day of June 1940, the hand that held the dagger has struck it into the back of its neighbor." Roosevelt's earlier "cash and carry" program of sales to belligerents had created a situation, at least in the Atlantic Ocean, similar to that which had drawn us into World War I: Great Britain's command of the seas manifestly isolated Germany from any possibilities of purchasing American goods. In September 1940, the Selective Service Act was passed. Defense agencies were already in existence, with more in the process of receiving legislative endorsement. Roosevelt's "Four Freedoms," defined January 6, 1941, compared strikingly with Wilson's old Fourteen Points.

The Four Freedoms

I address you, the Members of the Seventy-seventh Congress, at a moment unprecedented in the history of the Union. I use the word "unprecedented," because at no previous time has American security been as seriously threatened from without as it is today.

Since the permanent formation of our government under the Constitution, in 1789, most of the periods of crisis in our history have related to our domestic affairs. Fortunately, only one of these —the four year War between the States—ever threatened our national unity. Today, thank God, one hundred and thirty million Americans, in forty-eight States, have forgotten points of the compass in our national unity.

It is true that prior to 1914 the United States often had been disturbed by events in other Continents. We had even engaged in two wars with European nations and in a number of undeclared wars in the West Indies, in the Mediterranean and in the Pacific for the maintenance of American rights and for the principles of peaceful commerce. In no case, however, had a serious threat been raised against our national safety or our independence.

What I seek to convey is the historic truth that the United States as a Nation has at all times maintained opposition to any attempt to lock us in behind an ancient Chinese wall while the procession of civilization went past. Today, thinking of our children and their children, we oppose enforced isolation for ourselves or for any part of the Americas. . . .

Every realist knows that the democratic way of life is at this moment being directly assailed in every part of the world—assailed either by arms, or by secret spreading of poisonous propaganda by those who seek to destroy unity and promote discord in nations still at peace.

During sixteen months this assault has blotted out the whole pattern of democratic life in an appalling number of independent nations, great and small. The assailants are still on the march, threatening other nations, great and small.

Therefore, as your President, performing my constitutional duty to "give to the Congress information of the state of the Union," I find it necessary to report that the future and the safety of our country and of our democracy are overwhelmingly involved in events far beyond our borders.

Armed defense of democratic existence is now being gallantly waged in four continents. If that defense fails, all the population and all the resources of Europe, Asia, Africa and Australasia will be dominated by the conquerors. The total of those populations and their resources greatly exceed the sum total of the population and resources of the whole of the Western Hemisphere—many times over.

In times like these it is immature—and incidentally untrue—for anybody to brag that an unprepared America, single-handed, and with one hand tied behind its back, can hold off the whole world.

No realistic American can expect from a dictator's peace international generosity, or return of true independence, or world disarmament, or freedom of expression, or freedom of religion—or even good business.

Such a peace would bring no security for us or for our neighbors. "Those, who would give up essential liberty to purchase a little temporary safety, deserve neither liberty nor safety." . . .

There is much loose talk of our immunity from immediate and direct invasion from across the seas. Obviously, as long as the British Navy retains its power, no such danger exists. Even if there were no British Navy, it is not probable than any enemy would be stupid enough to attack us by landing troops in the United States from across thousands of miles of ocean, until it had acquired strategic bases from which to operate.

But we learn much from the lessons of the past years in Europe—particularly the lesson of Norway, whose essential seaports were captured by treachery and surprise built up over a series of years.

The first phase of the invasion of this Hemisphere would not be the landing of regular troops. The necessary strategic points would be occupied by secret agents and their dupes—and great numbers of them are already here, and in Latin America.

As long as the aggressor nations maintain the offensive, they —not we—will choose the time and the place and the method of their attack.

That is why the future of all American Republics is today in serious danger.

That is why this Annual Message to the Congress is unique in our history.

That is why every member of the Executive Branch of the Government and every member of the Congress faces great responsibility—and great accountability.

239

The need of the moment is that our actions and our policy should be devoted primarily—almost exclusively—to meeting this foreign peril. For all our domestic problems are now a part of the great emergency. . . .

Our national policy is this:

First, by an impressive expression of the public will and without regard to partisanship, we are committed to all-inclusive national defense.

Second, by an impressive expression of the public will and without regard to partisanship, we are committed to full support of all those resolute peoples, everywhere, who are resisting aggression and are thereby keeping war away from our Hemisphere. By this support, we express our determination that the democratic cause shall prevail; and we strengthen the defense and security of our own nation.

Third, by an impressive expression of the public will and without regard to partisanship we are committed to the proposition that principles of morality and considerations for our own security will never permit us to acquiesce in a peace dictated by aggressors and sponsored by appeasers. We know that enduring peace cannot be bought at the cost of other people's freedom.

In the recent national election there was no substantial difference between the two great parties in respect to that national policy. No issue was fought out on this line before the American electorate. Today, it is abundantly evident that American citizens everywhere are demanding and supporting speedy and complete action in recognition of obvious danger.

Therefore, the immediate need is a swift and driving increase in our armament production.

Leaders of industry and labor have responded to our summons. Goals of speed have been set. In some cases these goals are being reached ahead of time; in some cases we are on schedule; in other cases there are slight but not serious delays; and in some cases— and I am sorry to say very important cases—we are all concerned by the slowness of the accomplishment of our plans. . . .

To change a whole nation from a basis of peace time production of implements of peace to a basis of war time production of implements of war is no small task. And the greatest difficulty comes at the beginning of the program, when new tools and plant facilities and new assembly lines and ship ways must first be constructed before the actual material begins to flow steadily and speedily from them.

The Congress, of course, must rightly keep itself informed at all times of the progress of the program. However, there is certain information, as the Congress itself will readily recognize, which, in the interests of our own security and those of the nations we are supporting, must needs be kept in confidence.

New circumstances are constantly begetting new needs for our safety. I shall ask this Congress for greatly increased new appropriations and authorizations to carry on what we have begun.

I also ask this Congress for authority and for funds sufficient to manufacture additional munitions and war supplies of many kinds, to be turned over to those nations which are now in actual war with aggressor nations.

Our most useful and immediate role is to act as an arsenal for them as well as for ourselves. They do not need man power. They do need billions of dollars worth of the weapons of defense.

The time is near when they will not be able to pay for them in ready cash. We cannot, and will not, tell them they must surrender, merely because of present inability to pay for the weapons which we know they must have. . . .

Let us say to the democracies: "We Americans are vitally concerned in your defense of freedom. We are putting forth our energies, our resources and our organizing powers to give you the strength to regain and maintain a free world. We shall send you, in ever-increasing numbers, ships, planes, tanks, guns. This is our purpose and our pledge."

In fulfillment of this purpose we will not be intimidated by the threats of dictators that they will regard as a breach of international law and as an act of war our aid to the democracies which dare to resist their aggression. Such aid is not an act of war, even if a dictator should unilaterally proclaim it so to be.

When the dictators are ready to make war upon us, they will not wait for an act of war on our part. They did not wait for Norway or Belgium or the Netherlands to commit an act of war. . . .

Certainly this is no time to stop thinking about the social and economic problems which are the root cause of the social revolution which is today a supreme factor in the world. . . .

In the future days, which we seek to make secure, we look forward to a world founded upon four essential human freedoms.

The first is freedom of speech and expression—everywhere in the world.

The second is freedom of every person to worship God in his own way—everywhere in the world.

The third is freedom from want—which, translated into world terms, means economic understandings which will secure to every nation a healthy peace time life for its inhabitants—everywhere in the world.

The fourth is freedom from fear—which, translated into world terms, means a world-wide reduction, armaments to such a point and in such a thorough fashion that no nation will be in a position to commit an act of physical aggression against any neighbor—anywhere in the world.

That is no vision of a distant millennium. It is a definite basis for a kind of world attainable in our own time and generation. That kind of world is the very antithesis of the so-called new order of tyranny which the dictators seek to create with the crash of a bomb.

To that new order we oppose the greater conception—the moral order. A good society is able to face schemes of world domination and foreign revolutions alike without fear.

Since the beginning of our American history we have been engaged in change—in a perpetual peaceful revolution—a revolution which goes on steadily, quietly adjusting itself to changing conditions —without the concentration camp or the quick-lime in the ditch. The world order which we seek is the cooperation of free countries, working together in a friendly, civilized society.

This Nation has placed its destiny in the hands and heads and hearts of its millions of free men and women; and its faith in freedom under the guidance of God. Freedom means the supremacy of human rights everywhere. Our support goes to those who struggle to gain those rights or keep them. Our strength is in our unity of purpose.

To that high concept there can be no end save victory.

Winston Churchill had risen in all his magnificence to the defense of what was left of the Old World. Roosevelt had begun the determined feeding of weapons and supplies to Great Britain. Defense agencies like the Office of Production Management were being set up and set turning, preparing the country for any outbreak. Fifty over-age destroyers had gone to support the Battle for Britain. All eyes were upon it as, on March 12, 1941, the phrase "lend lease" entered into American parlance—a striking distance away from the now ancient "war debts."

Lend Lease

This Nation has felt that it was imperative to the security of America that we encourage the democracies' heroic resistance to aggressions, by not only maintaining but also increasing the flow of material assistance from this country. Therefore, the Congress has enacted and I have signed H. R. 1776.

Through this legislation, our country has determined to do its full part in creating an adequate arsenal of democracy. This great arsenal will be here in this country. It will be a bulwark of our own defense. It will be the source of the tools of defense for all democracies who are fighting to preserve themselves against aggression.

While the defense equipment produced under H. R. 1776 remains under the control of the United States until it is ready for disposition, it is the fixed policy of this Government to make for democracies every gun, plane, and munition of war that we possibly can.

To accomplish these objectives, I am transmitting an estimate in the amount of $7,000,000,000, the details of which are set forth in the accompanying letter from the Director of the Bureau of the Budget. I strongly urge the immediate enactment of this appropriation.

Respectfully,

Honorable Sam Rayburn,
Speaker, House of Representatives,
Washington, D. C.

America entered into an undeclared war with Germany, in the course of which what amounted to convoying activities in behalf of England brought an open declaration of war closer and closer. Iceland and Greenland became bases for American military units. On June 22, 1941, Hitler made his epochal decision to turn upon his former ally, Stalin, who had been calmly talking over Baltic and Balkan terrain while Nazi armies shed their blood on western fronts. Mechanized German divisions moved swiftly east, as Russians began a "scorched earth" campaign to slow them up and prepare for decisive battles. Antifascism began a new career, in America, as well as elsewhere.

American tankers and destroyers sailing the Atlantic Ocean were tor-

pedoed by German submarines; best remembered, thanks to a moving
ballad, would be "the good *Reuben James*," which sank on the night of
October 30, 1941, carrying 96 officers and men to their deaths.

Roosevelt and Churchill had already met secretly off Newfoundland
Coast, on the British warship HMS *Prince of Wales*, to cement their already firm friendship and understanding, and to draw up a statement of
their strategy and goals in pursuing a war on fascism. Roosevelt reported
the results of this meeting in his Message to Congress, August 21, 1941.

The Atlantic Charter

Over a week ago I held several important conferences at sea
with the British Prime Minister. Because of the factor of safety to
British, Canadian and American ships and their personnel no prior
announcement of these meetings could properly be made.

At the close, a public statement by the Prime Minister and the
President was made. I quote it for the information of the Congress
and for the record:

"The President of the United States and the Prime Minister,
Mr. Churchill, representing His Majesty's Government in the United
Kingdom, have met at sea.

"They have been accompanied by officials of their two Governments, including high ranking officers of their Military, Naval and
Air Services.

"The whole problem of the supply of munitions of war, as
provided by the Lend-Lease Act, for the Armed Forces of the
United States and for those countries actively engaged in resisting
aggression has been further examined.

"Lord Beaverbrook, the Minister of Supply of the British Government, has joined in these conferences. He is going to proceed
to Washington to discuss further details with appropriate officials
of the United States Government. These conferences will also cover
the supply problems of the Soviet Union.

"The President and the Prime Minister have had several conferences. They have considered the dangers to world civilization
arising from the policies of military domination by conquest upon
which the Hitlerite government of Germany and other governments
associated therewith have embarked, and have made clear the

steps which their countries are respectively taking for their safety in the face of these dangers.

"They have agreed upon the following joint declaration:

"Joint declaration of the President of the United States of America and the Prime Minister, Mr. Churchill, representing His Majesty's Government in the United Kingdom, being met together, deem it right to make known certain common principles in the national policies of their respective countries on which they base their hopes for a better future for the world.

"First, their countries seek no aggrandizement, territorial or other;

"Second, they desire to see no territorial changes that do not accord with the freely expressed wishes of the peoples concerned;

"Third, they respect the right of all peoples to choose the form of government under which they will live; and they wish to see sovereign rights and self government restored to those who have been forcibly deprived of them;

"Fourth, they will endeavor, with the respect of their existing obligations, to further the enjoyment by all States, great and small, victor or vanquished, of access, on equal terms, to the trade and to the raw materials of the world which are needed for their economic prosperity;

"Fifth, they desire to bring about the fullest collaboration between all nations in the economic field with the object of securing, for all, improved labor standards, economic advancement and social security;

"Sixth, after the final destruction of the Nazi tyranny, they hope to see established a peace which will afford to all nations the means of dwelling in safety within their own boundaries, and which will afford assurance that all the men in all the lands may live out their lives in freedom from fear and want;

"Seventh, such a peace should enable all men to traverse the high seas and oceans without hindrance;

"Eighth, they believe that all of the nations of the world, for realistic as well as spiritual reasons must come to the abandonment of the use of force. Since no future peace can be maintained if land, sea or air armaments continue to be employed by nations which threaten, or may threaten, aggression outside of their frontiers, they believe, pending the establishment of a wider and permanent system of general security, that the disarmament of such nations is essential. They will likewise aid and encourage all other practicable measures which will lighten for peace-loving peoples the crushing burden of armaments."

The Congress and the President having heretofore determined through the Lend-Lease Act on the national policy of American aid to the democracies which East and West are waging war against dictatorships, the military and naval conversations at these meetings made clear gains in furthering the effectiveness of this aid.

Furthermore, the Prime Minister and I are arranging for conferences with the Soviet Union to aid it in its defense against the attack made by the principal aggressor of the modern world—Germany.

Finally, the declaration of principles at this time presents a goal which is worth while for our type of civilization to seek. It is so clear cut that it is difficult to oppose in any major particular without automatically admitting a willingness to accept compromise with Nazism; or to agree to a world peace which would give to Nazism domination over large numbers of conquered nations. Inevitably such a peace would be a gift to Nazism to take breath—armed breath—for a second war to extend the control over Europe and Asia to the American Hemisphere itself.

It is perhaps unnecessary for me to call attention once more to the utter lack of validity of the spoken or written word of the Nazi government.

It is also unnecessary for me to point out that the declaration of principles includes of necessity the world need for freedom of religion and freedom of information. No society of the world organized under the announced principles could survive without these freedoms which are a part of the whole freedom for which we strive.

Americans had little sense of the spirit of Japan. Their own interest in history being intermittent and intended to soothe, rather than disturb, it was difficult to keep Americans aware of Japan's long hatred of them—for segregation policies in California, for immigration discriminations, for the simple fact that Americans could not concentrate upon the Japanese or take them seriously. Japanese aggression in Manchuria in 1931 flickered in the public consciousness and went out, though it continued into 1932 and 1933. The savage attacks on Chinese cities in succeeding years appeared and disappeared in the public press like forest and hotel fires or street riots in Central American countries. The staggering nature of the Japanese military build-up was unheralded and unsung. Even the sinking of the United States gunboat, *Panay,* in the Yangtze River, December 12, 1937, made a brief sensation and sank out of sight, once the Tokyo government had apologized, paid indemnities, and gone through other diplomatic formalities.

The Japanese government fell more heavily to the militarists. The United States government had maintained an attitude of moral condemnation of Japanese military brutalities while permitting the sale to Japan of oil, steel, and other materials essential to war. This policy was based on fears that Americans were not ready for battle, and that cutting off such supplies would send Japan off on another military adventure against the oil-bearing Dutch East Indies. The Japanese could, in effect, have soothed Americans while quietly making firmer their program of a "Monroe Doctrine for the Far East." Instead, their war party prepared for a great adventure. Their strategy was, essentially, that which had guided Germany in 1917: they would destroy American lifelines in the Pacific, and take over and make impregnable fortresses throughout the Far East before Americans were prepared to mount a counteroffensive. On December 6, 1941, Roosevelt, fully apprised of Japanese movements in the South Pacific, appealed to the Japanese emperor in behalf of peace.

Personal Appeal to Hirohito

Almost a century ago the President of the United States addressed to the Emperor of Japan a message extending an offer of friendship of the people of the United States to the people of Japan. That offer was accepted, and in the long period of unbroken peace and friendship which has followed, our respective Nations, through the virtues of their people and the wisdom of their rulers, have prospered and have substantially helped humanity.

Only in situations of extraordinary importance to our two countries need I address to Your Majesty messages on matters of state. I feel I should now so address you because of the deep and far-reaching emergency which appears to be in formation. . . .

More than a year ago Your Majesty's Government concluded an agreement with the Vichy Government by which five or six thousand Japanese troops were permitted to enter into Northern French Indo-China for the protection of Japanese troops which were operating against China further north. And this spring and summer the Vichy Government permitted further Japanese military forces to enter into Southern French Indo-China for the common defense of French Indo-China. I think I am correct in saying that no attack has been made upon Indo-China, nor that any has been contemplated.

During the past few weeks it has become clear to the world that Japanese military, naval, and air forces have been sent to Southern

Indo-China in such large numbers as to create a reasonable doubt on the part of other Nations that this continuing concentration in Indo-China is not defensive in its character.

Because these continuing concentrations in Indo-China have reached such large proportions and because they extend now to the southeast and the southwest corners of that peninsula, it is only reasonable that the people of the Philippines, of the hundreds of islands of the East Indies, of Malaya, and of Thailand itself are asking themselves whether these forces of Japan are preparing or intending to make attack in one or more of these many directions.

I am sure that Your Majesty will understand that the fear of all these peoples is a legitimate fear inasmuch as it involves their peace and their national existence. I am sure that Your Majesty will understand why the people of the United States in such large numbers look askance to the establishment of military, naval, and air bases manned and equipped so greatly as to constitute armed forces capable of measures of offense.

It is clear that a continuance of such a situation is unthinkable.

None of the peoples whom I have spoken of above can sit either indefinitely or permanently on a keg of dynamite.

There is absolutely no thought on the part of the United States of invading Indo-China if every Japanese soldier or sailor were to be withdrawn therefrom.

I think that we can obtain the same assurance from the Governments of the East Indies, the Governments of Malaya, and the Government of Thailand. I would even undertake to ask for the same assurance on the part of the Government of China. Thus a withdrawal of the Japanese forces from Indo-China would result in the assurance of peace throughout the whole of the South Pacific area.

I address myself to Your Majesty at this moment in the fervent hope that Your Majesty may, as I am doing, give thought in this definite emergency to ways of dispelling the dark clouds. I am confident that both of us, for the sake of the peoples not only of our own great countries but for the sake of humanity in neighboring territories, have a sacred duty to restore traditional amity and prevent further death and destruction in the world.

The Japanese saw no need for diplomatic niceties. American punctilio appeared to them a species of hypocrisy and stupidity. Captured films later showed Japanese air force personnel relaxing before taking off for

Pearl Harbor, listening with hilarity to a Honolulu broadcast of nightclub music. Several of them, to the amusement of their mates, mimicked American pilots dancing jazzily, their eyes rolled up to the ceiling in ecstasy. The Japanese planes struck Pearl Harbor with shattering effect on the morning of December 7, 1941. In less than two hours, 19 American ships had been sunk or disabled, five of them battleships. Some 2,400 men were dead. Aircraft to the number of 120 were shattered. The following day, a grim President went on the radio to address the American people. Forgotten were the blandishments of the Fireside and election promises. He offered leadership and issued a call to arms.

"A Date Which Will Live in Infamy"

Yesterday, December 7, 1941—a date which will live in infamy— the United States of America was suddenly and deliberately attacked by naval and air forces of the Empire of Japan.

The United States was at peace with that nation and, at the solicitation of Japan, was still in conversation with its government and its Emperor looking toward the maintenance of peace in the Pacific. Indeed, one hour after Japanese air squadrons had commenced bombing in Oahu, the Japanese ambassador to the United States and his colleague delivered to the Secretary of State a formal reply to a recent American message. While this reply stated that it seemed useless to continue the existing diplomatic negotiations, it contained no threat or hint of war or armed attack.

It will be recorded that the distance of Hawaii from Japan makes it obvious that the attack was deliberately planned many days or even weeks ago. During the intervening time the Japanese Government has deliberately sought to deceive the United States by false statements and expressions of hope for continued peace.

The attack yesterday on the Hawaiian Islands has caused severe damage to American naval and military forces. Very many American lives have been lost. In addition American ships have been reported torpedoed on the high seas between San Francisco and Honolulu.

Yesterday the Japanese government also launched an attack against Malaya.

Last night Japanese forces attacked Hong Kong.

Last night Japanese forces attacked Guam.

Last night Japanese forces attacked the Philippine Islands.

249

Last night the Japanese attacked Wake Island.

This morning the Japanese attacked Midway Island.

Japan has, therefore, undertaken a surprise offensive extending throughout the Pacific area. The facts of yesterday speak for themselves. The people of the United States have already formed their opinions and well understand the implications to the very life and safety of our nation.

As Commander-in-Chief of the Army and Navy, I have directed that all measures be taken for our defense.

Always will we remember the character of the onslaught against us.

No matter how long it may take us to overcome this premeditated invasion, the American people in their righteous might will win through to absolute victory.

I believe I interpret the will of the Congress and of the people when I assert that we will not only defend ourselves to the uttermost but will make very certain that this form of treachery shall never endanger us again.

Hostilities exist. There is no blinking at the fact that our people, our territory and our interests are in grave danger.

With confidence in our armed forces—with the unbounding determination of our people—we will gain the inevitable triumph —so help us God.

I ask that the Congress declare that since the unprovoked and dastardly attack by Japan on Sunday, December 7th, a state of war has existed between the United States and the Japanese Empire.

Miraculously, the Japanese failed to follow up their advantage. Attacks on Alaskan outposts and West Coast cities might well have bewildered a nation no longer habituated to storm and cooperation at home, and might have given Japan precious time for securing her hold on vital centers in the Far East. Instead, Americans were permitted time to mobilize their huge manpower and technology and resources for war purposes. The War Production Board was established, January 16, 1942. In succeeding months, the War Shipping Board, the National Housing Agency, the War Manpower Commission, the Office of War Information and other agencies went into high gear. Various commands were created: the European Theater of Operations, the Southwest Pacific Command, the Mediterranean Theater of Operations, and others in the Pacific, Caribbean, South America, the Middle East, and the Persian Gulf. Through the now mighty office of The Quartermaster General poured forth plans and orders that affected a major portion of the economy. American industry began its astounding feat—unachieved during World War I—of producing for war and domestic consumption at the same time. Scrap metal drives were curtailed, as industrial alloys made "tin" for canned foods available to the folks at home. There were rationed goods and difficulties in obtaining some services and commodities, but, by and large, sacrifices were at a minimum.

Heroes began to appear. U.S. Navy Lt. Edward H. O'Hare, attached to the aircraft carrier, *Lexington*, on February 20, 1942, separated from his teammates, "interposed his plane between his ship and an enemy formation of nine attacking twin-engined heavy bombers," and brought down five and damaged another, in the face of intense machine gun and cannon fire. General Jonathan Wainwright, defending Corregidor in the Philippines and isolated from American forces, fought on with exemplary devotion. The giant figure of General Douglas MacArthur, in the Pacific sector, captured the public imagination partly thanks to his distinguished figure and remarkable military prose. In the European Theater, which swarmed with notables of land, sea, and air, General Dwight D. Eisenhower less dramatically established his dependability and staying powers.

On December 4, 1942, the President gave WPA its "honorable discharge," last units being incorporated into defense activities. The Depression Era was officially ended; the outlines of the coming era were dim. Roosevelt struggled with war tasks, in June of 1943 coping with the coal miners, who had offered strikes and threats of strikes in furtherance of their demands. In August, he pledged independence to the Filipinos. The infinite war continued. The Russians, whom Allied leaders had feared might have been drained of military strength by their interparty bloodletting, and who had not appeared at their military best against "little Finland," fought with colossal courage and effect. They turned the defense of Stalingrad into a heroic victory. They lifted the sieges of Moscow and Leningrad. In North Africa, the Nazis were hard-driven by forces headed by English and American commanders. Readers of the daily press could hardly fail to note the increasing strength of American operations in the Pacific. They became acquainted with the Solomon Islands, the Coral Sea, Midway Island, and especially Guadalcanal. By November 1943, Americans had turned a defensive series of actions into an offensive operation.

Meanwhile, the President pondered peace. Of the League of Nations only a ghost remained. A new agency for world order would have to be created. But also, the victims of the war would have to be fed, if they were not to descend to riot and confusion, once the Axis powers were defeated. A halfway house to peace was created by the establishment of the United Nations Relief and Rehabilitation Administration, November 9, 1943.

UNRRA

Gentlemen, on behalf of the host Nations, I welcome you to this historic conference.

Here in the White House seated about a table in the historic East Room are representatives of 44 Nations—United Nations and those associated with them.

The people of these 44 Nations include approximately 80 percent of the human race, now united by a common devotion to the cause of civilization and by a common determination to build for the future a world of decency and security, and above all peace.

Representatives of these 44 Nations—you gentlemen who represent them—have just signed an agreement creating the United Nations Relief and Rehabilitation Administration—commonly known as U.N.R.R.A.

This agency will help to put into practical effect some of the high purposes that were set forth in the declaration of the United Nations on January 1, 1942.

Coming after the Declarations of Moscow recently, this agreement shows that we mean business in this war in a political and humanitarian sense, just as surely as we mean business in a military sense. It is one more strong link joining the United Nations and their associates in facing problems of mutual need and mutual interest.

The agreement which we have all just signed is based on a preamble in which the United Nations declare that they are ". . . determined that immediately upon the liberation of any area . . . the population thereof shall receive aid and relief from their sufferings, food, clothing and shelter, aid in the prevention of pestilence and in the recovery of the health of the people, and that preparation and arrangements shall be made for the return of prisoners and exiles to their homes and for assistance in the resumption of urgently needed agricultural and industrial production and the restoration of essential services." That is the preamble of the agreement which has just been signed here today.

All of the United Nations agree to cooperate and share in the work of U.N.R.R.A.—each Nation according to its own individual resources—and to provide relief and help in rehabilitation for the victims of German and Japanese barbarism.

It is hard for us to grasp the magnitude of the needs in occupied countries.

The Germans and the Japanese have carried on their campaigns of plunder and destruction with one purpose in mind: that in the lands they occupy there shall be left only a generation of half-men —undernourished, crushed in body and spirit, without strength or incentive to hope—ready, in fact, to be enslaved and used as beasts of burden by the self-styled master races.

The occupied countries have been robbed of their foodstuffs and raw materials, and even of the agricultural and industrial machinery upon which their workers must depend for employment. The Germans have been planning systematically to make the other countries economic vassals, utterly dependent upon, and completely subservient to the Nazi tyrants.

Responsibility for alleviating the suffering and misery occasioned by this so-called New Order must be assumed not by any individual Nation but by all of the united and associated Nations acting together. No one country could—or should, for that matter—attempt to bear the burden of meeting the vast relief needs—either in money or in supplies.

The work confronting U.N.R.R.A. is immediate and urgent. As it now begins its operations, many of the most fertile food regions of the world are either under Axis domination, or have been stripped by the practice of the dictatorships to make themselves self-sustaining on other peoples' lands. Additional regions will almost inevitably be blackened as the German and Japanese forces in their retreat scorch the earth behind them.

So, it will be the task of U.N.R.R.A. to operate in these areas of food shortages until the resumption of peaceful occupations enables the liberated peoples once more to assume the full burden of their own support. It will be for U.N.R.R.A., first to assure a fair distribution of available supplies among all of the liberated peoples, and second, to ward off death by starvation or exposure among these peoples.

It would be supreme irony for us to win a victory, and then to inherit world chaos simply because we were unprepared to meet what we know we shall have to meet. We know the human wants that will follow liberation. Many ruthlessly shattered cities and villages in Russia, China, and Italy provide horrible evidence of what the defeated retreating Germans and Japanese will leave behind.

It is not only humane and charitable for the United Nations to supply medicine and food and other necessities to the peoples freed from Axis control; it is a clear matter of enlightened self-interest— and of military strategic necessity. This was apparent to us even before the Germans were ousted from any of the territories under their control.

But we need not any longer speculate. We have had nearly a year of experience in French Africa—and later experience in Sicily and in Italy.

In French North Africa, the United Nations have given assistance in the form of seeds, agricultural supplies, and agricultural equipment, and have made it possible for the people there to increase their harvest.

After years of looting by the Germans, the people of French Africa are now able to supply virtually all of their own food needs. And that in just one year. Besides, they are meeting important needs of the Allied armed forces in French Africa, in Sicily, and Italy, and giving much of the civilian labor which assists our armed forces there in loading and unloading ships.

The assistance rendered to the liberated peoples of French Africa was a joint venture of Great Britain and the United States.

The next step, as in the case of other joint operations of the United Nations, is to handle the problems of supply for the liberated areas on a United Nations basis—rather than on the cooperation of only two Nations.

We have shown that while the war lasts, whenever we help the liberated peoples with essential supplies and services, we hasten the day of the defeat of the Axis powers.

When victory comes there can certainly be no secure peace until there is a return of law and order in the oppressed countries, until the peoples of these countries have been restored to a normal, healthy, and self-sustaining existence. This means that the more quickly and effectually we apply measures of relief and rehabilitation, the more quickly will our own boys overseas be able to come home.

We have acted together with the other United Nations in harnessing our raw materials, our production, and our other resources to defeat the common enemy. We have worked together with the United Nations in full agreement and action in the fighting on land, and on the sea and in the air. We are now about to take an additional step in the combined actions that are necessary to win the war and to build the foundation for a secure peace. . . .

As the giant work of construction and destruction went on, the world leaders considered battle strategy and objectives. F.D.R. treated these matters on a personal level; he undertook to win Stalin's good will, and called him "Uncle Joe," and he developed a dislike for the exiled Resistance leader, General Charles de Gaulle. Later, discussing the Near East with Ibn Saud of Saudi Arabia, he felt he had "learned more about that whole problem . . . by talking . . . for five minutes than I could have learned in exchange of two or three dozen letters." At Casablanca, in January 1943, he called for unconditional surrender of the enemy. He traveled to Quebec in August to discuss Anglo-American cooperation and war tactics. In December, he met with Churchill and Stalin at Teheran in order to initiate joint discussions at close range on war policy and the coming peace.

In May of 1944, he was asked if he intended to run for a fourth term of office. Time will tell, he answered. On July 14, he told the world that he would accept the office, reluctantly, "if I am so ordered by the Commander in Chief of us all—the sovereign people of the United States." Utilizing humor, drama, New Deal-type promises, the growing succession of victories in the field, confounding doubts about his health, and with a new vice-presidential candidate in tow, Senator Harry S. Truman of Missouri, he swept to a far from overwhelming victory—303,193 votes, out of 47,630,044 votes cast, redistributed among twelve states would have made Thomas E. Dewey President of the United States.*

Was Roosevelt wrong to press for a fourth term with his knowing of his ill health? Did he take too much upon himself in a personal diplomacy that served the Soviet Union probably more than it did the interests of the people of the United States? The President was but a man, who had given heart and leadership to a nation that dearly needed both. He was aided and opposed by formidable parties and personalities who had money and communication vehicles for trying to qualify such of his decisions as they could prove ill-advised and inadequate. The President had always rested his case in democratic processes. Now, in his Fourth Inaugural Address, January 20, 1945, he told his countrymen: "We have learned to be citizens of the world, members of the human community." At Yalta, the next month, he sought to implement this affirmation in decisions reached with Churchill and Stalin; the French were not invited to the conference. The three Allied chieftains anticipated the defeat of Germany and its occupation; the organization of a United Nations at San Francisco, April 25; plans for a democratic Poland, now in Red Army hands, and an anti-fascist Yugoslavia; as well as plans for regular meetings of their foreign secretaries, to organize "for peace as for war." F.D.R. explained his hopes for the Yalta agreement in his Message to Congress, March 1, 1945.

* Svend Petersen, *A Statistical History of the American Presidential Elections* (1963), p. 99.

Yalta

. . . I come from the Crimean Conference, my fellow Americans, with a firm belief that we have made a good start on the road to a world of peace.

There were two main purposes in this Crimean Conference. The first was to bring defeat to Germany with the greatest possible speed and the smallest possible loss of Allied men. That purpose is now being carried out in great force. The German Army, and the German people, are feeling the ever-increasing might of our fighting men and of the Allied armies. Every hour gives us added pride in the heroic advance of our troops over German soil, toward a meeting with the gallant Red Army.

The second purpose was to continue to build the foundation for an international accord which would bring order and security after the chaos of the war, and would give some assurance of lasting peace among the nations of the world.

Toward that goal, a tremendous stride has been made.

At Teheran, over a year ago, there were long-range military plans laid by the Chiefs of Staff of the three most powerful nations. Among the civilian leaders at Teheran, however, at that time, there were only exchanges of views and expressions of opinion. No political arrangements were made—and none was attempted.

At the Crimean Conference, however, the time had come for getting down to specific cases in the political field.

There was on all sides at this Conference an enthusiastic effort to reach agreement. Since the time of the Teheran Conference there had developed among all of us a greater facility in negotiating with each other, which augurs well for the peace of the world.

I had never for an instant wavered in my belief that an agreement to insure world peace and security can be reached.

The lapse of time between Teheran and Yalta without conferences of civilian representatives of the three major powers has proved to be too long—fourteen months. During this long period, local problems were permitted to become acute in places like Poland and Greece and Italy and Yugoslavia.

Therefore we decided at Yalta that even if circumstances made it impossible for the heads of the three Governments to meet more often in the future, we could make sure that there would be more frequent personal contacts for the exchange of views. Accordingly, we arranged for periodic meetings of the foreign secretaries of

Great Britain, Russia and the United States at intervals of three or four months. I feel very confident that under this arrangement there will be no recurrence of the incidents which this winter disturbed the friends of world-wide collaboration.

When we met at Yalta, in addition to laying our strategic and tactical plans for the final and complete victory over Germany, there were other problems of vital political consequence.

First, there were the problems of occupation and control of Germany after victory, the complete destruction of her military power, and the assurance that neither Nazism nor Prussian militarism could again be revived to threaten the peace and civilization of the world.

Second, there was the settlement of the few differences which remained among us with respect to the International Security Organization after the Dumbarton Oaks Conference.

Third, there were the general political and economic problems common to all of the areas that had been or would be liberated from the Nazi yoke.

Fourth, there were the special problems created by Poland and Yugoslavia.

Days were spent in discussing these momentous matters. We argued freely and frankly across the table. But at the end, on every point, unanimous agreement was reached. And more important even than the agreement of words, I may say we achieved a unity of thought and a way of getting along together.

It was Hitler's hope that we would not agree—that some slight crack might appear in the solid wall of Allied unity that would give him and his fellow gangsters one last hope of escaping their just doom. That is the objective for which his propaganda machine has been working for many months.

But Hitler has failed.

Never before have the major Allies been more closely united—not only in their war aims but in their peace aims. And they are determined to continue to be united with each other—and with all peace-loving nations—so that the ideal of lasting peace will become a reality.

The Soviet, British and United States Chiefs of Staff held daily meetings with each other, and conferred frequently with Marshal Stalin, with Prime Minister Churchill and with me, on the problems of coordinating the strategic and tactical efforts of all the Allied forces. They completed their plans for the final knock-out blows to Germany.

At the time of the Teheran Conference, the Russian front was so far removed from the American and British fronts that, while certain long-range strategic cooperation was possible, there could be no tactical, day-by-day coordination. But Russian troops have now crossed Poland and are fighting on the eastern soil of Germany; British and American troops are now on German soil close to the Rhine River in the west. It is a different situation today; a closer tactical liaison has become possible—for the first time in Europe— and, in the Crimean Conference, this has been accomplished.

Provision was made for daily exchange of information between the armies under command of General Eisenhower and those under command of the Soviet marshals on the Eastern Front, and our armies in Italy—without the necessity of going through the Chiefs of Staff in Washington or London, as in the past.

You have seen one result of this exchange of information in the recent bombings by American and English aircraft of points which are directly related to the Russian advance on Berlin.

From now on, American and British heavy bombers will be used —in the day-by-day tactics of the war—in direct support of Soviet armies, as well as in the support of our own in the Western Front.

They are now engaged in bombing and strafing in order to hamper the movements of German reserves, German materials, to the Eastern and Western Fronts from other parts of Germany and from Italy. . . .

There will be no respite for them. We will not desist for one moment from unconditional surrender. . . .

We made it clear again at Yalta, and I now repeat—that unconditional surrender does not mean the destruction or enslavement of the German people. The Nazi leaders have deliberately withheld that part of the Yalta Declaration from the German press and radio. They seek to convince the people of Germany that the Yalta Declaration does mean slavery and destruction for them—for that is how the Nazis hope to save their own skins, and to deceive their people into continued useless resistance.

We did, however, make it clear at the Conference just what unconditional surrender does mean for Germany.

It means the temporary control of Germany by Great Britain, Russia, France and the United States. Each of these nations will occupy and control a separate zone of Germany—and the administration of the four zones will be coordinated in Berlin by a Control Council composed of representatives of the four nations.

Unconditional surrender also means the end of Nazism and of the Nazi Party—and all of its barbaric laws and institutions.

It means the termination of all militaristic influence in the public, private and cultural life of Germany.

It means for the Nazi war criminals a punishment that is speedy and just—and severe.

It means the complete disarmament of Germany; the destruction of its militarism and its military equipment; the end of its production of armament; the dispersal of all its armed forces; the permanent dismemberment of the German General Staff, which has so often shattered the peace of the world.

It means that Germany will have to make reparations in kind for the damage which has been done to the innocent victims of its aggression.

By compelling reparations in kind—in plants and machinery and rolling stock and raw materials—we shall avoid the mistake that we and other people made after the last war of demanding reparations in the form of money, which Germany could never pay.

We do not want the German people to starve or become a burden on the rest of the world.

Our objective in handling Germany is simple—it is to secure the peace of the future world. Too much experience has shown that that objective is impossible if Germany is allowed to retain any ability to wage aggressive war.

That objective will not harm the German people. On the contrary, it will protect them from a repetition of the fate which the General Staff and Kaiserism imposed on them before, and which Hitlerism is now imposing on them again a hundredfold. It will be removing a cancer from the German body, which for generations has produced only misery and pain for the whole world. . . .

I had read about Warsaw and Lidice and Rotterdam and Coventry—but I *saw* Sevastopol and Yalta! And I know that there is not room enough on earth for both German militarism and Christian decency.

Of equal importance with the military arrangements at the Crimean Conference were the agreements reached with respect to a general international organization for lasting world peace. The foundations were laid at Dumbarton Oaks. . . .

A Conference of all the United Nations of the world will meet in San Francisco on April twenty-fifth, 1945. There, we all hope, and confidently expect, to execute a definite charter of organization under which the peace of the world will be preserved and the forces of aggression permanently outlawed.

This time we shall not make the mistake of waiting until the end of the war to set up the machinery of peace. This time, as we fight together to get the war over quickly, we work together to keep it from happening again.

I am well aware of the constitutional fact—as are all the United Nations—that this charter must be approved by two-thirds of the Senate of the United States—as will some of the other arrangements made at Yalta.

The Senate of the United States, through its appropriate representatives, has been kept continuously advised of the program of this Government in the creation of the International Security Organization.

The Senate and the House of Representatives will both be represented at the San Francisco Conference. The Congressional delegates will consist of an equal number of Republican and Democratic members. The American delegation is—in every sense of the word—bipartisan. . . .

The structure of world peace cannot be the work of one man, or one party, or one nation. It cannot be an American peace, or a British peace, or a Russian, or a French or a Chinese peace. It cannot be a peace of large nations—or of small nations. It must be a peace which rests on the cooperative effort of the whole world. . . .

The three most powerful nations have agreed that the political and economic problems of any area liberated from Nazi conquest, or any former Axis satellite, are a joint responsibility of all three Governments. They will join together, during the temporary period of instability after hostilities, to help the people of any liberated area, or of any former satellite state, to solve their own problems through firmly established democratic processes.

They will endeavor to see to it that interim governing authorities are as representative as possible of all democratic elements in the population, and that free elections are held as soon as possible.

Responsibility for political conditions thousands of miles overseas can no longer be avoided by this great nation. As I have said, it is a smaller world. The United States now exerts a vast influence in the cause of peace throughout all the world. We will continue to exert that influence only if we are willing to continue to share in the responsibility for keeping the peace. It would be our own tragic loss were we to shirk that responsibility.

Final decisions in these areas are going to be made jointly; and therefore they will often be a result of give-and-take compromise.

The United States will not always have its way one hundred per cent—nor will Russia, or Great Britain. We shall not always have ideal solutions to complicated international problems, even though we are determined continuously to strive toward the ideal. But I am sure that—under the agreements reached at Yalta—there will be a more stable political Europe than ever before. . . .

One outstanding example of joint action by the three major Allies in the liberated areas was the solution reached on Poland. The whole Polish question was a potential source of trouble in post-war Europe, and we came to the Conference determined to find a common ground for its solution. We did.

Our objective was to help create a strong, independent and prosperous nation with a Government ultimately to be selected by the Polish people themselves.

To achieve that objective, it was necessary to provide for the formation of a new Government, much more representative than had been possible while Poland was enslaved. Accordingly, steps were taken at Yalta to reorganize the existing Provisional Government in Poland on a broader democratic basis, so as to include democratic leaders now in Poland and those abroad. This new, reorganized Government will be recognized by all of us as the temporary Government of Poland.

However, the new Polish Provisional Government of National Unity will be pledged to hold a free election as soon as possible on the basis of universal suffrage and a secret ballot.

Throughout history, Poland has been the corridor through which attacks on Russia have been made. Twice in this generation, Germany has struck at Russia through this corridor. To insure European security and world peace, a strong and independent Poland is necessary. . . .

I am convinced that the agreement on Poland, under the circumstances, is the most hopeful agreement possible for a free, independent and prosperous Polish State.

The Crimean Conference was a meeting of the three major military powers on whose shoulders rest the chief responsibility and burden of the war. Although, for this reason, France was not a participant in the Conference, no one should detract from the recognition that was accorded of her role in the future of Europe and of the world. . . .

Agreement was reached on Yugoslavia, as announced in the communiqué, and is in process of fulfillment.

Quite naturally, the Crimean Conference concerned itself only with the European War and with the political problems of Europe —and not with the Pacific War.

At Yalta, however, our Combined British and American Staffs made their plans to increase the attack against Japan. . . .

It is still a tough, long road to Tokyo. The defeat of Germany will not mean the end of the war against Japan. On the contrary, America must be prepared for a long and costly struggle in the Pacific.

But the unconditional surrender of Japan is as essential as the defeat of Germany—if our plans for world peace are to succeed. For Japanese militarism must be wiped out as thoroughly as German militarism. . . .

HARRY S. TRUMAN

(1884–   )

The Party Line

Almost a year ago, in company with 16 free nations of Europe, we launched the greatest cooperative economic program in history. The purpose of that unprecedented effort is to invigorate and strengthen democracy in Europe, so that the free people of that continent can resume their rightful place in the forefront of civilization and can contribute once more to the security and welfare of the world.

Our efforts have brought new hope to all mankind. We have beaten back despair and defeatism. We have saved a number of countries from losing their liberty. Hundreds of millions of people all over the world now agree with us, that we need not have war—that we can have peace.

The initiative is ours.

Inaugural Address, *January 20, 1949*

PEOPLE were quickly becoming aware that F.D.R. looked old and sick—almost Wilsonian in his pallid and stricken features. Suddenly, on April 12, 1945, he was gone. At his Warm Springs, Georgia, home, while preparing a speech, he had complained: "I have a terrific headache." Soon after, he was dead of a cerebral hemorrhage, caused by progressive arteriosclerosis. Adolf Hitler, in his Berlin bunker, danced gleefully at the news, persuaded that fate was once more intervening in his behalf. Perhaps some Americans received word of the event with satisfaction, but most of them remembered a great and remarkable leader. Those who followed press accounts and the long radio requiem for the deceased learned of his unfinished speech, intended for delivery April 13, to commemorate Jefferson day. In it he spelled "democrats" with a small *d*, and compared the times of Jefferson with modern times of mighty armaments and Allied forces that were "destroying the makers of war, the breeders of hatred, in Europe and in Asia." But victory was not enough, he emphasized:

Today, as we move against the terrible scourge of war—as we go forward toward the greatest contribution that any generation of

263

human beings can make in this world—the contribution of lasting peace, I ask you to keep up your faith. I measure the sound, solid achievement that can be made at this time by the straight edge of your own confidence and your resolve. And to you, and to all Americans who dedicate themselves with us to the making of an abiding peace, I say:

The only limit to our realization of tomorrow will be our doubts of today. Let us move forward with strong and active faith.

He left the presidency to a man whom professional observers saw as small, untalented, insecure. No one questioned Harry Truman's personal probity, his willingness to give the best that he had, his homely character, or his good will and patriotism. But the utterly accidental nature of his rise to the presidency startled them. This son of a Missouri farmer was cut out for anything but world crisis leadership. Born and raised on the family farm, with weak eyes that lost him a West Point opportunity, he had worked at trifling jobs in Kansas City before returning for another ten years to farm life. He was a World War I hero who emerged a major, lost $15,000 in a haberdashery venture, and paid off the debt for the following fourteen years. Boss Tom Pendergast of Kansas City—then one of the wide open, gaudy, dissolute towns of America—helped him make a modest beginning as a county judge. "I'm a Jackson County Democrat," said Truman, years later, "and proud of it." He became a faithful, efficient administrator of some 64 road supervisers (who, under a less lavish budget—for which the impeccable Truman shared no responsibility—were reduced to 16) and administered three million dollars for the building of the county courthouse, emerging with a $36,000 surplus. For his faithful services he hoped, in 1934, to be given a $25,000 collectorship, but it had been promised to someone else, and Pendergast delivered himself of an immortal sentence: "The best I can do right now, Harry, is a U.S. Senatorship."

Pendergast voted the graveyards to put Truman into the Senate, and never asked him to do a dishonest deed. When, in 1939, Pendergast was indicted and sent to prison for gross corruption, Truman declared: "I won't desert a ship in distress." Moreover, he sought energetically to block the reappointment of United States District Attorney Maurice M. Milligan, who had sent Pendergast to prison. Ironically, Milligan helped advance Truman's career; by entering the Senatorial race in 1940, he split the votes of the anti-Truman faction and helped keep him in the Senate.

Truman applied for active duty when war began, but was turned down on the grounds of age. At his own expense he toured the country's military centers and observed the waste and confusion present in them. He returned to request a Senatorial committee to investigate the conduct of war preparations and production. His long years of plodding, patient, fair, and honest work sustained and established him, for his committee did not seek or create sensations: it acted as watchdog over war contracts and their execution. It investigated, and recommended, and played no favorites. F.D.R. approved such patently worthwhile industry, such patriotic service. Truman attracted respect. The Senate press gallery had voted him the civilian who next to the President "knows most about the war." F.D.R. was impatient with the incumbent Vice-President, Henry A. Wallace of Iowa. Truman had no interest in the vice presidency, but was persuaded to accept the nomination in 1944. The *Manchester Guardian* felt that the sloughing off of Wallace by the administration "may seem to many Americans to mark the end of the liberal epoch."

The *Guardian* failed to perceive the principles by which the trim grey man with the firm mouth and double-breasted suits operated. Those principles were not liberal or conservative. They involved personal and party loyalty, and a patriotism that had enabled him to criticize the White House itself, when it had appeared to his committee that the White House was responsible for defects in the war program. These principles Pendergast had respected, and Roosevelt had respected. They enabled Truman, when Germany fell, to felicitate Stalin on the event and to remark:

> You have demonstrated in all your campaigns what it is possible to accomplish when a free people under superlative leadership and with unfailing courage rise against the forces of barbarism.

And they enabled him to move into world politics with ease and without qualms. On June 26, 1945, he addressed the newly formed United Nations, picking up from where his late chief had left the enterprise.

U. N.

Mr. Chairman* and Delegates to the United Nations Conference on International Organization:

I deeply regret that the press of circumstances when this Conference opened made it impossible for me to be here to greet you in person. I have asked for the privilege of coming today, to express on behalf of the people of the United States our thanks for what you have done here, and to wish you Godspeed on your journeys home.

Somewhere is this broad country, every one of you can find some of our citizens who are sons and daughters, or descendants in

* Secretary of State Edward R. Stettinius.

some degree, of your own native land. All our people are glad and proud that this historic meeting and its accomplishments have taken place in our country. And that includes the millions of loyal and patriotic Americans who stem from the countries not represented at this Conference.

We are grateful to you for coming. We hope you have enjoyed your stay, and that you will come again.

You assembled in San Francisco nine weeks ago with the high hope and confidence of peace-loving people the world over.

Their confidence in you has been justified.

Their hope for your success has been fulfilled.

The Charter of the United Nations which you have just signed is a solid structure upon which we can build a better world. History will honor you for it. Between the victory in Europe and the final victory in Japan, in this most destructive of all wars, you have won a victory against war itself.

It was the hope of such a Charter that helped sustain the courage of stricken peoples through the darkest days of the war. For it is a declaration of great faith by the nations of the earth—faith that war is not inevitable, faith that peace can be maintained.

If we had had this Charter a few years ago—and above all, the will to use it—millions now dead would be alive. If we should falter in the future in our will to use it, millions now living will surely die.

It has already been said by many that this is only a first step to a lasting peace. That is true. The important thing is that all our thinking and all our actions be based on the realization that it is in fact only a first step. Let us all have it firmly in mind that we start today from a good beginning and, with our eye always on the final objective, let us march forward.

The Constitution of my own country came from a Convention which—like this one—was made up of delegates with many different views. Like this Charter, our Constitution came from a free and sometimes bitter exchange of conflicting opinions. When it was adopted, no one regarded it as a perfect document. But it grew and developed and expanded. And upon it there was built a bigger, a better, a more perfect union.

This Charter, like our own Constitution, will be expanded and improved as time goes on. No one claims that it is now a final or a perfect instrument. It has not been poured into any fixed mold. Changing world conditions will require readjustments—but they will be the readjustments of peace and not of war.

That we now have this Charter at all is a great wonder. It is also a cause for profound thinksgiving to Almighty God, who has brought us so far in our search for peace through world organization.

There were many who doubted that agreement could ever be reached by these fifty countries differing so much in race and religion, in language and culture. But these differences were all forgotten in one unshakable unity of determination—to find a way to end wars. . . .

We have tested the principle of cooperation in this war and have found that it works. Through the pooling of resources, through joint and combined military command, through constant staff meetings, we have shown what united strength can do in war. That united strength forced Germany to surrender. United strength will force Japan to surrender.

The United Nations have also had experience, even while the fighting was still going on, in reaching economic agreements for times of peace. What was done on the subject of relief at Atlantic City, food at Hot Springs, finance at Bretton Woods, aviation at Chicago, was a fair test of what can be done by nations determined to live cooperatively in a world where they cannot live peacefully any other way.

What you have accomplished in San Francisco shows how well these lessons of military and economic cooperation have been learned. You have created a great instrument for peace and security and human progress in the world.

The world must now use it! . . .

There is a time for making plans—and there is a time for action. The time for action is now! Let us, therefore, each in his own nation and according to its own way, seek immediate approval of this Charter—and make it a living thing.

I shall send this Charter to the United States Senate at once. I am sure that the overwhelming sentiment of the people of my country and of their representatives in the Senate is in favor of immediate ratification.

A just and lasting peace cannot be attained by diplomatic agreement alone, or by military cooperation alone. Experience has shown how deeply the seeds of war are planted by economic rivalry and by social injustice. The Charter recognizes this fact for it has provided for economic and social cooperation as well. It has provided for this cooperation as part of the very heart of the entire compact.

It has set up machinery of international cooperation which men and nations of good will can use to help correct economic and social causes for conflict.

Artificial and uneconomic trade barriers should be removed—to the end that the standard of living of as many people as possible throughout the world may be raised. For Freedom from Want is one of the basic Four Freedoms toward which we all strive. The large and powerful nations of the world must assume leadership in this economic field as in all others.

Under this document we have good reason to expect the framing of an international bill of rights, acceptable to all the nations involved. That bill of rights will be as much a part of international life as our own Bill of Rights is a part of our Constitution. The Charter is dedicated to the achievement and observance of human rights and fundamental freedoms. Unless we can attain those objectives for all men and women everywhere—without regard to race, language or religion—we cannot have permanent peace and security.

With this Charter the world can begin to look forward to the time when all worthy human beings may be permitted to live decently as free people.

The world has learned again that nations, like individuals, must know the truth if they would be free—must read and hear the truth, learn and teach the truth.

We must set up an effective agency for constant and thorough interchange of thought and ideas. For there lies the road to a better and more tolerant understanding among nations and among peoples.

All Fascism did not die with Mussolini. Hitler is finished—but the seeds spread by his disordered mind have firm root in too many fanatical brains. It is easier to remove tyrants and destroy concentration camps than it is to kill the ideas which gave them birth and strength. Victory on the battlefield was essential, but it was not enough. For a good peace, a lasting peace, the decent peoples of the earth must remain determined to strike down the evil spirit which has hung over the world for the last decade. . . .

No philosophical doubts disturbed Truman as the atom bomb became available. Before him was the alternative of a mass invasion of Japan by American armed forces—men who would have fallen by the tens of thousands, and meted out death in comparable numbers. The atom bomb offered the chance of a quick end to the war—as the result of a frightful and indiscriminate sowing of death, to be sure, but differing only in the novelty of the instrument from the "saturation" bombings that had devastated English and German, as well as Japanese, cities. On August 6, 1945, Truman issued the statement that separated the historic past from the present.

Hiroshima

Sixteen hours ago an American airplane dropped one bomb on Hiroshima, an important Japanese Army base. That bomb had more power than 20,000 tons of T.N.T. It had more than two thousand times the blast power of the British "Grand Slam" which is the largest bomb ever yet used in the history of warfare.

The Japanese began the war from the air at Pearl Harbor. They have been repaid many fold. And the end is not yet. With this bomb we have now added a new and revolutionary increase in destruction to supplement the growing power of our armed forces. In their present form these bombs are now in production and even more powerful forms are in development.

It is an atomic bomb. It is a harnessing of the basic power of the universe. The force from which the sun draws its power has been loosed against those who brought war to the Far East.

Before 1939, it was the accepted belief of scientists that it was theoretically possible to release atomic energy. But no one knew any practical method of doing it. By 1942, however, we knew that the Germans were working feverishly to find a way to add atomic energy to the other engines of war with which they hoped to enslave the world. But they failed. We may be grateful to Providence that the Germans got the V–1's and V–2's late and in limited quantities and even more grateful that they did not get the atomic bomb at all.

The battle of the laboratories held fateful risks for us as well as the battles of the air, land and sea, and we have now won the battle of the laboratories as we have won the other battles.

Beginning in 1940, before Pearl Harbor, scientific knowledge useful in war was pooled between the United States and Great Britain, and many priceless helps to our victories have come from that arrangement. Under that general policy the research on the atomic bomb was begun. With American and British scientists working together we entered the race of discovery against the Germans.

The United States had available the large number of scientists of distinction in the many needed areas of knowledge. It had the tremendous industrial and financial resources necessary for the project and they could be devoted to it without undue impairment of other vital war work. In the United States the laboratory work and the production plants, on which a substantial start had already been made, would be out of reach of enemy bombing, while at that time

Britain was exposed to constant air attack and was still threatened with the possibility of invasion. For these reasons Prime Minister Churchill and President Roosevelt agreed that it was wise to carry on the project here. We now have two great plants and many lesser works devoted to the production of atomic power. Employment during peak construction numbered 125,000 and over 65,000 individuals are even now engaged in operating the plants. Many have worked there for two and a half years. Few know what they have been producing. They see great quantities of material going in and they see nothing coming out of these plants, for the physical size of the explosive charge is exceedingly small. We have spent two billion dollars on the greatest scientific gamble in history—and won.

But the greatest marvel is not the size of the enterprise, its secrecy, nor its cost, but the achievement of scientific brains in putting together infinitely complex pieces of knowledge held by many men in different fields of science into a workable plan. And hardly less marvelous has been the capacity of industry to design, and of labor to operate, the machines and methods to do things never done before so that the brain child of many minds came forth in physical shape and performed as it was supposed to do. Both science and industry worked under the direction of the United States Army, which achieved a unique success in managing so diverse a problem in the advancement of knowledge in an amazingly short time. It is doubtful if such another combination could be got together in the world. What has been done is the greatest achievement of organized science in history. It was done under high pressure and without failure.

We are now prepared to obliterate more rapidly and completely every productive enterprise the Japanese have above ground in any city. We shall destroy their docks, their factories, and their communications. Let there be no mistake; we shall completely destroy Japan's power to make war.

It was to spare the Japanese people from utter destruction that the ultimatum of July 26 was issued at Potsdam. Their leaders promptly rejected that ultimatum. If they do not now accept our terms they may expect a rain of ruin from the air, the like of which has never been seen on this earth. Behind this air attack will follow sea and land forces in such numbers and power as they have not yet seen and with the fighting skill of which they are already well aware.

The Secretary of War, who has kept in personal touch with all phases of the project, will immediately make public a statement giving further details.

His statement will give facts concerning the sites at Oak Ridge near Knoxville, Tennessee, and at Richland near Pasco, Washington, and an installation near Santa Fe, New Mexico. Although the workers at the sites have been making materials to be used in producing the greatest destructive force in history they have not themselves been in danger beyond that of many other occupations, for the utmost care has been taken of their safety.

The fact that we can release atomic energy ushers in a new era in man's understanding of nature's forces. Atomic energy may in the future supplement the power that now comes from coal, oil, and falling water, but at present it cannot be produced on a basis to compete with them commercially. Before that comes there must be a long period of intensive research.

It has never been the habit of the scientists of this country or the policy of this Government to withhold from the world scientific knowledge. Normally, therefore, everything about the work with atomic energy would be made public.

But under present circumstances it is not intended to divulge the technical processes of production or all the military applications, pending further examination of possible methods of protecting us and the rest of the world from the danger of sudden destruction.

I shall recommend that the Congress of the United States consider promptly the establishment of an appropriate commission to control the production and use of atomic power within the United States. I shall give further consideration and make further recommendations to the Congress as to how atomic power can become a powerful and forceful influence towards the maintenance of world peace.

PART VII

The Cold War

The nation reconverted. Labor tensed itself to prevent cutbacks in wages and employment from its wartime highs. Debates got under way that ultimately would result, in 1947, in the passage of the Taft-Hartley Labor Management Relations Act. General Motors, steel, and, later, coal arbitrations were launched to prevent strikes. The President took steps to implement housing and urged the continuation of victory garden programs.

New Dealers began to leave Washington: Judge Samuel I. Rosenman, who had been a philosopher and friend to F.D.R.; Herbert H. Lehman, whose competence and honesty had been one of UNRRA's basic assets; Edward R. Stettinius, Chester Bowles, Malcolm D. Ross, and others. Friends and neighbors of Truman found berths in Washington and offices in the White House. John W. Snyder, who had served in World War I with Truman and was from St. Louis, was named Reconversion Director and later Secretary of the Treasury. Truman's executive secretary was one Sidney W. Souers, who had been president of the Piggly-Wiggly Stores. His military aide, Harry H. Vaughan, liked to sport uniforms and medals, and would be heard of again. John R. Steelman, of Alabama, the President's assistant, was attached to conservative economic policies.

On February 20, 1946, Truman signed into law an employment act that his admirers would deem a landmark in history. It declared that it was the government's duty to afford employment opportunities for those able, willing, and seeking work, and gave the President the responsibility of formulating programs in this connection.

Truman announced emergency measures to relieve the world food shortage, and Herbert Hoover reappeared in connection with the discussions about developing a food conservation program. Soon after, Hoover became honorary chairman of the Famine Emergency Committee, and visited Egypt, India, China, and Japan; Truman urged him to return "in order to bring directly home to the American people your eyewitness account of the necessity for greater assistance from this country." Thus, the President moved toward the doctrine he was to esteem as his major claim to fame.

The Cold War was under way. Soviet arms supported communist regimes in what were to have been Free Poland and a rebuilt Germany, and in Bulgaria, Rumania, and elsewhere. What Winston Churchill called the "Iron Curtain," on March 5, 1946, had fallen. Greece and Turkey were in danger of disappearing behind it. On March 12, 1947, the President delivered himself of a Message to Congress, which, two months later, that body approved.

Truman Doctrine

The gravity of the situation which confronts the world today necessitates my appearance before a joint session of the Congress. The foreign policy and the national security of this country are involved.

One aspect of the present situation, which I wish to present to you at this time for your consideration and decision, concerns Greece and Turkey. The United States has received from the Greek government an urgent appeal for financial and economic assistance. Preliminary reports from the American Economic Mission now in Greece and reports from the American Ambassador in Greece corroborate the statement of the Greek government that assistance is imperative if Greece is to survive as a free nation. I do not believe that the American people and the Congress wish to turn a deaf ear to the appeal of the Greek government.

Greece is not a rich country. Lack of sufficient natural resources has always forced Greek people to work hard to make both ends meet. Since 1940 this industrious and peace-loving country has suffered invasion, four years of cruel enemy occupation, and bitter internal strife.

When forces of liberation entered Greece they found that the retreating Germans had destroyed virtually all the railways, roads, port facilities, communications, and merchant marine. More than a thousand villages had been burned. Eighty-five per cent of the children were tubercular. Livestock, poultry, and draft animals had almost disappeared. Inflation had wiped out practically all savings. As a result of these tragic conditions a military minority, exploiting human want and misery, was able to create political chaos which, until now, has made economic recovery impossible.

Greece is today without funds to finance the importation of those goods which are essential to bare subsistence. Under these circumstances the people of Greece cannot make progress in solving their problems of reconstruction. Greece is in desperate need of financial and economic assistance to enable it to resume purchases of food, clothing, fuel, and seeds. These are indispensable for the subsistence of its people and are obtainable only from abroad. Greece must have help to import the goods necessary to restore internal order and security, so essential for economic and political recovery.

The Greek government has also asked for the assistance of experienced American administrators, economists, and technicians to insure that the financial and other aid given to Greece shall be used effectively in creating a stable and self-sustaining economy and in improving its public administration.

The very existence of the Greek state is today threatened by the terrorist activities of several thousand armed men, led by communists, who defy the government's authority at a number of points, particularly along the northern boundaries. A commission appointed by the United Nations Security Council is at present investigating disturbed conditions in northern Greece and alleged border violations along the frontier between Greece on the one hand and Albania, Bulgaria, and Yugoslavia on the other. Meanwhile, the Greek government is unable to cope with the situation. The Greek army is small and poorly equipped. It needs supplies and equipment if it is to restore the authority of the government throughout Greek territory.

Greece must have assistance if it is to become a self-supporting and self-respecting democracy. The United States must supply that assistance. We have already extended to Greece certain types of relief and economic aid, but these are inadequate. There is no other country to which democratic Greece can turn. No other nation is willing and able to provide the necessary support for a democratic Greek government.

The British government, which has been helping Greece, can give no further financial or economic aid after March 31. Great Britain finds itself under the necessity of reducing or liquidating its commitments in several parts of the world, including Greece.

We have considered how the United Nations might assist in this crisis. But the situation is an urgent one requiring immediate action, and the United Nations and its related organizations are not in a position to extend help of the kind that is required.

It is important to note that the Greek government has asked for our aid in utilizing effectively the financial and other assistance we may give to Greece and in improving its public administration. It is of the utmost importance that we supervise the use of any funds made available to Greece, in such a manner that each dollar spent will count toward making Greece self-supporting and will help to build an economy in which a healthy democracy can flourish.

No government is perfect. One of the chief virtues of a democracy, however, is that its defects are always visible and under democratic processes can be pointed out and corrected. The government of Greece is not perfect. Nevertheless it represents 85 per cent of the members of the Greek Parliament who were chosen in an election last year. Foreign observers, including 692 Americans, considered this election to be a fair expression of the views of the Greek people.

The Greek government has been operating in an atmosphere of chaos and extremism. It has made mistakes. The extension of aid by this country does not mean that the United States condones everything that the Greek government has done or will do. We have condemned in the past, and we condemn now, extremist measures of the Right or the Left. We have in the past advised tolerance, and we advise tolerance now.

Greece's neighbor Turkey also deserves our attention. The future of Turkey as an independent and economically sound state is clearly no less important to the freedom-loving peoples of the world than the future of Greece. The circumstances in which Turkey finds itself today are considerably different from those of Greece. Turkey has been spared the disasters that have beset Greece. And during the war the United States and Great Britain furnished Turkey with material aid.

Nevertheless, Turkey now needs our support. Since the war Turkey has sought financial assistance from Great Britain and the United States for the purpose of effecting that modernization necessary for the maintenance of its national integrity. That integrity is essential to the preservation of order in the Middle East. The British Government has informed us that, owing to its own difficulties, it can no longer extend financial or economic aid to Turkey. As in the case of Greece, if Turkey is to have the assistance it needs the United States must supply it. We are the only country able to provide that help.

I am fully aware of the broad implications involved if the United States extends assistance to Greece and Turkey, and I shall discuss these implications with you at this time.

One of the primary objectives of the foreign policy of the United States is the creation of conditions in which we and other nations will be able to work out a way of life free from coercion. This was a fundamental issue in the war with Germany and Japan. Our victory was won over countries which sought to impose their will and their way of life upon other nations.

To ensure the peaceful development of nations, free from coercion, the United States has taken a leading part in establishing the United Nations. The United Nations is designed to make possible lasting freedom and independence for all its members. We shall not realize our objectives, however, unless we are willing to help free people to maintain their free institutions and their national integrity against aggressive movements that seek to impose upon them totalitarian regimes. This is no more than a frank recognition that totalitarian regimes imposed on free peoples, by direct or indirect aggression, undermine the foundations of international peace and hence the security of the United States. . . .

I believe that it must be the policy of the United States to support free peoples who are resisting attempted subjugation by armed minorities or by outside pressures. I believe that we must assist free peoples to work out their own destinies in their own way. I believe that our help should be primarily through economic and financial aid, which is essential to economic stability and orderly political processes.

The world is not static, and the status quo is not sacred. But we cannot allow changes in the status quo in violation of the Charter of the United Nations by such methods as coercion, or by such subterfuges as political infiltration. In helping free and independent nations to maintain their freedom the United States will be giving effect to the principles of the Charter of the United Nations.

It is necessary only to glance at a map to realize that the survival and integrity of the Greek nation are of grave importance in a much wider situation. If Greece should fall under the control of an armed minority, the effect upon its neighbor Turkey would be immediate and serious. Confusion and disorder might well spread throughout the entire Middle East.

Moreover, the disappearance of Greece as an independent state would have a profound effect upon those countries in Europe whose peoples are struggling against great difficulties to maintain their freedoms and their independence while they repair the damages of war. It would be an unspeakable tragedy if these countries, which have struggled so long against overwhelming odds, should lose that victory for which they sacrificed so much. Collapse of free institutions and loss of independence would be disastrous not only for them but for the world. Discouragement and possibly failure would quickly be the lot of neighboring peoples striving to maintain their freedom and independence.

Should we fail to aid Greece and Turkey in this fateful hour, the effect will be far-reaching to the West as well as to the East. We must take immediate and resolute action.

I therefore ask the Congress to provide authority for assistance to Greece and Turkey in the amount of $400,000,000 for the period ending June 30, 1948. In requesting these funds I have taken into consideration the maximum amount of relief assistance which would be furnished to Greece out of the $350,000,000 which I recently requested that the Congress authorize for the prevention of starvation and suffering in countries devastated by the war.

In addition to funds I ask the Congress to authorize the detail of American civilian and military personnel to Greece and Turkey, at the request of those countries, to assist in the tasks of reconstruction and for the purpose of supervising the use of such financial and material assistance as may be furnished. I recommend that authority also be provided for the instruction and training of selected Greek and Turkish personnel.

Finally, I ask that the Congress provide authority which will permit the speediest and most effective use, in terms of needed commodities, supplies, and equipment, of such funds as may be authorized.

If further funds, or further authority, should be needed for purposes indicated in this message, I shall not hesitate to bring the situation before the Congress. On this subject the executive and legislative branches of the government must work together.

This is a serious course upon which we embark. I would not recommend it except that the alternative is much more serious.

The United States contributed $341,000,000,000 toward winning World War II. This is an investment in world freedom and world peace. The assistance that I am recommending for Greece and Turkey amounts to little more than one tenth of one per cent of this investment. It is only common sense that we should safeguard this investment and make sure that it was not in vain. . . .

Did American aid save Greece and Turkey from communism? and what did the rescue achieve? Without doubt, it began a process that put the United States in a constant cycle of aid giving. Isolationists cried angrily and repeatedly that funds and supplies were diverted from necessary domestic projects, and often reappeared in communist hands abroad. They accused Washington of giving away our substance, and receiving from the recipients little more than abuse. The sums dispensed were astronomical; the results imponderable.

Truman's Midwestern individualism did not shrink from large-scale aid. He had been too long accustomed to mass expenditures, from his old county courthouse days. New Deal projects and mass allocations were familiar to him. The unstinted war budgets, the largesse of UNNRA, stop-gap relief abroad, and Cold War allotments of funds were to him all old stories, old familiar stories. He now projected a fundamentally new peacetime program of spending which would essentially be maintained by his successors in the White House. It would be supported by taxing schedules that changed the American's basic view of earnings. It was justified on the ground that more Americans ate and lived better than they ever had before, while paying their unprecedented taxes, and while supporting an unprecedented military establishment, and while footing the foreign aid bill. Not until the 1960's would questions be raised respecting the accomplishments of foreign aid, the nature of the American economy, its effect on the American family, the city, and the farm. However these might be assayed, it was evident that an American public hastening to reconvert to peacetime pursuits had no plan to suggest for world cooperation more effective than this foreign aid plan.

On June 5, 1947, Truman's Secretary of State George C. Marshall spoke at Harvard University in behalf of a plan which would help put Europe back on its feet. Truman himself capped further discussions on the same theme with a Message to Congress, delivered December 19, 1947.

ERP: The Marshall Plan

It is of vital importance to the United States that European recovery be continued to ultimate success. The American tradition of extending a helping hand to people in distress, our concern for the building of a healthy world economy which can make possible ever-increasing standards of living for our people, and our overwhelming concern for the maintenance of a civilization of free men and free institutions, all combine to give us this great interest in European recovery.

The people of the United States have shown, by generous contributions since the end of hostilities, their great sympathy and concern for the many millions in Europe who underwent the trials of war and enemy occupation. Our sympathy is undiminished, but we know that we cannot give relief indefinitely, and so we seek practical measures which will eliminate Europe's need for further relief.

Considered in terms of our own economy, European recovery is essential. The last two decades have taught us the bitter lesson that no economy, not even one so strong as our own, can remain healthy and prosperous in a world of poverty and want.

In the past the flow of raw materials and manufactured products between Western Europe, Latin America, Canada, and the United States has integrated these areas in a great trading system. In the same manner Far Eastern exports to the United States have helped pay for the goods shipped from Europe to the Far East. Europe is thus an essential part of a world trading network. The failure to revive fully this vast trading system, which has begun to function again since the end of the war, would result in economic deterioration throughout the world. The United States, in common with other nations, would suffer.

Our deepest concern with European recovery, however, is that it is essential to the maintenance of the civilization in which the American way of life is rooted. It is the only assurance of the continued independence and integrity of a group of nations who constitute a bulwark for the principles of freedom, justice, and the dignity of the individual.

The economic plight in which Europe now finds itself has intensified a political struggle between those who wish to remain free men living under the rule of law and those who would use economic distress as a pretext for the establishment of a totalitarian state.

The next few years can determine whether the free countries of Europe will be able to preserve their heritage of freedom. If Europe fails to recover, the peoples of these countries might be driven to the philosophy of despair—the philosophy which contends that their basic wants can be met only by the surrender of their basic rights to totalitarian control. Such a turn of events would constitute a shattering blow to peace and stability in the world. It might well compel us to modify our own economic system and to forego, for the sake of our own security, the enjoyment of many of our freedoms and privileges.

It is for these reasons that the United States has so vital an interest in strengthening the belief of the people of Europe that freedom from fear and want will be achieved under free and democratic governments.

The end of the fighting in Europe left that continent physically devastated and its economy temporarily paralyzed. The immediate problem was to prevent widespread starvation and disease and to make a start toward economic recovery. In the first year and a half after V-E day the people of Western Europe, by their own diligent efforts and with the aid of the United States and other nations, made remarkable progress toward these objectives.

At the beginning of 1947, however, they were still short of the goal of economic recovery. Their difficulties were greatly increased during the present year, chiefly by a bitter winter followed by floods and droughts which cut Western Europe's grain crop to the lowest figure in generations and hampered production of many other products. Nevertheless it was clear by last spring that Europe had achieved sufficient political and economic stability to make possible an over-all plan for recovery.

European recovery is essentially a problem for the nations of Europe. It was therefore apparent that it could not be solved, even with outside aid, unless the European nations themselves would find a joint solution and accept joint responsibility for its execution. Such a co-operative plan would serve to release the full productive resources of Europe and provide a proper basis for measuring the need and effectiveness of further aid from outside Europe, and in particular from the United States.

These considerations led to the suggestion by the Secretary of State on June 5, 1947, that further help from the United States should be given only after the countries of Europe had agreed upon their basic requirements and the steps which they would take in order to give proper effect to additional aid from us.

In response to this suggestion representatives of sixteen European nations assembled in Paris in July, at the invitation of the British and French governments, to draw up a co-operative program of European recovery. They formed a Committee of European Economic Co-operation. The countries represented were Austria, Belgium, Denmark, France, Greece, Iceland, Ireland, Italy, Luxembourg, the Netherlands, Norway, Portugal, Sweden, Switzerland, Turkey, and the United Kingdom. Although Western Germany was not formally represented on the Committee, its requirements as well as its ability to contribute to European economic recovery were considered by the Committee.

The report of the European Committee was transmitted to the government of the United States late in September. The report describes the present economic situation of Europe and the extent to which the participating countries can solve their problem by individual and joint efforts. After taking into account these recovery efforts, the report estimates the extent to which the sixteen countries will be unable to pay for the imports they must have.

The report points out that the peoples of Western Europe depend for their support upon international trade. It has been possible for some 270,000,000 people occupying this relatively small area to enjoy a good standard of living only by manufacturing imported raw materials and exporting the finished products to the rest of the world. They must also import foodstuffs in large volume, for there is not enough farmland in Western Europe to support its population even with intensive cultivation and with favorable weather. They cannot produce adequate amounts of cotton, oil, and other raw materials. Unless these deficiencies are met by imports, the productive centers of Europe can function only at low efficiency if at all.

In the past these necessary imports were paid for by exports from Europe, by the performance of services such as shipping and banking, and by income from capital investments abroad. All these elements of international trade were so badly disrupted by the war that the people of Western Europe have been unable to produce in their own countries, or to purchase elsewhere, the goods essential to their livelihood. Shortages of raw materials, productive capacity, and exportable commodities have set up vicious circles of increasing scarcities and lowered standards of living.

The economic recovery of Western European countries depends upon breaking through these vicious circles by increasing production to a point where exports and services can pay for the imports they must have to live. The basic problem in making Europe self-supporting is to increase European production.

The sixteen nations presented in their report a recovery program designed to enable them and Western Germany to become economically self-supporting within a period of four years and thereafter to maintain a reasonable minimum standard of living for their people without special help from others. The program rests upon four basic points:

(1) A strong production effort by each of the participating countries.

(2) Creation of internal financial stability by each country.

(3) Maximum and continuing co-operation among the participating countries.

(4) A solution of the problem of the participating countries' trading deficit with the American continents, particularly by increasing European exports.

The nations represented on the European Committee agreed at Paris to do everything in their power to achieve these four aims. They agreed to take definite measures leading to financial, economic, and monetary stability, the reduction of trade barriers, the removal of obstacles to the free movement of persons within Europe, and a joint effort to use their common resources to the best advantage.

These agreements are a source of great encouragement. When the representatives of sixteen sovereign nations with diverse peoples, histories, and institutions jointly determine to achieve closer economic ties among themselves and to break away from the self-defeating actions of narrow nationalism, the obstacles in the way of recovery appear less formidable.

The report takes into account the productive capacities of the participating nations and their ability to obtain supplies from other parts of the world. It also takes into account the possibilities of obtaining funds through the International Bank for Reconstruction and Development, through private investment, and in some instances by the sale of existing foreign assets. The participating countries recognized that some commodities, particularly food, will remain scarce for years to come, and the diet they have set as their goal for 1951 is less adequate in most cases than their prewar diet. The report assumes that many countries will continue restrictions on the distribution of shortage items such as food, clothing, and fuel.

When all these factors had been considered the European Committee concluded that there will still be a requirement for large quantities of food, fuel, raw materials, and capital equipment for which the financial resources of the participating countries will be inadequate. With successful execution of the European recovery program, this requirement will diminish in each of the four years ahead, and the Committee anticipated that by 1952 Europe could again meet its needs without special aid. . . .

The war had created a challenge to the government to set an example of democracy at home. Negro agitation and threats had caused the creation in 1941 of the Fair Employment Practices Committee, through Roosevelt's Executive Order 8802. The worst scandal of the war was F.D.R.'s Japanese Relocation Order in 1942, which had uprooted over 100,000 Japanese-Americans, most of them of manifestly innocent and patriotic character, and subjected them to military authority. This accomplished little besides demoralizing many of these Americans, and was a blow to civil rights. Truman made many and repeated efforts to build an edifice of liberal practices. Although he believed in separation of the races,* he had a sweeping program for giving justice to the Negroes under

* ". . . I wish to make it clear that I am not appealing for social equality of the Negro. The Negro himself knows better than that, and the highest types of Negro leaders say quite frankly that they prefer the society of their own people. Negroes want justice, not social relations. . . ." *An Introductory Anthology of President Truman compiled by the Staff of the American Library in London and edited by Dr. Richard H. Heindel, Director* (April 1945), p. 30.

law. Most of his program did not survive Congressional debates and procedure. His Special Message to Congress of February 2, 1948, summarized much of his thought in the field.

Civil Rights

To the Congress of the United States: In the State of the Union message on January 7, 1948, I spoke of five great goals toward which we should strive in our constant effort to strengthen our democracy and improve the welfare of our people. The first of these is to secure fully our essential human rights. I am now presenting to the Congress my recommendations for legislation to carry us forward toward that goal.

This nation was founded by men and women who sought these shores that they might enjoy greater freedom and greater opportunity than they had known before. The founders of the United States proclaimed to the world the American belief that all men are created equal, and that governments are instituted to secure the inalienable rights with which all men are endowed. In the Declaration of Independence and the Constitution of the United States, they eloquently expressed the aspirations of all mankind for equality and freedom. . . .

Today, the American people enjoy more freedom and opportunity than ever before. Never in our history has there been better reason to hope for the complete realization of the ideals of liberty and equality.

We shall not, however, finally achieve the ideals for which this nation was founded so long as any American suffers discrimination as a result of his race, or religion, or color, or the land of origin of his forefathers.

Unfortunately, there are still examples—flagrant examples—of discrimination which are utterly contrary to our ideals. Not all groups of our population are free from the fear of violence. Not all groups are free to live and work where they please or to improve their conditions of life by their own efforts. Not all groups enjoy the full privileges of citizenship and participation in the government under which they live.

We cannot be satisfied until all our people have equal opportunities for jobs, for homes, for education, for health, and for political expression, and until all our people have equal protection under the law.

One year ago I appointed a committee of fifteen distinguished Americans and asked them to appraise the condition of our civil rights and to recommend appropriate action by federal, state, and local governments.

The committee's appraisal has resulted in a frank and revealing report. This report emphasizes that our basic human freedoms are better cared for and more vigilantly defended than ever before. But it also makes clear that there is a serious gap between our ideals and some of our practices. This gap must be closed. . . .

The federal government has a clear duty to see that constitutional guarantees of individual liberties and of equal protection under the laws are not denied or abridged anywhere in our union. That duty is shared by all three branches of the government, but it can be fulfilled only if the Congress enacts modern, comprehensive civil rights laws, adequate to the needs of the day, and demonstrating our continuing faith in the free way of life.

I recommend, therefore, that the Congress enact legislation at this session directed toward the following specific objectives:

1. Establishing a permanent commission on civil rights, a joint Congressional committee on civil rights, and a Civil Rights Division in the Department of Justice.

2. Strengthening existing civil rights statutes.

3. Providing federal protection against lynching.

4. Protecting more adequately the right to vote.

5. Establishing a Fair Employment Practice Commission to prevent unfair discrimination in employment.

6. Prohibiting discrimination in interstate transportation facilities.

7. Providing home rule and suffrage in presidential elections for the residents of the District of Columbia.

8. Providing statehood for Hawaii and Alaska and a greater measure of self-government for our island possessions.

9. Equalizing the opportunities for residents of the United States to become naturalized citizens.

10. Settling the evacuation claims of Japanese-Americans.

As a first step, we must strengthen the organization of the federal government in order to enforce civil-rights legislation more adequately and to watch over the state of our traditional liberties.

I recommend that the Congress establish a permanent commission on civil rights reporting to the President. The commission should continuously review our civil-rights policies and practices, study specific problems, and make recommendations to the President at frequent intervals. It should work with other agencies of the federal government, with state and local governments, and with private organizations.

I also suggest that the Congress establish a joint Congressional committee on civil rights. This committee should make a continuing study of legislative matters relating to civil rights and should consider means of improving respect for and enforcement of those rights.

These two bodies together should keep all of us continuously aware of the condition of civil rights in the United States and keep us alert to opportunities to improve their protection.

To provide for better enforcement of federal civil rights laws, there will be established a division of civil rights in the Department of Justice. I recommend that the Congress provide for an additional Assistant Attorney General to supervise this division.

I recommend that the Congress amend and strengthen the existing provisions of federal law which safeguard the right to vote and the right to safety and security of person and property. These provisions are the basis for our present civil rights enforcement program.

Section 51 of Title 18 of the United States Code, which now gives protection to citizens in the enjoyment of rights secured by the Constitution or federal laws, needs to be strengthened in two respects. In its present form this section protects persons only if they are citizens, and it affords protection only against conspiracies by two or more persons. This protection should be extended to all inhabitants of the United States, whether or not they are citizens, and should be afforded against infringement by persons acting individually as well as in conspiracy.

Section 52 of Title 18 of the United States Code, which now gives general protection to individuals against the deprivation of federally secured rights by public officers, has proved to be inadequate in some cases because of the generality of its language. An enumeration of the principal rights protected under this section is needed to make more definite and certain the protection which the section affords.

A specific federal measure is needed to deal with the crime of lynching—against which I cannot speak too strongly. It is a principle of our democracy, written into our Constitution, that every person accused of an offense against the law shall have a fair, orderly trial in an impartial court. We have made great progress towards this end, but I regret to say that lynching has not yet finally disappeared from our land. So long as one person walks in fear of lynching, we shall not have achieved equal justice under law. I call upon the Congress to take decisive action against this crime.

Under the Constitution the right of all properly qualified citizens to vote is beyond question. Yet the exercise of this right is still subject to interference. Some individuals are prevented from voting by isolated acts of intimidation. Some whole groups are prevented by outmoded policies prevailing in certain states or communities.

We need stronger statutory protection of the right to vote. I urge the Congress to enact legislation forbidding interference by public officers or private persons with the right of qualified citizens to participate in primary, special, and general elections in which federal officers are to be chosen. This legislation should extend to elections for state as well as federal officers insofar as interference with the right to vote results from discriminatory action by public officers based on race, color, or other unreasonable classification.

Requirements for the payment of poll taxes also interfere with the right to vote. There are still seven states which, by their constitutions, place this barrier between their citizens and the ballot box. The American people would welcome voluntary action on the part of these states to remove this barrier. Nevertheless, I believe the Congress should enact measures insuring that the right to vote in elections for federal officers shall not be contingent upon the payment of taxes.

I wish to make it clear that the enactment of the measures I have recommended will in no sense result in federal conduct of elections. They are designed to give qualified citizens federal protection of their right to vote. The actual conduct of elections, as always, will remain the responsibility of state governments.

We in the United States believe that all men are entitled to equality of opportunity. Racial, religious, and other invidious forms of discrimination deprive the individual of an equal chance to develop and utilize his talents and to enjoy the rewards of his efforts.

Once more I repeat my request that the Congress enact fair employment practice legislation prohibiting discrimination in employment based on race, color, religion, or national origin. The legislation should create a Fair Employment Practice Commission with authority to prevent discrimination by employers and labor unions, trade and professional associations, and government agencies and employment bureaus. The degree of effectiveness which the wartime Fair Employment Practice Committee attained shows that it is possible to equalize job opportunity by government action and thus to eliminate the influence of prejudice in employment.

The channels of interstate commerce should be open to all Americans on a basis of complete equality. The Supreme Court has recently declared unconstitutional state laws requiring segregation on public carriers in interstate travel. Company regulations must not be allowed to replace unconstitutional state laws. I urge the Congress to prohibit discrimination and segregation, in the use of interstate transportation facilities, by both public officers and the employees of private companies.

I am in full accord with the principle of local self-government for residents of the District of Columbia. In addition, I believe that the Constitution should be amended to extend suffrage in presidential elections to the residents of the District.

The District of Columbia should be a true symbol of American freedom and democracy for our own people and for the people of the world. It is my earnest hope that the Congress will promptly give the citizens of the District of Columbia their own local elective government. They themselves can then deal with the inequalities arising from segregation in the schools and other public facilities, and from racial barriers to places of public accommodation which now exist for one third of the District's population.

The present inequalities in essential services are primarily a problem for the District itself, but they are also of great concern to the whole nation. Failing local corrective action in the near future, the Congress should enact a model civil rights law for the nation's capital.

The present political status of our territories and possessions impairs the enjoyment of civil rights by their residents. I have in the past recommended legislation granting statehood to Alaska and Hawaii, and organic acts for Guam and American Samoa, including a grant of citizenship to the people of these Pacific islands. I repeat these recommendations.

Furthermore, the residents of the Virgin Islands should be granted an increasing measure of self-government, and the people of Puerto Rico should be allowed to choose their form of government and their ultimate status with respect to the United States.

All properly qualified legal residents of the United States should be allowed to become citizens without regard to race, color, religion, or national origin. The Congress has recently removed the bars which formerly prevented persons from China, India, and the Philippines from becoming naturalized citizens. I urge the Congress to remove the remaining racial or nationality barriers which stand in the way of citizenship for some residents of our country.

During the last war more than 100,000 Japanese-Americans were evacuated from their homes in the Pacific states solely because of their racial origin. Many of these people suffered property and business losses as a result of this forced evacuation and through no fault of their own. The Congress has before it legislation establishing a procedure by which claims based upon these losses can be promptly considered and settled. I trust that favorable action on this legislation will soon be taken.

The legislation I have recommended for enactment by the Congress at the present session is a minimum program if the federal government is to fulfill its obligation of insuring the Constitutional guarantees of individual liberties and of equal protection under the law. . . .

We in the United States are working in company with other nations who share our desire for enduring world peace and who believe with us that, above all else, men must be free. We are striving to build a world family of nations—a world where men may live under governments of their own choosing and under laws of their own making.

As part of that endeavor the Commission on Human Rights of the United Nations is now engaged in preparing an international bill of human rights by which the nations of the world may bind themselves by international covenant to give effect to basic human rights and fundamental freedoms. We have played a leading role in this undertaking designed to create a world order of law and justice fully protective of the rights and the dignity of the individual. . . .

We know the way. We need only the will.

Truman grew more firm and positive in manner with the passing months. He had particularly hardened in his approach to the communists abroad. The end of the war had seen the collapse of the Grand Alliance. Russia had settled herself firmly among the satellites. Czechoslovakia was now wholly in communist control. Germany had become East Germany and West Germany, with Berlin a divided city. In April 1948, the Russians made an effort to seal off West Berlin from American aid; only a determined airlift discouraged this sullen effort. Truman put himself to organizing a military alliance of North Atlantic powers that would be prepared for any crisis precipitated by the Soviets.

Nevertheless, many observers concluded he was too much burdened with outmoded New Deal psychology, too much a shadow of F.D.R., to be able to aspire to election in his own person. Also, it seemed that Americans were ready for a change. Although Democratic supporters derided Thomas E. Dewey as "the little man on the wedding cake," he had campaigned effectively in 1944, and done well, considering that there was a war on, and his opponent was F.D.R. Now the war was over, and he faced Truman. The New York rackets buster and governor was certain that his reputation for courage and efficiency would carry him without effort into the White House. The Republican bands played over and over again, "What Do We Do on a Dew, Dew, Dewy Day?" The official polls gave their standard-bearer the election.

A cheerful and fighting Truman—almost alone in his certainty of victory—ridiculed his opponents as poll happy. Their candidate, he asserted, was offering the people sleeping polls. But Truman did not believe they would be fooled. The Dixiecrats had split off from the Democratic Party in resentment of civil rights legislation. The exalted followers of Henry A. Wallace's Progressive Party had split off on the other extreme of that party. But Truman fought boldly in the center for votes. It would later be remarked how vigorously he had appealed to the American farmers to recognize and sustain their friends. (The Dixiecrats had foolishly sung, at the convention, despite their own agrarian background: "Let's send Harry back to the farm,—Right back where he started from. . . .") Truman's unique insight into the strategic importance of the dwindling farm vote—in a nation closely divided by labor and capital—was to chasten politicians for the next while.

Dewey's speeches were not inspired or inspiring, and he proved insensitive to public attitudes. At one whistle-stop, the train engineer inadvertently backed his car, but without accident, into a crowd. A startled Dewey, possibly intending to be jocund, remarked: "That's the first lunatic I've had for an engineer. He probably should be shot at sunrise, but we'll let him off this time, since no one was hurt." The engineer, on learning of this, shot back: "I think just about as much of Dewey as I did before and that's not very much." Truman was not similarly inept, and, whether his speeches were inspired or not, they were spirited. His Pittsburgh address of October 23, 1948, was a fair sample of his style.

"Doctor" Dewey and the Republican Record

I think a Presidential campaign is one of the most important elements in our democratic process. It's a chance to get things out in

291

the open and discuss them and make decisions. I am an old campaigner, and I enjoy it.

I would enjoy it even more if my opponent had the courage to discuss the issues. The American people have the right to know where I stand and where my opponent stands on the issues that affect every person in this country.

The people know where I stand. But the Republican candidate refuses to tell where he stands.

My opponent is conducting a very peculiar campaign. He has set himself up as a kind of doctor with a magic cure for all the ills of mankind.

Let's imagine that we, the American people, are going to see this doctor. It's just our usual routine check-up which we have every four years.

We go into the doctor's office.

"Doctor," we say, "we're feeling fine."

"Is that so?" says the doctor. "You been bothered much by issues lately?"

"Not bothered, exactly," we say. "Of course, we've had quite a few. We've had the issues of high prices, and housing, education and social security, and a few others."

"That's bad," says the doctor. "You shouldn't have so many issues."

"Is that right?" we say. "We thought that issues were a sign of political health."

"Not at all," says the doctor. "You shouldn't think about issues. What you need is my brand of soothing syrup—I call it 'unity.' "

Then the doctor edges up a little closer.

"Say, you don't look so good," he says.

We say to him, "Well, that seems strange to me, Doc. I never felt stronger, never had more money, and never had a brighter future. What is wrong with me?"

Well, the doctor looks blank and says, "I never discuss issues with a patient. But what you need is a major operation."

"Will it be serious, Doc?" we say.

"No, not very serious," he says. "It will just mean taking out the complete works and putting in a Republican Administration."

That's the kind of campaign you're getting from the Republicans. They won't talk about the issues, but they insist that a major operation is necessary.

Take this vague talk of the Republican candidate about the "failures" of the present Administration. That puzzled me for a bit.

292

I thought of the fact that our national income is now running at the rate of over 220 billion dollars a year—over five times as much as it was in 1932. Is that what he calls a failure?

Or perhaps he was worried about the profits of corporations. In 1932, corporations lost 43 billion dollars. Now corporate profits are running at the rate of 19 billion dollars a year. Is that what he calls a failure?

Or perhaps he was thinking about our mighty undertakings to assist the free nations of the world to protect themselves against the inroads of Communism. These efforts are proving successful. Is that what he calls a failure?

In his speech here in Pittsburgh just a few days ago, the Republican candidate pretended to be upset about the way my Administration has treated labor—about the terrible condition that labor was in in 1946. That's the excuse he gives for the passage of the Taft-Hartley law. All right, let's examine that.

In 1946 more people had jobs than ever before. Unions were healthier and had more members than ever before. And the working men and women of the United States produced more goods in 1946 than in any previous peacetime year.

The world wasn't perfect in 1946. But before any Republican begins complaining about that, he had better take a look at 1932—the last Republican year.

The Republican candidate talks about the work-days lost from strikes in 1946. Our industrial production in 1946 was three times as much as it was in 1932. And the days lost from strikes in 1946 were less than one and one-half per cent of the total days worked that year.

Republicans don't like to talk about 1932—and I don't blame them. But it is a good year for you to remember when you start out to vote on election day.

When the Republican candidate finished telling you, here in Pittsburgh, how labor had suffered under my Administration, he told you who had come to the rescue.

Who do you guess it was? It was the Republicans.

And how do you suppose they did it? They did it with the Taft-Hartley Act.

Yes, sir. The Republican candidate marched up proudly and embraced the Taft-Hartley law—lock, stock, and barrel. No working man can have any doubt about that any more.

And in praising the Taft-Hartley law, he displayed his characteristic tendency of claiming credit where no credit is due. He tried to tell you that it is the Taft-Hartley Act that is driving the Communists out of labor unions.

If you want to know how much truth there is in this claim, ask Bill Green—ask Phil Murray. They'll tell you who is cleaning up the Communists in the labor unions. It's being done in the good American way—by the unions themselves.

Now in this speech he made here in Pittsburgh, the Republican candidate admitted, with characteristic modesty, that he was going to lead the country—and, indeed, the whole world—out of all our troubles. And he made a lot of promises.

He opened his mouth and closed his eyes, and swallowed the terrible record of the Republican 80th Congress.

Four years ago this same Presidential candidate went around the country saying that he was in favor of what the Democrats had done, but he could do it better. He said he was in favor of the National Labor Relations Act, the Wage and Hour Act, the Social Security Act, and "all the other Federal statutes designed to promote and protect the welfare of American working men and women"—but he could do it better. For some reason or other the American people did not believe him in 1944.

This year the same candidate is back with us, and he is saying much the same thing; that he likes our Democratic laws, but that he can run them better than we can.

It sounds like the same old phonograph record; but this year the record has a crack, and the needle gets stuck in it. The crack was provided by the Republican 80th Congress.

In 1948, every time the candidate says, "I can do it better," the crack says, "We're against it."

So the sounds coming out of the Republican Party this year are not very harmonious. And they are even less believable than they were in 1944.

The candidate said: "The present minimum wage set by law is far too low and it will be raised." That's fine. We're right with the candidate on that. In fact, we are 'way ahead of him.

Time and time again in the last two years I urged the Republican 80th Congress to raise the minimum wage from the present 40 cents an hour to at least 75 cents an hour. But the Republican Congress—the crack in the phonograph record—said, "Nothing doing—we're against it." And the minimum wage stayed where it was.

Let's look at another song on the record the candidate played for you here in Pittsburgh.

The candidate said: "We will overhaul the Social Security System for the unemployed and the aged, and go forward to extend its coverage and increase its benefits." That sounds good, although it's a little vague. But that's the candidate speaking. Where do the Republicans actually stand on social security?

As your President, I made every effort to get the Republican 80th Congress to extend social security coverage and increase social security benefits. What did the Congress do? They took social security benefits AWAY from nearly a million people.

What do you believe—campaign promises, or the plain facts of Republican action?

Again, the crack in the record gives them away. It says, "We're against it."

In my recommendations to the special do-nothing session of Congress in July, I pointed out the desperate need to increase old-age insurance benefits by at least 50 per cent. At the present time the average insurance benefit payment for an old couple is less than $40 a month.

The Republican Congress did nothing about it—and neither did the Republican candidate.

He was silent as the tomb while the Congress was in session. Now while he's campaigning, he suddenly takes quite an interest in increasing social security benefits. Now, I ask you: "Can you believe that kind of campaign promise?"

Take another promise in that Pittsburgh speech. The Republican candidate said: "We will make the Labor Department equal in actual Cabinet status to Commerce and Agriculture. It will make an important contribution to the national welfare."

That promise is ridiculous in the face of what the Republicans in the 80th Congress did. The Republican 80th Congress stripped the Mediation and Conciliation Service from the Labor Department. The Republican 80th Congress stripped the United States Employment Service from the Labor Department. The Republican 80th Congress cut the appropriations for the Bureau of Labor Statistics almost in half—apparently to prevent the Bureau from showing what's happening to the cost of living. That's the plain factual record of what the Republicans have done to the Labor Department in the last two years.

Remember, the Republican candidate has said he is proud of the record of the 80th Congress. That is the crack in the phonograph record that gives them away.

Here's another one of his promises. Here in Pittsburgh, the Republican candidate said: "We will bring a new and vigorous leadership to the Federal Conciliation and Mediation Service so that major disputes are settled before they become strikes."

Now that's a very peculiar promise. The present director of the Mediation Service is a well-known industrial leader named Cyrus Ching. Mr. Ching has been widely praised for his work in mediation. I think the Republican candidate is a bit confused here.

Let's take another campaign promise. Here in Pittsburgh the Republican candidate said: "We will encourage unions to grow in responsibility and strengthen the processes of collective bargaining." I know it's hard to believe but that's exactly what he said. And he said it in the very same speech in which he went all out for the Taft-Hartley law.

In this case, the candidate has fallen in the crack with the Republican Congress. He makes a promise, but the record says they're both against it.

Here's another promise by the Republican candidate: "We will vigorously and consistently enforce and strengthen our anti-trust laws against business monopolies."

Now that's really fantastic. The Republican Party is notoriously favorable toward big business monopolies. The record of the Republican 80th Congress furnishes plenty of proof. They passed over my veto a bill to exempt the railroads from the anti-trust laws. And at the same time they refused to pass, as I recommended, the O'Mahoney-Kefauver bill to plug loopholes in the anti-trust laws.

In the face of that record, the candidate now claims that the Republicans will strengthen the anti-trust laws. How can the Republican candidate say such things with a straight face?

But here's another. Here in Pittsburgh he said: "We will break the log jam in housing so that decent houses may be provided at reasonable cost for our people." For two solid years I tried in every way I knew to get the Republican 80th Congress to break the log jam in housing by passing the Taft-Ellender-Wagner Bill. But the Republicans would not act.

In the face of pleading and urging from Governors and Mayors, from veterans and plain people all over the country, the Republicans in Congress refused to pass the housing bill.

But now—now in the middle of the campaign—the Republican candidate has the gall to promise that the Republicans will take action on housing. I wouldn't have believed it if I hadn't seen it in print.

Let me quote just one more campaign promise from that incredible Pittsburgh speech. "We will make sure," said the Republican candidate, "we will make sure that soaring prices do not steal food and clothing and other necessities from American families." That one stops me completely.

Everybody in this country knows that the Republican 80th Congress refused, time and time again, to pass the laws we need to stop high prices. In November, 1947, in January, 1948, in July, 1948, I asked that Republican Congress to act against inflation. They did nothing.

And neither did the Republican candidate. All through the time when the Congress was in session, stalling and blocking anti-inflation legislation, the Republican candidate was silent as the grave.

But now—now that he's trying to persuade people to vote for him —the Republican candidate says the Republicans will do something about high prices. It looks to me as though it's a little late in the game for that promise.

The candidate says, "Me, too." But the Republican record still says, "We're against it." These two phrases, "me, too" and "we're against it," sum up the whole Republican campaign. But it isn't funny.

This soft talk and double talk, this combination of crafty silence and resounding misrepresentation, is an insult to the intelligence of the American voter. It proceeds upon the assumption that you *can* fool all the people—or enough of them—all the time.

In this campaign you don't have to rely on promises. This time, you have the record.

You don't have to play just the Republican side of the record. Turn it over. Our side—the Democratic side—doesn't say, "We're against it." It says, "We can do it." Our side of the record is the Victory March—victory on November 2nd for all the people and for the people's party.

Republicans were confident; they anticipated success. The day after election showed a happy Truman holding up a copy of the *Chicago Tribune,* sent out prematurely into the streets with the luckless headline: "DEWEY DEFEATS TRUMAN." And now Truman, President in his own right, in his Inaugural Address, January 20, 1949, outlined the program of his administration. It was a comprehensive program that featured Point Four, the summation of Truman's experiences with foreign aid.

Inaugural Address: Point Four

Today marks the beginning not only of a new administration, but of a period that will be eventful, perhaps decisive, for us and for the world.

It may be our lot to experience, and in large measure to bring about, a major turning point in the long history of the human race. The first half of this century has been marked by unprecedented and brutal attacks on the rights of man and by the two most frightful wars in history. The supreme need of our time is for men to learn to live together in peace and harmony. . . .

The American people stand firm in the faith which has inspired this nation from the beginning. We believe that all men have a right to equal justice under law and equal opportunity to share in the common good. We believe that all men have the right to freedom of thought and expression. We believe that all men are created equal because they are created in the image of God. From this faith we will not be moved.

The American people desire, and are determined to work for, a world in which all nations and all peoples are free to govern themselves as they see. fit and to achieve a decent and satisfying life. Above all else our people desire, and are determined to work for, peace on earth—a just and lasting peace based on genuine agreement freely arrived at by equals.

In the pursuit of these aims the U. S. and other like-minded nations find themselves directly opposed by a regime with contrary aims and a totally different concept of life. That regime adheres to a false philosophy which purports to offer freedom, security, and greater opportunity to mankind. Misled by this philosophy, many peoples have sacrificed their liberties only to learn to their sorrow that deceit and mockery, poverty and tyranny, are their reward. . . .

Since the end of hostilities the United States has invested its substance and its energy in a great constructive effort to restore peace, stability, and freedom to the world. We have sought no territory and we have imposed our will on none. We have asked for no privileges we would not extend to others. We have constantly and vigorously supported the United Nations and related agencies as a means of applying democratic principles to international relations. We have consistently advocated and relied upon peaceful settlement of disputes among nations. We have made every effort to secure agreement on effective international control of our most powerful weapon, and we have worked steadily for the limitation and control of all armaments. We have encouraged, by precept and example, the expansion of world trade on a sound and fair basis.

Almost a year ago, in company with sixteen free nations of Europe, we launched the greatest co-operative economic program in history. The purpose of that unprecedented effort is to invigorate and strengthen democracy in Europe, so that the free people of that continent can resume their rightful place in the forefront of civilization and can contribute once more to the security and welfare of the world.

Our efforts have brought new hope to all mankind. We have beaten back despair and defeatism. We have saved a number of countries from losing their liberty. Hundreds of millions of people all over the world now agree with us that we need not have war— that we can have peace.

The initiative is ours.

We are moving on with other nations to build an even stronger structure of international order and justice. We shall have as our partners countries which, no longer solely concerned with the problem of national survival, are now working to improve the standards of living of all their people. We are ready to undertake new projects to strengthen the free world.

In the coming years our program for peace and freedom will emphasize four major courses of action.

First, we will continue to give unfaltering support to the U.N. and related agencies, and we will continue to search for ways to strengthen their authority and increase their effectiveness. We believe that the U.N. will be strengthened by the new nations which are being formed in lands now advancing toward self-government under democratic principles.

Second, we will continue our programs for world economic recovery. This means, first of all, that we must keep our full weight behind the European Recovery Program. We are confident of the success of this major venture in world recovery. We believe that our partners in this effort will achieve the status of self-supporting nations once again. In addition we must carry out our plans for reducing the barriers to world trade and increasing its volume. Economic recovery and peace itself depend on increased world trade.

Third, we will strengthen freedom-loving nations against the dangers of aggression.

We are now working out with a number of countries a joint agreement designed to strengthen the security of the North Atlantic area. Such an agreement would take the form of a collective defense arrangement within the terms of the United Nations Charter. We have already established such a defense pact for the Western Hemisphere by the treaty of Rio de Janeiro. The primary purpose of these agreements is to provide unmistakable proof of the joint determination of the free countries to resist armed attack from any quarter. Each country participating in these arrangements must contribute all it can to the common defense.

If we can make it sufficiently clear in advance that any armed attack affecting our national security would be met with overwhelming force, the armed attack might never occur.

I hope soon to send to the Senate a treaty respecting the North Atlantic security plan. In addition we will provide military advice and equipment to free nations which will co-operate with us in the maintenance of peace and security.

Fourth, we must embark on a bold new program for making the benefits of our scientific advances and industrial progress available for the improvement and growth of underdeveloped areas.

More than half the people of the world are living in conditions approaching misery. Their food is inadequate. They are victims of disease. Their economic life is primitive and stagnant. Their poverty is a handicap and a threat both to them and to more prosperous areas. For the first time in history humanity possesses the knowledge and the skill to relieve the suffering of these people.

The U. S. is pre-eminent among nations in the development of industrial and scientific techniques. The material resources which we can afford to use for the assistance of other peoples are limited. But our imponderable resources in technical knowledge are constantly growing and are inexhaustible. I believe that we should make available to peace-loving peoples the benefits of our store of technical knowledge in order to help them realize their aspirations for a better life. And in co-operation with other nations we should foster capital investment in areas needing development.

Our aim should be to help the free peoples of the world, through their own efforts, to produce more food, more clothing, more materials for housing, and more mechanical power to lighten their burdens.

We invite other countries to pool their technological resources in this undertaking. Their contributions will be warmly welcomed. This should be a co-operative enterprise in which all nations work together through the United Nations and its specialized agencies wherever practicable. It must be a world-wide effort for the achievement of peace, plenty, and freedom.

With the co-operation of business, private capital, agriculture, and labor in this country, this program can greatly increase the industrial activity in other nations and can raise substantially their standards of living.

Such new economic developments must be devised and controlled to benefit the peoples of the areas in which they are established. Guarantees to the investor must be balanced by guarantees in the interest of the people whose resources and whose labor go into these developments.

The old imperialism—exploitation for foreign profit—has no place in our plans. What we envisage is a program of development based on the concepts of democratic fair dealing.

All countries, including our own, will greatly benefit from a constructive program for the better use of the world's human and natural resources. Experience shows that our commerce with other countries expands as they progress industrially and economically. Greater production is the key to prosperity and peace. And the key to greater production is a wider and more vigorous application of modern scientific and technical knowledge.

Only by helping the least fortunate of its members to help themselves can the human family achieve the decent, satisfying life that is the right of all people.

Democracy alone can supply the vitalizing force to stir the peoples of the world into triumphant action, not only against their human oppressors, but also against their ancient enemies hunger, misery, and despair. . . .

In due time, as our stability becomes manifest, as more and more nations come to know the benefits of democracy and to participate in growing abundance, I believe that those countries which now oppose us will abandon their delusions and join with the free nations of the world in a just settlement of international differences.

Events have brought our American democracy to new influence and new responsibilities. They will test our courage, our devotion to duty, and our concept of liberty. But I say to all men, what we have achieved in liberty we will surpass in greater liberty. Steadfast in our faith in the Almighty, we will advance toward a world where man's freedom is secure. To that end we will devote our strength, our resources, and our firmness of resolve. With God's help the future of mankind will be assured in a world of justice, harmony, and peace.

Truman anticipated a growing democratic network of nations and achievements around the world, and at its center the increasingly strong and affluent American society, united in prosperity and world leadership. The year 1949 was a dark one for these prospects. The North Atlantic Treaty Organization (NATO) was, indeed, launched, and was intended as a shield against communist aggressions. But, suddenly—for Americans had not been following events in the Far East closely—the Chinese Red army developed an offensive against the pro-American government of Chiang Kai-shek, and drove it into the sea. Chiang took up a position on the nearby island of Formosa, protected by the United States fleet. The U.S.S.R. exploded its own atom bomb; Americans no longer controlled this ultimate weapon alone.

A wave of fear and anger swept over Americans. They recalled that foreign communists had been treated as democratic allies, freely granted Lend Lease funds, permitted to absorb the Iron Curtain countries without challenge. They recalled the tolerance that had been accorded domestic communists, sympathizers, "fellow travellers," and other categories of pro-Soviet friends and agents. In 1948, the Hiss case had been opened by Whittaker Chambers, suggesting dark veins of subversion in and out of the government. Alger Hiss had been a trusted and influential official at Yalta and in other sensitive spots. Anticommunist spokesmen began to speak out boldly. Martin Dies of the House Un-American Activities Committee had lost his following and fame, because of U.S.-U.S.S.R. wartime collaboration, but the committee continued to press investigations; and the new voice of Senator Joseph R. McCarthy, of the Senate Committee on Government Operations, began to be heard in the land.

Moreover, the year 1949 created uncomfortable visions of the inner workings of an administration dedicated to a worldwide democratic crusade. The "five percenters" made headlines: influence peddlers in Washington who found friends in the administration to expedite government contracts and loans for their clients. As Blair Bolles explained in a 1952 analysis of the "Truman scandals," agencies that had been set up for depression purposes took on a different cast under Cold War prosperity conditions. The new tax structure tempted business to subvert Internal Revenue Bureau agents. The RFC, once concerned with stimulating lagging, key industries, was now a great udder of funds available for milking. The Federal Power Commission, the Maritime Commission, the Defense Production Administration were in similar situations.

Under such muddled circumstances, public feeling rose against communists and abettors of communism, as traitors who had helped speed up Soviet discovery of the atom bomb. During 1947, some 830 persons had been dropped from government posts on suspicion of disloyalty. The Congressional committees concerned with the issue eagerly sought witnesses and information that could reveal further breaches in American security, and were often not unhappy to identify traitors with the Roosevelt or Truman administrations. In a 1948 report, the House Un-American Activities Committee complained of lack of cooperation from the President. In a press conference, December 16, 1948, he denounced their work as no more than uncovering "red herrings," a phrase that pleased the embattled liberals and administration supporters, but was condemned by its critics. On April 24, 1950, Truman expanded his views on loyalty and security in an address before the Federal Bar Association.

"Red Herrings"

We've been fully aware of the threat of communist subversion within our own borders. Through the Federal Bureau of Investigation and other security forces, through prosecutions in the courts by the Department of Justice, through our federal employee loyalty program, and in many other ways, we. have vigorously attacked communists wherever their activities become a threat to our liberty.

There's been so much confusion recently about who's doing what to defeat communism in this country that I think the record should be set straight.

This administration has fought communism with action and not just with words. We've carried on this fight with every law on the statute books, and we've recommended new laws when we found they were necessary and could be framed without impairing the very freedoms we are seeking to protect.

No known instance of communist subversion—or any other kind of subversion—has gone uninvestigated.

No case where the facts warranted has gone unprosecuted.

We have prosecuted and obtained convictions of eleven top-ranking members of the Communist party in this country. We have successfully prosecuted many other persons for crimes related to communism. We have also prosecuted and obtained conviction of a large number of alleged communists on charge of contempt for refusing to testify before federal grand juries or Congressional committees.

And these prosecutions have been carried on by the Attorney General's office in the executive part of the government.

We now have under investigation the cases of over 1,000 citizens to determine whether steps should be taken to revoke their citizenship on grounds involving subversive activities. One hundred and thirty-eight persons are under orders of deportation on grounds involving communism.

There is no area of American life in which the Communist party is making headway, except, maybe, in the deluded minds of some people. The communists have done their best to penetrate labor unions and the government, but they are being successfully fought on both fronts. Labor has been doing a splendid job of cleaning its house. In the federal government the employee loyalty program has been an outstanding success, and your government lawyers have contributed greatly to its results.

I set up the employee loyalty program three years ago with two objectives in mind.

I was determined, as far as it was humanly possible, to see that no disloyal person should be employed by our government, whether he was a communist or a native American fascist of the Silver Shirt or Ku Klux Klan variety. I was equally determined that loyal government employees should be protected against accusations which were false, malicious, and ill founded. And that's just as important as the other part of the program.

The loyalty program was drafted by able and experienced persons to protect the security of the government and to safeguard the rights of its employees. It is the first time in the history of this country that we have had such a program. The communists and their friends, as well as some sincere idealists, say that it is too drastic. The false patriots and even some honest reactionaries say that it is entirely too mild. They want us to dismiss employees on the basis of unsupported charges. They actually resent the democratic safeguards of the loyalty program. All this confirms me in the conviction that it is a sound and effective program conceived and carried out in the American tradition. And that's just what it is.

The F.B.I., the agency loyalty boards, the Loyalty Review Board have quietly and effectively carried out their job of protecting the integrity and security of the government of the United States. The Loyalty Review Board is the central organization which directs the whole program. It is divided about half and half between Democrats and Republicans and is headed by a distinguished Republican lawyer, Mr. Seth Richardson, who served as Assistant Attorney General of the United States under President Hoover.

Under the supervision of this board the loyalty program has rid the government of all employees who were found to be disloyal—and they were only a tiny fraction of one per cent. . . .

A large part of the hue and cry about the loyalty program has centered on my refusal to turn over to a Congressional committee confidential loyalty files concerning individual employees. I've already stated several times the reasons why these files must not be disclosed. I want to restate them briefly, now.

The preservation of the strictest confidence with respect to loyalty files is the single most important element in operating a loyalty program which provides effective security for the government and justice for the individual employee.

The disclosures of these files would not only destroy the whole loyalty program, but it would seriously damage the future usefulness of the F.B.I. Information is given to the F.B.I. in confidence, which the F.B.I. has sworn to protect. Breaking the confidence would not only greatly embarrass and even endanger the informants involved, but would gravely impair the F.B.I.'s ability to get future information from other confidential sources.

Opening these files would reveal F.B.I. procedures and methods. It might reveal highly secret information vital to our national security and of great value to foreign nations.

Disclosure of the files would result in serious injustice to the reputation of many innocent persons. This is true because the F.B.I. investigative files do not contain proved information only. They include unverified charges and statements, as well as mere suspicions which, upon investigation, are found to be untrue.

If I should now open these files, I would create a precedent for future cases in which access to these files is demanded—and there would be many of those requirements. This would completely destroy the loyalty program, since, as experience shows, it would mean an attempt to try all loyalty cases over again in newspaper headlines, although they had already been carefully considered and fairly decided by a bipartisan board of loyal and distinguished Americans. . . .

Despite the historic precedents, with which I was thoroughly familiar, I gave the most careful consideration to the recent request of the Senate committee for access to the loyalty files. I obtained the views of Attorney General McGrath, the Loyalty Review Board chairman, Seth Richardson, and the F.B.I. director, Edgar Hoover, before I reached my decision to deny this request. All three were

305

unanimous in recommending to me in the strongest possible terms that I refuse to make the files available. The decision was mine to make, and I made it. I am confident that no President, whatever his party, would have acted otherwise. I'd do it again if necessary.

Now, the federal employee loyalty program has demonstrated that the United States has the most loyal civil service in the world. It's a splendid organization, and I'm proud to head it.

Of course, in an organization as large as the United States government it is always possible, despite the greatest precautions, that there may be a few bad individuals. We shall not for one minute relax our vigilant efforts to protect the security of the government of the United States. That's what I have sworn to do, and that's what I intend to proceed to do to the best of my ability.

The present Attorney General and his predecessor have repeatedly asked that if any person has any information about the presence of any communist in the government it be furnished to them.

I now repeat that request. . . .

There is a right way and a wrong way to fight communism. This administration is doing it the right way and the sensible way.

Our attack on communism is embodied in a positive threefold program:

One, we are strengthening our own defenses and aiding free nations in other parts of the world so that we and they can effectively resist communist aggression.

Two, we are working to improve our democracy so as to give further proof, both to our own citizens and to people in other parts of the world, that democracy is the best system of government that men have yet devised.

Three, we are working quietly but effectively, without headlines or hysteria, against communist subversion in this country wherever it appears, and we are doing this within the framework of the democratic liberties we cherish.

That's the way this administration is fighting communism. That's the way it's going to continue to fight communism.

Now I'm going to tell you how we are not going to fight communism. We are not going to transform our fine F.B.I. into a Gestapo secret police. That's what some people would like to do. We are not going to try to control what our people read and say and think. We are not going to turn the United States into a Right-Wing totalitarian country in order to deal with a Left-Wing totalitarian threat.

In short, we're not going to end democracy. We're going to keep the Bill of Rights on the books. We're going to keep those ancient, hard-earned liberties which you lawyers have done so much to preserve and protect.

If we all work together to maintain and strengthen our democratic ideals, communism will never be a serious threat to our American way of life. The example we set for free men everywhere will help to roll back the tide of communist imperialism in other parts of the world.

Now, I have outlined for you my program against communism.

This is the way I've worked against it.

This is the way I shall continue to work against it.

And now, I call on all fair-minded men and women to join me in this good fight.

Americans were not destined to enjoy peaceful isolation, as they entered into the second half of the century. Crises in every part of the world were interpreted as Soviet challenges to freedom and democracy. The fear of atomic warfare magnified the implications of each particular duel on the international arena. In 1948, a "People's Republic" was set up in North Korea, sponsored by the Soviet Union. A "democratic" republic in South Korea, under the arbitrary rule of President Syngman Rhee, was supported by the United States. In June 1950, North Korean troops invaded the South and posed a problem for President Truman. Should he let events take their course, or extend United States aid and take a chance that the Soviets would not join the other side, possibly beginning World War III? He concluded that the Russians must be stopped, that permitting the fall of the Republic of Korea (or R.O.K., as newspapers took to calling it) would simply encourage the communists to open attacks on democratic-supported nations elsewhere. Truman marshalled strength in the United Nations. American troops were hastily dispatched to hold up the sagging and inadequate lines of a little R.O.K. army in full retreat. General Douglas MacArthur, heading the United Nations forces, plotted the counter-strategy for a difficult and mountainous terrain. From June 25, when the first North Korean units crossed the 38th parallel dividing the country, till July 19, Truman made no report to Congress or the general public. On that date he first reviewed the situation for Congress. That evening, he spoke to the nation.

Korea

My fellow citizens: At noon today I sent a message to the Congress about the situation in Korea. I want to talk to you tonight about that situation, and about what it means to the security of the United States and to our hopes for peace in the world.

Korea is a small country, thousands of miles away, but what is happening there is important to every American.

On Sunday, June 25, Communist forces attacked the Republic of Korea. This attack has made it clear beyond all doubt that the international communist movement is willing to use armed invasion to conquer independent nations. An act of aggression such as this creates a very real danger to the security of all free nations.

The attack upon Korea was an outright breach of the peace and a violation of the Charter of the United Nations. By their actions in Korea communist leaders have demonstrated their contempt for the basic moral principles on which the United Nations is founded.

This is a direct challenge to the efforts of free nations to build the kind of world in which men can live in freedom and peace. This challenge has been presented squarely. We must meet it squarely.

It is important for all of us to understand the essential facts as to how the situation in Korea came about.

Before and during World War II Korea was subject to Japanese rule. When the fighting stopped it was agreed that troops of the Soviet Union would accept the surrender of the Japanese soldiers in the northern part of Korea and that American forces would accept the surrender of the Japanese in the southern part. For this purpose the 38th parallel was used as the dividing line.

Later the United Nations sought to establish Korea as a free and independent nation. A commission was sent out to supervise a free election in the whole of Korea. However, this election was held only in the southern part of the country, because the Soviet Union refused to permit an election for this purpose to be held in the northern part. Indeed, Soviet authorities even refused to permit the United Nations Commission to visit Northern Korea.

Nevertheless the United Nations decided to go ahead where it could. In August 1948 the Republic of Korea was established as a free and independent nation in that part of Korea south of the 38th parallel.

In December 1948 the Soviet Union stated that it had withdrawn its troops from Northern Korea and that a local government had been established there. However, the communist authorities never have permitted the United Nations observers to visit Northern Korea to see what was going on behind that part of the Iron Curtain. It was from that area, where the communist authorities have been unwilling to let the outside world see what was going on, that the attack was launched against the Republic of Korea on June 25. That attack came without provocation and without warning. It was an act of raw aggression, without a shadow of justification.

I repeat that it was an act of raw aggression. It had no justification whatever.

The communist invasion was launched in great force, with planes, tanks, and artillery. The size of the attack and the speed with which it was followed up make it perfectly plain that it had been plotted long in advance.

As soon as word of the attack was received, Secretary of State [Dean] Acheson called me at Independence, Missouri, and informed me that, with my approval, he would ask for an immediate meeting of the United Nations Security Council. The Security Council met just twenty-four hours after the communist invasion began.

One of the main reasons the Security Council was set up was to act in such cases as this—to stop outbreaks of aggression in a hurry before they develop into general conflicts. In this case the Council passed a resolution which called for the invaders of Korea to stop fighting and withdraw. The Council called on all members of the United Nations to help carry out this resolution. The communist invaders ignored the action of the Security Council and kept right on with their attack.

The Security Council then met again. It recommended that the members of the United Nations help the Republic of Korea repel the attack and help restore peace and security in that area. Fifty-two of the fifty-nine countries which are members of the United Nations have given their support to the action taken by the Security Council to restore peace in Korea.

These actions by the United Nations and its members are of great importance. The free nations have now made it clear that lawless aggression will be met with force. The free nations have learned the fateful lesson of the 1930's. That lesson is that aggression must be met firmly. Appeasement leads only to further aggression and ulti-mate war.

The principal effort to help the Koreans preserve their independence and to help the United Nations restore peace has been made by the United States. We have sent land, sea, and air forces to assist in these operations. We have done this because we know that what is at stake here is nothing less than our own national security and the peace of the world.

So far two other nations, Australia and Great Britain, have sent planes to Korea; and six other nations, Australia, Canada, France, Great Britain, the Netherlands, and New Zealand, have made naval forces available. Under the flag of the United Nations a unified command has been established for all forces of the members of the United Nations fighting in Korea. General Douglas MacArthur is the commander of this combined force.

The prompt action of the United Nations to put down lawless aggression and the prompt response to this action by free peoples all over the world will stand as a landmark in mankind's long search for a rule of law among nations.

Only a few countries have failed to indorse the efforts of the United Nations to stop the fighting in Korea. The most important of these is the Soviet Union. The Soviet Union has boycotted the meetings of the United Nations Security Council. It has refused to support the actions of the United Nations with respect to Korea. The United States requested the Soviet government, two days after the fighting started, to use its influence with the North Koreans to have them withdraw. The Soviet government refused. The Soviet government has said many times that it wants peace in the world, but its attitude toward this act of aggression against the Republic of Korea is in direct contradiction of its statements.

For our part, we shall continue to support the United Nations action to restore peace in the world. We know that it will take a hard, tough fight to halt the invasion, to drive the communists back. The invaders have been provided with enough equipment and supplies for a long campaign. They overwhelmed the lightly armed defense forces of the Korean Republic in the first few days and drove southward. Now, however, the Korean defenders have been reorganized and are making a brave fight for their liberty, and an increasing number of American troops have joined them. Our forces have fought a skillful rear guard delaying action, pending the arrival of reinforcements. Some of these reinforcements are now arriving; others are on the way from the United States. . . .

The long shadow of MacArthur dominated the building up of retaliatory forces and the campaign to drive the North Koreans out of the land.

A brilliant flanking action in September forced the communists into hasty retreat and raised the question of what ought next to be done. Truman opposed any plan that might bring Red China into the war. MacArthur believed the North Korean government could be wiped out with no threat to world peace. A thrust toward the Yalu River revealed that the Chinese Communists had not been off guard. Over 800,000 of their troops stood ready to engage the United Nations soldiers in battle. On December 15, 1950, Truman proclaimed a national emergency. His plan was to hold the line of battle against the Chinese, neither retreating nor trying for a decisive victory; a war of attrition would establish a working compromise that would stave off dangerous showdowns. MacArthur disagreed. In March of 1951, he made blunt demands of the Chinese. He recommended the use of Nationalist Chinese troops in the campaign—especially provocative to the communists. In a letter to the House Republican leader in Congress, Joseph W. Martin, he wrote: "There is no substitute for victory." Truman determined to rid himself of his distinguished but, to his mind, unreliable subordinate. On April 10 he released documents intended to prove that MacArthur had acted in defiance of his directives—a charge MacArthur's headquarters denied—and announced the general's removal. On the radio, the following evening, the President defended his action.

MacArthur

My fellow Americans:

I want to talk to you tonight about what we are doing in Korea and about our policy in the Far East.

In the simplest terms what we are doing in Korea is this: We are trying to prevent a third world war.

I think most people in this country recognized that fact last June. And they warmly supported the decision of the government to help the Republic of Korea against the communist aggressors. Now many persons, even some who applauded our decision to defend Korea, have forgotten the basic reason for our action.

It is right for us to be in Korea now. It was right last June. It is right today.

I want to remind you why this is true.

The communists in the Kremlin are engaged in a monstrous conspiracy to stamp out freedom all over the world. If they were to succeed, the United States would be numbered among their principal victims. It must be clear to everyone that the United States cannot and will not sit idly by and await foreign conquest. The only question is: When is the best time to meet the threat and how?

The best time to meet the threat is in the beginning. It is easier to put out a fire in the beginning when it is small than after it has become a roaring blaze.

And the best way to meet the threat of aggression is for the peace-loving nations to act together. If they don't act together, they are likely to be picked off one by one.

If they had followed the right policies in the 1930's—if the free countries had acted together to crush the aggression of the dictators, and if they had acted in the beginning, when the aggression was small—there probably would have been no World War II.

If history has taught us anything, it is that aggression anywhere in the world is a threat to the peace everywhere in the world. When that aggression is supported by the cruel and selfish rulers of a powerful nation who are bent on conquest, it becomes a clear and present danger to the security and independence of every free nation.

This is a lesson that most people in this country have learned thoroughly. This is the basic reason why we have joined in creating the United Nations. And since the end of World War II we have been putting that lesson into practice—we're working with other free nations to check the aggressive designs of the Soviet Union before they can result in a third world war.

That is what we did in Greece, when that nation was threatened by the aggression of international Communists. The attack against Greece could have led to general war. But this country came to the aid of Greece. The United Nations supported Greek resistance. With our help the determination and efforts of the Greek people defeated the attack on the spot.

Another big Communist threat to peace was the Berlin blockade. That, too, could have led to war. But again it was settled because free men would not back down in an emergency.

The aggression against Korea is the boldest and most dangerous move the Communists have yet made. The attack on Korea was part of a greater plan for conquering all of Asia. . . .

The whole communist imperialism is back of the attack on peace in the Far East. It was the Soviet Union that trained and equipped the North Koreans for aggression. The Chinese communists massed forty-four well trained and well equipped divisions on the Korean frontier. These were the troops they threw into battle when the North Korean communists were beaten.

The question we have had to face is whether the communist plan of conquest can be stopped without a general war. Our government and other countries associated with us in the United Nations believe that the best chance of stopping it without a general war is to meet the attack in Korea and defeat it there. That is what we have been doing. It is a difficult and bitter task. But so far it has been successful. So far, we have prevented World War III. So far, by fighting a limited war in Korea we have prevented aggression from succeeding, and bringing on a general war. And the ability of the whole free world to resist communist aggression has been greatly improved.

We have taught the enemy a lesson. He has found out that aggression is not cheap or easy. Moreover, men all over the world who want to remain free have been given new courage and new hope. They know now that the champions of freedom can stand up and fight and that they will stand up and fight. Our resolute stand in Korea is helping the forces of freedom now fighting in Indochina and other countries in that part of the world. It has already slowed down the timetable of conquest.

In Korea itself there are signs that the enemy is building up his ground forces for a new mass offensive. We also know that there have been large increases in the enemy's available air forces. If a new attack comes, I feel confident it will be turned back. The United Nations fighting forces are tough and able and well equipped. They are fighting for a just cause. They are proving to all the world that the principle of collective security will work. We are proud of all these forces for the magnificent job they have done against heavy odds. We pray that their efforts may succeed, for upon their success may hinge the peace of the world.

The communist side must now choose its course of action. The communist rulers may press the attack against us. They may take further action which will spread the conflict. They have that choice, and with it the awful responsibility for what may follow. The communists also have the choice of a peaceful settlement which could lead to a general relaxation of the tensions in the Far East. The decision is theirs, because the forces of the United Nations will strive to limit the conflict if possible.

We do not want to see the conflict in Korea extended. We are trying to prevent a world war, not to start one. And the best way to do that is to make it plain that we and the other free countries will continue to resist the attack.

But you may ask, Why can't we take other steps to punish the aggressor? Why don't we bomb Manchuria and China itself? Why don't we assist the Chinese Nationalist troops to land on the main-land of China?

If we were to do these things we would be running a very grave risk of starting a general war. If that were to happen, we would have brought about the exact situation we are trying to prevent. If we were to do these things we would become entangled in a vast conflict on the continent of Asia, and our task would become immeasurably more difficult all over the world. What would suit the ambitions of the Kremlin better than for our military forces to be committed to a full-scale war with Red China?

It may well be that, in spite of our best efforts, the communists may spread the war. But it would be wrong, tragically wrong, for us to take the initiative in extending the war.

The dangers are great. Make no mistake about it. Behind the North Koreans and Chinese communists in the front lines stand additional millions of Chinese soldiers. And behind the Chinese stand the tanks, the planes, the submarines, the soldiers, and the scheming rulers of the Soviet Union.

Our aim is to avoid the spread of the conflict. The course we have been following is the one best calculated to avoid an all-out war. It is the course consistent with our obligation to do all we can to maintain international peace and security. Our experience in Greece and Berlin shows that it is the most effective course of action we can follow. . . .

A number of events have made it evident that General MacArthur did not agree with that policy. I have therefore considered it essential to relieve General MacArthur so that there would be no doubt or confusion as to the real purpose and aim of our policy.

It was with the deepest personal regret that I found myself com-pelled to take this action. General MacArthur is one of our greatest military commanders. But the cause of world peace is more im-portant than any individual.

The change in commands in the Far East means no change what-ever in the policy of the United States. We will carry on the fight in Korea with vigor and determination in an effort to bring the war to a speedy and successful conclusion. The new commander, Lieu-tenant General Matthew Ridgway, has already demonstrated that he has the good qualities of military leadership needed for the task. . . .

Congress listened appreciatively to MacArthur's rhetorical defense of his course in Korea. San Francisco, New York, and other American cities received him with frantic joy and admiration. Sanguine politicians thought they saw in him a spectacular military man who might win the presidency in 1952. Instead he faded from public sight* as had, in earlier years, Admiral George Dewey and General John J. Pershing.

In the meantime, a phenomenon had entered American life. Senator Joseph R. McCarthy had sought an issue for arresting public attention. In what was to become a notorious speech in Wheeling, West Virginia, he waved a document before his audience that he claimed contained the names of Communist Party members who were still in the Department of State and still helping to make public policy. As subsequently exploited, the alleged names and their actual number were always contradictory and confused, and quite obviously of only demagogic significance. But an embittered portion of public opinion was quite ready to credit McCarthy's wild and often aimless charges. Most remarkable was his denunciation of Professor Owen Lattimore, then of Johns Hopkins University, who had been involved in Far Eastern policymaking.** McCarthy continued to improvise irresponsible charges. Truman had already expressed his distaste for anticommunist legislation dangerous to civil rights and security, in his veto of the McCarran-Wood Act of 1950. During the presidential campaign of 1952, on November 1, he paid his respects to the methods employed by the Senator from Wisconsin.

McCarthyism

Americans have no more precious possession than the Bill of Rights. Those few paragraphs in the Constitution of the United States were the product of centuries of struggle by mankind against tyranny. They are a code of conduct for men in public life everywhere to assure that, no matter what happens, America will remain a land of freedom, of liberty, and justice.

But eternal vigilance is still the price of liberty. There is no assurance that the ideals embodied in our Bill of Rights will survive if there is a determined effort by men in positions of leadership to snuff them out.

A powerful group of men in the Republican party is now deter-

* But not from public memory; thirteen years later, when MacArthur died, thousands of Americans in New York, Washington and Norfolk made a point of filing past the old soldier's bier.
** Louis Filler, *A Dictionary of American Social Reform* (1963), pp. 567-569.

mined to rise to power through a method of conduct as hostile to American ideals as anything we have ever seen. This method has come to be known as McCarthyism.

This method tries people by accusation and slander instead of by evidence and proof.

It destroys reputations by repeated utterances of gigantic falsehoods. It spares neither the lowly government clerk nor men of the towering stature of General George C. Marshall.

This new method of American politics has already been used with a terrifying degree of success. It defeated a distinguished Senator, Tydings of Maryland, in 1950, and helped to defeat several others.

Now, for the first time, it is being used in a presidential election. The Republican candidate for Vice-President has made it his stock in trade in this campaign. Senator McCarthy himself was a featured speaker at the Republican convention—and was provided a national radio and television hook-up in this campaign, to see if he could do to Governor Stevenson what was done to Senator Tydings.

I would have expected the Republican candidate for President to be against this kind of thing. I would have expected him to defend the name of his old friend and benefactor, George Marshall, against those detractors.

But he did not do it. Instead, he just uttered a few generalities about the American tradition of justice. And he went on to say that Senators McCarthy and Jenner were on his team and should be reelected. And he himself has been using the same kind of innuendo and distortion in his own speeches.

We must get rid of McCarthyism in our public life.

In his State of the Union Address of January 5, 1949, Truman had said: "Every segment of our population and every individual has a right to expect from his government a fair deal." The phrase caught on as the motto of his administration. As Truman prepared to wind up his term as President of the United States, observers assayed his achievements. He had been at the helm in the final phases of the world war. He had made the ultimate decision on the dropping of the A-bomb. He had seen his country into the U.N., and formulated with the prime ministers of the United Kingdom and Canada the Declaration of Atomic Energy (November 15, 1946) which kept that ultimate weapon in American hands, pending security agreements with other nations. (The Soviet Union had demanded that the manufacture of the bomb be outlawed, and stockpiles destroyed.) Truman's Loyalty Order of March 22, 1947, had disturbed liberals, who had been only partially appeased by his denunciations of Red hunters and McCarthyism, and by his unsuccessful veto of the McCarren Internal Security Act, September 23, 1950. He had also vetoed without effect the Taft-Hartley Act of June 23, 1947, which had placed restrictions on the operations of labor, now rapidly evolving into "big labor." He had done nothing whatever about corruption in government or racketeering in labor or otherwise. He had spoken ringingly on civil rights, though little legislation materialized as a result of any of his statements. Foreign aid programs had finally culminated in the Mutual Security Act of October 10, 1951, which coordinated military and economic aid to nations whom the United States hoped to influence or, at least, neutralize. During the Korean War, Truman had taken it upon himself to stop steelworkers from striking, and to assume mill operations, on the grounds that the nation was in a state of national emergency. This display of executive authority the Supreme Court overruled. What was the sum of Truman's efforts in foreign and domestic affairs? He gave his own view of them in his final State of the Union Address, January 7, 1953.

The Fair Deal in Retrospect

We are still so close to recent controversies that some of us may find it hard to understand the accomplishments of these past eight years. But the accomplishments are real and very great, not as the President's, not as the Congress', but as the achievements of our country and all the people in it.

Let me remind you of some of the things we have done since I first assumed my duties as President of the United States.

I took the oath of office on April 12, 1945. In May of that same year the Nazis surrendered. Then, in July, that great white flash of light, man-made at Alamogordo, heralded swift and final victory in World War II—and opened the doorway to the atomic age.

Consider some of the great questions that were posed for us by sudden total victory in World War II. Consider also how well we as a nation have responded.

Would the American economy collapse after the war? That was one question. Would there be another depression here—a repetition of 1921 or 1929? The free world feared and dreaded it. The communists hoped for it and built their policies upon that hope. We answered that question—answered it with a resounding "No."

Our economy has grown tremendously. Free enterprise has flourished as never before. Sixty-two million people are now gainfully employed, compared with fifty-one million seven years ago. Private businessmen and farmers have invested more than $200,000,000,000 in new plant and equipment since the end of World War II. Prices have risen further than they should have done; but incomes, by and large, have risen even more, so that real living standards are now considerably higher than seven years ago. Aided by sound government policies, our expanding economy has shown the strength and flexibility for swift and almost painless reconversion from war to peace, in 1945 and 1946; for quick reaction and recovery—well before Korea—from the beginnings of recession in 1949. Above all, this live and vital economy of ours has now shown the remarkable capacity to sustain a great mobilization program for defense, a vast outpouring of aid to friends and allies all around the world—and still to produce more goods and services for peaceful use at home than we have ever known before.

This has been our answer, up to now, to those who feared or hoped for a depression in this country.

How have we handled our national finances? That was another question arising at war's end. In the administration of the government no problem takes more of the President's time, year in and year out, than fashioning the budget and the related problem of managing the public debt.

Financing World War II left us with a tremendous public debt, which reached $279,000,000,000 at its peak in February 1946.

Beginning in July 1946, when war and reconversion financing had ended, we have held quite closely to the sound standard that in times of high employment and high national income the federal budget should be balanced and the debt reduced. . . .

Now let me turn to another question we faced at the war's end. Would we take up again, and carry forward, the great projects of social welfare—so badly needed, so long overdue—that the New Deal had introduced into our national life? Would our government continue to have a heart for the people, or was the progress of the New Deal to be halted in the aftermath of war as decisively as the progress of Woodrow Wilson's New Freedom had been halted after the First World War?

This question, too, we have answered. We have answered it by doubling old-age insurance benefits and extending coverage to ten million more people. We have answered it by increasing our mini-

318

mum wage. We have answered by the three million privately constructed homes that the federal government has helped finance since the war and the 155,000 units of low-rent public housing placed under construction since 1949.

We have answered with the 42,000 new hospital beds provided since 1946 through the joint efforts of the federal government and local communities.

We have answered by helping 8,000,000 veterans of World War II to obtain advanced education, 196,000 to start in business, and 64,000 to buy farms.

We have answered by continuing to help farmers obtain electric power, until today nearly ninety per cent of our farms have power line electric service.

In these and other ways we have demonstrated, up to now, that our democracy has not forgotten how to use the powers of the government to promote the people's welfare and security.

Another of the big postwar questions was this: What we would do with the nation's natural resources—its soils and water, forests and grasslands. Would we continue the strong conservation movement of the 1930's, or would we, as we did after the First World War, slip back into the practices of monopoly, exploitation, and waste?

The answer is plain. All across our country the soil conservation movement has spread, aided by government programs, enriching private and public lands, preserving them from destruction, improving them for future use. In our river basins we have invested nearly $5,000,000,000 of public funds in the last eight years—invested them in projects to control floods, irrigate farmlands, produce low-cost power and get it to the housewives and farmers and businessmen who need it. We have been vigilant in protecting the people's property—lands and forests and oil and minerals.

We have had to fight hard against those who would use our resources for private greed; we have met setbacks; we have had to delay work because of defense priorities. But on the whole we can be proud of our record in protecting our natural heritage and in using our resources for the public good.

Here is another question we had to face at the war's close: Would we continue, in peace as well as war, to promote equality of opportunity for all our citizens, seeking ways and means to guarantee for all of them the full enjoyment of their civil rights?

During the war we achieved great economic and social gains for millions of our fellow citizens who had been held back by prejudice. Were we prepared, in peacetime, to keep on moving toward full realization of the democratic promise? Or would we let it be submerged, wiped out, in postwar riots and reactions, as after World War I?

We answered these questions in a series of forward steps at every level of government and in many spheres of private life. In our armed forces, our civil service, our universities, our railway trains, the residential districts of our cities, in stores and factories all across the nation, in the polling booths as well, the barriers are coming down. This is happening, in part, at the mandate of the courts; in part at the insistence of federal, state, and local governments; in part through the enlightened action of private groups and persons in every region and every walk of life.

There has been a great awakening of the American conscience on the issues of civil rights. And all this progress—still far from complete but still continuing—has been our answer, up to now, to those who questioned our intention to live up to the promises of equal freedom for us all.

There was another question posed for us at the war's end, which equally concerned the future course of our democracy: Could the machinery of government and politics in this republic be changed, improved, adapted rapidly enough to carry through, responsibly and well, the vast new complicated undertakings called for in our time?

We have answered this question, too, answered it by tackling the most urgent, most specific problems which the war experience itself had brought into sharp focus. The reorganization of the Congress in 1946; the unification of our armed services, beginning in 1947; the closer integration of foreign and military policy through the National Security Council created that same year; and the executive reorganizations, before and after the Hoover-Acheson Commission report in 1949—these are landmarks in our continuing endeavor to make government an effective instrument of service to the people.

DWIGHT D. EISENHOWER
(1890–   )

Dead Center

My friends, before I begin the expression of those thoughts that I deem appropriate to this moment, would you permit me the privilege of uttering a little private prayer of my own. And I ask that you bow your heads.

Almighty God, as we stand here at this moment my future associates in the executive branch of government join me in beseeching that Thou will make full and complete our dedication to the service of the people in this throng, and their fellow citizens everywhere.

Give us, we pray, the power to discern clearly right from wrong, and allow all our words and actions to be governed thereby, and by the laws of this land. Especially we pray that our concern shall be for all the people regardless of station, race, or calling.

May cooperation be permitted and be the mutual aim of those who, under the concepts of our Constitution, hold to differing political faiths; so that all may work for the good of our beloved country and Thy glory. Amen.

First Inaugural Address, *January 20, 1953*

H E WAS General Eisenhower before he became "Ike," but there was no exact point at which the transition occurred. He became center man in a swarm of devastating operations enlisting millions of soldiers, pilots, seamen, and civilians, and requiring such glamorous American personalities as Generals Mark Clark, George E. Patton, and Omar N. Bradley, to say nothing of the famous Montgomery, Tedder, Alexander, and others of the European Theater of Operations. Eisenhower made momentous and irrevocable decisions, but he was informal, positive in his thinking, and interested in the men under him, and with the smile of a comrade. So, as the battle turned in favor of the Allies, he became Ike, and more and more involved in social and diplomatic decisions as they affected Allied forces landing in North Africa, France and Italy.

His individual qualities became more distinct. Their source lay in a

Kansas boyhood. He had enjoyed an average West Point youth, made notable by football ability. He had then built a remarkably varied army career through competence and a universal interest in military affairs. Ike was transparently modest, good humored, and concerned with results. Although he had lived all his life on the humble stipend of a professional soldier between wars—as late as August 12, 1943, his permanent rank was no more than lieutenant colonel—he accepted the exclusive contacts and regal services of a four-star general without excitement or a revision of his objectives.

Eisenhower had trained himself to study the facts and to act on them in the interests of the several "bosses" he obeyed. MacArthur later patronized him as the "best clerk who ever served under me." (MacArthur was upset by Eisenhower's rapid rise, partly at his expense, for the European Theater had been better provisioned than the Pacific Theater.) Ike drily recalled that he had "studied dramatics under [MacArthur] for five years in Washington and four in the Philippines."

Ike had known how to take orders, and, given his great chance by Chief of Staff General George C. Marshall, he learned to give orders. He found vanity useless and repugnant to his personality. In one interview, after his rise to greatness, he asked reporters to pass their versions of his direct statements through one of his officers, "so that you can correct any errors I might make, at least in grammar." He shunned complexities. A sound plan, he thought, should be capable of summary on one page. His sole aim during hostilities was victory. Morale must not be harmed by antipathies of any kind between officers and men. He met ultimate military showdowns with full awareness of their difficulties, and with a curious boldness of expression that later escaped intellectuals: "Whenever you attack, you have got dreams, then you have got hopes, then you have got expectations and then you have got just what you have got to get. I mean there are many things."

He honored the American G.I. His visit to German concentration camps was as deep an experience as he ever had. Otherwise, he was undisturbed by ideologies, except as they affected official American goals. In the postwar period, he spoke easily and without embarrassment to foreign assemblies and on American terrain: on campuses, at the Metropolitan Museum of Art in New York, and, on one and the same day, before the CIO and the Economic Club of New York, an organization of financiers. His subjects were as catholic as his audiences: peace, tolerance, education, the needs of war veterans. He became president of Columbia University. A liberal canard had it that the trustees had confused him with his brother Milton, a college president. Eisenhower was, at least, admired by his administrative associates. He avoided efforts to get him to run for President of the United States in 1948. In 1950, Truman asked him to head the NATO armed forces. In 1952, he turned over these duties to others, resigned from the army and became a candidate for the presidency.

What did Ike believe? He had concluded that the Republican Party best comported with his political views. He thought free enterprise the keystone of democracy. Yet he also favored cooperation. His ideals lay somewhere between those of Woodrow Wilson and Herbert Hoover. His ultimate achievement during the war had been to reconcile bitter disputes between Allied commanders. Intelligent people, he thought, were not isolationists. As for domestic issues, in a speech before the American Bar Association, September 5, 1949, he had emphasized that "increased productivity . . . alone can better the position of labor, of management, of all America." He was frank in his reverence for small-town ideals. During the election campaign of 1952, the Democrats ridiculed his folksiness and his sometimes awkward efforts to gear it to national audiences. They mocked Eisenhower's offer, if elected, to visit Korea in person and see the unresolved battlefront for himself. His opponent, Adlai E. Stevenson, asked what Ike hoped to learn that military and Department of State reports could not tell him better. Although the Democratic machine held together, enough voters were unimpressed by Stevenson's "egghead" approach to give him no more than 44.38 percent of the popular vote, and 89 Electoral Votes to Ike's 442.

The new President held that he had a mandate for change. He removed price controls. He supported his Mormon Secretary of Agriculture Ezra T. Benson's effort to create a program of "flexible" price supports for farm products. He was willing to give greater responsibility and freedom of action to unions than Taft-Hartley allowed. He was for curbing government expenses. He believed in holding his party together, and for that reason endured the campaign embraces of Senator Joseph R. McCarthy, and even of Senator William Jenner of Indiana, who had denounced his own revered General Marshall as a "front man for traitors." He chose as Secretary of Defense Charles E. Wilson, who was to utter, among other immortal thoughts, that "what is good for our country is good for General Motors, and vice versa."

Major areas wanting definition included foreign affairs, slated to be dominated by Secretary of State John Foster Dulles, and civil rights. The latter area remained shadowed by charges of official tolerance of communist pawns and by the drastic biddings for public attention of Senator McCarthy. On June 14, 1953, during Dartmouth College commencement exercises, the President offered an impromptu statement on freedom of inquiry which heartened those who hoped he would help halt McCarthy's Nero-like destructiveness.

"Don't Join the Book Burners"

Your president possesses a brash bravery approaching foolhardiness when he gives to me this platform in front of such an audience, with no other admonition except to speak informally, and giving me no limits of any other kind.

He has forgotten, I think, that old soldiers love to reminisce, and that they are, in addition, notoriously garrulous. But I have certain limitations of my own I learned throughout these many years, and I think they will serve to keep me from offending too deeply. But even if I do offend, I beg, in advance, the pardon of those families and friends, sweethearts that are waiting to greet these new graduates with a chaste handshake of congratulations, and assure you that any overstaying of my time was unintentional and just merely a product of my past upbringing. . . .

Now, with your permission, I want to talk about two points—two qualities—today that are purely personal. . . .

I am going to talk about fun—joy—happiness, just fun in life. I am going to talk a little about courage.

Now, as to fun: to get myself straight at once, for fear that in my garrulous way I might stray from my point, I shall say this: unless each day can be looked back upon by an individual as one in which he has had some fun, some joy, some real satisfaction, that day is a loss. It is un-Christian and wicked, in my opinion, to allow such a thing to occur.

Now, there are many, many different things and thoughts and ideas that will contribute—any acts of your own—that will contribute to the fun you have out of life. You can go along the bank of a stream in the tropics, and there is a crocodile lying in the sun. He looks the picture of contentment. They tell me that often they live to be a great age—a hundred years or more—and still lying in the sun and that is all they do.

Now, by going to Dartmouth, by coming this far along the road, you have achieved certain standards. One of those standards is: it is no longer so easy for you to have fun, and you can't be like a crocodile and sleep away your life and be satisfied. You must do something, and normally it must involve others, something you do for them. The satisfaction—it's trite but it's true—the satisfaction of a clear conscience, no matter what happens. . . .

Whatever you do—a little help to someone along the road—

something you have achieved because you worked hard for it, like your graduation diploma today, those things have become worth while, and in your own estimation will contribute to your happiness. They will measure up to your standards because your standards have become those that only you know, but they have become very high. And if you do those things, they are the kind of things that will satisfy you and make life something that is joyous, that will cause your face to spread out a little, instead of going this way [*indicating a long face*]. There's too much of that in the world, anyway.

You are leaders. You are bound to be leaders because you have had advantages that make you leader to someone, whether you know it or not. There will be tough problems to solve. You have heard about them. You can't solve them with long faces— they don't solve problems, not when they deal with humans. Humans have to have confidence. You have got to help give it to them.

This brings me up to my second little topic, which is courage. I forget the author, but one many years ago, you know, uttered that famous saying, "The coward dies a thousand deaths, but the brave man dies but once." In other words, you can live happily if you have courage, because you are not fearing something that you can't help.

You must have courage to look at all about you with honest eyes—above all, yourself. And we go back to our standards. Have you actually measured up? If you have, it is that courage to look at yourself and say, well, I failed miserably there, I hurt someone's feelings needlessly, I lost my temper—which you must never do except deliberately. You did not measure up to your own standards. . . .

Look at your country. Here is a country of which we are proud, as you are proud of Dartmouth and all about you, and the families to which you belong. But this country is a long way from perfection—a long way. We have the disgrace of racial discrimination, or we have prejudice against people because of their religion. We have crime on the docks. We have not had the courage to uproot these things, although we know they are wrong. And we with our standards, the standards given us at places like Dartmouth, we know they are wrong.

Now, that courage is not going to be satisfied—your sense of satisfaction is not going to be satisfied, if you haven't the courage to look at these things and do your best to help correct them, because that is the contribution you shall make to this beloved country in your time. Each of us, as he passes along, should strive to add something.

It is not enough merely to say I love America, and to salute the flag and take off your hat as it goes by, and to help sing the Star Spangled Banner. Wonderful! We love to do them, and our hearts swell with pride, because those who went before you worked to give to us today, standing here, this pride.

And this is a pride in an institution that we think has brought great happiness, and we know has brought great contentment and freedom of soul to many people. But it is not yet done. You must add to it.

Don't join the book burners. Don't think you are going to conceal faults by concealing evidence that they ever existed. Don't be afraid to go in your library and read every book, as long as that document does not offend our own ideas of decency. That should be the only censorship.

How will we defeat communism unless we know what it is, and what it teaches, and why does it have such an appeal for men, why are so many people swearing allegiance to it? It is almost a religion, albeit one of the nether regions.

And we have got to fight it with something better, not try to conceal the thinking of our own people. They are part of America. And even if they think ideas that are contrary to ours, their right to say them, their right to record them, and their right to have them at places where they are accessible to others is unquestioned, or it isn't America. . . .

On March 5, 1953, Stalin died. A "thaw" in Soviet foreign policy and national life began that many people outside the Iron Curtain countries hoped would lead to a more democratic relationship between the Russians and their satellites. Apparently, the very possibility stirred unrest in those captive nations. On June 17, riots broke out in East Germany which the Russians were compelled to put down with force. Photographs of Germans expressing their feelings about Russian tanks with stones and paving bricks stirred indignation and interest in the United States. But what steps could the American government initiate that might help the yoked peoples? In those early months of his administration, Eisenhower adopted a program of watchful waiting and of faith that Soviet brutality would be its own undoing. He expressed his sentiments in a letter dated July 25, 1963, to Konrad Adenauer, the West German leader.

East Germany

My dear Mr. Chancellor:

During the development of the conversations between the U.S. Secretary of State and the Foreign Ministers of Great Britain and France, it occurred to me that it might be helpful if I were to write you a letter in amplification of the thoughts so tightly compressed in the final communique.

It seems to me that certain definite patterns are emerging from the situation in East Germany and the Eastern European satellite countries—patterns which will unquestionably have a profound effect upon the future, including the proposed meeting of the Foreign Ministers of the Four Powers.

I think, therefore, that it will be useful for me to share my thoughts with you in some detail at this time.

Great historical developments, such as the recent Berlin and East German anti-Communist demonstrations, rarely have single roots. Nevertheless, I am quite certain that future historians, in their analysis of the causes which will have brought about the disintegration of the Communist Empire, will single out those brave East Germans who dared to rise against the cannons of tyranny with nothing but their bare hands and their stout hearts, as a root cause. I think also that those same historians will record your own extraordinary steadfastness in the cause of European peace and freedom over many, many years.

In analyzing these recent developments, there appear to be five points of greatest significance.

First, this eruption against Communist oppression was spontaneous. I know that I need not go into any elaborate denial with you of the fantastic explanation put out by Moscow that the uprising was caused by American provocateurs. No provocateur of any nationality can persuade human beings to stand up in front of rumbling tanks with sticks and stones. Such action comes from the heart and not from any foreign purse.

Second, this uprising was not just a momentary flash of desperation. The continuing news of disorders in Eastern Germany indicates a fundamental and lasting determination to be fully and finally free, despite long years of stern Sovietization.

Third, nowhere were the rioters "bourgeois reactionaries" or "capitalist warmongers." They were workers. Therefore, the martyrs who fell before Russian Communist guns were the very same workers in whose name the Kremlin has falsely and cynically built their empire of oppression, their far-flung "workers' paradise."

Fourth, the fact of the uprising, the conduct of the German Communist leaders during the event and their actions since the event, all indicate the complete political bankruptcy of the SED.

Fifth, and to me of utmost significance, when the riots developed in the Russian sector of Berlin, the workers' chant was, "We want free elections." In this phrase, the people clearly and simply summed up their yearning for the alleviation of their grievances and sufferings.

The combination of these five facts actually forms the background for that portion of the July 15 Foreign Ministers' communique dealing with German unification and free elections. And the communique itself, as you know, is actually the diplomatic confirmation of your own earlier statements, of my June 26 cable to you, and most important, of the Resolution of the German Bundestag of June 10.

For the past many months there have been endless arguments and debates on both sides of the Atlantic over the respective priorities of such words and phrases as "unification," "peace treaty," "free elections," "withdrawal of occupation troops," etc.

It has always seemed to me—and these recent events, to me at least, clearly confirm the thought—that there can be no solution without free elections and the formation of a free all-German government, leading to unification. From that point on can flow a logical, orderly sequence of events, culminating in an honorable peace treaty and the re-emergence of a new united German Republic, dedicated to the welfare of its own people, as a friendly and peaceful member of the European family of nations.

To this first step of free elections, the Government of the United States will continue to lend the full force of its political, diplomatic, and moral support.

There are sincere people in Germany, in the nations of Western Europe, and even in my own country, who have come to believe that free elections, and therefore the unification of Germany, contradict and possibly exclude the concept of the European Defense Community which has been ratified by both your Houses of Parliament and is now before your Constitutional Court. I do not and have never accepted this theory that the EDC and unification of Germany are mutually exclusive. Quite the contrary.

As the three Foreign Ministers stated at the conclusion of their recent meeting in Washington, since the European community corresponds to the lasting needs of its members and their people for peace, security and welfare, it is looked upon as necessary in itself and not linked up with existing international tensions.

It has long been my conviction that the strengthening of the Federal Republic, through adoption of the EDC, the contractual agreements and further progress in the integration of Western Europe, can only enhance the prospects for the peaceful unification of Germany, by increasing the attractive power of this prosperous Western Germany vis-à-vis the Soviet Zone, an attractive power which has already been demonstrated by the steady stream of refugees in recent months, as well as the demonstrations which began on June 17. This increasing contrast between Western and Eastern Germany, the latter with its bankrupt regime and impoverished economy, will in the long run produce conditions which should make possible the liquidation of the present Communist dictatorship and of the Soviet occupation.

While a future all-German Government must obviously be free to choose the degree to which it wishes to enter into defensive and other arrangements compatible with the principles of the United Nations, I can hardly imagine that it would seek the path of complete and premature disarmament in the presence of other nations still heavily armed. I believe this is a matter worthy of serious attention. Those who in Germany believe they can suggest an easy, safe solution through defenseless neutralization should carefully ponder the true wisdom and safety of such a course.

Speaking for America, and I believe the rest of the free world share this view, I can say that there has been enough bloodshed and enough misery and enough destruction in the past fifty years, to deter any people or any Government of the West from any ideas of military aggression. But the peace we all so dearly seek cannot be maintained through weakness. EDC will be the simplest, most unequivocal, and most self-evident demonstration of strength for peace.

No one can foretell what the unfolding months will bring, but it can certainly be said that the workers of Berlin's Soviet Sector and the workers of East Germany, with the workers of Czechoslovakia, have started something that will have an important place on the pages of history. May the concluding chapter of that history record the reemergence of freedom, of peace, and of happiness.

With kindest personal regard,

Sincerely,

In his first Annual Message to Congress, February 2, 1953, Eisenhower had called the Korean war "the worst painful phase of Communist aggression throughout the world." This judgment failed to take in the aggression that had bent Czechoslovakia and other European nations to communist purposes, but it helped spell out the President's strategy. He would, essentially, continue Truman's program: to contain communism, rather than force it to a showdown. He would thus avoid the possibility of another world war. With his Defense Department head and his Secretary of State, he would place his faith in the atom bomb (though he had, in 1945, opposed dropping it on Japan), cutting back on the maintenance of ground and air forces. This strategy would also save tax money, giving the country, in Charles E. Wilson's phrase, "more bang for the buck." Eisenhower embraced other views that were controversial. He maintained, in his first Annual Message to Congress, that the presence of the United States Seventh Fleet in Formosan waters had shielded the Red Chinese from an attack by Chinese Nationalists, forcing "the United States Navy . . . to serve as a defensive arm of Communist China." Eisenhower did not probe the possibility that American forces were protecting the Formosan Nationalists from being overwhelmed by Red Chinese armies, as they had been on the mainland. Thus, a note of conjecture entered into his foreign policy which urgently required realistic debate. The President's eminence in military matters made such a debate close to impossible.

The state of public interest and opinion did not help. American soldiers and pilots were dying daily in Korea, but their deaths were mainly mourned in private homes. On June 19, 1953, Eisenhower declined to intervene to prevent the execution of Julius and Ethel Rosenberg, who had been convicted of betraying atom bomb secrets to the Russians. Eisenhower believed that "by immeasurably increasing the chances of atomic war the Rosenbergs may have condemned to death tens of millions of innocent people all over the world." Thus, it was the fear of atom bombs striking the American soil that troubled Americans, rather than wars anywhere else.

The Korean war came to an ignominious end. Eisenhower called his countrymen to prayerful rededication. In doing so, he honored the Korean leadership in terms such as he had used to encourage Allied unity during World War II; he said nothing to suggest their incompetence and corruption, and nothing about removing these leaders or eradicating their evils.

Korean Armistice

My fellow citizens:

Tonight we greet, with prayers of thanksgiving, the official news that an armistice was signed almost an hour ago in Korea. It will quickly bring to an end the fighting between the United Nations forces and the Communist armies. For this Nation the cost of repelling aggression has been high. In thousands of homes it has been incalculable. It has been paid in terms of tragedy.

With special feelings of sorrow—and of solemn gratitude—we think of those who were called upon to lay down their lives in that far-off land to prove once again that only courage and sacrifice can keep freedom alive upon the earth. To the widows and orphans of this war, and to those veterans who bear disabling wounds, America renews tonight her pledge of lasting devotion and care. . . .

Soldiers, sailors, and airmen of 16 different countries have stood as partners beside us throughout these long and bitter months. America's thanks go to each. In this struggle we have seen the United Nations meet the challenge of aggression—not with pathetic words of protest, but with deeds of decisive purpose. It is proper that we salute particularly the valorous armies of the Republic of Korea, for they have done even more than prove their right to freedom. Inspired by President Syngman Rhee, they have given an example of courage and patriotism which again demonstrates that men of the West and men of the East can fight and work and live together side by side in pursuit of a just and noble cause.

And so at long last the carnage of war is to cease and the negotiations of the conference table is [*sic*] to begin. On this Sabbath evening each of us devoutly prays that all nations may come to see the wisdom of composing differences in this fashion before, rather than after, there is resort to brutal and futile battle. . . .

Throughout the coming months, during the period of prisoner screening and exchange, and during the possibly longer period of the political conference which looks toward the unification of Korea, we and our United Nations Allies must be vigilant against the possibility of untoward developments.

And as we do so, we shall fervently strive to insure that this armistice will, in fact, bring free peoples one step nearer to their goal of a world at peace.

My friends, almost 90 years ago, Abraham Lincoln at the end

of a war delivered his second Inaugural Address. At the end of that speech he spoke some words that I think more nearly express the true feelings of America tonight than would any other words ever spoken or written. You will recall them:

"With malice toward none; with charity for all; with firmness in the right as God gives us to see the right, let us strive on to finish the work we are in . . . to do all which may achieve and cherish a just and a lasting peace, among ourselves, and with all nations."

This is our resolve and our dedication.

PART VIII
The Search for Peace

A major problem facing the Eisenhower administration was the conservative wing of his party, revitalized by growing popular sentiment against liberal and international thinking. It produced the Bricker Amendment, product of the thought of an Ohio Senator, which would have seriously limited the power of the President to negotiate foreign treaties, and which failed of passage in the Senate by a narrow margin. Yet the problem of U.S.-U.S.S.R. relations remained. On August 12, 1953, the Russians exploded their first hydrogen bomb, and public fears of catastrophe were heightened. Eisenhower's strategy was to persuade Americans that atomic energy could truly destroy them, but also that the United States had the capacity to deliver a death blow to its antagonist. And that, finally, both these facts required an energetic search for a peaceful solution to the atom problem.

The difficulty lay in building up, at the same time, a foreign policy that would discourage communist aggression. Americans were divided on whether or not the Allied democracies ought to take a strong stand against communists, as in Indochina, where French rule was being seriously threatened. Democratic Party spokesmen criticized the President and his Secretary of State for doing too little to prevent the communists from taking over parts of the "free" world piece by piece. Yet many of them had also defended, under Truman, the tolerance of communist maneuvers that had partially, perhaps inadvertently, followed the Yalta agreements.

In Southeast Asia, the communists were gaining ground not because of superior armaments, but because they were better able to win the cooperation and devotion of peasants than were the "democratic" allies of pro-Western powers, some of whom apparently plotted their military strategy from headquarters on the Riviera. Could Americans produce dedicated fighters for freedom everywhere, who studied the languages and traditions of the peoples they aspired to help, and who could set examples of selflessness and endurance in order to win their admiration and support? These lacking, Americans could only offer foreign aid—guns, technicians, drillmasters, food—and hope that it would not be mismanaged by inept friends of America.

The American public continued to respond not to the democratic challenge, as it was being indivisibly posed in a dozen incandescent places around the world, but to the possibility of a major atomic attack. Eisenhower met their fears, and the fears of a large part of the western world, with the major appeal of his administration, one which gained the United States substantial world sympathy. On December 8, 1953, he appeared before the U.N. and urged the establishment of an international agency to control the atom.

Atoms for Peace

When Secretary General Hammarskjold's invitation to address this General Assembly reached me in Bermuda, I was just beginning a series of conferences with the Prime Ministers and Foreign Ministers of Great Britain and of France. Our subject was some of the problems that beset our world.

During the remainder of the Bermuda Conference, I had constantly in mind that ahead of me lay a great honor. That honor is mine today as I stand here, privileged to address the General Assembly of the United Nations.

At the same time that I appreciate the distinction of addressing you, I have a sense of exhilaration as I look upon this Assembly.

Never before in history has so much hope for so many people been gathered together in a single organization. Your deliberations and decisions during these somber years have already realized part of those hopes. . . .

I know that the American people share my deep belief that if a danger exists in the world, it is a danger shared by all—and equally, that if hope exists in the mind of one nation, that hope should be shared by all.

Finally, if there is to be advanced any proposal designed to ease even by the smallest measure the tensions of today's world what more appropriate audience could there be than the members of the General Assembly of the United Nations?

I feel impelled to speak today in a language that in a sense is new—one which I, who have spent so much of my life in the military profession, would have preferred never to use.

That new language is the language of atomic warfare.

The atomic age has moved forward at such a pace that every citizen of the world should have some comprehension, at least in comparative terms, of the extent of this development of the utmost significance to every one of us. Clearly, if the peoples of the world are to conduct an intelligent search for peace, they must be armed with the significant facts of today's existence.

My recital of atomic danger and power is necessarily stated in United States terms, for these are the only incontrovertible facts that I know. I need hardly point out to this Assembly, however, that this subject is global, not merely national in character.

On July 16, 1945, the United States set off the world's first atomic explosion. Since that date in 1945, the United States of America has conducted 42 test explosions.

Atomic bombs today are more than 25 times as powerful as the weapons with which the atomic age dawned, while hydrogen weapons are in the ranges of millions of tons of TNT equivalent.

Today, the United States' stockpile of atomic weapons, which, of course, increases daily, exceeds by many times the explosive equivalent of the total of all bombs and all shells that came from every plane and every gun in every theatre of war in all of the years of World War II.

A single air group, whether afloat or land-based, can now deliver to any reachable target a destructive cargo exceeding in power all the bombs that fell on Britain in all of World War II.

In size and variety, the development of atomic weapons has been no less remarkable. The development has been such that atomic weapons have virtually achieved conventional status within our armed services. In the United States, the Army, the Navy, the Air Force, and the Marine Corps are all capable of putting this weapon to military use.

But the dread secret, and the fearful engines of atomic might, are not ours alone.

In the first place, the secret is possessed by our friends and allies, Great Britain and Canada, whose scientific genius made a tremendous contribution to our original discoveries, and the designs of atomic bombs.

The secret is also known by the Soviet Union.

The Soviet Union has informed us that, over recent years, it has devoted extensive resources to atomic weapons. During this period, the Soviet Union has exploded a series of atomic devices, including at least one involving thermo-nuclear reactions.

If at one time the United States possessed what might have been called a monopoly of atomic power, that monopoly ceased to exist several years ago. Therefore, although our earlier start has permitted us to accumulate what is today a great quantitative advantage, the atomic realities of today comprehend two facts of even greater significance.

First, the knowledge now possessed by several nations will eventually be shared by others—possibly all others.

Second, even a vast superiority in numbers of weapons, and a consequent capability of devastating retaliation, is no preventive, of itself, against the fearful material damage and toll of human lives that would be inflicted by surprise aggression.

The free world, at least dimly aware of these facts, has naturally embarked on a large program of warning and defense systems. That program will be accelerated and expanded.

But let no one think that the expenditure of vast sums for weapons and systems of defense can guarantee absolute safety for the cities and citizens of any nation. The awful arithmetic of the atomic bomb does not permit of any such easy solution. Even against the most powerful defense, an aggressor in possession of the effective minimum number of atomic bombs for a surprise attack could probably place a sufficient number of his bombs on the chosen targets to cause hideous damage.

Should such an atomic attack be launched against the United States, our reactions would be swift and resolute. But for me to say that the defense capabilities of the United States are such that they could inflict terrible losses upon an aggressor—for me to say that the retaliation capabilities of the United States are so great that such an aggressor's land would be laid waste—all this, while fact, is not the true expression of the purpose and the hope of the United States. . . .

It is with the book of history, and not with isolated pages, that the United States will ever wish to be identified. My country wants to be constructive, not destructive. It wants agreements, not wars, among nations. It wants itself to live in freedom, and in the confidence that the people of every other nation enjoy equally the right of choosing their own way of life.

So my country's purpose is to help us move out of the dark chamber of horrors into the light, to find a way by which the minds of men, the hopes of men, the souls of men everywhere, can move forward toward peace and happiness and well being.

In this quest, I know that we must not lack patience.

I know that in a world divided, such as ours today, salvation cannot be attained by one dramatic act.

I know that many steps will have to be taken over many months before the world can look at itself one day and truly realize that a new climate of mutually peaceful confidence is abroad in the world.

But I know, above all else, that we must start to take these steps—*now*.

The United States and its allies, Great Britain and France, have over the past months tried to take some of these steps. Let no one say that we shun the conference table.

On the record has long stood the request of the United States,

Great Britain, and France to negotiate with the Soviet Union the problems of a divided Germany.

On that record has long stood the request of the same three nations to negotiate an Austrian Peace Treaty.

On the same record still stands the request of the United Nations to negotiate the problems of Korea.

Most recently, we have received from the Soveit Union what is in effect an expression of willingness to hold a Four Power Meeting. Along with our allies, Great Britain and France, we were pleased to see that this note did not contain the unacceptable preconditions previously put forward.

As you already know from our joint Bermuda communique, the United States, Great Britain, and France have agreed promptly to meet with the Soviet Union.

The Government of the United States approaches this conference with hopeful sincerity. We will bend every effort of our minds to the single purpose of emerging from that conference with tangible results toward peace—the only true way of lessening international tension.

We never have, we never will, propose or suggest that the Soviet Union surrender what is rightfully theirs.

We will never say that the peoples of Russia are an enemy with whom we have no desire ever to deal or mingle in friendly and fruitful relationship.

On the contrary, we hope that this coming Conference may initiate a relationship with the Soviet Union which will eventually bring about a free intermingling of the peoples of the East and of the West—the one sure, human way of developing the understanding required for confident and peaceful relations. . . .

But I do not wish to rest either upon the reiteration of past proposals or the restatement of past deeds. The gravity of the time is such that every new avenue of peace, no matter how dimly discernible, should be explored.

There is at least one new avenue of peace which has not yet been well explored—an avenue now laid out by the General Assembly of the United Nations.

In its resolution of November 18th, 1953, this General Assembly suggested—and I quote—"that the Disarmament Commission study the desirability of establishing a sub-committee consisting of representatives of the Powers principally involved, which should seek in private an acceptable solution . . . and report on such a solution

338

to the General Assembly and to the Security Council not later than 1 September 1954."

The United States, heeding the suggestion of the General Assembly of the United Nations, is instantly prepared to meet privately with such other countries as may be "principally involved," to seek "an acceptable solution" to the atomic armaments race which overshadows not only the peace, but the very life, of the world.

We shall carry into these private or diplomatic talks a new conception.

The United States would seek more than the mere reduction or elimination of atomic materials for military purposes.

It is not enough to take this weapon out of the hands of the soldiers. It must be put into the hands of those who will know how to strip its military casing and adapt it to the arts of peace. . . .

To hasten the day when fear of the atom will begin to disappear from the minds of people, and the governments of the East and West, there are certain steps that can be taken now.

I therefore make the following proposals:

The Governments principally involved, to the extent permitted by elementary prudence, to begin now and continue to make joint contributions from their stockpiles of normal uranium and fissionable materials to an International Atomic Energy Agency. We would expect that such an agency would be set up under the aegis of the United Nations.

The ratios of contributions, the procedures and other details would properly be within the scope of the "private conversations" I have referred to earlier.

The United States is prepared to undertake these explorations in good faith. Any partner of the United States acting in the same good faith will find the United States a not unreasonable or ungenerous associate.

Undoubtedly initial and early contributions to this plan would be small in quantity. However, the proposal has the great virtue that it can be undertaken without the irritations and mutual suspicions incident to any attempt to set up a completely acceptable system of world-wide inspection and control.

The Atomic Energy Agency could be made responsible for the impounding, storage, and protection of the contributed fissionable and other materials. The ingenuity of our scientists will provide special safe conditions under which such a bank of fissionable material can be made essentially immune to surprise seizure.

The more important responsibility of this Atomic Energy Agency would be to devise methods whereby the fissionable material would be allocated to serve the peaceful pursuits of mankind. Experts would be mobilized to apply atomic energy to the needs of agriculture, medicine, and other peaceful activities. A special purpose would be to provide abundant electrical energy in the power-starved areas of the world. Thus the contributing powers would be dedicating some of their strength to serve the needs rather than the fears of mankind.

The United States would be more than willing—it would be proud to take up with others "principally involved" the development of plans whereby such peaceful use of atomic energy would be expedited.

Of those "principally involved" the Soviet Union must, of course, be one.

I would be prepared to submit to the Congress of the United States, and with every expectation of approval, any such plan that would:

First—encourage world-wide investigation into the most effective peacetime uses of fissionable material, and with the certainty that they had all the material needed for the conduct of all experiments that were appropriate;

Second—begin to diminish the potential destructive power of the world's atomic stockpiles;

Third—allow all peoples of all nations to see that, in this enlightened age, the great powers of the earth, both of the East and of the West, are interested in human aspirations first, rather than in building up the armaments of war;

Fourth—open up a new channel for peaceful discussion, and initiate at least a new approach to the many difficult problems that must be solved in both private and public conversations, if the world is to shake off the inertia imposed by fear, and is to make positive progress toward peace.

Against the dark background of the atomic bomb, the United States does not wish merely to present strength, but also the desire and the hope for peace.

The coming months will be fraught with fateful decisions. In this Assembly; in the capitals and military headquarters of the world; in the hearts of men everywhere, be they governors or governed, may they be the decisions which will lead this world out of fear and into peace.

To the making of these fateful decisions, the United States pledges before you—and therefore before the world—its determination to help solve the fearful atomic dilemma—to devote its entire heart and mind to find the way by which the miraculous inventiveness of man shall not be dedicated to his death, but consecrated to his life. . . .

Eisenhower's speech, and his subsequent efforts to begin experimentation with peaceful uses of the atom, were impressive but totally dependent on Congress for implementation. Beginnings of sorts were attained in 1955, and an Atoms-for-Peace Treaty was actually achieved in 1957. But the significance of all such actions rested mainly in what they promised; the future lay in armies and diplomats, rather than scientists.

The Congressional elections of 1954 prompted Eisenhower to rally his forces to maintain, if he could, his Republican majority in Congress. He entered into this unsuccessful work with genuine interest. It was a favorite quotation of his, from Woodrow Wilson, that "the highest form of efficiency is the spontaneous cooperation of a free people," and much of his thought, as President, went into seeking cooperation. He had to face the challenge of the Democrats, who had not been idle in seeking to undermine his public image. They made much of his golf playing, and highlighted every vacation as an escape from reality.

For a "Citizens for Eisenhower" meeting on October 28, 1954, Ike recalled the spirit of the 1952 campaign and urged Republican workers to go out once more and infuse others with their faith and enthusiasm. He reviewed the achievements, as he saw them, of his administration. A transition to peace had been made without economic setbacks. Government was now clean and efficient. Its spending had been "slashed by billions." Social security and unemployment insurance had been extended. (Eisenhower did not emphasize that the country was fighting off a "recession"—despite a current joke: It's a recession if you lose your job; it becomes a depression when I lose mine.) The President found no reason to discuss the Dixon-Yates affair. Although liberal spokesmen had been fearful that the contract sponsored by these worthies would begin to undermine the great TVA power facilities in the interests of private enterprise, Eisenhower saw no great principle at stake. Private enterprise *was* preferable, he thought, when it could offer comparable services; and Eisenhower disapproved of "creeping socialism" and what he saw as subsidized industry in the Tennessee Valley, drawing private industry away from other states and creating unemployment in their industrial towns.

His report on world affairs was optimistic. The French had, to be sure, been severely beaten in Indochina; Vietnam had been divided like Korea, and all of Southeast Asia stood exposed to communist plans and stratagems. But it sufficed for Ike that "a security coalition has at last been developed." He had developed a propaganda, rather than an educational view of troubled spots. It satisfied him, at least for campaign purposes, that "Strategic Iran, with its vast oil riches, threw off a threat of Communist domination and came strongly to our side." He barely mentioned Guatemala by name, in stating that "The Communist foothold in our hemisphere was eliminated," though the act had taken direct United States intervention, if only in terms of the delivery of aircraft bombers to the opponents of the leftist regime. Ike's view of "two . . . friends," England and Egypt, as having "solved long-standing differences over Suez" would return to mock him.

There were rifts of light. The incredible buffooneries of Senator McCarthy had finally led him to challenge the loyalty of tried and high-ranking army officers. The President held grimly to his policy of not engaging in personalities, but he did speak out in defense of civil rights and in defense of the army. Events led to the televised hearings of April and May 1954, which featured McCarthy, his aides Cohn and Schine, and Joseph N. Welch, Boston counsel for the army. Some observers had it that the President permitted McCarthy to have much of his own way in order to expose his total incapacity. What was certain was that McCarthy's decline, following these unprecedented hearings and a vote of censure against him by the Senate, was swift and remorseless. McCarthyism, as the phrase went, became McCarthywasm.

It was time, again, for another attempt at reconciling differences between the United States and the Soviets: to make an effort to achieve the unification of Germany, to offer hope that there would be an easing of Russian pressure on her satellites, and, above all, to probe possibilities for disarmament. A "summit" conference was arranged for July of 1955, to bring together representatives of Great Britain, France, the United States and the U.S.S.R. Eisenhower brought with him a plan for aerial inspection that had been prepared by Nelson A. Rockefeller in association with a group of military experts, technical personnel, and others. The Soviet representatives brought to Geneva a disarmament plan of their own which called for a simple ban on nuclear weapons. The American plan was the more practical of the two, but it was Eisenhower's moral fervor and eloquence which on July 21, 1955, gave him his second resounding success in the area.

Open Skies at the Summit

Mr. Chairman, Gentlemen:

Disarmament is one of the most important subjects on our agenda. It is also extremely difficult. In recent years the scientists have discovered methods of making weapons many, many times more destructive of opposing armed forces—but also of homes, and industries and lives—than ever known or even imagined before. The same scientific discoveries have made much more complex the problems of limitation and control and reduction of armament.

After our victory as Allies in World War II, my country rapidly disarmed. Within a few years our armament was at a very low level. Then events occurred beyond our borders which caused us to realize that we had disarmed too much. For our own security and to safeguard peace we needed greater strength. Therefore we proceeded to rearm and to associate with others in a partnership for peace and for mutual security.

The American people are determined to maintain and if necessary increase this armed strength for as long a period as is necessary to safeguard peace and to maintain our security.

But we know that a mutually dependable system for less armament on the part of all nations would be a better way to safeguard peace and to maintain our security.

It would ease the fears of war in the anxious hearts of people everywhere. It would lighten the burdens upon the backs of the people. It would make it possible for every nation, great and small, developed and less developed, to advance the standards of living of its people, to attain better food, and clothing, and shelter, more of education and larger enjoyment of life.

Therefore the United States government is prepared to enter into a sound and reliable agreement making possible the reduction of armament. I have directed that an intensive and thorough study of this subject be made within our own government. From these studies, which are continuing, a very important principle is emerging to which I referred in my opening statement on Monday.

No sound and reliable agreement can be made unless is is completely covered by an inspection and reporting system adequate to support every portion of the agreement.

The lessons of history teach us that disarmament agreements without adequate reciprocal inspection increase the dangers of war and do not brighten the prospects of peace.

Thus it is my view that the priority attention of our combined study of disarmament should be upon the subject of inspection and reporting.

Questions suggest themselves.

How effective an inspection system can be designed which would be mutually and reciprocally acceptable within our countries and the other nations of the world? How would such a system operate? What could it accomplish?

Is certainty against surprise aggression attainable by inspection? Could violations be discovered promptly and effectively counteracted?

We have not as yet been able to discover any scientific or other inspection method which would make certain of the elimination of nuclear weapons. So far as we are aware no other nation has made such a discovery. Our study of this problem is continuing. We have not as yet been able to discover any accounting or other inspection method of being certain of the true budgetary facts of total expenditures for armament. Our study of this problem is continuing. We by no means exclude the possibility of finding useful checks in these fields.

As you can see from these statements, it is our impression that many past proposals of disarmament are more sweeping than can be insured by effective inspection.

Gentlemen, since I have been working on this memorandum to present to this Conference, I have been searching my heart and mind for something that I could say here that could convince everyone of the great sincerity of the United States in approaching this problem of disarmament.

I should address myself for a moment principally to the Delegates from the Soviet Union, because our two great countries admittedly possess new and terrible weapons in quantities which do give rise in other parts of the world, or reciprocally, to the fears and dangers of surprise attack.

I propose, therefore, that we take a practical step, that we begin an arrangement, very quickly, as between ourselves—immediately. These steps would include:

To give to each other a complete blueprint of our military establishments, from beginning to end, from one end of our countries to the other; lay out the establishments and provide the blueprints to each other.

Next, to provide within our countries facilities for aerial photography to the other country—we to provide you the facilities within our country, ample facilities for aerial reconnaissance, where you can make all the pictures you choose and take them to your own country to study, you to provide exactly the same facilities for us and we to make these examinations, and by this step to convince the world that we are providing as between ourselves against the possibility of great surprise attack, thus lessening danger and relaxing tension. Likewise we will make more easily attainable a comprehensive system of inspection and disarmament, because what I propose, I assure you, would be but a beginning.

Now from my statements I believe you will anticipate my suggestion. It is that we instruct our representatives in the Subcommittee on Disarmament in discharge of their mandate from the United Nations to give priority effort to the study of inspection and reporting. Such a study could well include a step by step testing of inspection and reporting methods.

The United States is ready to proceed in the study and testing of a reliable system of inspections and reporting, and when that system is proved, then to reduce armaments with all others to the extent that the system will provide assured results.

The successful working out of such a system would do much to develop the mutual confidence which will open wide the avenues of progress for all our peoples.

The quest for peace is the statesman's most exacting duty. Security of the nation entrusted to his care is his greatest responsibility. Practical progress to lasting peace is his fondest hope. Yet in pursuit of his hope he must not betray the trust placed in him as guardian of the people's security. A sound peace—with security, justice, wellbeing, and freedom for the people of the world—*can* be achieved, but only by patiently and thoughtfully following a hard and sure and tested road.

On September 24, 1955, the President suffered a heart attack. Public responses to the crisis indicated that the majority of Americans preferred to wait and observe whether he had been incapacitated, and whether his cabinet, operating under the executive direction of his Vice-President, was able to maintain the smooth operation of public affairs. By and large, the public agreed that it was. Eisenhower later thanked his cabinet for as efficient and cooperative a performance as he had ever known. Still later, he credited his heart attack with having helped him decide to run for re-election. It had persuaded him that other Republicans, though competent for the position of President, did not have a prestige and drawing power comparable to his own for waging a successful campaign. Ike suffered a brief recurrence of his illness in 1957, which the public accepted without alarm. People unsympathetic to the Eisenhower administration were annoyed by what seemed to them popular complacency. The major significance of the episode was that it temporarily concentrated attention on the importance of the office of Vice-President.

On February 24-25, 1956, Premier Nikita Khrushchev, in a speech before the Russian Communist Party chieftains, denounced their late leader Stalin as a tyrant and murderer. This speech created a world sensation, and began a process of re-evaluation that ultimately ended in Stalin's removal from Lenin's tomb and simple reburial beside other, lesser communist leaders by the Kremlin wall. The speech raised hopes that the famous "thaw" would deepen and affect communist modes of behavior and administration inside and outside of Russia. The writhings of satellites under Russian domination reached their peak in the great effort of the Poles and the Hungarians to reassert their national feelings. The Poles no more than protested against the forms of Soviet power, and, in the quarrels and negotiations which followed, gained a measure of independence. The Hungarians made a heroic effort to reassume sovereignty, through street fighting and the proclamation of Hungarian autonomy.

Meanwhile, Eisenhower was compelled to face dangerous developments in the Middle East. It had been his hope that the United States might be able to help Egypt—center of the Arab world—to build its Aswan Dam, as a step toward modernizing Egypt's economy and providing positive leadership to its Arab-speaking allies. The Arabs were slow to rise to the opportunity, and cotton growers in the American South were loath to aid their Egyptian competitors in the production of cotton. Under such circumstances, Egyptian leaders found it convenient to discuss favors with the Russians, and to feed nationalistic fervor by taking over the Suez Canal. They also exploited and encouraged hatred of the Israelis and urged that they be driven into the Mediterranean. Eisenhower on October 31, 1956, approaching Election Day, summed up in what was the outstanding foreign policy statement of his administration, the dilemmas facing his countrymen.

Agonized Reappraisals: Hungary and Suez

My Fellow Americans:

Tonight I report to you as your President.

We all realize that the full and free debate of a political campaign surrounds us. But the events and issues I wish to place before you this evening have no connection whatsoever with matters of partisanship. They are concerns of every American—his present and his future.

I wish, therefore, to give you a report of essential facts so that

346

you—whether belonging to either one of our two great parties, or to neither—may give thoughtful and informed consideration to this swiftly changing world scene. The changes of which I speak have come in two areas of the world—Eastern Europe and the Mid-East.

I.

In Eastern Europe there is the dawning of a new day. It has not been short or easy in coming.

After World War II, the Soviet Union used military force to impose on the nations of Eastern Europe, governments of Soviet choice—servants of Moscow.

It has been a consistent United States policy—without regard to political party—to seek to end this situation. We have sought to fulfill the wartime pledge of the United Nations that these countries, over-run by wartime armies, would once again know sovereignty and self-government.

We could not, of course, carry out this policy by resort to force. Such force would have been contrary both to the best interests of the Eastern European peoples and to the abiding principles of the United Nations. But we did help to keep alive the hope of these peoples for freedom. . . .

A few days ago, the people of Poland—with their proud and deathless devotion to freedom—moved to secure a peaceful transition to a new government. And this government, it seems, will strive genuinely to serve the Polish people.

And, more recently, all the world has been watching dramatic events in Hungary where this brave people, as so often in the past, have offered their very lives for independence from foreign masters. Today, it appears, a new Hungary is rising from this struggle, a Hungary which we hope from our hearts will know full and free nationhood.

We have rejoiced in all these historic events.

Only yesterday the Soviet Union issued an important statement on its relations with all the countries of Eastern Europe. This statement recognized the need for review of Soviet policies, and the amendment of these policies to meet the demands of the people for greater national independence and personal freedom. The Soviet Union declared its readiness to consider the withdrawal of Soviet "advisers"—who have been, as you know, the effective ruling force in Soviet occupied countries—and also to consider withdrawal of Soviet forces from Poland, Hungary and Rumania.

We cannot yet know if these avowed purposes will be truly carried out.

But two things are clear.

First, the fervor and the sacrifice of the peoples of these countries, in the name of freedom, have themselves brought real promise that the light of liberty soon will shine again in this darkness.

And second, if the Soviet Union indeed faithfully acts upon its announced intention, the world will witness the greatest forward stride toward justice, trust and understanding among nations in our generation.

These are the facts. How has your government responded to them?

The United States has made clear its readiness to assist economically the new and independent governments of these countries. We have already—some days since—been in contact with the new Government of Poland on this matter. We have also publicly declared that we do not demand of these governments their adoption of any particular form of society as a condition upon our economic assistance. Our one concern is that they be free—for their sake, and for freedom's sake.

We have also—with respect to the Soviet Union—sought clearly to remove any false fears that we would look upon new governments in these Eastern European countries as potential military allies. We have no such ulterior purpose. We see these peoples as friends, and we wish simply that they be friends who are free.

II.

I now turn to that other part of the world where, at this moment, the situation is somber. It is not a situation that calls for extravagant fear or hysteria. But it invites our most serious concern.

I speak, of course, of the Middle East. This ancient crossroads of the world was, as we all know, an area long subject to colonial rule. This rule ended after World War II, when all countries there won full independence. Out of the Palestinian mandated territory was born the new State of Israel.

These historic changes could not, however, instantly banish animosities born of the ages. Israel and her Arab neighbors soon found themselves at war with one another. And the Arab nations showed continuing anger toward their former colonial rulers, notably France and Great Britain.

The United States—through all the years since the close of World War II—has labored tirelessly to bring peace and stability to this area.

We have considered it a basic matter of United States policy to support the new State of Israel and—at the same time—to strengthen our bonds both with Israel and with the Arab countries. But, unfortunately through all these years, passion in the area threatened to prevail over peaceful purposes, and in one form or another, there has been almost continuous fighting.

This situation recently was aggravated by Egyptian policy including rearmament with Communist weapons. We felt this to be a misguided policy on the part of the Government of Egypt. The State of Israel, at the same time, felt increasing anxiety for its safety. And Great Britain and France feared more and more that Egyptian policies threatened their "life line" of the Suez Canal.

These matters came to a crisis on July 26th of this year, when the Egyptian Government seized the Universal Suez Canal Company. For ninety years—ever since the inauguration of the Canal—that Company has operated the Canal, largely under British and French technical supervision.

Now there were some among our allies who urged an immediate reaction to this event by use of force. We insistently urged otherwise, and our wish prevailed—through a long succession of conferences and negotiations for weeks—even months—with participation by the United Nations. And there, in the United Nations, only a short while ago, on the basis of agreed principles, it seemed that an acceptable accord was within our reach.

But the direct relations of Egypt with both Israel and France kept worsening to a point at which first Israel—then France—and Great Britain also—determined that, in their judgment, there could be no protection of their vital interests without resort to force.

Upon this decision, events followed swiftly. On Sunday the Israeli Government ordered total mobilization. On Monday, their armed forces penetrated deeply into Egypt and to the vicinity of the Suez Canal, nearly one hundred miles away. And on Tuesday, the British and French Governments delivered a 12-hour ultimatum to Israel and Egypt—now followed up by armed attack against Egypt.

The United States was not consulted in any way about any phase of these actions. Nor were we informed of them in advance.

As it is the manifest right of any of these nations to take such decisions and actions, it is likewise our right—if our judgment so dictates—to dissent. We believe these actions to have been taken in error. For we do not accept the use of force as a wise or proper instrument for the settlement of international disputes.

To say this—in this particular instance—is in no way to minimize our friendship with these nations—nor our determination to maintain those friendships.

And we are fully aware of the grave anxieties of Israel, of Britain and of France. We know that they have been subjected to grave and repeated provocations.

The present fact, nonetheless, seems clear: the action taken can scarcely be reconciled with the principles and purposes of the United Nations to which we have all subscribed. And, beyond this, we are forced to doubt that resort to force and war will for long serve the permanent interest of the attacking nations.

Now—we must look to the future.

In the circumstances I have described, there will be no United States involvement in these present hostilities. I therefore have no plan to call the Congress in Special Session. Of course, we shall continue to keep in contact with Congressional leaders of both parties. . . .

At the same time it is—and it will remain—the dedicated purpose of your government to do all in its power to localize the fighting and to end the conflict.

We took our first measure in this action yesterday. We went to the United Nations with a request that the forces of Israel return to their own land and that hostilities in the area be brought to a close. This proposal was not adopted—because it was vetoed by Great Britain and by France.

The processes of the United Nations, however, are not exhausted. It is our hope and intent that this matter will be brought before the United Nations General Assembly. There—with no veto operating— the opinion of the world can be brought to bear in our quest for a just end to this tormenting problem. In the past the United Nations has proved able to find a way to end bloodshed. We believe it can and that it will do so again.

My fellow citizens, as I review the march of world events in recent years, I am ever more deeply convinced that the processes of the United Nations represent the soundest hope for peace in the world. For this very reason, I believe that the processes of the United Nations need further to be developed and strengthened. I speak particularly of increasing its ability to secure justice under international law.

In all the recent troubles in the Middle East, there have indeed been injustices suffered by all nations involved. But I do not believe that another instrument of injustice—war—is the remedy for these wrongs.

There can be no peace—without law. And there can be no law—if we were to invoke one code of international conduct for those who oppose us—and another for our friends. . . .

The Russians promised the Hungarians talks, then brought up heavy tanks and reinforcements to crush the insurrectionists. Last, tragic radio appeals told the West that the Hungarian uprising was dead. Eleven years of foreign affairs had created no policy for helping any people free itself from Soviet-imposed authority. The American government offered condolences, visas, and some jobs to exiles, but could do no more.

In the Middle East, the Egyptian dictator Gamal Abdel Nasser was rescued from his Israeli and English opponents. Nasser, more vigorously than ever, began to work toward a Middle Eastern union of Arab states. Communist or communist-inspired groups were also active throughout the region; if they were to seize power suddenly, they could threaten Western ability to prevent another Vietnam. Eisenhower rose to the crisis, and, in a Message to Congress, January 5, 1957, enunciated a policy that became one of the foundation stones of American foreign policy.

The Eisenhower Doctrine

. . . In my forthcoming State of the Union Message, I shall review the international situation generally. There are worldwide hopes which we can reasonably entertain, and there are worldwide responsibilities which we must carry to make certain that freedom—including our own—may be secure.

There is, however, a special situation in the Middle East which I feel I should, even now, lay before you. . . .

I.

The Middle East has abruptly reached a new and critical stage in its long and important history. In past decades many of the countries in that area were not fully self-governing. Other nations exercised considerable authority in the area and the security of the region was largely built around their power. But since the First World War there has been a steady evolution toward self-government and independence. This development the United States has welcomed and has encouraged. Our country supports without reservation the full sovereignty and independence of each and every nation in the Middle East. . . .

II.

Russia's rulers have long sought to dominate the Middle East. That was true of the Czars and it is true of the Bolsheviks. The reasons are not hard to find. They do not affect Russia's security, for no one plans to use the Middle East as a base for aggression against Russia. Never for a moment has the United States entertained such a thought.

The Soviet Union has nothing whatsoever to fear from the United States in the Middle East, or anywhere else in the world, so long as its rulers do not themselves first resort to aggression.

That statement I make solemnly and emphatically.

Neither does Russia's desire to dominate the Middle East spring from its own economic interest in the area. Russia does not appreciably use or depend upon the Suez Canal. In 1955 Soviet traffic through the Canal represented only about three fourths of 1% of the total. The Soviets have no need for, and could provide no market for, the petroleum resources which constitute the principal natural wealth of the area. Indeed, the Soviet Union is a substantial exporter of petroleum products.

The reason for Russia's interest in the Middle East is solely that of power politics. Considering her announced purpose of Communizing the world, it is easy to understand her hope of dominating the Middle East.

This region has always been the crossroads of the continents of the Eastern Hemisphere. The Suez Canal enables the nations of Asia and Europe to carry on the commerce that is essential if these countries are to maintain well-rounded and prosperous economies. The Middle East provides a gateway between Eurasia and Africa.

It contains about two thirds of the presently known oil deposits of the world and it normally supplies the petroleum needs of many nations of Europe, Asia and Africa. The nations of Europe are peculiarly dependent upon this supply, and this dependency relates to transportation as well as to production! This has been vividly demonstrated since the closing of the Suez Canal and some of the pipelines. Alternate ways of transportation and, indeed, alternate sources of power can, if necessary, be developed. But these cannot be considered as early prospects. . . .

Then there are other factors which transcend the material. The Middle East is the birthplace of three great religions—Moslem, Christian and Hebrew. Mecca and Jerusalem are more than places on the map. They symbolize religions which teach that the spirit has supremacy over matter and that the individual has a dignity and rights of which no despotic government can rightfully deprive him. It would be intolerable if the holy places of the Middle East should be subjected to a rule that glorifies atheistic materialism.

International Communism, of course, seeks to mask its purposes of domination by expressions of good will and by superficially attractive offers of political, economic and military aid. But any free nation, which is the subject of Soviet enticement, ought, in elementary wisdom, to look behind the mask.

Remember Estonia, Latvia and Lithuania! In 1939 the Soviet Union entered into mutual assistance pacts with these then independent countries; and the Soviet Foreign Minister, addressing the Extraordinary Fifth Session of the Supreme Soviet in October 1939, solemnly and publicly declared that "we stand for the scrupulous and punctilious observance of the pacts on the basis of complete reciprocity, and we declare that all the nonsensical talk about the Sovietization of the Baltic countries is only to the interest of our common enemies and of all anti-Soviet provocateurs." Yet in *1940*, Estonia, Latvia and Lithuania were forcibly incorporated into the Soviet Union. . . .

Stalin's death brought hope that this pattern would change. And we read the pledge of the Warsaw Treaty of 1955 that the Soviet Union would follow in satellite countries "the principles of mutual respect for their independence and sovereignty and noninterference in domestic affairs." But we have just seen the subjugation of Hungary by naked armed force. In the aftermath of this Hungarian tragedy, world respect for and belief in Soviet promises have sunk to a new low. International Communism needs and seeks a recognizable success. . . .

III.

Our thoughts naturally turn to the United Nations as a protector of small nations. Its charter gives it primary responsibility for the

353

maintenance of international peace and security. Our country has given the United Nations its full support in relation to the hostilities in Hungary and in Egypt. The United Nations was able to bring about a cease-fire and withdrawal of hostile forces from Egypt because it was dealing with governments and peoples who had a decent respect for the opinions of mankind as reflected in the United Nations General Assembly. But in the case of Hungary, the situation was different. The Soviet Union vetoed action by the Security Council to require the withdrawal of Soviet armed forces from Hungary. And it has shown callous indifference to the recommendations, even the censure, of the General Assembly. The United Nations can always be helpful, but it cannot be a wholly dependable protector of freedom when the ambitions of the Soviet Union are involved.

IV.

Under all the circumstances I have laid before you, a greater responsibility now devolves upon the United States. We have shown, so that none can doubt, our dedication to the principle that force shall not be used internationally for any aggressive purpose and that the integrity and independence of the nations of the Middle East should be inviolate. Seldom in history has a nation's dedication to principle been tested as severely as ours during recent weeks. . . .

If the Middle East is to continue its geographic role of uniting rather than separating East and West; if its vast economic resources are to serve the well-being of the peoples there, as well as that of others; and if its cultures and religions and their shrines are to be preserved for the uplifting of the spirits of the peoples, then the United States must make more evident its willingness to support the independence of the freedom-loving nations of the area.

V.

Under these circumstances I deem it necessary to seek the cooperation of the Congress. Only with that cooperation can we give the reassurance needed to deter aggression, to give courage and confidence to those who are dedicated to freedom and thus prevent a chain of events which would gravely endanger all of the free world.

There have been several Executive declarations made by the United States in relation to the Middle East. There is the Tripartite Declaration of May 25, 1950, followed by the Presidential assurance of October 31, 1950, to the King of Saudi Arabia. There is the Presidential declaration of April 9, 1956, that the United States will within constitutional means oppose any aggression in the area. There is our Declaration of November 29, 1956, that a threat to the territorial integrity or political independence of Iran, Iraq, Pakistan, or Turkey would be viewed by the United States with the utmost gravity.

Nevertheless, weaknesses in the present situation and the increased danger from International Communism, convince me that basic United States policy should now find expression in joint action by the Congress and the Executive. Furthermore, our joint resolve should be so couched as to make it apparent that if need be our words will be backed by action.

VI.

It is nothing new for the President and the Congress to join to recognize that the national integrity of other free nations is directly related to our own security.

We have joined to create and support the security system of the United Nations. We have reinforced the collective security system of the United Nations by a series of collective defense arrangements. Today we have security treaties with 42 other nations which recognize that our peace and security are intertwined. We have joined to take decisive action in relation to Greece and Turkey and in relation to Taiwan. . . .

The action which I propose would have the following features.

It would, first of all, authorize the United States to cooperate with and assist any nation or group of nations in the general area of the Middle East in the development of economic strength dedicated to the maintenance of national independence.

It would, in the second place, authorize the Executive to undertake in the same region programs of military assistance and cooperation with any nation or group of nations which desires such aid.

It would, in the third place, authorize such assistance and cooperation to include the employment of the armed forces of the United States to secure and protect the territorial integrity and political independence of such nations, requesting such aid, against overt armed aggression from any nation controlled by International Communism.

These measures would have to be consonant with the treaty obligations of the United States, including the Charter of the United Nations and with any action or recommendations of the United Nations. They would also, if armed attack occurs, be subject

355

to the overriding authority of the United Nations Security Council in accordance with the Charter.

The present proposal would, in the fourth place, authorize the President to employ, for economic and defensive military purposes, sums available under the Mutual Security Act of 1954, as amended, without regard to existing limitations. . . .

VII.

This program will not solve all the problems of the Middle East. Neither does it represent the totality of our policies for the area. There are the problems of Palestine and relations between Israel and the Arab States, and the future of the Arab refugees. There is the problem of the future status of the Suez Canal. These difficulties are aggravated by International Communism, but they would exist quite apart from that threat. It is not the purpose of the legislation I propose to deal directly with these problems. The United Nations is actively concerning itself with all these matters, and we are supporting the United Nations. The United States has made clear, notably by Secretary Dulles' address of August 26, 1955, that we are willing to do much to assist the United Nations in solving the basic problems of Palestine. . . .

It is my hope and belief that if our purpose be proclaimed, as proposed by the requested legislation, that very fact will serve to halt any contemplated aggression. We shall have heartened the patriots who are dedicated to the independence of their nations. They will not feel that they stand alone, under the menace of great power. And I should add that patriotism is, throughout this area, a powerful sentiment. It is true that fear sometimes perverts true patriotism into fanaticism and to the acceptance of dangerous enticements from without. But if that fear can be allayed, then the climate will be more favorable to the attainment of worthy national ambitions.

And as I have indicated, it will also be necessary for us to contribute economically to strengthen those countries, or groups of countries, which have governments manifestly dedicated to the preservation of independence and resistance to subversion. Such measures will provide the greatest insurance against Communist inroads. Words alone are not enough. . . .

At home, another great issue was taking shape. The United States Supreme Court, headed by Eisenhower's appointee, Chief Justice Earl Warren, had, on May 17, 1954, made its historic decision desegregating the public schools of the land. The force of this decision was increased by the dissatisfaction of Negro middle-class elements at home, who had discovered that respectability, excellent salaries, and other signs of well-being and readiness for equality did not add up to equality. They were unimpressed by the segregationist "equal but separate" doctrine. They argued that separateness did not in fact give them equality. And elements of the Negro people, in addition, were seized by a more principled insistence on the brotherhood of man, of which they felt themselves deprived. Such feelings were augmented by the fact that Africa was in ferment, and was producing numerous spectacular proponents of Negro nationalism. Negroes who had once been offended at being thought of as Africa-related could feel a new pride of association with those vast and varied terrains.

Eisenhower took a moderate view of the great decision, and awaited events. The decision was underscored by the May 31, 1955, Supreme Court decision which reaffirmed the findings of the previous year but recognized the need for gradual but unequivocal action. Eisenhower himself continued the process initiated under Truman of desegregating areas and services under direct governmental control, fighting the tendencies toward racial quotas and other discriminations which pervaded social and official life.

Meanwhile desegregation moved scarcely at all. Terroristic incidents warned Negroes against challenging the status quo. A pitiful case that won headlines was the murder in Mississippi of a Negro boy, visiting from Chicago, who had perpetrated the social error of whistling appreciatively at a presumably pretty white woman. The South was girding for battle. September 9, 1957, Congress approved establishment of a Civil Rights Commission. Initial trouble broke out in Little Rock, Arkansas, where the National Association for the Advancement of Colored People attempted to give vitality to the desegregation decision by opening the local high school to Negro children. Governor Orval Faubus took the lead in preventing such an occurrence. On September 23, 1957, Eisenhower warned that he would not tolerate the flouting of Federal law. The next day he initiated government action in the field and explained his purposes to the radio and television audience.

Little Rock

Good Evening, My Fellow Citizens:

For a few minutes this evening I want to speak to you about the serious situation that has arisen in Little Rock. To make this talk I have come to the President's office in the White House. I could have spoken from Rhode Island, where I have been staying recently, but I felt that, in speaking from the house of Lincoln, of Jackson and of Wilson, my words would better convey both the sadness I feel in the action I was compelled today to take and the firmness with which I intend to pursue this course until the orders of the Federal Court at Little Rock can be executed without unlawful interference.

In that city, under the leadership of demagogic extremists, disorderly mobs have deliberately prevented the carrying out of proper orders from a Federal Court. Local authorities have not eliminated that violent opposition and, under the law, I yesterday issued a Proclamation calling upon the mob to disperse.

This morning the mob again gathered in front of the Central High School of Little Rock, obviously for the purpose of again preventing the carrying out of the Court's order relating to the admission of Negro children to that school.

Whenever normal agencies prove inadequate to the task and it becomes necessary for the Executive Branch of the Federal Government to use its powers and authority to uphold Federal Courts, the President's responsibility is inescapable.

In accordance with that responsibility, I have today issued an Executive Order directing the use of troops under Federal authority to aid in the execution of Federal law at Little Rock, Arkansas. This became necessary when my Proclamation of yesterday was not observed, and the obstruction of justice still continues.

It is important that the reasons for my action be understood by all our citizens.

As you know, the Supreme Court of the United States has decided that separate public educational facilities for the races are inherently unequal and therefore compulsory school segregation laws are unconstitutional.

Our personal opinions about the decision have no bearing on the matter of enforcement; the responsibility and authority of the Supreme Court to interpret the Constitution are very clear. Local Federal Courts were instructed by the Supreme Court to issue such orders and decrees as might be necessary to achieve admission to public schools without regard to race—and with all deliberate speed.

During the past several years, many communities in our Southern States have instituted public school plans for gradual progress in

358

the enrollment and attendance of school children of all races in order to bring themselves into compliance with the law of the land.

They thus demonstrated to the world that we are a nation in which laws, not men, are supreme.

I regret to say that this truth—the cornerstone of our liberties—was not observed in this instance.

It was my hope that this localized situation would be brought under control by city and State authorities. If the use of local police powers had been sufficient, our traditional method of leaving the problems in those hands would have been pursued. But when large gatherings of obstructionists made it impossible for the decrees of the Court to be carried out, both the law and the national interest demanded that the President take action.

Here is the sequence of events in the development of the Little Rock school case.

In May of 1955, the Little Rock School Board approved a moderate plan for the gradual desegregation of the public schools in that city. It provided that a start toward integration would be made at the present term in the high school, and that the plan would be in full operation by 1963. Here I might say that in a number of communities in Arkansas integration in the schools has already started and without violence of any kind. Now this Little Rock plan was challenged in the courts by some who believed that the period of time as proposed in the plan was too long.

The United States Court at Little Rock, which has supervisory responsibility under the law for the plan of desegregation in the public schools, dismissed the challenge, thus approving a gradual rather than an abrupt change from the existing system. The court found that the school board had acted in good faith in planning for a public school system free from racial discrimination.

Since that time, the court has on three separate occasions issued orders directing that the plan be carried out. All persons were instructed to refrain from interfering with the efforts of the school board to comply with the law.

Proper and sensible observance of the law then demanded the respectful obedience which the nation has a right to expect from all its people. This, unfortunately, has not been the case at Little Rock. Certain misguided persons, many of them imported into Little Rock by agitators, have insisted upon defying the law and have sought to bring it into disrepute. The orders of the court have thus been frustrated. . . .

359

Now, let me make it very clear that Federal troops are not being used to relieve local and state authorities of their primary duty to preserve the peace and order of the community. Nor are the troops there for the purpose of taking over the responsibility of the School Board and the other responsible local officials in running Central High School. The running of our school system and the maintenance of peace and order in each of our States are strictly local affairs and the Federal Government does not interfere except in a very few special cases and when requested by one of the several States. In the present case the troops are there, pursuant to law, solely for the purpose of preventing interference with the orders of the Court.

The proper use of the powers of the Executive Branch to enforce the orders of a Federal Court is limited to extraordinary and compelling circumstances. Manifestly, such an extreme situation has been created in Little Rock. This challenge must be met and with such measures as will preserve to the people as a whole their lawfully-protected rights in a climate permitting their free and fair exercise.

The overwhelming majority of our people in every section of the country are united in their respect for observance of the law—even in those cases where they may disagree with that law.

They deplore the call of extremists to violence.

The decision of the Supreme Court concerning school integration, of course, affects the South more seriously than it does other sections of the country. In that region I have many warm friends, some of them in the city of Little Rock. I have deemed it a great personal privilege to spend in our Southland tours of duty while in the military service and enjoyable recreational periods since that time.

So from intimate personal knowledge, I know that the over-whelming majority of the people in the South—including those of Arkansas and of Little Rock—are of good will, united in their efforts to preserve and respect the law even when they disagree with it. . . .

At a time when we face grave situations abroad because of the hatred that Communism bears toward a system of government based on human rights, it would be difficult to exaggerate the harm that is being done to the prestige and influence, and indeed to the safety, of our nation and the world.

Our enemies are gloating over this incident and using it everywhere to misrepresent our whole nation. We are portrayed as a violator of those standards of conduct which the peoples of the world united to proclaim in the Charter of the United Nations. There they affirmed "faith in fundamental human rights" and "in the dignity and worth of the human person" and they did so "without distinction as to race, sex, language or religion."

And so, with deep confidence, I call upon the citizens of the State of Arkansas to assist in bringing to an immediate end all interference with the law and its processes. If resistance to the Federal Court orders ceases at once, the further presence of Federal troops will be unnecessary and the City of Little Rock will return to its normal habits of peace and order and a blot upon the fair name and high honor of our nation in the world will be removed.

Thus will be restored the image of America and of all its parts as one nation, indivisible, with liberty and justice for all.

Good night, and thank you very much.

Troops patrolled Little Rock until May 8, 1958. Actual desegregation was little more than token; the entire incident had only symbolic significance. The President took advantage of the summer recess to remove the Federal troops and to express his hope that thereafter local officials and citizens would assume responsibility for maintaining the laws.

The "Eisenhower Era" was entering its last phase. A species of stability seemed to be settling over world and domestic affairs. There was less general fear of an atomic explosion. Public discussion over bomb shelters waned; fewer Hollywood stars built elaborate shelters stocked with entertainment facilities and edibles. There were, indeed, interesting discussions. One individual asserted that he would shoot strangers who tried to gain entry into his shelter, and thoughtful citizens studied the pros and cons of what was owed to one's own family, as compared with society. Another controversy raged over how much torture an American soldier could be expected reasonably to endure before telling his captors everything he knew. Sometimes a plaintive editorial voice asked what had happened to the spirit of Nathan Hale. Joseph McCarthy died in 1957, puzzled, disillusioned, and largely forgotten. Intellectuals registered discontent with a society which the scabrous writer, Henry Miller, had once described as an "air-conditioned nightmare." The 1930's were totally forgotten. Youngsters gave "twenties" parties and talked familiarly of "Scott" Fitzgerald. Yet there was anxiety. Men who had eaten meagerly during the depression crisis were not even permitted to enjoy their expanded waistlines. Advertisements bewilderingly offered them hearty meals in one column and denounced them for being fat in the next. Scandal, probably unfairly, hit the Eisenhower administration in charges that the President's assistant, ex-governor Sherman Adams of New Hampshire had received favors from a manufacturer who turned out to be most interested in giving and receiving favors. Democrats made the most of the incident, and Adams resigned to

361

avoid embarrassing the President. In May of 1958, Vice-President Richard M. Nixon was subjected to demonstrations and attacks during his South American good will tour. Eisenhower's own tour south, early in 1960, elicited more good will and warmth than it did light. Eisenhower denied Soviet contentions that the United States had been imperialistic in its dealings with South American nations. "In all history," he declared, "no nation has had a more honorable record in its dealings with other countries than the United States." Eisenhower had once derogated the use of such phrases as "in all history."

He continued to aspire to a summit meeting that would permit further probing of the possibilities for peace between the United States and the U.S.S.R. Such a meeting was arranged to convene in Paris in May of 1960. He arrived in Paris May 15 and expressed the pleasure he anticipated in meeting his old friends President de Gaulle and British Prime Minister Harold Macmillan. He voiced his willingness to meet Khrushchev "halfway in every honest effort" to make a new beginning. Suddenly, the world was electrified by news that an American U-2 plane had been brought down in Soviet territory. Its pilot was alive and in captivity, and the Russians were roused by being victims of espionage. A proper atmosphere for a summit conference had been shattered. Eisenhower met the issue in his statement released the following day of May 16.

U–2

Having been informed yesterday by General de Gaulle and Prime Minister Macmillan of the position which Mr. Khrushchev has taken in regard to this conference during his calls yesterday morning on them, I gave most careful thought as to how this matter should best be handled. Having in mind the great importance of this conference and the hopes that the peoples of all the world have reposed in this meeting, I concluded that in the circumstances it was best to see if at today's private meeting any possibility existed through the exercise of reason and restraint to dispose of this matter of the overflights, which would have permitted the conference to go forward.

I was under no illusion as to the probability of success of any such approach but I felt that in view of the great responsibility resting on me as President of the United States this effort should be made.

In this I received the strongest support of my colleagues President de Gaulle and Prime Minister Macmillan. Accordingly, at this morning's private session, despite the violence and inaccuracy of Mr. Khrushchev's statements, I replied to him on [sic] the following terms:

"I had previously been informed of the sense of the statement just read by Premier Khrushchev.

"In my statement of May 11th and in the statement of Secretary [Christian A.] Herter* of May 9th, the position of the United States was made clear with respect to the distasteful necessity of espionage activities in a world where nations distrust each other's intentions. We pointed out that these activities had no aggressive intent but rather were to assure the safety of the United States and the free world against surprise attack by a power which boasts of its ability to devastate the United States and other countries by missiles armed with atomic warheads. As is well known, not only the United States but most other countries are constantly the targets of elaborate and persistent espionage of the Soviet Union.

"There is in the Soviet statement an evident misapprehension on one key point. It alleges that the United States has through official statements, threatened continued overflights. The importance of this alleged threat was emphasized and repeated by Mr. Khrushchev. The United States has made no such threat. Neither I nor my government has intended any. The actual statements go no further than to say that the United States will not shirk its responsibility to safeguard against surprise attack.

"In point of fact, these flights were suspended after the recent incident and are not to be resumed. Accordingly, this cannot be the issue.

"I have come to Paris to seek agreements with the Soviet Union which would eliminate the necessity for all forms of espionage, including overflights. I see no reason to use this incident to disrupt the conference.

"Should it prove impossible, because of the Soviet attitude, to come to grips here in Paris with this problem and the other vital issues threatening world peace, I am planning in the near future to submit to the United Nations a proposal for the creation of a United Nations aerial surveillance to detect preparations for attack. This plan I had intended to place before this conference. This surveillance system would operate in the territories of all nations prepared to accept such inspection. For its part, the United States is prepared not only to accept United Nations aerial surveillance, but to do everything in its power to contribute to the rapid organization and successful operation of such international surveillance.

"We of the United States are here to consider in good faith the important problems before this conference. We are prepared either to

* Secretary of State Dulles had died on May 24, 1959.

363

carry this point no further, or to undertake bilateral conversations between the United States and the U.S.S.R. while the main conference proceeds."

My words were seconded and supported by my Western colleagues who also urged Mr. Khrushchev to pursue the path of reason and common sense, and to forget propaganda. Such an attitude would have permitted the conference to proceed. Mr. Khrushchev was left in no doubt by me that his ultimatum would never be acceptable to the United States.

Mr. Khrushchev brushed aside all arguments of reason, and not only insisted upon this ultimatum, but also insisted that he was going to publish his statement in full at the time of his own choosing.

It was thus made apparent that he was determined to wreck the Paris conference.

In fact, the only conclusion that can be drawn from his behavior this morning was that he came all the way from Moscow to Paris with the sole intention of sabotaging this meeting on which so much of the hopes of the world have rested.

In spite of this serious and adverse development, I have no intention whatsoever to diminish my continuing efforts to promote progress toward a peace with justice. This applies to the remainder of my stay in Paris as well as thereafter.

So the summit meeting came to nothing. Eisenhower made stops in Portugal. In Lisbon, speaking to the staff of the U. S. Embassy and the American community, he asked: "Did you see that cartoon not long ago where it says, 'The next speaker needs all the introduction he can get'? Well, I rather feel that way, after coming from this last meeting in Paris." He offered a detailed report to the American people, on his return, on May 25, concluding: "long ago I pledged to you that I would journey anywhere in the world to promote the cause of peace. I remain pledged to pursue a peace of dignity, of friendships, of honor, of justice."

But his time as President was running out. Attention centered on the coming nominating conventions. He concerned himself with areas that were suffering "labor surpluses." He visited Manila and Taipei, over which loomed the guns of the Seventh Fleet as well as the less friendly cannon of the Chinese Reds, and he visited Korea again. He grew "deeply perplexed" by the course of the Cuban revolution and its leader Fidel Castro, whose advent at the beginning of 1959 had been received with interest and good wishes. Popular motion picture and television personalities had visited Castro and given him their attention. Now the Cubans were revealing tendencies that promised no good, Eisenhower thought. They were sharp in their criticism of Americans. They were friendly toward Russia.

Ike thought Castro's suspicions of the United States were offensive and unfounded. "The United States," he affirmed, January 26, 1960, "adheres strictly to the policy of non-intervention in the domestic affairs of other countries, including Cuba." His government had viewed with increasing concern "the tendency of spokesmen of the Cuban government, including Prime Minister Castro, to create the illusion of aggressive acts and conspiratorial activities aimed at the Cuban government and attributed to the United States officials or agencies." Cuban seizure of U. S. property, American changes in the Cuban sugar quota, Cuban trade relations with Soviet Russia—all this and more culminated, January 3, 1961, in the termination of diplomatic relations between the United States and Cuba. Eisenhower declared that American friendship for the Cuban people was not affected. "[O]ur sympathy goes out to the people of Cuba now suffering under the yoke of a dictator."

Eisenhower said that he did his best for the Republican presidential candidate in the November elections, and afterwards felicitated the successful Democratic candidate. He closed up his affairs as President, and, on January 17, 1961, offered his final thoughts in office to the American people.

Farewell Address

My fellow Americans:

Three days from now, after half a century in the service of our country, I shall lay down the responsibilities of office as, in traditional and solemn ceremony, the authority of the Presidency is vested in my successor.

This evening I come to you with a message of leave-taking and farewell, and to share a few final thoughts with you, my countrymen.

Like every other citizen, I wish the new President, and all who will labor with him, Godspeed. I pray that the coming years will be blessed with peace and prosperity for all.

Our people expect their President and the Congress to find essential agreement on issues of great moment, the wise resolution of which will better shape the future of the Nation.

My own relations with the Congress, which began on a remote and tenuous basis when, long ago, a member of the Senate appointed me to West Point, have since ranged to the intimate during the war and immediate post-war period, and, finally, to the mutually interdependent during these past eight years.

In this final relationship, the Congress and the Administration have, on most vital issues, cooperated well, to serve the national good rather than mere partisanship, and so have assured that the business of the Nation should go forward. So, my official relationship with the Congress ends in a feeling, on my part, of gratitude that we have been able to do so much together.

II.

We now stand ten years past the midpoint of a century that has witnessed four major wars among great nations. Three of these involved our own country. Despite these holocausts America is today the strongest, the most influential and most productive nation in the world. Understandably proud of this pre-eminence, we yet realize that America's leadership and prestige depend, not merely upon our unmatched material progress, riches and military strength, but on how we use our power in the interests of world peace and human betterment.

III.

Throughout America's adventure in free government, our basic purposes have been to keep the peace; to foster progress in human achievement, and to enhance liberty, dignity and integrity among people and among nations. To strive for less would be unworthy of a free and religious people. Any failure traceable to arrogance, or our lack of comprehension or readiness to sacrifice would inflict upon us grievous hurt both at home and abroad.

Progress toward these noble goals is persistently threatened by the conflict now engulfing the world. It commands our whole attention, absorbs our very beings. We face a hostile ideology—global in scope, atheistic in character, ruthless in purpose, and insidious in method. Unhappily the danger it poses promises to be of indefinite duration. To meet it successfully, there is called for, not so much the emotional and transitory sacrifices of crisis, but rather those which enable us to carry forward steadily, surely, and without complaint the burdens of a prolonged and complex struggle—with liberty the stake. Only thus shall we remain, despite every provocation, on our charted course toward permanent peace and human betterment.

Crises there will continue to be. In meeting them, whether foreign or domestic, great or small, there is a recurring temptation to feel that some spectacular and costly action could become the miraculous solution to all current difficulties. A huge increase in newer elements of our defense; development of unrealistic programs to cure every ill in agriculture; a dramatic expansion in basic and applied research—these and many other possibilities, each possibly promising in itself, may be suggested as the only way to the road we wish to travel.

But each proposal must be weighed in the light of a broader consideration: the need to maintain balance in and among national programs—balance between the private and the public economy, balance between cost and hoped for advantage—balance between the clearly necessary and the comfortably desirable; balance between our essential requirements as a nation and the duties imposed by the nation upon the individual; balance between actions of the moment and the national welfare of the future. Good judgment seeks balance and progress; lack of it eventually finds imbalance and frustration.

The record of many decades stands as proof that our people and their government have, in the main, understood these truths and have responded to them well, in the face of stress and threat. But threats, new in kind or degree, constantly arise. I mention two only.

IV.

A vital element in keeping the peace is our military establishment. Our arms must be mighty, ready for instant action, so that no potential aggressor may be tempted to risk his own destruction.

Our military organization today bears little relation to that known by any of my predecessors in peacetime, or indeed by the fighting men of World War II or Korea.

Until the latest of our world conflicts, the United States had no armaments industry. American makers of plowshares could, with time and as required, make swords as well. But now we can no longer risk emergency improvisation of national defense; we have been compelled to create a permanent armaments industry of vast proportions. Added to this, three and a half million men and women are directly engaged in the defense establishment. We annually spend on military security more than the net income of all United States corporations.

This conjunction of an immense military establishment and a large arms industry is new in the American experience. The total influence—economic, political, even spiritual—is felt in every city, every State house, every office of the Federal government. We recognize the imperative need for this development. Yet we must not fail to comprehend its grave implications. Our toil, resources and livelihood are all involved; so is the very structure of our society.

In the councils of government, we must guard against the acquisition of unwarranted influence, whether sought or unsought, by the military-industrial complex. The potential for the disastrous rise of misplaced power exists and will persist.

We must never let the weight of this combination endanger our liberties or democratic processes. We should take nothing for granted. Only an alert and knowledgeable citizenry can compel the proper meshing of the huge industrial and military machinery of defense with our peaceful methods and goals, so that security and liberty may prosper together.

Akin to, and largely responsible for the sweeping changes in our industrial-military posture, has been the technological revolution during recent decades.

In this revolution, research has become central; it also becomes more formalized, complex, and costly. A steadily increasing share is conducted for, by, or at the direction of, the Federal government.

Today, the solitary inventor, tinkering in his shop, has been overshadowed by task forces of scientists in laboratories and testing fields. In the same fashion, the free university, historically the fountainhead of free ideas and scientific discovery, has experienced a revolution in the conduct of research. Partly because of the huge costs involved, a government contract becomes virtually a substitute for intellectual curiosity. For every old blackboard there are now hundreds of new electronic computers.

The prospect of domination of the nation's scholars by Federal employment, project allocations, and the power of money is ever present—and is gravely to be regarded.

Yet, in holding scientific research and discovery in respect, as we should, we must also be alert to the equal and opposite danger that public policy could itself become the captive of a scientific-technological elite.

It is the task of statesmanship to mold, to balance, and to integrate these and other forces, new and old, within the principles of our democratic system—ever aiming toward the supreme goals of our free society. . . .

VII.

So—in this my last good night to you as your President—I thank you for the many opportunities you have given me for public service

368

in war and peace. I trust that in that service you find some things worthy; as for the rest of it, I know you will find ways to improve performance in the future.

You and I—my fellow citizens—need to be strong in our faith that all nations, under God, will reach the goal of peace with justice. May we be ever unswerving in devotion to principle, confident but humble with power, diligent in pursuit of the Nation's great goals.

To all the peoples of the world, I once more give expression to America's prayerful and continuing aspiration:

We pray that peoples of all faiths, all races, all nations, may have their great human needs satisfied; that those now denied opportunity shall come to enjoy it to the full; that all who yearn for freedom may experience its spiritual blessings; that those who have freedom will understand, also, its heavy responsibilities; that all who are insensitive to the needs of others will learn charity; that the scourges of poverty, disease and ignorance will be made to disappear from the earth, and that, in the goodness of time, all peoples will come to live together in a peace guaranteed by the binding force of mutual respect and love.

JOHN FITZGERALD KENNEDY

(1917–1963)

New Frontiers

We dare not forget today that we are the heirs of that first revolution. Let the word go forth from this time and place, to friend and foe alike, that the torch has been passed to a new generation of Americans—born in this century, tempered by war, disciplined by a hard and bitter peace, proud of our ancient heritage—and unwilling to witness or permit the slow undoing of those human rights to which this Nation has always been committed, and to which we are committed today at home and around the world.

Inaugural Address, *January 20, 1961*

HE WAS a young man of wealth, but this did not distinguish him from many young men of wealth who had chosen a career in politics. He was part of a large, aggressive, capable family which was very helpful to him in his work, but did not by itself explain his phenomenal ascent. He met the problem of all ambitious young men: of standing for something, and also of finding the words and gestures that would persuade the vast electorate to prefer him over his opponent.

He had been a good student, but, though he read the New York *Times* industriously at his exclusive Choate School, aged fourteen, he was also interested in football and swimming. In 1938, he buckled down to work, visited Europe and the Middle East, returned to Harvard to work on an honors thesis in political science. He graduated *cum laude* and revised his thesis into his first book, *Why England Slept* (1940). With England under air attack by Hitler's bombers, it became a best seller. It was a remarkable production for a twenty-three-year old. Henry R. Luce, of *Time-Life,* who introduced it, said that if its author was "characteristic of the younger generation—and I believe he is—many of us would be happy to have the destinies of this Republic handed over to his generation at once."

The book probed the psychology of the Britisher and of every man: "It takes time to change men's minds, and it takes violent shocks to change an entire nation's psychology." The English had responded to the slogan of economy in government expenditures, they had hoped for disarmament, had put their faith in bombers rather than defensive fighter planes. They had misread statistics. Even when events had at last alarmed them, they had been half-hearted, with an attitude like that "of a man who, in noticing that his suit is getting shabby, decides he had better order a new one. But, if he must choose between food or the new suit, a man will naturally take the food." There was a lesson in all this for America: "Any system of government will work when everything is going well. It's the system that functions in the pinches that survives."

In the spring of 1941, Kennedy was turned down as an enlistee by the army because of an old back injury. He worked to strengthen his back, and was accepted by the navy. There followed service in the Pacific as a PT commander which almost cost him his life in August of 1943. He returned a war hero, and his ambitious father's hope in politics. In 1946, he was elected to Congress. He was adept at building up his personal political machine, and spent energy and money freely. Having been re-elected three times, he ran in 1952 for the Senate against Henry Cabot Lodge, who was also a fortunate and capable man, and the scion of a more patrician family than Kennedy's. The older Lodge had, in 1916, beaten Kennedy's grandfather, "Honey Fitz" John F. Fitzgerald, who had been mayor of Boston. But Kennedy's multimillionaire father worked strenuously in his behalf; his mother's teas for his constituents became legendary; his brothers and sisters and their relatives outdid themselves in putting his name before possible voters. He himself shook more hands, made more promises, traveled more extensively than ever before.

A vignette of the campaign* has him worried over an amendment cutting foreign aid to Israel, which he had offered in the House in 1951. It had not passed, but it disturbed his Jewish constituents. With Republicans reminding them of the deed, Kennedy asked House Speaker John W. McCormack for help; the worldly-wise fellow Democrat had warned him this would happen. McCormack appeared at a "hastily arranged rally in Ward 14—where he is fondly known as Rabbi John"—and there falsely confided that he had himself secretly prepared the young man's amendment, in order to head off the plot of "powerful forces" who planned more drastic cuts in aid to the Israelis. Kennedy won. He later advised a new congressman to "stick with John McCormack, and you'll be all right."

The young Senator developed a social welfare program that grew out of ward politics patronage and was refined into New Deal and Fair Deal measures. He fought for housing legislation. He opposed Taft-Hartley. He endorsed increased social security and argued for a lowering of immigration bars. In a muddled period, highlighted by Korea and Red China on one side of the world and Iron Curtain problems on the other, he made sharp and not wholly consistent stands that emphasized

* *Saturday Evening Post,* March 21, 1964, p. 68.

his old cause, defense at home and abroad. His argumentative views made more conspicuous his attractive and vigorous young personality. He made trips abroad and returned to offer reports of his personal observations. His father's fame as a New Deal stalwart and ambassador to the Court of St. James helped him, but the residue of regard, purposefulness, political articulateness and effectiveness was his own.

Now happily married and in the powerful Senate, the fortunate youth set himself to building roads into national politics. He resisted being considered a spokesman for Catholics, but approved aid for parochial schools. He fought for economy in government, but not at the expense of welfare measures and what he deemed to be necessary foreign aid. He erected an impressive personal staff of loyal and adroit workers, and though he had been active in furthering Adlai E. Stevenson's candidacy in 1952, he did not forget his own. He bore down on issues of interest to his Massachusetts constituency, and took steps to avoid being firmly identified with liberal causes. In an atmosphere heated by Senator McCarthy, on whose Committee on Government Operations he served, he studied deliberation and noncommitment. His strategy in 1954 was comparable to Abraham Lincoln's as a Congressman during the crisis that brought on the Mexican war. Lincoln had refused to become emotional over whether or not Mexicans had crossed the boundary to attack and kill part of a detachment of American dragoons. Lincoln had suggested an inquiry into whether, in fact, the line had been crossed. "Line" Lincoln, his critics called him, satirically. The young Massachusetts Senator was equally legalistic as to whether McCarthy was or was not transgressing civil rights. His caution offended some liberals, and also some Catholics who thought a more ardent anticommunism was proper to 1954. However, his emphasis on law and unwillingness to join issue, like Eisenhower's, enabled him to survive a politically dangerous era. It enabled him to avoid being tarred as demagogically anticommunist, as happened to the young Senator from California, Richard M. Nixon, who had served on the House Un-American Activities Committee.

A serious operation all but incapacitated the young Massachusetts Senator. His family, friends, and staff rallied to give him stimulation and profitable work during his convalescence. The preface to his completed and published *Profiles in Courage* (1955) bristled with the names of people who counted in journalism and academic work, who had collected materials for him, helped prepare chapters, offered "suggestions, understanding cooperation and initial encouragement." Yet the book was his own. He had simply, more than others, known how to bring together efficient and convinced associates, and to profit from their talents. *Profiles in Courage* was a sensational and continuing best seller. It repaid his years of interest in reading, his respect for knowledge and history, his curiosity about people, which had always kept his practical arts as a politician from becoming ends in themselves.

The book made Kennedy more famous than had his day-in day-out political work. He voted, to be sure, the straight Democratic Party history ticket on strategic aspects of his tale, but he was hardly to be blamed for the stupidity of his opponents. Thus, he praised John Quincy Adams for having broken with his Federalist associates to support President Jefferson's embargo policy of 1807-9. Only in passing—in a passing phrase—did *Profiles in Courage* note that Adams's long battle against the infamous Gag Rule—a Democratic Party-sponsored anticivil liberties measure—was, much later, "the brightest chapter of his history." The young Senator's historical interests were as well controlled as were all other aspects of his career. But they emphasized concern for the Union, and included brave views on political morality and the need for independence, all of which the reading public found admirable.

Kennedy was surprisingly strong in the 1956 Democratic National Convention fight for the vice-presidential nomination. Observers later thought he was fortunate in having been edged out by Estes Kefauver of Tennessee, thus avoiding the drastic Democratic defeat of that year. But granted his charming, intelligent personality, the nomination might well have been yet another rung in his ladder to the presidency. Following the election, he continued with his forging of a national machine. Nixon was now a Vice-President who had made international headlines, and acted as presidential stand-in during Eisenhower's illness. Critics later noted how often the dedicated Senator was off addressing a Pulaski Day dinner in Milwaukee, a student convocation at U.C.L.A., a Conference of the American Friends of Vietnam, the National Conference of Christians and Jews, a Democratic Party dinner in San Juan, Puerto Rico, or the Loyola College Alumni Association banquet, often at the expense of direct service in the Senate. During the 1960 elections, misguided Republican Party speakers attempted to make political capital of these activities. But Americans never appeared to take to heart the political junketing of lawyers who never seemed to practice law, or governors who were rarely in their state capitals. Apparently, they realized that political aspirants who, like Kefauver, stuck to the business for which they were elected, were best suited to such business.

Early in 1960, Kennedy published *The Strategy of Peace,* a collection of his speeches on many subjects, with an introduction by Allan Nevins, who combined wide popularity with scholarly status. The collection, in effect, called Kennedy's forces together for the long drive to the presidency. The young Senator made a spectacular showing in the primaries of that year. Once the Democrats had convened for the main event, his political organization moved with startling efficiency. Such an old pro as Lyndon B. Johnson had his eye on the major plum, and Johnson was famous, almost notorious, for his ability to organize, to get things done, to effect compromises. He now complained that Kennedy was not yet ready for the major political role; but he could not stop the swing to the young Senator's hard-fighting organization. When he received the Vice-Presidential nomination, he displayed a unity smile, but of the weakest sort.

Eisenhower later said that he would not have consented to television debates, which were only calculated to make the young Democratic nominee better known than he was. Whatever his rationale, Nixon consented. He wore the firm, responsible look of a man who had already been tried in presidential matters, all but lecturing his somewhat younger opponent on manners and proper politics. The Democrat's manner was more uncertain; he had a tendency toward hoarseness, and toward talking up to the Vice-President. But he fought with his usual vigor, he was earnest, he was better looking, and his promises were more clearly in the New Deal giving tradition than were the Vice-President's. Nixon, knowing the power of the big city machines, "ran scared." Both, tied to an electorate which cared nothing about foreign affairs, were fantastic on the subject of Cuba, being concerned not for Cuba at all, but for being elected President. The young Democrat professed concern for Soviet superiority in the "space race," but also addressed street crowds in Los Angeles with the charming familiarity he had employed in Boston. In the morning hours of November 3, it was not clear if Americans had elected a President. Rumor had it that Nixon's forces might refuse to accept the Illinois vote because of the patent fraud practiced in Cook County. Apparently, a countereffort was being planned by Democrats to challenge the California returns on the same grounds. Nixon concluded to concede the title to his opponent, and a new, excited, exultant group prepared to take office.

On January 20, J.F.K. delivered his Inaugural Address. It was accepted by friends and critics as one of the greatest of Inaugural Addresses. Even those who were unhappy with the tendencies of the New Frontier associates referred to them as representing a comedown from the views and expectations which the Inaugural Address had prepared.

Inaugural

Vice President Johnson, Mr. Speaker, Mr. Chief Justice, President Eisenhower, Vice President Nixon, President Truman, Reverend Clergy, fellow citizens:

We observe today not a victory of a party but a celebration of freedom—symbolizing an end as well as a beginning—signifying renewal as well as change. For I have sworn before you and Almighty

God the same solemn oath our forebears prescribed nearly a century and three quarters ago.

The world is very different now. For man holds in his mortal hands the power to abolish all forms of human poverty and all forms of human life. And yet the same revolutionary beliefs for which our forebears fought are still at issue around the globe—the belief that the rights of man come not from the generosity of the state but from the hand of God.

We dare not forget today that we are the heirs of that first revolution. Let the word go forth from this time and place, to friend and foe alike, that the torch has been passed to a new generation of Americans—born in this century, tempered by war, disciplined by a hard and bitter peace, proud of our ancient heritage—and unwilling to witness or permit the slow undoing of those human rights to which this Nation has always been committed, and to which we are committed today at home and around the world.

Let every nation know, whether it wishes us well or ill, that we shall pay any price, bear any burden, meet any hardship, support any friend, oppose any foe to assure the survival and success of liberty.

This much we pledge—and more.

To those old allies whose cultural and spiritual origins we share, we pledge the loyalty of faithful friends. United, there is little we cannot do in a host of cooperative ventures. Divided, there is little we can do—for we dare not meet a powerful challenge at odds and split asunder.

To those new states whom we welcome to the ranks of the free, we pledge our word that one form of colonial control shall not have passed away merely to be replaced by a far more iron tyranny. We shall not always expect to find them supporting our view. But we shall always hope to find them strongly supporting their own freedom —and to remember that, in the past, those who foolishly sought power by riding the back of the tiger ended up inside.

To those peoples in the huts and villages of half the globe struggling to break the bonds of mass misery, we pledge our best efforts to help them help themselves, for whatever period is required —not because the Communists may be doing it, not because we seek their votes, but because it is right. If a free society cannot help the many who are poor, it cannot save the few who are rich.

To our sister republics south of our border, we offer a special pledge—to convert our good words into good deeds—in a new alliance for progress—to assist free men and free governments in casting off the chains of poverty. But this peaceful revolution of hope cannot become the prey of hostile powers. Let all our neighbors know that we shall join with them to oppose aggression or subversion anywhere in the Americas. And let every other power know that this hemisphere intends to remain the master of its own house.

To that world assembly of sovereign states, the United Nations, our last best hope in an age where the instruments of war have far outpaced the instruments of peace, we renew our pledge of support—to prevent it from becoming merely a forum for invective—to strengthen its shield of the new and the weak—and to enlarge the area in which its writ may run.

Finally, to those nations who would make themselves our adversary, we offer not a pledge but a request: that both sides begin anew the quest for peace, before the dark powers of destruction unleashed by science engulf all humanity in planned or accidental self-destruction.

We dare not tempt them with weakness. For only when our arms are sufficient beyond doubt can we be certain beyond doubt that they will never be employed.

But neither can two great and powerful groups of nations take comfort from our present course—both sides overburdened by the cost of modern weapons, both rightly alarmed by the steady spread of the deadly atom, yet both racing to alter that uncertain balance of terror that stays the hand of mankind's final war.

So let us begin anew—remembering on both sides that civility is not a sign of weakness, and sincerity is always subject to proof. Let us never negotiate out of fear. But let us never fear to negotiate.

Let both sides explore what problems unite us instead of belaboring those problems which divide us. Let both sides, for the first time, formulate serious and precise proposals for the inspection and control of arms—and bring the absolute power to destroy other nations under the absolute control of all nations.

Let both sides seek to invoke the wonders of science instead of its terrors. Together let us explore the stars, conquer the deserts, eradicate disease, tap the ocean depths and encourage the arts and commerce.

Let both sides unite to heed in all corners of the earth the command of Isaiah—to "undo the heavy burdens . . . [and] let the oppressed go free."

And if a beach-head of cooperation may push back the jungle of suspicion, let both sides join in a new endeavor, not a new balance of power, but a new world of law, where the strong are just and the weak secure and the peace preserved.

All this will not be finished in the first one hundred days. Nor will it be finished in the first one thousand days, nor in the life of this Administration, nor even perhaps in our lifetime on this planet. But let us begin.

In your hands, my fellow citizens, more than mine, will rest the final success or failure of our course. Since this country was founded, each generation of Americans has been summoned to give testimony to its national loyalty. The graves of young Americans who answered the call to service surround the globe.

Now the trumpet summons us again—not as a call to bear arms, though arms we need—not as a call to battle, though embattled we are—but a call to bear the burden of a long twilight struggle, year in and year out, "rejoicing in hope, patient in tribulation"—a struggle against the common enemies of man: tyranny, poverty, disease and war itself.

Can we forge against these enemies a grand and global alliance, North and South, East and West, that can assure a more fruitful life for all mankind? Will you join in that historic effort?

In the long history of the world, only a few generations have been granted the role of defending freedom in its hour of maximum danger. I do not shrink from this responsibility—I welcome it. I do not believe that any of us would exchange places with any other people or any other generation. The energy, the faith, the devotion which we bring to this endeavor will light our country and all who serve it—and the glow from that fire can truly light the world.

And so, my fellow Americans: Ask not what your country can do for you—ask what you can do for your country.

My fellow citizens of the world: Ask not what America will do for you, but what together we can do for the freedom of man.

Finally, whether you are citizens of America or citizens of the world, ask of us here the same high standards of strength and sacrifice which we ask of you. With a good conscience our only sure reward, with history the final judge of our deeds, let us go forth to lead the land we love, asking His blessing and His help, but knowing that here on earth God's work must truly be our own.

J.F.K.'s major aspiration was to continue the New Deal. Unfortunately, he was too much affected by a mere literary knowledge of its workings to be able to assess its relevant features for current circumstances. Thus, he was aware of the economically depressed conditions in West Virginia, where his fight for the presidential nomination was given its first good push. He conceived of a Civilian Conservation Corps that could employ empty-handed young people in healthy, constructive work. His Congressional critics reviewed these suggestions and set them down as nonsense. There were numerous social agencies, they asserted, to deal with such problems; a new CCC would merely add another bureau to the many others. Had J.F.K. concentrated on the sordid jungles of the cities, he might have outraged their local politicians who were administering patronage in time-honored ways, but he might also have raised an antipoverty slogan that could have inspired progressive urban elements to work with him at mending their old frontier.

Social amelioration at home was a swift failure. But its equivalent abroad gave the new administration one of its most promising slogans, one of its best advertising missions abroad: only a beginning, to be sure, but one which increasingly won popularity and adherents. On March 1, 1961, Kennedy signed the order establishing the Peace Corps.

Peace Corps

I have today signed an Executive Order* providing for the establishment of a Peace Corps on a temporary pilot basis. I am also sending to Congress a message proposing authorization of a permanent Peace Corps. This Corps will be a pool of trained American men and women sent overseas by the U.S. Government or through private institutions and organizations to help foreign countries meet their urgent needs for skilled manpower.

It is our hope to have 500 or more people in the field by the end of the year.

The initial reactions to the Peace Corps proposal are convincing proof that we have, in this country, an immense reservoir of such men and women—anxious to sacrifice their energies and time and toil to the cause of world peace and human progress.

In establishing our Peace Corps we intend to make full use of the resources and talents of private institutions and groups. Universities, voluntary agencies, labor unions and industry will be asked to share in this effort—contributing diverse sources of energy and imagination—making it clear that the responsibility for peace is the responsibility of our entire society.

We will only send abroad Americans who are wanted by the host

* Executive Order 10924, 26 F.R. 1789.

country—who have a real job to do—and who are qualified to do that job. Programs will be developed with care, and after full negotiation, in order to make sure that the Peace Corps is wanted and will contribute to the welfare of other people. Our Peace Corps is not designed as an instrument of diplomacy or propaganda or ideological conflict. It is designed to permit our people to exercise more fully their responsibilities in the great common cause of world development.

Life in the Peace Corps will not be easy. There will be no salary and allowances will be at a level sufficient only to maintain health and meet basic needs. Men and women will be expected to work and live alongside the nationals of the country in which they are stationed—doing the same work, eating the same food, talking the same language.

But if the life will not be easy, it will be rich and satisfying. For every young American who participates in the Peace Corps—who works in a foreign land—will know that he or she is sharing in the great common task of bringing to man that decent way of life which is the foundation of freedom and a condition of peace.

J.F.K. was well aware of the challenge to American effectiveness abroad. With respect to Vietnam, there was little he could do but maintain a holding action; Americans could not concentrate on Vietnam under him anymore than under Ike. Kennedy had some sense of the seething unrest throughout Central and South America, and the fact that something would have to be done to keep the countries there from falling into hopelessness —ripe for communist, as distinguished from republican, demagogues. He projected an aid and cooperation program that was one of the best conceived of his largescale plans for augmenting American influence in the world—a precursor of the $20 billion bill he signed August 17.

His address to members of Congress and the diplomatic corps of the Latin American Republics, at a White House reception, March 13, 1961, expressed the vision that he anticipated would be made real by dedicated elements at home and south of the border.

Alliance for Progress

It is a great pleasure for Mrs. Kennedy and for me, for the Vice-President and Mrs. Johnson, and for the Members of Congress, to welcome the Ambassadorial Corps of our Hemisphere, our long time friends, to the White House today. One hundred and thirty-nine years ago this week the United States, stirred by the heroic struggle of its fellow Americans, urged the independence and recognition of the new Latin American Republics. It was then, at the dawn of freedom throughout this hemisphere, that Bolívar spoke of his desire to see the Americas fashioned into the greatest region in the world, "greatest," he said, "not so much by virtue of her area and her wealth, as by her freedom and her glory."

Never in the long history of our hemisphere has this dream been nearer to fulfillment, and never has it been in greater danger.

The genius of our scientists has given us the tools to bring abundance to our land, strength to our industry, and knowledge to our people. For the first time we have the capacity to strike off the remaining bonds of poverty and ignorance—to free our people for the spiritual and intellectual fulfillment which has always been the goal of our civilization.

Yet at this very moment of maximum opportunity, we confront the same forces which have imperiled America throughout its history —the alien forces which once again seek to impose the despotisms of the Old World on the people of the New.

I have asked you to come here today so that I might discuss these challenges and these dangers.

We meet together as firm and ancient friends, united by history and experience and by our determination to advance the values of American civilization. For this New World of ours is not a mere accident of geography. Our continents are bound together by a common history, the endless exploration of new frontiers. Our nations are the product of a common struggle, the revolt from colonial rule. And our people share a common heritage, the quest for the dignity and the freedom of man.

The revolutions which gave us birth ignited, in the words of Thomas Paine, "a spark never to be extinguished." And across vast, turbulent continents these American ideals still stir man's struggle for national independence and individual freedom. But as we welcome the spread of the American revolution to other lands, we must also remember that our own struggle—the revolution which began in Philadelphia in 1776, and in Caracas in 1811—is not yet finished. Our hemisphere's mission is not yet completed. For our unfulfilled task is to demonstrate to the entire world that man's unsatisfied aspiration for economic progress and social justice can best be achieved by free men working within a framework of democratic institutions. If we can do this in our own hemisphere, and for our own people, we may yet realize the prophecy of the great Mexican patriot, Benito Juarez, that "democracy is the destiny of future humanity."

As a citizen of the United States let me be the first to admit that we North Americans have not always grasped the significance of this common mission, just as it is also true that many in your own countries have not fully understood the urgency of the need to lift people from poverty and ignorance and despair. But we must turn from these mistakes—from the failures and the misunderstandings of the past to a future full of peril, but bright with hope.

Throughout Latin America, a continent rich in resources and in the spiritual and cultural achievements of its people, millions of men and women suffer the daily degradations of poverty and hunger. They lack decent shelter or protection from disease. Their children are deprived of the education or the jobs which are the gateway to a better life. And each day the problems grow more urgent. Population growth is outspacing economic growth—low living standards are further endangered—and discontent—the discontent of a people who know that abundance and the tools of progress are at last within their reach—that discontent is growing. In the words of José Figueres, "once dormant peoples are struggling upward toward the sun, toward a better life."

If we are to meet a problem so staggering in its dimensions, our approach must itself be equally bold—an approach consistent with the majestic concept of Operation Pan America. Therefore I have called on all people of the hemisphere to join in a new Alliance for Progress—*Alianza para Progreso*—a vast cooperative effort, unparalleled in magnitude and nobility of purpose, to satisfy the basic needs of the American people for homes, work and land, health and schools—*techo, trabajo y tierra, salud y escuela.*

First, I propose that the American Republics begin on a vast new Ten Year Plan for the Americas, a plan to transform the 1960's into a historic decade of democratic progress.

These 10 years will be the years of maximum progress-maximum effort, the years when the greatest obstacles must be overcome, the years when the need for assistance will be the greatest.

And if we are successful, if our effort is bold enough and determined enough, then the close of this decade will mark the beginning of a new era in the American experience. The living standards of every American family will be on the rise, basic education will be available to all, hunger will be a forgotten experience, the need for massive outside help will have passed, most nations will have entered a period of self-sustaining growth, and though there will be still much to do, every American Republic will be the master of its own revolution and its own hope and progress.

Let me stress that only the most determined efforts of the American nations themselves can bring success to this effort. They, and they alone, can mobilize their resources, enlist the energies of their people, and modify their social patterns so that all, and not just a privileged few, share in the fruits of growth. If this effort is made, then outside assistance will give vital impetus to progress; without it, no amount of help will advance the welfare of the people.

Thus if the countries of Latin America are ready to do their part, and I am sure they are, then I believe the United States, for its part, should help provide resources of a scope and magnitude sufficient to make this bold development plan a success—just as we helped to provide, against equal odds nearly, the resources adequate to help rebuild the economies of Western Europe. For only an effort of towering dimensions can ensure fulfillment of our plan for a decade of progress.

Secondly, I will shortly request a ministerial meeting of the Inter-American Economic and Social Council, a meeting at which we can begin the massive planning effort which will be at the heart of the Alliance for Progress.

For if our Alliance is to succeed, each Latin nation must formulate long-range plans for its own development, plans which establish targets and priorities, ensure monetary stability, establish the machinery for vital social change, stimulate private activity and initiative, and provide for a maximum national effort. These plans will be the foundation of our development effort, and the basis for the allocation of outside resources.

A greatly strengthened IA-ECOSOC, working with the Economic Commission for Latin America and the Inter-American Development Bank, can assemble the leading economists and experts of the hemisphere to help each country develop its own development plan —and provide a continuing review of economic progress in this hemisphere.

Third, I have this evening signed a request to the Congress for $500 million as a first step in fulfilling the Act of Bogotá. This is the first large-scale Inter-American effort, instituted by my predecessor President Eisenhower, to attack the social barriers which block economic progress. The money will be used to combat illiteracy, improve the productivity and use of their land, wipe out disease, attack archaic tax and land tenure structures, provide educational opportunities, and offer a broad range of projects designed to make the benefits of increasing abundance available to all. We will begin to commit these funds as soon as they are appropriated.

Fourth, we must support all economic integration which is a genuine step toward larger markets and greater competitive opportunity. The fragmentation of Latin American economies is a serious barrier to industrial growth. Projects such as the Central American common market and free trade areas in South America can help to remove these obstacles.

Fifth, the United States is ready to cooperate in serious, case-by-case examinations of commodity market problems. Frequent violent change is commodity prices seriously injure the economies of many Latin American countries, draining their resources and stultifying their growth. Together we must find practical methods of bringing an end to this pattern.

Sixth, we will immediately step up our Food for Peace emergency program, help establish food reserves in areas of recurrent drought, help provide school lunches for children, and offer feed grains for use in rural development. For hungry men and women cannot wait for economic discussions or diplomatic meetings—their need is urgent—and their hunger rests heavily on the conscience of their fellow men.

Seventh, all the people of the hemisphere must be allowed to share in the expanding wonders of science—wonders which have captured man's imagination, challenged the powers of his mind, and given him the tools for rapid progress. I invite Latin American scientists to work with us in new projects in fields such as medicine and agriculture, physics and astronomy, and desalinization, to help plan for regional research laboratories in these and other fields, and to strengthen cooperation between American universities and laboratories.

We also intend to expand our science teacher training programs to include Latin American instructors, to assist in establishing such programs in other American countries, and translate and make available revolutionary new teaching materials in physics, chemistry, biology, and mathematics, so that the young of all nations may contribute their skills to the advance of science.

Eighth, we must rapidly expand the training of those needed to man the economies of rapidly developing countries. This means expanded technical training programs, for which the Peace Corps, for example, will be available when needed. It also means assistance to Latin American universities, graduate schools, and research institutes.

We welcome proposals in Central America for intimate cooperation in higher education—cooperation which can achieve a regional effort of increased effectiveness and excellence. We are ready to help fill the gap in trained manpower, realizing that our ultimate goal must be a basic education for all who wish to learn.

Ninth, we reaffirm our pledge to come to the defense of any American nation whose independence is endangered. As its confidence in the collective security system of the OAS spreads, it will be possible to devote to constructive use a major share of those resources now spent on the instruments of war. Even now, as the government of Chile has said, the time has come to take the first steps toward sensible limitations of arms. And the new generation of military leaders has shown an increasing awareness that armies cannot only defend their countries—they can, as we have learned through our own Corps of Engineers, they can help to build them.

Tenth, we invite our friends in Latin America to contribute to the enrichment of life and culture in the United States. We need teachers of your literature and history and tradition, opportunities for our young people to study in your universities, access to your music, your art, and the thought of your great philosophers. For we know we have much to learn.

In this way you can help bring a fuller spiritual and intellectual life to the people of the United States—and contribute to understanding and mutual respect among the nations of the hemisphere.

With steps such as these, we propose to complete the revolution of the Americas, to build a hemisphere where all men can hope for a suitable standard of living, and all can live out their lives in dignity and in freedom. . . .

Cuba rankled as a recalcitrant element at the very heel of America, an open sore festering with communism. It pleased editors and analysts to denounce its leader, Castro, as a Marxist, a dictator, a wind-bag. But Cuba remained, and there appeared to be no diplomatic way of easing out its regime and acquiring one more satisfactory to the State Department. An American who had achieved respectable academic status, C. Wright Mills, wrote a tract, *Listen Yankee: the revolution in Cuba* (1960) which sought to persuade its readers that Cuba appeared one way to the Cubans in

Cuba, and another to the expatriates in Florida. But it was the latter who received sympathy and attention.

Admirers of the new administration praised J.F.K. for his interest in details. He not only read memoranda; he insisted on examining the actual original sources. Presumably he read them on the subject of Cuba. (Afterwards, experts in aspects of Latin American affairs—terrain, economics, social classes—noted that they had not been consulted on Cuban realities.) Kennedy was persuaded that the Cuban government could be overthrown without direct American intervention and without difficulty. Vast branches of the government were synchronized to carry out a plan that should have blown the Marxists on the little island into the sea. The succeeding catastrophe produced astounding results.

J.F.K.'s popularity rose to 83 per cent. It was conjectured that Americans had been proud of his readiness to assume the blame for the appalling failure, even though Democratic journalists had unloaded as much of it as they could on Eisenhower. It was equally possible that the implications of the weird effort were totally beyond the understanding of Americans, who continued to respond to anti-Castro jokes, and automatically closed ranks behind their incumbent Chief. On April 20, 1961, he offered his summary of the situation.

Cuba I

Mr. [Turner] Catledge, members of the American Society of Newspaper Editors, ladies and gentlemen:

The president of a great democracy such as ours, and the editors of great newspapers such as yours, owe a common obligation to the people: an obligation to present the facts, to present them with candor, and to present them in perspective. It is with that obligation in mind that I have decided in the last 24 hours to discuss briefly at this time the recent events in Cuba.

On that unhappy island, as in so many other arenas of the contest for freedom, the news has grown worse instead of better. I have emphasized before that this was a struggle of Cuban patriots against a Cuban dictator. While we could not be expected to hide our sympathies, we made it repeatedly clear that the armed forces of this country would not intervene in any way.

Any unilateral American intervention, in the absence of an external attack upon ourselves or an ally, would have been contrary to our traditions and to our international obligations. But let the record show that our restraint is not inexhaustible. Should it ever appear that the inter-American doctrine of non-interference merely conceals or excuses a policy of nonaction—if the nations of this Hemisphere should fail to meet their commitments against outside Communist penetration—then I want it clearly understood that this Government will not hesitate in meeting its primary obligations which are to the security of our Nation!

Should that time ever come, we do not intend to be lectured on "intervention" by those whose character was stamped for all time on the bloody streets of Budapest! Nor would we expect or accept the same outcome which this small band of gallant Cuban refugees must have known that they were chancing, determined as they were against heavy odds to pursue their courageous attempts to regain their Island's freedom.

But Cuba is not an island unto itself; and our concern is not ended by mere expressions of nonintervention or regret. This is not the first time in either ancient or recent history that a small band of freedom fighters has engaged the armor of totalitarianism.

It is not the first time that Communist tanks have rolled over gallant men and women fighting to redeem the independence of their homeland. Nor. is it by any means the final episode in the eternal struggle of liberty against tyranny, anywhere on the face of the globe, including Cuba itself.

Mr. Castro has said that these were mercenaries. According to press reports, the final message to be relayed from the refugee forces on the beach came from the rebel commander when asked if he wished to be evacuated. His answer was: "I will never leave this country." That is not the reply of a mercenary. He has gone now to join in the mountains countless other guerrilla fighters, who are equally determined that the dedication of those who gave their lives shall not be forgotten, and that Cuba must not be abandoned to the Communists. And we do not intend to abandon it either!

The Cuban people have not yet spoken their final piece. And I have no doubt that they and their Revolutionary Council, led by Dr. Miró Cardona*—and members of the families of the Revolutionary Council, I am informed by the Doctor yesterday, are involved themselves in the Islands—will continue to speak up for a free and independent Cuba.

Meanwhile we will not accept Mr. Castro's attempts to blame this

* President of the Cuban Revolutionary Council.

386

nation for the hatred which his onetime supporters now regard his repression. But there are from this sobering episode useful lessons for us all to learn. Some may be still obscure, and await further information. Some are clear today.

First, it is clear that the forces of communism are not to be underestimated, in Cuba or anywhere else in the world. The advantages of a police state—its use of mass terror and arrests to prevent the spread of free dissent—cannot be overlooked by those who expect the fall of every fanatic tyrant. If the self-discipline of the free cannot match the iron discipline of the mailed fist—in economic, political, scientific and all the other kinds of struggles as well as the military—then the peril to freedom will continue to rise.

Secondly, it is clear that this Nation, in concert with all the free nations of this hemisphere, must take an ever closer and more realistic look at the menace of external Communist intervention and domination in Cuba. The American people are not complacent about Iron Curtain tanks and planes less than 90 miles from their shore. But a nation of Cuba's size is less a threat to our survival than it is a base for subverting the survival of other free nations throughout the hemisphere. It is not primarily our interest or our security but theirs which is now, today, in the greater peril. It is for their sake as well as our own that we must show our will. . . .

Third, and finally, it is clearer than ever that we face a relentless struggle in every corner of the globe that goes far beyond the clash of armies or even nuclear armaments. The armies are there, and in large number. The nuclear armaments are there. But they serve primarily as the shield behind which subversion, infiltration, and a host of other tactics steadily advance, picking off vulnerable areas one by one in situations which do not permit our own armed intervention. . . .

The message of Cuba, of Laos, of the rising din of Communist voices in Asia and Latin America—these messages are all the same. The complacent, the self-indulgent, the soft societies are about to be swept away with the debris of history. Only the strong, only the industrious, only the determined, only the courageous, only the visionary who determine the real nature of our struggle can possibly survive. . . .

We intend to profit from this lesson. We intend to reexamine and reorient our forces of all kinds—our tactics and our institutions here in this community. We intend to intensify our efforts for a struggle

387

in many ways more difficult than war, where disappointment will often accompany us. . . .

In the following year, there were many momentary sensations. The space race gave the administration followers a lift. Americans were orbited; popular idols, they represented a new type of American hero, more appropriate to a serious time. Later, J.F.K. would conceive of the "great, new enterprise" of putting a man on the moon by 1970. Still later, he would ask for a joint moon flight by Soviet and American space men. (By the spring of 1964, the subject had disappeared from the newspapers.) Kennedy traveled to Vienna to discuss world problems with Khrushchev, then resumed nuclear testing. He forced the steel companies to rescind a price rise that he held to be inflationary, threatening them with an investigation. Business spokesmen complained that the Administration did not employ similar tones in connection with official labor. J.F.K. developed a "bold, new" foreign trade policy intended to revitalize American business relations abroad. East and West Germany continued to present problems.

Still, the Cuban fiasco rankled. Castro took on the proportions of an American leader competing with the United States for hemisphere attention. The émigré Cubans became a permanent and unhappy feature of Florida life, forgotten everywhere else. Then, suddenly, there were developments. On October 14, 1962, word came that the Russians had established missile bases in Cuba. The White House organized for the emergency. On October 22, the President made his second major report to the nation on the crisis that had brought Soviet power to the very shores of the United States.

Cuba II

Good evening, my fellow citizens:

This Government, as promised, has maintained the closest surveillance of the Soviet military buildup on the island of Cuba. Within the past week, unmistakable evidence has established the fact that a series of offensive missile sites is now in preparation on that imprisoned island. The purpose of these bases can be none other than to provide a nuclear strike capability against the Western Hemisphere.

Upon receiving the first preliminary hard information of this nature last Tuesday morning at 9 a.m., I directed that our surveillance be stepped up. And having now confirmed and completed our evaluation of the evidence and our decision on a course of action, this Government feels obliged to report this new crisis to you in fullest detail.

The characteristics of these new missile sites indicate two distinct types of installations. Several of them include medium range ballistic missiles, capable of carrying a nuclear warhead for a distance of more than 1,000 nautical miles. Each of these missiles, in short, is capable of striking Washington, D.C., the Panama Canal, Cape Canaveral, Mexico City, or any other city in the southeastern part of the United States, in Central America, or in the Caribbean area.

Additional sites not yet completed appear to be designed for intermediate range ballistic missiles—capable of traveling more than twice as far—and thus capable of striking most of the major cities in the Western Hemisphere, ranging as far north as Hudson Bay, Canada, and as far south as Lima, Peru. In addition, jet bombers, capable of carrying nuclear weapons, are now being uncrated and assembled in Cuba, while the necessary air bases are being prepared.

This urgent transformation of Cuba into an important strategic base—by the presence of these large, long-range, and clearly offensive weapons of sudden mass destruction—constitutes an explicit threat to the peace and security of all the Americas, in flagrant and deliberate defiance of the Rio Pact of 1947, the traditions of this Nation and hemisphere, the joint resolution of the 87th Congress, the Charter of the United Nations, and my own public warnings to the Soviets on September 4 and 13. This action also contradicts the repeated assurances of Soviet spokesmen, both publicly and privately delivered, that the arms buildup in Cuba would retain its original defensive character, and that the Soviet Union had no need or desire to station strategic missiles on the territory of any other nation.

The size of this undertaking makes clear that it has been planned for some months. Yet only last month, after I had made clear the distinction between any introduction of ground-to-ground missiles and the existence of defensive antiaircraft missiles, the Soviet Government publicly stated on September 11 that, and I quote, "the armaments and military equipment sent to Cuba are designed exclusively for defensive purposes," that, and I quote the Soviet Government, "there is no need for the Soviet Government to shift its weapons . . . for a retaliatory blow to any other country, for instance Cuba," and that, and I quote their government, "the Soviet Union has so powerful rockets to carry these nuclear warheads that there is no need to search for sites for them beyond the boundaries of the Soviet Union." That statement was false.

Only last Thursday, as evidence of this rapid offensive buildup was already in my hand, Soviet Foreign Minister Gromyko told me in my office that he was instructed to make it clear once again, as he said his government had already done, that Soviet assistance to Cuba, and I quote, "pursued solely the purpose of contributing to the defense capabilities of Cuba," that, and I quote him, "training by Soviet specialists of Cuban nationals in handling defensive armaments was by no means offensive, and if it were otherwise," Mr. Gromyko went on, "the Soviet Government would never become involved in rendering such assistance." That statement also was false.

Neither the United States of America nor the world community of nations can tolerate deliberate deception and offensive threats on the part of any nation, large or small. We no longer live in a world where only the actual firing of weapons represents a sufficient challenge to a nation's security to constitute maximum peril. Nuclear weapons are so destructive and ballistic missiles are so swift, that any substantially increased possibility of their use or any sudden change in their deployment may well be regarded as a definite threat to peace.

For many years, both the Soviet Union and the United States, recognizing this fact, have deployed strategic nuclear weapons with great care, never upsetting the precarious status quo which insured that these weapons would not be used in the absence of some vital challenge. Our own strategic missiles have never been transferred to the territory of any other nation under a cloak of secrecy and deception; and our history—unlike that of the Soviets since the end of World War II—demonstrates that we have no desire to dominate or conquer any other nation or impose our system upon its people. Nevertheless, American citizens have become adjusted to living daily on the bull's eye of Soviet missiles located inside the U.S.S.R. or in submarines.

In that sense, missiles in Cuba add to an already clear and present danger—although it should be noted the nations of Latin America have never previously been subjected to a potential nuclear threat.

But this secret, swift, and extraordinary buildup of Communist missiles—in an area well known to have a special and historical relationship to the United States and the nations of the Western Hemisphere, in violation of Soviet assurances, and in defiance of American and hemispheric policy—this sudden, clandestine decision to station strategic weapons for the first time outside of Soviet soil— is a deliberately provocative and unjustified change in the status quo which cannot be accepted by this country, if our courage and our commitments are ever to be trusted again by either friend or foe.

The 1930's taught us a clear lesson: aggressive conduct, if allowed to go unchecked and unchallenged, ultimately leads to war. This nation is opposed to war. We are also true to our word. Our unswerving objective, therefore, must be to prevent the use of these missiles against this or any other country, and to secure their withdrawal or elimination from the Western Hemisphere.

Our policy has been one of patience and restraint, as befits a peaceful and powerful nation, which leads a worldwide alliance. We have been determined not to be diverted from our central concerns by mere irritants and fanatics. But now further action is required— and it is under way; and these actions may only be the beginning. We will not prematurely or unnecessarily risk the costs of worldwide nuclear war in which even the fruits of victory would be ashes in our mouth—but neither will we shrink from that risk at any time it must be faced.

Acting, therefore, in the defense of our own security and of the entire Western Hemisphere, and under the authority entrusted to me by the Constitution as endorsed by the resolution of the Congress, I have directed that the following *initial* steps be taken immediately:

First: To halt this offensive buildup, a strict quarantine on all offensive military equipment under shipment to Cuba is being initiated. All ships of any kind bound for Cuba from whatever nation or port will, if found to contain cargoes of offensive weapons, be turned back. This quarantine will be extended, if needed, to other types of cargo and carriers. We are not at this time, however, denying the necessities of life as the Soviets attempted to do in their Berlin blockade of 1948.

Second: I have directed the continued and increased close surveillance of Cuba and its military buildup. The foreign ministers of the OAS, in their communique of October 6, rejected secrecy on such matters in this hemisphere. Should these offensive military preparations continue, thus increasing the threat to the hemisphere, further action will be justified. I have directed the Armed Forces to prepare for any eventualities; and I trust that in the interest of both the Cuban people and the Soviet technicians at the sites, the hazards to all concerned of continuing this threat will be recognized.

Third: It shall be the policy of this Nation to regard any nuclear missile launched from Cuba against any nation in the Western Hemisphere as an attack by the Soviet Union on the United States, requiring a full retaliatory response upon the Soviet Union.

Fourth: As a necessary military precaution, I have reinforced our base at Guantanamo, evacuated today the dependents of our personnel there, and ordered additional military units to be on a standby alert basis.

Fifth: We are calling tonight for an immediate meeting of the Organ of Consultation under the Organization of American States, to consider this threat to hemispheric security and to invoke articles 6 and 8 of the Rio Treaty in support of all necessary action. The United Nations Charter allows for regional security arrangements—and the nations of this hemisphere decided long ago against the military presence of outside powers. Our other allies around the world have also been alerted.

Sixth: Under the Charter of the United Nations, we are asking tonight that an emergency meeting of the Security Council be convoked without delay to take action against this latest Soviet threat to world peace. Our resolution will call for the prompt dismantling and withdrawal of all offensive weapons in Cuba, under the supervision of U.N. observers, before the quarantine can be lifted.

Seventh and finally: I call upon Chairman Khrushchev to halt and eliminate this clandestine, reckless, and provocative threat to world peace and to stable relations between our two nations. I call upon him further to abandon this course of world domination, and to join in an historic effort to end the perilous arms race and to transform the history of man. He has an opportunity now to move the world back from the abyss of destruction—by returning to his government's own words that it had no need to station missiles outside its own territory, and withdrawing these weapons from Cuba—by refraining from any action which will widen or deepen the present crisis—and then by participating in a search for peaceful and permanent solutions.

This Nation is prepared to present its case against the Soviet threat to peace, and our own proposals for a peaceful world, at any time and in any forum—in the OAS, in the United Nations, or in any other meeting that could be useful—without limiting our freedom of action. We have in the past made strenuous efforts to limit the spread of nuclear weapons. We have proposed the elimination of all arms and military bases in a fair and effective disarmament treaty. We are prepared to discuss new proposals for the removal of tensions on both sides—including the possibilities of a genuinely independent Cuba, free to determine its own destiny. We have no wish to war with the Soviet Union—for we are a peaceful people who desire to live in peace with all other peoples.

But it is difficult to settle or even discuss these problems in an atmosphere of intimidation. That is why this latest Soviet threat—

or any other threat which is made either independently or in response to our actions this week—must and will be met with determination. Any hostile move anywhere in the world against the safety and freedom of peoples to whom we are committed—including in particular the brave people of West Berlin—will be met by whatever action is needed. . . .

In his book *John F. Kennedy, President,* Hugh Sidey reported the opening of the 88th Congress in January 1963, noting that the President faced Congress with a confidence that had been lacking two years before, but with less of the earlier élan, and with more of a somber sense of responsibility and of the political necessities he would have to meet. In January of 1961, he had noted critical problems and adverse tides, but called the nation to "proud and memorable" deeds. Now he called for a tax cut, as overshadowing "all other domestic problems in this Congress." The rationale for his view of priorities appeared in his State of the Union Address of January 14.

Tax Cut

Mr. Vice President, Mr. Speaker, Members of the 88th Congress, I congratulate you all—not merely on your electoral victory but on your selected role in history. For you and I are privileged to serve the great Republic in what could be the most decisive decade of its life. The choices we make, for good or ill, may well shape the state of the Union for generations yet to come.

Little more than a hundred weeks ago I assumed the office of President of the United States. In seeking the help of the Congress and my countrymen, I pledged no easy answers. I pledged—and asked— only toil and dedication. These the Congress and the people have given in good measure. And today, having witnessed in recent months a heightened respect for our national purpose and power—having seen the courageous calm of a united people in a perilous hour—and having observed a steady improvement in the opportunities and well-being of our citizens—I can report to you that the state of this old but youthful Union, is good.

In the world beyond our borders, steady progress has been made in building a world of order. The people of West Berlin remain free and secure. A settlement, though still precarious, has been reached in Laos. The spearpoint of aggression has been blunted in South

Vietnam. The end of agony may be in sight in the Congo. The doctrine of troika is dead. And, while danger continues, a deadly threat has been removed from Cuba.

At home, the recession is behind us. Well over a million more men and women are working today than were working 2 years ago. The average factory workweek is once again more than 40 hours; our industries are turning out more goods than ever before; and more than half of the manufacturing capacity that lay silent and wasted 100 weeks ago is humming with activity.

In short, both at home and abroad, there may now be a temptation to relax. For the road has been long, the burden heavy, and the pace consistently urgent.

But we cannot be satisfied to rest here. This is the side of the hill, not the top. The mere absence of war is not peace. The mere absence of recession is not growth. We have made a beginning—but we have only begun.

Now the time has come to make the most of our gains—to translate the renewal of our national strength into the achievement of our national purpose.

II

America has enjoyed 22 months of uninterrupted economic recovery. But recovery is not enough. If we are to prevail in the long run, we must expand the longrun strength of our economy. We must move along the path to a higher rate of growth and full employment.

For this would mean tens of billions of dollars more each year in production, profits, wages, and public revenues. It would mean an end to the persistent slack which has kept unemployment at or above 5 percent for 61 out of 62 months—and an end to the growing pressures for such restrictive measures as the 35-hour week, which alone could increase hourly labor costs by as much as 14 percent, start a new wage-price spiral of inflation, and undercut our efforts to compete with other nations.

To achieve these greater gains, one step, above all, is essential— the enactment this year of a substantial reduction and revision in Federal income taxes.

For it is increasingly clear—to those in Government, business, and labor who are responsible for our economy's success—that our obsolete tax system exerts too heavy a drag on private purchasing power, profits, and employment. Designed to check inflation in earlier years, it now checks growth instead. It discourages extra effort and risk. It distorts the use of resources. It invites recurrent recessions, depresses our Federal revenues, and causes chronic budget deficits.

Now, when the inflationary pressures of the war and postwar years no longer threaten, and the dollar commands new respect— now, when no military crisis strains our resources—now is the time to act. We cannot afford to be timid or slow. For this is the most urgent task confronting the Congress in 1963.

In an early message, I shall propose a permanent reduction in tax rates which will lower liabilities by $13.5 billion. Of this, $11 billion results from reducing individual tax rates, which now range between 20 and 91 percent, to a more sensible range of 14 to 65 percent with a split in the present first bracket. Two and one-half billion dollars results from reducing corporate tax rates, from 52 percent— which gives the Government today a majority interest in profits—to the permanent pre-Korean level of 47 percent. This is in addition to the more than $2 billion cut in corporate tax liabilities resulting from last year's investment credit and depreciation reform. . . .

This net reduction in tax liabilities of $10 billion will increase the purchasing power of American families and business enterprises in every tax bracket, with the greatest increase going to our low-income consumers. It will, in addition, encourage the initiative and risk taking on which our free enterprise system depends—induce more investment, production, and capacity use—help provide the 2 million new jobs we need every year—and reinforce the American principle of additional reward for additional effort.

I do not say that a measure for tax reduction and reform is the only way to achieve these goals.

No doubt a massive increase in Federal spending could also create jobs and growth—but, in today's setting, private consumers, employers, and investors should be given a full opportunity first.

No doubt a temporary tax cut could provide a spur to our economy —but a longrun problem compels a longrun solution.

No doubt a reduction in either individual or corporation taxes alone would be of great help—but corporations need customers and jobseekers need jobs.

No doubt tax reduction without reform would sound simpler and more attractive to many—but our growth is also hampered by a host of tax inequities and special preferences which have distorted the flow of investment.

And, finally, there are no doubt some who would prefer to put off a tax cut in the hope that ultimately an end to the cold war would make possible an equivalent reduction in Government expenditures

—but that end is not in view and to wait for it would be costly and self-defeating.

In submitting a tax program which will, of course, temporarily increase the deficit but can, I believe, ultimately end it—and in recognition of the need to control expenditures—I will shortly submit a fiscal 1964 administrative budget which, while allowing for needed rises in defense, space, and fixed interest charges, holds total expenditures for all other purposes below this year's level.

This requires the reduction or postponement of many desirable programs—the absorption of a large part of last year's Federal pay raise through personnel and other economies—the termination of certain installations and projects—and the substitution in several programs of private for public credit. But I am convinced that the enactment this year of tax reduction and tax reform overshadows all other domestic problems in this Congress. For we cannot lead for long the cause of peace and freedom, if we ever cease to set the pace at home.

III

Tax reduction alone, however, is not enough to strengthen our society, to provide opportunities for the 4 million new Americans who are born every year, to improve the lives of the 32 million Americans who still live on the outskirts of poverty.

The quality of American life must keep pace with the quantity of American goods.

This country cannot afford to be materially rich and spiritually desperately poor.

Therefore, by holding down the budgetary cost of existing programs to keep within the limitations I have set, it is both possible and imperative to adopt other new measures that we cannot afford to postpone.

These measures are based on a series of fundamental premises, grouped under four related headings:

First, we need to strengthen our Nation by investing in our youth:

The future of any country which is dependent on the will and wisdom of its citizens is damaged, and irreparably damaged, whenever any of its children are not educated to the fullest extent of his capacity, from grade school through graduate school. Today, an estimated 4 out of every 10 students in the fifth grade will never finish high school—and that is a waste we cannot afford.

In addition, there is no reason why 1 million young Americans, out of school and out of work, should all remain unwanted and often untrained on our city streets when their energies can be put to good use.

Finally, the oversea success of our Peace Corps volunteers, most of them young men and women carrying skills and ideals to needy people, suggests the merit of a similar corps serving our own community needs: in mental hospitals, on Indian reservations, in centers for the aged or for young delinquents, in schools for the illiterate or the handicapped. As the idealism of our youth has served world peace, so can it serve the domestic tranquility.

Second, we need to strengthen our Nation by safeguarding its health:

Our working men and women—instead of being forced to ask for help from public charity once they are old and ill—should start contributing now to their own retirement health program through the social security system.

Moreover, all our miracles of medical research will count for little if we cannot reverse the growing nationwide shortage of doctors, dentists, and nurses, and the widespread shortages of nursing homes and modern urban hospital facilities. Merely to keep the present ratio of doctors and dentists from declining any further, this country must over the next 10 years increase the capacity of our medical schools by 50 percent and our dental schools by 100 percent.

Finally, and of deep concern, I believe that the abandonment of the mentally ill and the mentally retarded to the grim mercy of custodial institutions too often inflicts on them and their families a needless cruelty which this Nation should not endure. The incidence of mental retardation in the United States of America is three times as high as that of Sweden, for example—and that figure can and must be reduced.

Third, we need to strengthen our Nation by protecting the basic rights of its citizens:

The right to competent counsel must be assured to every man accused of crime in Federal court, regardless of his means.

And the most precious and powerful right in the world, the right to vote in a free American election, must not be denied to any citizen on grounds of his race or his color.

I wish that all qualified Americans permitted to vote were willing to vote—but surely, in this centennial year of the Emancipation, all those who are willing to vote should always be permitted.

Fourth, we need to strengthen our Nation by making the best and the most economical use of its resources and facilities:

Our economic health depends on having healthy transportation arteries; and I believe the way to a more modern, economical choice of national transportation service is through increased competition and decreased regulation. Local mass transit, faring even worse, is as essential a community service as highways. Nearly three-fourths of our citizens live in urban areas, which occupy only 2 percent of our land—and if local transit is to survive and relieve the congestion of these cities, it needs Federal stimulation and assistance.

Next, this Government is in the storage and stockpile business to the melancholy tune of $16 billion. We must continue to support farm income, but we should not pile more farm surpluses on top of the $7.5 billion worth we already own. We must maintain a stockpile of strategic materials, but the $8.5 billion worth we have acquired—for reasons both good and bad—is much more than we need; and we should be empowered to dispose of the excess in ways which will not cause market disruption.

Finally, our already overcrowded national parks and recreation areas will have twice as many visitors 10 years from now. If we do not plan today for the future growth of these and other great natural assets—not only parks and forests but wildlife and wilderness preserves, and water projects of all kinds—our children and their children will be poorer in every sense of the word. Proposals will be made to the Congress in the coming days to meet these challenges. . . .

J.F.K.'s budget troubled his Congressional friends and enemies. Senator Karl Mundt, a Republican, saw it as having "a chilling effect on the understandable desire to cut taxes." Senator John Sparkman, Alabama Democrat and running mate of Stevenson in 1952, thought that his fellow legislators would be "hesitant to vote large tax cuts with a heavy deficit." The attendant discussion wandered off, to become the theme of specialized papers at professional associations.

The President himself found more inspiring his recollections of the second Cuban crisis, which had brought him popular approval and had contributed to some Democratic victories in the fall elections. J.F.K. had made up, as mementos for those who shared the crisis with him, 32 copies in silver of a calendar for the month of October 1962, with the dates 16 to 28 embossed more heavily than the other dates, memorializing the challenge he had met, and the agreement which had been reached to dismantle the missile bases.

Meanwhile, racial unrest had mounted enormously since Little Rock. "Freedom riders" had flouted Southern segregationists in various states; "We Shall Overcome" had become the prayerful anthem of the martyrs, in jails, at bus terminals, at schools, in department stores. They and their friends pressed for civil rights legislation and government action. On May

20, 1961, J.F.K. had called on Alabama authorities to put an end to racial violence. In Mississippi, James H. Meredith, a Negro, enrolled at the university, creating a perpetual threat of violence. The use of dogs to dismay and discourage demonstrators horrified the North and disgraced the nation in world opinion. In Birmingham, in May of 1963, negotiations intended to make for a peaceful settlement of differences broke down. "Quislings" and "gutless traitors," the city's mayor called the white would-be peacemakers. Negro demonstrators were met with dogs and firehoses. J.F.K.'s actions in the crisis were moderate, stepped up over Little Rock in proportion to the higher magnitude of trouble throughout the South. His statement of May 12, 1963, explained his purposes and hopes, while readying troops for possible use in Birmingham.

Birmingham

I am deeply concerned about the events which occurred in Birmingham, Ala., last night. The home of Rev. A. D. King was bombed and badly damaged. Shortly thereafter the A. G. Gaston motel was also bombed.

These occurrences led to rioting, personal injuries, property damage and various reports of violence and brutality. This Government will do whatever must be done to preserve order, to protect the lives of its citizens and to uphold the law of the land. I am certain that the vast majority of the citizens of Birmingham, both white and Negro—particularly those who labored so hard to achieve the peaceful, constructive settlement of last week—can feel nothing but dismay at the efforts of those who would replace conciliation and good will with violence and hate.

The Birmingham agreement was and is a fair and just accord. It recognized the fundamental right of all citizens to be accorded equal treatment and opportunity. It was a tribute to the process of peaceful negotiation and to the good faith of both parties. The Federal Government will not permit it to be sabotaged by a few extremists on either side who think they can defy both law and the wishes of responsible citizens by inciting or inviting violence.

I call upon all the citizens of Birmingham, both Negro and white, to live up to the standards their responsible leaders set in reaching the agreement of last week, to realize that violence only breeds more violence and that good will and good faith are most important now to restore the atmosphere in which last week's agreement can be carried out. There must be no repetition of last night's incidents by any group. To make certain that this Government is prepared to carry out its statutory and constitutional obligations, I have ordered the following three initial steps:

1. I am sending Assistant Attorney-General Burke Marshall to Birmingham this evening to consult with local citizens. He will join Assistant Deputy Attorney-General Joseph F. Dolan and other Justice Department officials who were sent back to Birmingham this morning.

2. I have instructed Secretary of Defense McNamara to alert units of the armed forces trained in riot control and to dispatch selected units to military bases in the vicinity of Birmingham.

3. Finally I have directed that the necessary preliminary steps to calling the Alabama National Guard into Federal service be taken now so that units of the guard will be promptly available should their services be required.

It is my hope, however, that the citizens of Birmingham themselves maintain standards of responsible conduct that will make outside intervention unnecessary and permit the city, the state and the country to move ahead in protecting the lives and the interests of those citizens and the welfare of our country.

J.F.K. continued to offer softening words while reaffirming the necessity for law and order. He pleaded with Governor George C. Wallace of Alabama to give his "constructive" cooperation to building up a "sense of justice and foresight" in Birmingham. On June 11, 1963, he deplored the "fires of discord" that had accompanied the forced admission of two Negroes into the University of Alabama, and pleaded for public support of his policy. Since the Governor's inaugural address had emphasized "segregation now, segregation tomorrow, segregation forever," it was evident that no final word on the situation had yet been offered.

On July 26, 1963, the President had the satisfaction of announcing that "a shaft of light [had] cut into the darkness" of U.S.-U.S.S.R. differences. A ban on all nuclear tests in the atmosphere, in outer space and under water had been reached. It was a limited treaty, there was much yet to be negotiated . . . but a beginning had perhaps been made. In August, the President was to see the completion of a "hot line" teletype link from Washington to Moscow, permitting immediate discussion between himself and the Russian premier, in case of a threat of war.

Meanwhile, it appeared to him to be time for fence mending. His civil rights efforts had disturbed valued voters in the South. A great civil rights march in August in Washington was widely discussed in the press. It had been made almost respectably sober and unaggressive—in a city that was rapidly turning into a Negro community. Had the march advanced civil rights? Kennedy said yes. Militant civil libertarians were skeptical. Southern segregationists took it as a direct attack upon their hopes of maintaining white supremacy, and pondered alternatives to Kennedy. Northern optimists spoke of the million or more new Negro votes that would appear in the South in time for the 1964 elections. But no one truly knew how many such votes there would be, and for whom. J.F.K. decided to strengthen his organization in the South.

James Reston of *The New York Times* put it that he would win reelection simply because he was already in office, though Reston sensed a "vague feeling of doubt and disappointment in the country about his first term." He thought Kennedy had touched the intellect of the nation, but not its heart. He talked of "international liquidity" and "multilateral forces" and other remote matters. One man-in-the-street was quoted as saying he did not know what Kennedy was talking about most of the time; however, another was also quoted as saying that all he knew was that there was work and peace.

It was politics as usual as November got under way. Midwest lobbies sought an atom project, presumably so that they could do their part in assuring American strength. Several Congressmen who visited Paris at public expense took along a headwaiter. House Speaker John W. McCormack defended their action as "a wonderful thing." "This is a land of opportunity," he said. "[The headwaiter] is a fine person." One Bobby Baker further illustrated the opportunities America offered. A former secretary of the Democratic Senate majority, he had become inspiringly wealthy. His fellow Democrats were incurious about the secret of his success.

On November 14, at Elkton, Maryland, the President cut a blue-and-gray ribbon stretched across the Mason-Dixon Line, opening part of a North-South highway. Pickets on the northern, Delaware side held signs reading: "Mr. President, you've opened highway No. 95. Now, help us open public accommodations." In New York, the following day, the President told the AFL-CIO Convention that jobs were more important than rights or education, being anterior to them. *The New York Times* took issue with him; a war on ignorance and a welcome to automation seemed the better slogan to its editors.

On Saturday, November 16, J.F.K. visited Cape Canaveral. He attended church the next day in West Palm Beach, and worked on speeches. On November 18, he was in Florida, warmly received by crowds at the Tampa baseball park and at the Miami airport. He told the Florida Chamber of Commerce that he had no plan to "soak the rich." Before a press group, he denounced the "small band of conspirators" who had made Cuba "a victim of foreign imperialism." But Castro, he thought, was in decline: "his torch is flickering." Kennedy was winsome, and promised to return next year and make a longer speech.

On November 20, some Texas Democrats professed anger at the $100 dinners being planned for the President on what was being officially called a nonpolitical tour, though it was well known that he hoped to reconcile warring Texas factions in the Democratic Party. One hundred dollars was beyond the means of thousands of Texans who had voted for the President in 1960. His party critics feared, too, that the revenue from these dinners might not be used equitably for opposing party groups. Pierre Salinger, for the White House, gave assurances that "Every faction in Texas will be taken care of."

On November 22, in the morning, J.F.K. spoke at Fort Worth. He offered his always felicitous compliments and quips, but he spoke also of national defense: his old, old theme of 1940. He then moved on to Dallas.

Undelivered Dallas Speech

I am honored to have this invitation to address the annual meeting of the Dallas Citizens Council, joined by the members of the Dallas Assembly—and pleased to have this opportunity to salute the Graduate Research Center of the Southwest.

It is fitting that these two symbols of Dallas progress are united in the sponsorship of this meeting. For they represent the best qualities, I am told, of leadership and learning in this city—and leadership and learning are indispensable to each other.

The advancement of learning depends on community leadership for financial and political support—and the products of that learning, in turn, are essential to the leadership's hopes for continued progress and prosperity. It is not a coincidence that those communities possessing the best in research and graduate facilities—from M.I.T. to Cal Tech—tend to attract the new and growing industries. I congratulate those of you here in Dallas who have recognized these basic facts through the creation of the unique and forward-looking graduate research center.

This link between leadership and learning is not only essential at the community level. It is even more indispensable in world affairs. Ignorance and misinformation can handicap the progress of a city or a company—but they can, if allowed to prevail in foreign policy, handicap this country's security. In a world of complex and continuing problems, in a world full of frustrations and irritations, America's leadership must be guided by the lights of learning and reason—or else those who confuse rhetoric with real[i]ty and the plausible with the

402

possible will gain the popular ascendancy with their seemingly swift and simple solutions to every world problem.

There will always be dissident voices heard in the land, expressing opposition without alternatives, finding fault but never favor, perceiving gloom on every side and seeking influence without responsibility. Those voices are inevitable.

But today other voices are heard in the land—voices preaching doctrines wholly unrelated to reality, wholly unsuited to the sixties, doctrines which apparently assume that words will suffice without weapons, that vituperation is as good as victory and that peace is a sign of weakness.

At a time when the national debt is steadily being reduced in terms of its burden on our economy, they see that debt as the greatest single threat to our security. At a time when we are steadily reducing the number of Federal employes serving every thousand citizens, they fear those supposed hordes of civil servants far more than the actual hordes of opposing armies.

We cannot expect that everyone, to use the phrase of a decade ago, will "talk sense to the American people." But we can hope that fewer people will listen to nonsense. And the notion that this nation is headed for defeat through deficit, or that strength is but a matter of slogans, is nothing but just plain nonsense.

I want to discuss with you today the status of our strength and our security because this question clearly calls for the most responsible qualities of leadership and the most enlightened products of scholarship. For this nation's strength and security are not easily or cheaply obtained—nor are they quickly and simply explained.

There are many kinds of strength and no one kind will suffice. Overwhelming nuclear strength cannot stop a guerrilla war. Formal pacts of alliance cannot stop internal subversion. Displays of material wealth cannot stop the disillusionment of diplomats subjected to discrimination.

Above all, words alone are not enough. The United States is a peaceful nation. And where our strength and determination are clear, our words need merely to convey conviction, not belligerence. If we are strong, our strength will speak for itself. If we are weak, words will be no help.

I realize that this nation often tends to identify turning-points in world affairs with the major addresses which preceded them. But it was not the Monroe Doctrine that kept all Europe away from this hemisphere—it was the strength of the British fleet and the width of the Atlantic Ocean. It was not General Marshall's speech at Harvard which kept Communism out of Western Europe—it was the strength and stability made possible by our military and economic assistance.

In this Administration also it has been necessary at times to issue specific warnings that we could not stand by and watch the Communists conquer Laos by force, or intervene in the Congo, or swallow West Berlin or maintain offensive missiles on Cuba.

But while our goals were at least temporarily obtained in those and other instances, our successful defense of freedom was due— not to the words we used—but to the strength we stood ready to use on behalf of the principles we stand ready to defend.

This strength is composed of many different elements, ranging from the most massive deterrents to the most subtle influences. And all types of strength are needed—no one kind could do the job alone. Let us take a moment, therefore, to review this nation's progress in each major area of strength.

First, as Secretary McNamara made clear in his address last Monday, the strategic nuclear power of the United States has been so greatly modernized and expanded in the last 1,000 days, by the rapid production and deployment of the most modern missile systems, that any and all potential aggressors are clearly confronted now with the impossibility of strategic victory—and the certainty of total destruction—if by reckless attack they should ever force upon us the necessity of a strategic reply.

In less than three years, we have increased by 50 per cent the number of Polaris submarines scheduled to be in force by the next fiscal year—increased by more than 70 per cent our total Polaris purchase program—increased by 50 per cent the portion of our strategic bombers on 15-minute alert—and increased by 100 per cent the total number of nuclear weapons available in our strategic alert forces.

Our security is further enhanced by the steps we have taken regarding these weapons to improve the speed and certainty of their response, their readiness at all times to respond, their ability to survive an attack and their ability to be carefully controlled and directed through secure command operations.

But the lessons of the last decade have taught us that freedom cannot be defended by strategic nuclear power alone. We have, therefore, in the last three years accelerated the development and deployment of tactical nuclear weapons—and increased by 60 per cent the tactical nuclear forces deployed in Western Europe.

Nor can Europe or any other continent rely on nuclear forces alone, whether they are strategic or tactical. We have radically improved the readiness of our conventional forces—increased by 45 per cent the number of combat ready army divisions—increased by 100 per cent the procurement of modern army weapons and equipment—increased by 100 per cent our ship construction, conversion and modernization program—increased by 100 per cent our procurement of tactical aircraft—increased by 30 per cent the number of tactical air squadrons—and increased the strength of the Marines.

As last month's Operation Big Lift—which originated here in Texas—showed so clearly, this nation is prepared as never before to move substantial numbers of men in surprisingly little time to advanced positions anywhere in the world. We have increased by 175 per cent the procurement of airlift aircraft—and we have already achieved a 75 per cent increase in our existing strategic airlift capability. Finally, moving beyond the traditional roles of our military forces, we have achieved an increase of nearly 600 per cent in our special forces—those forces that are prepared to work with our allies and friends against the guerrillas, saboteurs, insurgents and assassins who threaten freedom in a less direct but equally dangerous manner.

But American military might should not and need not stand alone against the ambitions of international Communism. Our security and strength, in the last analysis, directly depend on the security and strength of others—and that is why our military and economic assistance plays such a key role in enabling those who live on the periphery of the Communist world to maintain their independence of choice.

Our assistance to these nations can be painful, risky and costly— as is true in Southeast Asia today. But we dare not weary of the task. For our assistance makes possible the stationing of 3.5 million allied troops along the Communist frontier at one-tenth the cost of maintaining a comparable number of American soldiers. A successful Communist breakthrough in these areas, necessitating direct United States intervention, would cost us several times as much as our entire foreign aid program—and might cost us heavily in American lives as well.

About 70 per cent of our military assistance goes to nine key countries located on or near the borders of the Communist bloc— nine countries confronted directly or indirectly with the threat of Communist aggression—Vietnam, free China, Korea, India, Pakistan, Thailand, Greece, Turkey and Iran. No one of these countries possesses on its own the resources to maintain the forces which our own chiefs of staff think needed in the common interest.

Reducing our efforts to train, equip and assist their armies can only encourage Communist penetration and require in time the increased overseas deployment of American combat forces. And reducing the economic help needed to bolster these nations that undertake to help defend freedom can have the same disastrous result. In short, the $50 billion we spend each year on our own defense could well be ineffective without the $4 billion required for military and economic assistance.

Our foreign aid program is not growing in size—it is, on the contrary, smaller now than in previous years. It has had its weaknesses—but we have undertaken to correct them—and the proper way of treating weaknesses is to replace them with strength, not to increase those weaknesses by emasculating essential programs.

Dollar for dollar, in or out of Government, there is no better form of investment in our national security than our much-abused foreign aid program. We cannot afford to lose it. We can afford to maintain it. We can surely afford, for example, to do as much for our 19 needy neighbors of Latin America as the Communist bloc is sending to the island of Cuba alone.

I have spoken of strength largely in terms of the deterrence and resistance of aggression and attack. But, in today's world, freedom can be lost without a shot being fired, by ballots as well as bullets. The success of our leadership is dependent upon respect for our mission in the world as well as our missiles—on a clearer recognition of the virtues of freedom as well as the evils of tyranny.

That is why our information agency has doubled the shortwave broadcasting power of the Voice of America and increased the number of broadcasting hours by 30 per cent—increased Spanish-language broadcasting to Cuba and Latin-American listeners—and taken a host of other steps to carry our message of truth and freedom to all the far corners of the earth.

And that is also why we have regained the initiative in the exploration of outer space—making an annual effort greater than the combined total of all space activities undertaken during the fifties—launching more than 130 vehicles into earth orbit—putting into actual operation valuable weather and communications satellites —and making it clear to all that the United States of America has no intention of finishing second in space.

This effort is expensive—but it pays its own way, for freedom and for America. For there is no longer any fear in the free world that a Communist lead in space will become a permanent assertion of supremacy and the basis of military superiority. There is no longer any doubt about the strength and skill of American science, American industry, American education and the American free enterprise system. In short, our national space effort represents a great gain in and a great resource of, our national strength—and both Texas and Texans are contributing greatly to this strength.

Finally, it should be clear by now that a nation can be no stronger abroad than she is at home. Only America which practices what it preaches about equal rights and social justice will be respected by those whose choice effects our future. Only an America which has fully educated its citizens is fully capable of tackling the complex problems and perceiving the hidden dangers of the world in which we live. And only an America which is growing and prospering economically can sustain the worldwide defense of freedom, while demonstrating to all concerned the opportunities of our system and society.

It is clear, therefore, that we are strengthening our security as well as our economy by our recent record increases in national income and output—by surging ahead of most of Western Europe in the rate of business expansion.

And the margin of corporate profits—by maintaining a more stable level of prices than almost any of our overseas competitors—and by cutting personal and corporate income taxes by some $11 billion, as I have proposed, to assure this nation of the longest and strongest expansion in our peacetime economic history.

This nation's total output—which three years ago was at the $500 billion mark—will soon pass $600 billion, for a record rise of over $100 billion in 3 years. For the first time in history we have 70 million men and women at work. For the first time in history average factory earnings have exceeded $100 a week. For the first time in history corporation profits after taxes—which have risen 43 per cent in less than 3 years—have reached an annual level of $27.4 billion.

My friends and fellow citizens: I cite these facts and figures to make it clear that America today is stronger than ever before. Our adversaries have not abandoned their ambitions—our dangers have not diminished—our vigilance cannot be relaxed. But now we have the military, the scientific and the economic strength to do whatever must be done for the preservation and promotion of freedom.

That strength will never be used in pursuit of aggressive ambitions —it will always be used in pursuit of peace. It will never be used to promote provocations—it will always be used to promote the peaceful settlement of disputes.

We in this country, in this generation, are—by destiny rather than choice—the watchmen on the walls of world freedom. We ask, therefore, that we may be worthy of our power and responsibility— that we may exercise our strength with wisdom and restraint—and that we may achieve in our time and for all time the ancient vision of peace on earth, good will toward men. That must always be our goal—and the righteousness of our cause must always underlie our strength. For as was written long ago: "Except the Lord keep the city, the watchman waketh but in vain."

LYNDON BAINES JOHNSON
(1908–   )

State of the Union Message

Mr. Speaker, Mr. President, Members of the House and Senate, my fellow Americans:

I will be brief, for our time is necessarily short and our agenda is already long.

Last year's Congressional session was the longest in peacetime history. And with that foundation, let us work together to make this year's session the best in the nation's history.

Let this session of Congress be known as the session which did more for civil rights than the last 100 sessions combined; as the session which enacted the most far-reaching tax cut of our time; as the session which declared all-out war on human poverty and unemployment in these United States; as the session which finally recognized the health needs of all of our older citizens; as the session which reformed our tangled transportation and transit policies; as the session which achieved the most effective, efficient foreign aid program ever, and as the session which helped to build more homes and more schools and more libraries and more hospitals than any single session of Congress in the history of our republic.

All this and more can and must be done.

It can be done by this summer.

And it can be done without any increase in spending.

In fact, under the budget that I shall shortly submit, it can be done with an actual reduction in Federal expenditures and Federal employment.

We have, in 1964, a unique opportunity and obligation to prove the success of our system, to disprove those cynics and critics at home and abroad who question our purpose and our competence.

If we fail, if we fritter and fumble away our opportunity in needless, senseless quarrels between Democrats and Republicans, or between the House and the Senate, or between the South and the North, or between the Congress and the Administration, then history will rightly judge us harshly.

But if we succeed, if we can achieve these goals by forging in this country a greater sense of union, then, and only then, can we take full satisfaction in the state of the Union.

Here in the Congress you can demonstrate effective legislative leadership by discharging the public business with clarity and dispatch, voting each important proposal up or voting it down, but at least bringing it to a fair and a final vote.

Let us carry forward the plans and programs of John Fitzgerald Kennedy, not because of our sorrow or sympathy, but because they are right.

And in his memory today, I especially ask all members of my own political faith, in this election year, to put your country ahead of your party and to always debate principles; never debate personalities.

For my part, I pledge a progressive administration which is efficient, and honest and frugal.

The budget to be submitted to the Congress shortly is in full accord with this pledge.

It will cut our deficit in half, from $10 billion to $4.9 billion.

It will be, in proportion to our national output, the smallest budget since 19 and 51.

It will call for a substantial reduction in Federal employment, a feat accomplished only once before in the last 10 years.

While maintaining the full strength of our combat defenses, it will call for the lowest number of civilian personnel in the Department of Defense since 19 and 50.

It will call for total expenditures of $97.7 billion, compared to $98.4 for the current year, a reduction of more than $500 million.

It will call for new obligation authority of $103.8 billion, a reduction of more than $4 billion below last year request of $107.9 billion.

But it is not a stand-still budget, for America cannot afford to stand still. Our population is growing. Our economy is more complex. Our people's needs are expanding.

But by closing down obsolete installations, by curtailing less-urgent programs, by cutting back where cutting back seems to be wise, by insisting on a dollar's worth for a dollar spent, I am able to recommend in this reduced budget the most Federal support in history for education, for health, for retraining the unemployed and for helping the economically and the physically handicapped.

This budget, and this year's legislative program, are designed to help each and every American citizen fulfill his basic hopes:

His hopes for a fair chance to make good.

His hopes for fair play from the law.

His hopes for a full-time job on full-time pay.

His hopes for a decent home for his family in a decent community.

His hopes for a good school for his children with good teachers.

And his hopes for security when faced with sickness, or unemployment or old age.

Unfortunately, many Americans live on the outskirts of hope, some because of their poverty and some because of their color, and all too many because of both.

Our task is to help replace their despair with opportunity.

And this Administration today, here and now, declares unconditional war on poverty in America, and I urge this Congress and all Americans to join with me in that effort.

It will not be a short or easy struggle, no single weapon or strategy will suffice, but we shall not rest until that war is won.

The richest nation on earth can afford to win it.

We cannot afford to lose it.

One thousand dollars invested in salvaging an unemployable youth today can return $40,000 or more in his lifetime.

Poverty is a national problem, requiring improved national organization and support. But this attack, to be effective, must also be organized at the state and the local level, and must be supported and directed by state and local efforts.

For the war against poverty will not be won here in Washington. It must be won in the field, in every private home, in every public office, from the courthouse to the White House.

The program I shall propose will emphasize this cooperative approach. To help that one-fifth of all American families with income too small to even meet their basic needs, our chief weapons in a more pinpointed attack will be better schools and better health and better homes and better training and better job opportunities to help more Americans, especially young Americans, escape from squalor and misery and unemployment rolls, where other citizens help to carry them.

Very often a lack of jobs and money is not the cause of poverty, but the symptom.

The cause may lie deeper in our failure to give our fellow citizens a fair chance to develop their own capacities, in a lack of education and training, in a lack of medical care and housing, in a lack of decent communities in which to live and bring up their children. But whatever the cause, our joint Federal-local effort must pursue poverty, pursue it wherever it exists. In city slums, in small towns, in sharecroppers' shacks or in migrant worker camps, on Indian reservations, among whites as well as Negroes, among the young as well as the aged, in the boomtowns and in the depressed areas.

Our aim is not only to relieve the symptom of poverty, but to cure it, and, above all, to prevent it.

No single piece of legislation, however, is going to suffice:

We will launch a special effort in the chronically distressed areas of Appalachia.

We must expand our small but our successful area redevelopment program.

We must enact youth employment legislation to put jobless, aimless, hopeless youngsters to work on useful projects.

We must distribute more food to the needy through a broader food stamp program.

We must create a National Service Corps to help the economically handicapped of our own country, as the Peace Corps now helps those abroad.

We must modernize our unemployment insurance and establish a high-level commission on automation. If we have the brain power to invent these machines, we have the brain power to make certain that they are a boon and not a bane to humanity.

We must extend the coverage of our minimum wage laws to more than 2 million workers now lacking this basic protection of purchasing power.

We must, by including special school aid funds as part of our education program, improve the quality of teaching and training and counseling in our hardest-hit areas.

We must build more libraries in every area, and more hospitals and nursing homes under the Hill-Burton Act, and train more nurses to staff them.

We must provide hospital insurance for our older citizens, financed by every worker and his employer under Social Security contributing no more than $1 a month during the employe's working career to protect him in his old age in a dignified manner, without cost to the Treasury, against the devastating hardship of prolonged or repeated illness.

We must, as a part of a revised housing and urban renewal program, give more help to those displaced by slum clearance; provide more housing for our poor and our elderly, and seek as our ultimate goal in our free enterprise system a decent home for every American family.

We must help obtain more modern mass transit within our communities as well as low-cost transportation between them.

Above all, we must release $11 billion of tax reduction into the private spending stream to create new jobs and new markets in every area of this land.

These programs are obviously not for the poor or the under-privileged alone.

Every American will benefit by the extension of Social Security to cover the hospital costs of their aged parents.

Every American community will benefit from the construction or modernization of schools and libraries and hospitals and nursing homes, from the training of more nurses, and from the improvement of urban renewal and public transit.

And every individual American taxpayer, and every corporate taxpayer, will benefit from the earliest possible passage of the pending tax bill, from both the new investment it will bring and the new jobs that it will create.

That tax bill has been thoroughly discussed for a year. Now we need action.

The new budget clearly allows it.

Our taxpayers surely deserve it.

Our economy strongly demands it.

And every month of delay dilutes its benefits in 19 and 64 for consumption, for investment and for employment.

For until the bill is signed, its investments incentives cannot be deemed certain, and the withholding rate cannot be reduced.

And the most damaging and devastating thing you can do to any businessman in America is to keep him in doubt, and to keep him guessing, on what our tax policy is.

And I say that we should now reduce to 14 per cent, instead of 15 per cent, our withholding rate. And I therefore urge the Congress to take final action on this bill by the first of February, if at all possible.

For, however proud we may be of the unprecedented progress of our free enterprise economy over the last three years, we should not, and we cannot, permit it to pause.

In 1963, for the first time in history, we crossed the 70 million job mark, but we will soon need more than 70 million jobs.

In 1963, our gross national product reached the $600 billion level, $100 billion higher than when we took office. But it easily could, and it should, be still $30 billion higher today than it is.

Wages and profits and family income are also at their highest level in history, but I would remind you that 4 million workers and 13 per cent of our industrial capacity are still idle today.

We need a tax cut now to keep this country moving.

For our goal is not merely to spread the work. Our goal is to create more jobs.

I believe the enactment of a 35-hour week would sharply increase costs, would invite inflation, would impair our ability to compete and merely share instead of creating employment.

But I am equally opposed to the 45 or 50-hour week in those industries where consistently excessive use of overtime causes increased unemployment.

So, therefore, I recommend legislation authorizing the creation of a tripartite industry committee to determine on an industry-by-industry basis as to where a higher penalty rate for overtime would increase job openings without unduly increasing costs and authorizing the establishment of such higher rates.

Let me make one principle of this Administration abundantly clear. All of these increased opportunities in employment and education, in housing and in every field must be open to Americans of every color. As far as the writ of Federal law will run, we must abolish not some, but all, racial discrimination. For this is not merely an economic issue, or a social, political or international issue. It is a moral issue, and it must be met by the passage this session of the bill now pending in the House.

All members of the public should have equal access to facilities open to the public.

All members of the public should be equally eligible for Federal benefits that are financed by the public.

All members of the public should have an equal chance to vote for public officials and to send their children to good public schools, and to contribute their talents to the public good.

Today Americans of all races stand side by side in Berlin and in Vietnam. They died side by side in Korea. Surely they can work and eat and travel side by side in their own country.

We must also lift by legislation the bars of discrimination against those who seek entry into our country, particularly those with much needed skills and those joining their families. In establishing preferences, a nation that was built by the immigrants of all lands can ask those who now seek admission: What can you do for our country? But we should not be asking: In what country were you born?

For our ultimate goal is a world without war. A world made safe for diversity, in which all men, goods and ideas can freely move across every border and every boundary.

We must advance toward this goal in 1964 in at least 10 different ways, not as partisans but as patriots.

First, we must maintain—and our reduced defense budget will maintain—that margin of military safety and superiority obtained through three years of steadily increasing both the quality and the quantity of our strategic, our conventional and our antiguerrilla forces.

In 1964 we will be better prepared than ever before to defend the cause of freedom, whether it is threatened by outright aggression or by the infiltration practiced by those in Hanoi and Havana who ship arms and men across international borders to foment insurrection.

And we must continue to use that strength, as John Kennedy used it in the Cuban crisis and for the test-ban treaty, to demonstrate both the futility of nuclear war and the possibilities of lasting peace.

Second, we must take new steps—and we shall make new proposals at Geneva—toward the control and the eventual abolition of arms. Even in the absence of agreement, we must not stockpile arms beyond our needs, or seek an excess of military power that could be provocative as well as wasteful.

And it is in this spirit that in this fiscal year we are cutting back our production of enriched uranium by 25 per cent; we are shutting down four plutonium piles; we are closing many nonessential military installations. And it is in this spirit that we today call on our adversaries to do the same.

Third, we must make increased use of our food as an instrument of peace, making it available by sale or trade or loan or donation to hungry people in all nations which tell us of their needs and accept proper conditions of distribution.

Fourth, we must assure our preeminence in the peaceful exploration of outer space, focusing on an expedition to the moon in this decade, in cooperation with other powers, if possible, alone, if necessary.

Fifth, we must expand world trade. Having recognized, in the act of 1962, that we must buy as well as sell, we now expect our trading partners to recognize that we must sell as well as buy. We are willing to give them competitive access to our market, asking only that they do the same for us.

Sixth, we must, continue, through such measures as the interest equalization tax as well as the cooperation of other nations, our recent progress toward balancing our international accounts.

This Administration must and will preserve the present gold value of the dollar.

Seventh, we must become better neighbors with the free states of the Americas, working with the councils of the O.A.S., with a stronger

415

Alliance for Progress and with all the men and women of this hemisphere who really believe in liberty and justice for all.

Eighth, we must strengthen the ability of free nations everywhere to develop their independence and raise their standards of living and thereby frustrate those who prey on poverty and chaos. To do this, the rich must help the poor and we must do our part. We must achieve a more rigorous administration of our development assistance, with larger roles for private investors, for other industrialized nations and for international agencies and for the recipient nations themselves.

Ninth, we must strengthen our Atlantic and Pacific partnership, maintain our alliances and make the United Nations a more effective instrument for national independence and international order.

Tenth, and finally, we must develop with our allies new means of bridging the gap between the East and the West, facing dangers boldly wherever danger exists. But being equally bold in our search for new agreements which can enlarge the hopes of all while violating the interests of none.

In short, I would say to the Congress that we must be constantly prepared for the worst and constantly acting for the best.

We must be strong enough to win any war and we must be wise enough to prevent one.

We shall neither act as aggressors nor tolerate acts of aggression.

We intend to bury no one, and we do not intend to be buried.

We can fight, if we must, as we have fought before, but we pray that we will never have to fight again.

My good friends and my fellow Americans, in these last sorrowful weeks we have learned anew that nothing is so enduring as faith and nothing is so degrading as hate.

John Kennedy was a victim of hate, but he was also a great builder of faith—faith in our fellow Americans, whatever their creed or their color or their station in life; faith in the future of man, whatever his divisions and differences.

This faith was echoed in all parts of the world. On every continent and in every land to which Mrs. Johnson and I traveled, we found faith and hope and love toward this land of America and toward our people.

So I ask you now, in the Congress and in the country, to join with me in expressing and fulfilling that faith, in working for a nation, a nation that is free from want, and a world that is free from hate.

A world of peace and justice and freedom and abundance for our time and for all time to come.